Arresting Citizenship

Chicago Studies in American Politics

A SERIES EDITED BY BENJAMIN I. PAGE, SUSAN HERBST,
LAWRENCE R. JACOBS, AND ADAM BERINSKY

Also in the series:

HOW THE STATES SHAPED THE NATION:
AMERICAN ELECTORAL INSTITUTIONS AND
VOTER TURNOUT, 1920–2000 *by Melanie
Jean Springer*

THE AMERICAN WARFARE STATE: THE
DOMESTIC POLITICS OF MILITARY SPENDING
by Rebecca U. Thorpe

CHANGING MINDS OR CHANGING
CHANNELS? PARTISAN NEWS IN AN AGE
OF CHOICE *by Kevin Arceneaux and
Martin Johnson*

TRADING DEMOCRACY FOR JUSTICE:
CRIMINAL CONVICTIONS AND THE DECLINE
OF NEIGHBORHOOD POLITICAL
PARTICIPATION *by Traci Burch*

WHITE-COLLAR GOVERNMENT: THE HIDDEN
ROLE OF CLASS IN ECONOMIC POLICY
MAKING *by Nicholas Carnes*

HOW PARTISAN MEDIA POLARIZE AMERICA
by Matthew Levendusky

THE POLITICS OF BELONGING: RACE, PUBLIC
OPINION, AND IMMIGRATION *by Natalie
Masuoka and Jane Junn*

POLITICAL TONE: HOW LEADERS TALK
AND WHY *by Roderick P. Hart, Jay P.
Childers, and Colene J. Lind*

THE TIMELINE OF PRESIDENTIAL ELECTIONS:
HOW CAMPAIGNS DO (AND DO NOT) MATTER
by Robert S. Erikson and Christopher Wlezien

LEARNING WHILE GOVERNING: EXPERTISE
AND ACCOUNTABILITY IN THE EXECUTIVE
BRANCH *by Sean Gailmard and John W. Patty*

ELECTING JUDGES: THE SURPRISING EFFECTS
OF CAMPAIGNING ON JUDICIAL LEGITIMACY
by James L. Gibson

FOLLOW THE LEADER? HOW VOTERS RESPOND
TO POLITICIANS' POLICIES AND PERFORMANCE
by Gabriel S. Lenz

List continues after index.

Arresting Citizenship

*The Democratic Consequences
of American Crime Control*

AMY E. LERMAN AND
VESLA M. WEAVER

THE UNIVERSITY OF CHICAGO PRESS   CHICAGO AND LONDON

AMY E. LERMAN is assistant professor in the Goldman School of Public Policy at the University of California, Berkeley, and the author of *The Modern Prison Paradox*. VESLA M. WEAVER is assistant professor in the Department of African American Studies and the Department of Political Science at Yale University. She is coauthor of *Creating a New Racial Order*.

The University of Chicago Press, Chicago 60637
The University of Chicago Press, Ltd., London
© 2014 by The University of Chicago
All rights reserved. Published 2014.
Printed in the United States of America

23 22 21 20 19 18 17 16 15 14 1 2 3 4 5

ISBN-13: 978-0-226-13766-7 (cloth)
ISBN-13: 978-0-226-13783-4 (paper)
ISBN-13: 978-0-226-13797-1 (e-book)
DOI: 10.7208/chicago/9780226137971.001.0001

Library of Congress Cataloging-in-Publication Data

Lerman, Amy E., 1978– author.
    Arresting citizenship : the democratic consequences of American crime control /
Amy E. Lerman and Vesla M. Weaver.
        pages cm
        (Chicago studies in American politics)
    ISBN 978-0-226-13766-7 (cloth : alk. paper)
    ISBN 978-0-226-13783-4 (pbk. : alk. paper)
    ISBN 978-0-226-13797-1 (e-book)
    1. Criminal justice, Administration of—United States.   2. Discrimination in
criminal justice administration—United States.   I. Weaver, Vesla M., 1979–
author.   II. Title.   III. Series: Chicago studies in American politics.
HV9950.L475 2014
364.973–dc23

                                                                    2013043364

TO THE MANY WHO SHARED THEIR THOUGHTS AND EXPERIENCES WITH US FOR THIS BOOK, AND TO THE MILLIONS WHOSE VOICES HAVE NOT YET BEEN HEARD.

Contents

Acknowledgments   ix

CHAPTER 1.   Arresting Citizenship   1

CHAPTER 2.   Thinking about Crime and the Custodial Citizen   30

CHAPTER 3.   Democratic Ideals and Institutional Design   58

CHAPTER 4.   Assessing the Effects of Criminal Justice   92

CHAPTER 5.   "Democracy don't get you a second chance":
(Un)Learning Citizenship   110

CHAPTER 6.   "You in their house now":
Learning about the State and Control   139

CHAPTER 7.   "We're free, but we're not *free*": Black Custodial
Citizenship and Complex Racial Narratives   157

CHAPTER 8.   "I better stay below the radar":
Fear, Alienation, and Withdrawal   199

CHAPTER 9.   Where We Go from Here   231

Appendix A   Quantitative Data   261

Appendix B   Qualitative Data   269

Appendix C   Three Strategies to Address Causality   275

Notes   281

Index   321

Acknowledgments

What does the expansion of the carceral state mean for citizens who experience punishment and surveillance? Over the past few years, answering this question has been our central ambition. It has led us on an intellectual journey that shaped us as scholars and people. It required us to go beyond the methods we were comfortable with to undertake an ethnography of custodial citizens. It required more imagination than we sometimes felt we had. It required us to learn how not to treat the topic at arm's length, as we had become accustomed, but to "spend a day in their shoes." We are indebted to an enormous number of people for their support, participation, ideas, and enthusiasm over the long road we have traveled toward completing this book.

This book was shaped first and most fundamentally by the many people who you will come to know shortly, who generously shared their experiences with us and let us in to their worlds. Their voices made a deep imprint on the theories and ideas we developed here. We wrote this book for their sake alone, because we believed their voices should be heard and their stories told. In the process, though, they made it impossible for us to forget that their unique experience of democracy revealed something deeper about the current character of the American polity. Their particular stories were about criminal justice but also about contemporary citizenship and democracy in America; one cannot be understood without the other. Even when we don't quote them, their thoughts and experiences are written on every page. It is to them that the book is dedicated.

We might never have met Silas, Darcy, Marshall, and the others had we not had the support of organizations that already knew and worked closely with them. These organizations not only helped us reach these folks, but sometimes offered us spaces to talk with them and helped to coordinate the comlex task of scheduling. Thanks in particular to Offender Aid and Restoration in Charlottesville and to Ross Carew; the Haven in Charlottesville; Albert "Bo" Robinson in Trenton and Helping Arms in Trenton, especially Cynthia Morgan and Ralph Fretz; and AmeriCorps in New Orleans. A very special thanks to Leonard Ward from the New Jersey State Parole Board, Tina Chiu from the Vera Institute of Justice, and also to Kathleen Whalen and the staff of the Partnership for Youth Development in New Orleans who helped to connect us to the people and organizations in their communities. The financial support of our institutions seeded our research; The Bobst Center at Princeton and the University of Virginia faculty research grants provided us with resources to conduct our interviews.

The conversations we had with individual interviewees were often deeply emotional experiences. We were equipped with two phenomenal graduate students, Meredith Sadin and Michelle Phelps, who not only had experience in interviewing, but had the intellectual and emotional mettle to undertake this endeavor with us. They traveled with us to Charlottesville and New Orleans and came ready with reserves of energy, passion, and ideas. They should read these pages knowing how central they were to this project.

There are some folks who not only read chapters when we called on them but who took an interest in our book before it could be called that. Vesla frequently went across the hall to her confidant, Melvin Rogers, who should have learned to close his door, but always was more than happy to discuss some concept or thought. The products of those many conversations, debates, and advice-giving are within these pages. We will never forget his off-the-cuff analogies, which pushed us to understand that democracy as a whole was harmed through the indignities our subjects faced. Chris Lebron was incredibly generous in time and spirit, reading every page, sometimes more than once or twice. We are grateful for the many(!) epiphanies the conversations with him helped inspire. His abiding excitement for the project along with his love of justice, critical eye, and penchant for prose crucially shaped not just the content, but also the scope of this project. His readership made the text less timid and the theoretical insights more precise, pushing us to recognize the crucial distinction between antidemocratic and undemocratic institutions.

In addition, Amy would like to express an inordinate awe of and gratitude toward her brilliant and brave coauthor. Vesla embodies the incredibly rare combination of a first-rate mind and a boundless intellectual generosity, and I have been the lucky beneficiary of both. She has an extraordinary ability to put thoughts to paper and turn them into beautiful prose, and I have learned so very much by watching her work. She pushes me to think smarter and work harder. I could not have dreamt a better companion for this long and winding road.

Vesla could not have imagined a more inspiring, more hardworking, more lovely coauthor and gives thanks that Amy walked right up to her when they were both starting new jobs fresh out of graduate training. At the time, so few people were studying criminal justice within political science that it was a lonely intellectual space; years of conversations later, Amy was more than mere company in this project, she was key in articulating a broader vision of how central criminal justice was to critically analyzing American political life and governance. Along the way, Amy became that person who I could call on with an entirely too-rough idea and she would make it sing. Research and writing were smarter, bolder, and more fun with her.

To the remarkably generous group of scholars who came to our book conference and gave us a wealth of their insights, suggestions and time, including Alec Ewald, Michael Dawson, Jeff Fagan, James Forman Jr., Jennifer Hochschild, Glenn Loury, Lisa Miller, Christopher Muller, and Tom Tyler: Your comments on our manuscript made an immeasurable impact on the resulting book. Thanks also to those who gave extensive feedback at other stages of this book's progression, especially Chris Achen, Beth Colgan, Martin Gilens, Mary Katzenstein, Michael Owens, Markus Prior, Adrienne Smith, Joe Soss, and Chris Wildeman. We are especially indebted to Suzanne Mettler, who not only gave us the benefit of her wonderful ideas, but helped us connect with the folks at the University of Chicago Press.

We have had the good fortune of presenting various pieces of this work along the way and have received valuable insights from the audiences at these talks. Thanks go to the politics faculties at each of these places, including Yale, Harvard, Columbia, Penn, Emory, Georgetown, Minnesota, Princeton, Ohio State, University of Virginia, Cornell, MIT, NYU, GW, and UC Berkeley. In addition, an earlier version of some of the analysis in the empirical chapters appeared in Vesla Weaver and Amy Lerman, "Political Consequences of the Carceral State," *Ameri-*

can Political Science Review 104, no. 4 (2010): 817–33, and we are grateful to both the journal editors and anonymous reviewers for their helpful feedback.

We are extremely appreciative of the willingness of Chris Uggen and Cathy Cohen (and her associates at the Black Youth Project) to share their data with us. Many thanks also to ISPS at Yale University for hosting our book conference and to Pamela Greene for going above and beyond in helping us organize schedules, travel and food. Thanks, too, go to Helene Wood for helping to organize travel on the Princeton end.

We are grateful to the research assistants who provided us with help in shepherding this project to completion: Matt Incantalupo, Katherine McCabe, and Matt Tokeshi at Princeton, Claire Burks at UVA, and Chayma Boussayoud, Charles Decker, and Adina Hemley-Bronstein at Yale. We especially thank Adam Hughes at UVA who took on the vast task of transcribing our interviews. Many thanks to Brian Slattery for his assistance with copyediting and preparing our manuscript for publication.

Thanks also to the amazing people at the University of Chicago Press, most especially Rodney Powell and John Tryneski. Larry Jacobs was the keenest of series editors and we were so fortunate to have his extensive feedback at several points in the process. And thanks to the anonymous reviewers for giving the manuscript such a thorough read and reporting.

Finally, an enormous amount of gratitude to our families for their support and encouragement during this process. We could not have completed this project without having them behind us. And especially to our favorite guys, big and small. Chris, Lennox, and Noah: we adore you. Thank you for your patience and love throughout the writing of this book.

CHAPTER ONE

Arresting Citizenship

"Hard," he replied.

We had barely finished asking Renard how he would describe government in America when his single syllable pierced the room and hung there, simple but strange. Unwavering, Renard repeated himself. "The government is hard." After a long pause, he found more words to explain. "Government is like freedom," he said, "but not freedom. We're free but we're not *free*."

When we met him, Renard was working for a social service program in Louisiana along with two friends, Xavier and Reggie. These three young adults, with their contagious energy and outgoing smiles, had grown up together in Covington, a small town on the edge of New Orleans. Together they knew quite a lot about government. What they described, however, in the two hours that we interviewed them, bears little resemblance to the government depicted in most scholarly accounts of American politics. They did not refer to political parties vying for office in the legislature, municipal leaders making decisions in city hall, or even mundane bureaucratic practices like going to the post office or filing taxes. Indeed, nearly all of what these three young men described about government broke from the formal definitions learned in high school civics courses, practiced in the American electoral arena, and displayed in the rich civic traditions of town-hall meetings, civic associations, and bowling leagues.

Instead, most of what Renard, Xavier, and Reggie know and understand about government was born of their direct experiences with the state institutions that most directly structured the daily dramas of their communal and individual lives. As Xavier illustrated, reaching for the salt shakers and sugar packets to map out a small replica of his town on the table, government in his community formed a Bermuda Triangle of sorts: in the left corner a police station; in the right corner a court; and at the apex a jail. A majority of what these young men had come to believe about government derived primarily from their interactions with these and other institutions of criminal justice—encounters with Covington police and probation officers, going to court and meeting with the public defender, visiting a brother in prison for life, and spending nights on the cold floor of the overcrowded Saint Tammany jail.

Reggie, Xavier, and Renard are just three of the many people whose voices and experiences are documented through the surveys and interviews described in this book. What does American democracy look like to this large and growing group of citizens? What practices do they see enshrined in government, what lessons do they hear it espouse, and what have they come to expect from their elected officials and political institutions? Most basically, how do these individuals experience citizenship in America today? Our central argument in this book is that criminal justice institutions have come to play a socializing role in the lives of a substantial subset of Americans, fundamentally influencing how they come to conceptualize the democratic state and their place in it.

In the time we spent with Renard and his friends, it became clear that their experiences with criminal justice had taught them important lessons about their social and political standing in America. They described how, by virtue of being young, black, and poor, they and those like them were subjected to frequent police stops, during which they were treated with suspicion. "They got to look at people as people," Xavier explained to us. "It's like they're hunting tigers or something. Or lions. . . . If you get to know me, I'm the funniest person. But me, I'm black. I got a mouthful of gold, tattoos on me. I'm already looking like a drug dealer." Renard similarly related his feeling that they were the inevitable targets of negative attention from authorities: "We got that bull's eye on our back as soon as we're born," he said. And once they were "in the system," having been arrested or fingerprinted, they felt permanently stigmatized. "Once you mess up, you given your life over to the government, because they got you. . . . Democracy don't get you a second chance."

A great deal of scholarship has emerged to show that the frequency of contact with criminal justice that Renard and his friends describe makes them far from unique. By young adulthood, fully 24 percent of Americans have been arrested at least once, 12 percent have been convicted of a crime, and 5 percent have been incarcerated.[1] Many more have been stopped and questioned by police. The experiences of Renard and his friends are especially common among their particular demographic: nearly one in four blacks who did not complete high school is now confined in a juvenile correctional facility, jail, or prison.[2] For low-income black men coming of age today, contact with government through police stops, arrest, adjudication, probation, incarceration, and parole has become the de facto rule rather than a notable exception; it has become an "experience of the expected."[3]

These high rates of exposure to criminal justice grew out of dramatic shifts in criminal justice practices in cities and counties across America. In New York City alone, police stopped and questioned almost 700,000 people in 2011, an increase of more than 600 percent from a decade earlier. Other areas of criminal justice likewise witnessed tremendous expansion; rates of citizen contact with courts, probation offices, prisons and jails have experienced exponential growth since the 1970s. Four decades ago, 5 percent of adult men had ever been convicted of a felony and 2 percent had ever been to prison; by 2004, this proportion had swelled considerably, such that 13 percent of adult men have a felony on their record and 5 percent have been incarcerated.[4] Otherwise stated, men are more than twice as likely to have experienced incarceration or to have a felony record in 2004 as they were in 1968.

Our inquiry in this book goes beyond these frequently cited statistics, however. More important, we suggest, is that in contrast to an earlier era, the relationship between criminal behavior and contact with criminal justice has become increasingly tenuous. For instance, just one in ten of the abovementioned police stops in New York resulted in the individual being arrested or charged with a crime.[5] Put another way, in about 90 percent of cases there was insufficient evidence that the individuals who were stopped were actually engaging in criminal behavior. Rather, the criteria used to detain them were often circumstantial. In nearly two-thirds of police stops in New York, a contributing factor was that the individual was "walking in a high crime area." Many others were stopped because they "fit the description" of a suspect, made "furtive movements," or were "wearing clothes commonly used in a crime." The result of these practices is that, in a representative sample of young Americans, fully 20 percent report having been stopped and questioned at least once by police but never arrested, and about half that number have been arrested but never convicted of a crime.[6] Again, the proportions are significantly higher among young black men.[7]

It is hard to imagine that these experiences leave no mark. Yet existing models of American politics provide little theorizing to help make legible the perceptions and experiences voiced by Renard and others like him. Most frequently, scholars of American politics portray citizens' reticence to engage the political process as passive: They have not been mobilized by a candidate or campaign; they do not have the time, money, or knowledge to get involved in political life; they do not have any stake in the process because they do not receive (or are unaware that they receive) some type of direct benefit from government.[8] This is true even in extant scholarship on those with criminal convictions, as the existing literature has focused primarily on felon disenfranchisement and other legal restrictions that bar individuals from expressing their political voice.[9] These studies provide important insights into American political psychology and behavior, but fall short in helping us explain the experiences of Xavier and Reggie, who retained the right to legally participate in elections but chose not to do so. Nor do they fully explain the political orientations of Renard, who was disenfranchised due to a felony conviction but whose negative perceptions of government and sense of stigmatized citizenship had caused him to withdraw even from the other avenues of participation that remained open to him.

By any measure, money and education were not in abundance in the small community where Renard and his friends were raised. But for these young men, political disengagement had a distinctly different source: As they put it, "All we know about government is bad. We don't know the good aspects. And it might really be good in some spots, some parts. But we don't know that." From their direct experience of nonelectoral institutions, they had learned that government was not predominantly about redistribution or social supports or even about elected officials passing laws for the good of the people; it was about surveillance, punishment, and control—"keeping people in line." Thus, nonengagement for them was not passive abstention stemming from a lack of will or resources. Rather, they believed their best strategy was to intentionally stay invisible, to actively avoid authorities, and to keep a low profile. "You got to stay out of their view," Xavier explained. "Okay? If you be seen too much, [the police assume] you're doing something."

We are not the first to trace the growth of the carceral state, nor are we the first to suggest that custodial citizens occupy a "semi-citizenship."[10] Like us, these scholars suggest that criminal justice and its effects are not epiphenomenal to discussions of American democracy. The shifts in America's form and style of governance that we trace in this book are a political experiment that has no equal; no fully democratic system has ever attempted to operate with such intensive surveillance of its citizens and such demographically and geographically concentrated levels of punishment. This book sets out to trace the effects of these unprecedented historical developments for the practice of democracy and citizenship today. While our analyses are concerned with criminal justice policy and its consequences, ours is therefore a broader argument. This is not only a book about how punitive a society we have become; at its core, this book is about the character of the American state and the increasingly defining role of its least democratic institutions.

The Carceral State and American Democracy

It is often taken as an article of faith that the United States has always been centered in a strong democratic tradition, in which citizens were "born equal, instead of becoming so."[11] Indeed, a core tenet of American exceptionalism is that democracy in the United States did not emerge from an authoritarian past, but was instead "ordain[ed] and establish[ed]" as "a more perfect Union."[12] In this telling, the nation's antidemocratic periods are historical pitfalls overcome in the forward march toward democratic inclusion. Political struggles for equality—to end slavery, enfranchise blacks, extend the vote to women, and secure civil rights—progressively built on one another over time to bring the country's practice of democracy into line with its promise. In his most famous speech on race, then-candidate Barack Obama reminded voters that, through the struggles and sacrifice of "Americans in successive generations," the nation had "narrow[ed] that gap between the promise of our ideals and the reality of our time."[13]

Yet while national rhetoric often portrays democratization in the United States as "a tale of steady progress," scholars have long noted that extending citizenship to all Americans took many years, was hotly contested, and endured significant and repeated periods of backsliding during which democracy remained elusive. As Desmond King and Robert Lieberman rightly note, America's "democratic character has varied greatly—over time, across regions, and across groups of citizens and claimants to citizenship."[14] Democratic practices took hold only "gradually and haltingly," with advances accompanied by significant contractions, during which whole groups were purged from citizenship and entire regions of the country remained "authoritarian enclaves." In this view, America has been on an "unsteady march," blending liberal democratic tenets with rival, illiberal ideologies of ascriptive hierarchy.[15] For most of our history, American democracy was at best "incomplete," better understood as a "restricted democracy."[16]

Even those who have been attentive to variations in American democratic institutions and citizenship over time, however, most often end their accounts of our formally undemocratic past in the 1960s or soon thereafter. A consensus holds in many quarters that the United States by that period had rid itself of antidemocratic practices and illiberal citizenship and was now approaching, if it had not already arrived at, formal democratic enlightenment. Relying on T. H. Marshall's tripartite conception of citizenship, most democratic theorists broadly concurred that at least the first two tenets of citizenship—civil and political rights—were firmly institutionalized in America by the second half of the twentieth century, even if social rights remained elusive.[17] Speaking of the main instruments of democracy—universal suffrage, free speech and political expression, freedom to organize politically, and equality before the law—Sidney Verba stated plainly: "Equal political rights are fairly well established in the United States."[18] The massive civil rights mobilizations of the 1960s were the nail in the coffin of state-sanctioned inequality in America, and the Civil and Voting Rights Acts "ushered in a new era of democracy."[19] These important reforms assured that the essentials of the democratic ambition laid out by Verba, Robert Dahl, and others were in place by century's end, and we could now take "more or less for granted the fundamental democratic nature of the American regime." Accordingly, as America's undemocratic epochs receded into the past, "nondemocratic outcomes cannot help but appear as anomalies."[20]

We believe this accepted narrative of the nation's democratic arc is inaccurate or, at best, incomplete. In the chapters that follow, we address the complex question of whether American democracy is "alive and well" in American criminal justice. We bring a host of evidence to bear, from which we make two arguments that together form the basis of our claim that the criminal justice system has carved out an important exception to our democratic norms and, in so doing, has undercut the forward trajectory of equality and inclusion in America today.

The Carceral State and the Custodial Citizen

Criminal justice institutions have not only grown more pervasive over time, as numerous studies attest. In many ways, we argue, they also have grown more antidemocratic in character. We mean two things by this. First, we refer to changes in the systems' institutional features. As scholars of felon disenfranchisement have already noted, a significant collateral consequence of American crime control is that many individuals have been formally cut off from the democratic process. By losing important political and social rights of citizenship—the vote, jury service, ability to pursue many jobs and to access the social safety net—felons undergo a form of "civil death."[21] However, by focusing solely on the ways in which felons are legally excluded from suffrage and other democratic rights and privileges, scholars have missed the more complex but no less crucial ways in which the *lived experience* of American citizenship has changed for a growing group of Americans. Our argument is that criminal justice practices have broken significantly with the democratic norms that govern most American institutions: instead of embodying the commitments of a democratic republic, they undermine equality, restrict citizen voice, and insulate public officials from accountability and responsiveness. Thus, even those citizens who formally retain the right to vote are exposed to a set of institutions that systematically deny them the basic rights of a full and equal democratic citizen.

This was not always true and was not at all inevitable. As we point out in chapter 3, other nations—and earlier periods in American history—provide concrete examples of state and national criminal justice systems that employ a wide array of policies and institutions designed to deter and punish crime, without resorting to tools that depart from their core democratic principles. As we detail, the criminal justice system in the 1960s witnessed a marked expansion of rights and birthed a political movement that urged greater transparency and responsiveness from police and correctional authorities. This period exemplified the notion that while punishing and controlling crime often involved constraining liberties, it could do so without violating democratic norms.

It was short-lived, however. By the late 1970s, Congress and the courts had begun to scale back these gains by reducing access to litigation through the Prison Litigation Reform Act, limiting rights to speech and association among the incarcerated, insulating criminal justice agents by expanding legal immunity, and weakening institutional channels through which suspects and inmates could express their grievances. Through these and other developments, institutions of criminal justice have become places where citizens' voices are not often heard or responded to. At each stage of contact, from police stops to court adjudication to incarceration, custodial citizens experience a state-within-a state that reflects few of our core democratic values.

The significance of this divergence from democratic norms is compounded by the fact that criminal justice interventions have implicated greater numbers of citizens. As we detail in chapter 2, the scale of citizen contact with the American criminal justice system is unmatched in the nation's history. At least one estimate suggests that nearly a third of the total US adult population—roughly 65 million individuals over the age of eighteen—has a criminal record on file in at least one state (not counting some misdemeanants who were not fingerprinted).[22] In addition, 2.2 million adults—one in every 107—was behind bars at the close of 2011 and another 4.8 million are under some form of correctional jurisdiction (on probation, on parole) on any given day.[23] Many more have previously been wards of the state, including 20 million who have been imprisoned at some prior point in their lives.[24] The effective outcome of this overall growth is that a large group of Americans is exposed to a part of our democracy that, in practice, looks little like our democratic system in theory.

Some readers may think that this is appropriate, given that these people have violated the promise of a stable or "good" society by breaking the law. As we show in chapter 2, however, a large proportion of this group, who we refer to throughout the book as custodial citizens,—indeed, the majority of this group in some locales—*have never been found guilty of any crime in a court of law.* In particular, expanded police discretion to stop people for "reasonable suspicion" means that a majority of police stops in certain cities do not produce substantial evidence of wrongdoing, or lead to an arrest or summons. In addition, a large proportion of arrests never lead to a conviction, most often due to a lack of evidence.[25] And finally, even when police contact leads to arrests, most involve relatively low-level misdemeanors, such as loitering, graffiti, public intoxication, or smoking marijuana in public view, rather than violent or otherwise "serious" crimes. In recent years, this type of nonviolent infraction accounted for fully 80 percent of state court caseloads.[26]

In this we see a second aspect of carceral expansion that is anti-

democratic: that American policies and practices of crime control increasingly sort citizens into criminal justice institutions predicated as
much on their race and class as whether they are law-abiding or not. As
is by now well known, racial minorities are disproportionately likely
to be stopped, arrested, and incarcerated. A third of all black men in
their young adult years (25–29) are under correctional supervision at any
given time, and fully 11 percent (ages 20–34) are currently locked up in
a jail or prison.[27] The most underserved and marginal blacks are even
more likely to encounter the criminal justice system: prisons and jails
have been home to almost 70 percent of black male dropouts born since
the mid-1970s.[28]

Less well known is evidence suggesting that these groups experience
contact with criminal justice at rates that are disproportionate to their
share of criminal offending. For instance, national surveys show that,
with the exception of crack cocaine, blacks consistently report using
drugs at lower levels than whites.[29] Some studies also suggest that blacks
are engaged in drug trafficking at lower levels.[30] Yet, once we account
for their share of the population, blacks are ten times as likely to spend
time in prison for offenses related to drugs. In 2006, blacks accounted
for fully 45 percent of those held in state prison on drug charges. [31]

Our purpose in this book is not to argue that crime control policy
does not serve an important goal; it clearly does. Despite the importance
of determining whether and to what extent crime control policies meet
their intended goal of discouraging criminality, this is not our central
concern. Nor do we mean to suggest here that crime and victimization
are not pressing issues; they are. Indeed, as we discuss at some length
in chapter 2, the populations most directly affected by American crime
control policies are also those most directly harmed by the scourge of
violence.

Our primary goal in this book is not to estimate the efficacy of criminal justice policies in America or to document their scope. Rather, we
assess here the *character* of criminal justice in America, holding it up
against the traditional benchmarks of a democratic state. We set out
here to determine whether American crime control has become antidemocratic in ways that challenge our most basic notions of what constitutes a legitimate democratic system—and in ways which are not inevitable aspects of controlling crime, but are instead specific to American
policymaking in the modern era.

Political Socialization and Custodial Citizenship

In this book, we map the myriad ways that citizens' extraordinary rates of contact with criminal justice help to transform subjective conceptions of American citizenship. The antidemocratic features of criminal justice that we describe in chapters 2 and 3 matter not just because they go against the grain of democratic norms; they are important for what they convey to citizens about the nature of American democracy and citizenship. Thus, our second argument in this book concerns the individual-level political consequences of the expansion and antidemocratic character of the carceral state: The way criminal justice has grown and changed has deep consequences for the citizens it produces.

Most centrally, exposure to criminal justice institutions has implications for how individual citizens understand the political world they inhabit—how they see and seek to make claims on government, how they understand their political standing, and whether they perceive their group as a valued political equal in an ongoing scheme of cooperation. Instead of developing the tools and ethos of engaged citizens, they learn to stay quiet, make no demands, and be wary and distrustful of political authorities. In short, the democratic deficits of criminal justice institutions are reflected in the citizens that are its primary clientele.

Why would being exposed to a criminal justice intervention affect one's orientation to the political process or shape one's sense of citizenship and belonging? Citizens come to learn about their government through their direct contacts with it.[32] Interactions between citizen and state help form ideas about how government functions—its competence, for instance—but more important, about the democratic values, practices, and norms it embodies. Michael Lipsky argues that interactions with representatives of the government "socialize citizens to expectations of government service and a place in the political community . . . in a sense street-level bureaucrats implicitly mediate aspects of the constitutional relationship of citizens to the state."[33] Marc Landy has described this process as "a teaching" that "instruct[s] the public about the aims of government and the rights and responsibilities of citizens."[34] Through experiences within particular policy domains and with various government agencies, we the citizenry draw general conclusions about how government works, its underlying values and core commitments, and the political standing of the various social groups to which we belong.

Writing in this vein, T. H. Marshall was perhaps the first to show that one of the benefits of universal social programs in Britain was in teaching citizens that the state had responsibilities toward them.[35] Modern scholars of the welfare state echo this narrative; Suzanne Mettler argues that the GI Bill served not only to provide direct benefits to returning veterans, but also promoted civic obligation "by offering people a highly positive experience of government and public provision."[36] This civic-mindedness yielded higher rates of political activity and civic engagement among program participants that went above and beyond the direct effects of greater educational attainment. Likewise, according to Joe Soss, citizens who routinely interacted with government through the Social Security Disability Insurance (SSDI) program learned that government responds to them and treats them with respect.[37] In contrast, clients of the welfare system saw a government that stigmatized them and acted arbitrarily, with rules and processes that were difficult to navigate and understand.

Recipients of these and other social benefits come to view their contacts with the state as "a microcosm of government," generalizing their experience within the program to the broader nature and goals of the political system. Lessons learned through contact with social programs are lessons learned about government writ large, as contact with one part of government forms a "bridge" to perceptions of other aspects of the state. In his interviews with welfare recipients, Soss found that clients saw government as "one big system," often not distinguishing their views about welfare caseworkers from attitudes toward other government officials and bodies: "Experiences at the welfare agency come to be understood as an instructive and representative example of their broader relationship with government as a whole."[38] Similarly, Jennifer Lawless and Richard Fox found that "bad experiences with the welfare system transcended into other facets of government." As one woman with whom they spoke recounted, "I know all there is to know about government from welfare workers."[39] In a large analysis of over 3,000 citizens in Sweden, another scholar found that experiences with more empowering welfare institutions—health care and child care—affected general political orientations. Those who reported being satisfied with their treatment in this one domain voiced greater support for the political system as a whole, higher levels of satisfaction with democracy, and more trust in politicians.[40] In contrast, experiences with agencies that were disempowering—job assistance, housing assistance, and welfare—were more likely to increase political distrust and dissatisfaction with democracy.

Taken together, this work suggests that opinions about a specific agency are shaped through face-to-face interaction with physical institutions, but the resultant "teaching" is broader and more basic: It affects how we perceive the fundamental properties and commitments of our government and political system.

At the same time that they glean lessons about the nature of government, interactions with the state influence individuals' perceptions of their own political standing, membership, and efficacy. Institutions allow us to observe how the state treats and responds to people "like us"; through government contact, citizens "may acquire a sense of their own status in the polity, of how people like them are regarded—for instance, with respect or with stigma—and the extent to which they are included among the citizenry."[41] For example, community action programs were premised on the idea of empowering citizens to get involved in bettering their communities through direct action. This was accomplished by providing them with civic training, but also by conferring on them positions of worth and equal standing. In the same vein, Mettler argues that the GI Bill increased the political participation of returning soldiers not only because it provided them with the direct benefits of education, but also because it communicated respect and gratitude for their service.[42] In contrast, welfare positions recipients as "undeserving" through stigmatizing rules and requirements for receiving aid. In some places, for instance, individuals receiving benefits must submit to home searches and drug tests, toil in prisonlike garb along highways, and take any job given them.[43]

Related to these lessons about how the state values and treats us is the idea that government institutions can develop—or hinder—citizens' civic capacities, habits, and character. The idea is a simple one: citizens learn democracy by doing. According to Carole Pateman, as well as scholars of politics from Aristotle to John Stuart Mill and de Tocqueville, democratic participation helps develop an individual's faculties. As Pateman argues, "the experience of participation . . . will develop and foster the 'democratic' personality," one that resists hierarchy.[44] Participating in the democratic decisions of the state elevates a citizen's character and helps develop a consciousness that the citizen is a member of a political community. Moreover, participation begets participation. Through experience, the norms and practice of democratic life are incorporated into the political habitus, or way of being in and understanding the world.[45]

Thus, the design of political institutions is politically consequential because it provides a direct view of how government works, what role individuals are expected to play, and their worth vis-à-vis other citizens and the state. Through social programs, citizens garner important material resources, but also receive a blueprint of the character, capabilities, and commitments of the state. These lessons feed back into citizen participation and engagement. As Swedish political scientist Staffan Kumlin reminds us, "the structure of the contact interface between citizen and institution is just as important as the generosity of the transfers and services" it provides.[46] Institutions that promote and embody ideals of responsiveness and participation inculcate democratic habits among citizens. Institutions that send the message to individuals that they are valued and respected provide citizens with a symbolic civic resource of political standing.[47] Conversely, institutions that fail to reflect democratic values may inhibit civic skills, transmit ideas about government that demobilize, and inform citizens that they are not worthy of "equal concern and respect."[48]

Creating the Carceral Lifeworld

These existing accounts of how policies and institutions affect political socialization give us the conceptual tools for understanding how political institutions transmit ideas about the nature of the state and one's role in the democratic community or, put simply, how policies shape politics. The scholarship of Suzanne Mettler, Joe Soss, Andrea Campbell, Theda Skocpol, and others has indicated that people come to know about their government through their interactions with it. Jane Mansbridge instructs that "the character of the regime will affect the character of the citizens."[49] In short, interactions with government—whether through a welfare agency, a public library, the military, or a public school—"are the most direct source of information about how government works."[50]

In previous studies, however, scholars interested in how policies and institutions shape citizens have trained their eyes mainly on one side of the state—that concerned with social provision. Criminal justice is an increasingly routine point of contact between Americans and their state, a point we return to frequently in this book. We expect, therefore, that like welfare and other loci of state activity, the criminal justice system plays an important role in defining the status of citizens and imparting specific lessons about government, shaping political action and thought.

But the relationship between the citizen and the state in criminal justice interactions is fundamentally distinct from the citizen-state relationship in social welfare programs. Most basically, and in contrast to political experiences in other domains, contact with the carceral state is involuntary. It can have long-lasting and sometimes permanent effects, diverting the custodial citizen into a parallel system with a different set of rights, privileges, and rules. And it exposes individuals to authorities who are not elected trustees or social service bureaucrats, but judicial and law enforcement officials who wield immense and far-reaching control over their wards. For men and women who are more likely to encounter police than elected representatives, for youth who see probation officers more often than guidance counselors, and in neighborhoods where the greatest fiscal investment is in punishment rather than social welfare, how do citizens conceptualize the democracy they are inhabiting?

To understand the role of criminal justice in citizens' political lives, we explored a number of large social surveys, which included nationally representative samples and also subsamples of young and black Americans. These surveys allowed us to examine whether carceral contact, even accounting for its correlates of low income and low education, was related to particular views of government and politics. In addition to this extensive quantitative data, we went directly to the source, conducting intensive one-on-one interviews with individuals residing in three cities that have varied criminal justice systems and politics: Charlottesville, Virginia; New Orleans, Louisiana; and Trenton, New Jersey. All together, we sat down with about a hundred people, many of whom were racial minorities and living in poverty. Most of our interviewees had been stopped by police, slept on jail beds, or been confined to state prison at least once; many had extensive experience of this kind. However, we also sat down with a comparison group in Charlottesville, a set of about a dozen mostly low-income and minority citizens who had never had personal contact with criminal justice. Our interviewees told us stories of anguish, of losing families, jobs, and homes, but they also revealed their deeply held perceptions of the way government works. In their own words, they characterized the political system as they saw it, described how they felt about participating in the political process, and gave their account of race and inequality in twenty-first-century America.

In the quantitative data, there is often considerable overlap in the attitudes of custodial citizens and others who experience systematic disadvantage. Across our interview sample, too, nearly all of the individuals with whom we spoke described feeling that political participation was an exercise in futility, and that the voices of people "like them" carried little weight in the public sphere. Most spoke of government as distant and unhelpful, of politicians as untrustworthy and even corrupt. However, our data suggest that the political orientations of custodial citizens are distinct in both degree and kind.

Our interviews made clear that custodial citizens, in contrast to the others with whom we spoke, maintain a distinctive "lifeworld."[51] This custodial *lifeworld* has several primary distinguishing features. First, for a substantial number of those we interviewed, encounters with criminal justice authorities were their most proximate (and memorable) experience of government; as one individual we interviewed put it, "that's the only government I know." Because their frame of reference for considering the character of government centers on their personal experience with criminal justice, custodial citizens come to view the political system as being at least in part, if not primarily, about control, authority, and dominance. Through criminal justice contact, custodial citizens learn that government is not about distributing benefits, being a trustee of the public, or securing the collective good. Instead, government's primary purpose is keeping people in line.

Second, custodial citizens often develop a distinct set of rules and norms governing how to move through the social world, what we call the Code of Prohibitions and the Rules of the Game. What our interviewees learned through criminal justice was not simply about the punishment and surveillance they experienced; it was also about their social standing and about the many behaviors that were off-limits to "people like them." Chapters 5 and 6 show that the end result of citizen encounters with police, criminal courts, and correctional institutions is that custodial citizens develop a deep and sometimes totalizing sense of political alienation: "a subjective condition in which feelings of inefficacy or the belief that formal political decision-making is impenetrable to the average citizen conjoin with feelings of cynicism and distrust toward the government."[52] In stark contrast to the ideal character of the democratic citizen, who is "active" and "non-servile," an engaged participant wielding power in the political sphere, we find that custodial citizens become deeply distrustful of political authorities, have little faith that the state will respond to the will of the people, and believe they are not "full and equal."

In addition to creating political frameworks and thought in the citizenry, we find that contact with criminal justice helps to organize racial knowledge. That is to say, American institutions, beyond merely reflecting social understandings, actively cultivate and structure racial membership, identity, and perceptions. Not surprisingly, blacks who undergo contact with law enforcement exhibit a diminished faith in racial equality and greater discontent with government treatment of blacks. And yet, our ethnographic data reveal more complexity. In fact, two opposing transcripts are evident among the custodial citizens with whom we spoke, one focused on racial oppression and the other on personal choices and personal responsibility. These divergent narratives are rooted, we argue, in the counterposed messages of the criminal justice system itself. Key institutional developments like the emergence of colorblind jurisprudence and personal responsibility frameworks prevented the development of a unified narrative among custodial black citizens. Each of these narratives helped individuals make sense of their experiences with criminal justice—as well as with poverty, unemployment, and other social ills. However, neither provided a mobilized consciousness and effective discourse with which custodial citizens might challenge the racial disproportionality they witnessed in criminal justice institutions.

Finally, custodial citizens perceive government not only as failing to adequately assist them, as do most other low-income people, but also as actively doing harm. Theirs is an adversarial state that does not respond to their needs, it limits their chances and movements; where they are not voluntary participant in democratic politics, but involuntary subject to intervention from the state. This feature of the carceral lifeworld means that custodial citizens come to see participation in political life not only as something that is unlikely to yield returns, but as something to be actively avoided. In chapter 8 we show that those with criminal justice contact are less likely to participate in civic groups or express their political voice in elections. However, our interviews make clear that custodial citizens do not only fail to participate; they actively recoil from political life.

In sum, by attending to the prevalence of punitive interventions in citizens' lives, we show that punishment is not only an important aspect of the modern American state because it transforms the social and economic relationships of citizens, as previous studies have discussed. In addition, criminal justice is important because it transforms citizens' relationships to the polity. In both our interviews and survey data, we find that custodial citizens express a diminished belief in equality of citizenship and less optimism about their life chances. They voice lower levels of political trust and efficacy, and participate in politics at lower rates than those who have not had criminal justice contact. This remains true even once we account for race, socioeconomic status, self-reported engagement in criminal behavior, and other potential confounders.

Rather than learning that American government is accountable, responsive, and supportive of citizen participation and social equality—the hallmarks of a democratic polity and the American creed—custodial citizens come to view government as a closed, hierarchical system that minimizes their voice and allows authorities to act on them with relative impunity. Even more troubling, our results suggest that a growing number of citizens now regularly question whether they are, in fact, truly full and equal citizens, a fundamental offense against the core ideal of democratic citizenship. They believe they are unequal in the eyes of the state and harbor ideas about racial equality that do not reflect an egalitarian America. Worse, as we show in chapter 8, they fear the government and withdraw from civic and political life. Feeling disempowered and defamed, they make no demands and stay below the radar. In short, the carceral state carries deep implications for who is included—and how they are included—in the polity.

Contributions

A great deal of ink has been spilled examining the phenomenal growth in the punitive activities of American government over the past half-century. However, the transformations in the American state's capacity and desire to punish, as well as the repercussions for citizens and democracy, have engendered shockingly little discussion.[53] On the one hand, while political scientists and policy scholars are quite attentive to the ways that public policy, political institutions, and governance shape the citizenry, they have been much slower to evaluate the supervisory role of government compared to its redistributive functions, even as these functions have grown. On the other hand, because criminal justice has remained primarily the preserve of sociologists and legal scholars, they have produced scores of studies on modern trends in crime and punishment, but so far have not fully explored the *political* implications of the criminal justice system for citizens, communities, and the nation as a whole. "Criminologists have continued to study the causes, shape, and

consequences of carceral trends strictly in relation to crime and its suppression," Loïc Wacquant observes, with little regard for the "broader
reconstruction of the American state of which these trends are but one
fractional indicator."[54]

Excepting a few notable studies examining felon disenfranchisement
policies, sociologists and criminologists have excluded political attitudes
and behavior from their list of salient outcomes, focusing instead on variables related to employment, health, family, and criminality.[55] In these
studies, scholars have traced criminal justice contact to a wide range of
social and economic outcomes. To name just a few: researchers estimate
that incarceration predicts about a 6 percent decrease in employment
rates and between a 15 and 26 percent decrease in wages, that the black-
white disparity in marriage is cut in half without incarceration, and that
incarceration explains 70 percent of racial health disparities.[56] These developments are alarming, to say the least, but they miss whether and how
the decades-long expansion in the use of punitive interventions has re-
shaped citizenship and democracy. In several ways, then, our analyses in
this book urge a reconceptualization of the American state over the past
half-century, and shed a new light on the role of criminal justice in the
political life of the nation.

Locating Criminal Justice as a Central State Activity

Our work places the criminal justice reforms of the past half-century in
the broader context of American democratic governance. Despite its un-
yielding growth and scale, coercive state expansion remains a relatively
hidden development in our scholarship on American politics, a particularly remarkable oversight given the volumes dedicated to other developments in our nation's recent history. Scholars have focused on the rise
and dismantling of the welfare state and the growth of the administrative state. They have examined shifts in the interest group universe, the
decline of federated associations and labor unions, and changes in party
rules and procedures. They have explored social movements, civil rights
expansions, and immigration, and in striving to understand each of these
developments, they have probed their attendant meaning for political
life—whether and how they have prompted declining trust, shrinking social capital, widening polarization, political inequality, and other political phenomena.

Yet while scholars of American politics have even ferreted out aspects of the American state that are more subterranean, "out of sight," or "submerged," one of the most visible and transformative modern interventions has somehow escaped our notice.[57] For example, in *The Transformation of American Politics*, Paul Pierson and Theda Skocpol note that "the domestic role of the American national state underwent a stunning expansion" as the United States built an activist state over the past half century.[58] They trace the growth of several instruments of political authority; no mention is made of the expansion in punishment. By treating crime policy and carceral state growth as outside its purview, scholars of American politics have missed a central aspect of what makes the American state unique, captured only a fraction of state expansion, and misdiagnosed the consequences of shifts in American governance in the modern era.

A few scholars have urged us to consider the carceral state as a key feature of American political development and the organization of authority over time. In their work, these authors have described how criminal justice has enlarged state capacity and become central to the way we govern. With her groundbreaking book, *The Prison and the Gallows*, Marie Gottschalk was one of the first scholars—and still one of the only—to emphasize how punishment helped construct the early modern state; her book put the lie to the conception of America as a weak state, showing that at crucial moments in our nation's history, the United States expanded its power to punish. Through a sweeping historical analysis, Gottschalk shows that debates about crime were actually central to debates about state power and authority for much of the nation's history.[59]

Jonathan Simon is also attentive to how criminal justice affected state building and the broader political order. In recent work, he argues that criminal justice institutions became an important area for "constructing state government" and ultimately, the prison became a solution to the dilemma of governing after the New Deal, "a positive project of state legitimacy."[60] For Simon, shifts in policy and governance in the post–Great Society era are indicative of a broader movement toward "governing through crime," whereby, in a host of contexts, government has been reorganized around the problem of crime—from immigration to welfare to education.

Nowhere is this more evident than in how we govern the poor. Indeed, Loïc Wacquant pushes us to see prison expansion as linked to a "broader restructuring of government" by which the penal state replaced the welfare state for citizens at the bottom of the class structure.[61] Specifically,

Wacquant argues that penality was the American state's response to dealing with the social insecurities caused by the jobless ghetto and de-regulation of the market economy. In his view, criminal justice was not simply targeted at the poor; it became the primary way the state man-ages, regulates, and controls its poor in light of downsizing of the wel-fare state. Relatedly, Joe Soss, Richard Fording, and Sanford Schram ar-gue that shifts in welfare and criminal justice policy that have increased surveillance and punishment of poor citizens are part of a broader neo-liberal trend in poverty governance, one that means "low-income Amer-icans face a governing regime today that differs dramatically from the systems in place only a handful of decades ago."[62]

We extend these important analyses in the first half of this book, where we focus on crime control and the American state. In centralizing criminal justice, our book joins the handful of projects that have tack-led criminal justice as an integral part of state activity, concerned ex-plicitly with how the carceral state has developed over time. In deploy-ing the term *carceral state*, they (and we) mean to call attention to the network of institutions that are a key aspect of American government, much like the term *welfare state* refers not only to cash aid, but to a sys-tem of social provision that is politically constructed through policies, social movements, and institutions. These works force a new view of po-litical history, one that challenges our traditional view of American gov-ernance as weak or stateless. By incorporating criminal justice into the narrative of American state development, we highlight that government activism has been more uneven and also more robust than is tradition-ally appreciated.

Creating a New and Durable Social Cleavage

These shifts in governance are not only worthy of attention because they built state capacity, laws, and institutions or because they provided a way to manage social insecurities. They also matter, we suggest, because they changed the face of the state in citizens' lives. Suzanne Mettler and An-drew Milstein, in a piece concerned with state developments "from citi-zens' perspective," find a rapid "departure of government from the lives of nonelderly, low-income citizens in the latter twentieth century."[63] But if we broaden the field of state interventions to include criminal justice, we see a very different picture: The United States has witnessed a steady and consequential transformation of the state's role in the lives of its citizens. Despite claims of formal equality, custodial citizens are regularly and involuntarily exposed to institutions that systematically deny them equal voice, are unresponsive to their claims, and treat them as demonstrably unequal. That these characteristics of criminal justice institutions are purposive and intentional—that they are this way *by design*—is notable for what it helps to illuminate about modern political inequality.

Current debates over citizenship and democracy often center on the third of Marshall's pillars of citizenship—social rights—and on how unequal access to social and economic goods continues to structure civic and political inclusion. In the very first paragraph of *Inequality and American Democracy*, which seeks to set a new agenda for understanding political inequality, Lawrence Jacobs and Theda Skocpol state powerfully:

> Equal political voice and democratically responsive government are widely cherished American ideals—yet as the United States aggressively promotes democracy abroad, these principles are under growing threat in an era of persistent and rising inequalities at home. Disparities of income, wealth, and access to opportunity are growing more sharply in the United States than in many other nations, and gaps between races and ethnic groups persist. Progress toward expanding democracy may have stalled, and in some arenas reversed.[64]

Others have also cast the new threat to democracy in economic terms, demonstrating how inequalities in individual resources translate into inequalities in political voice and representation. Larry Bartels warns that "economic inequality impinges powerfully on the political process, frustrating the egalitarian ideals of American democracy."[65] Martin Gilens proclaims in equally strong language that "representational biases [favoring the rich] of this magnitude call into question the very democratic character of our society."[66] Scholars in this tradition often decry the erosion of social benefits born in the New Deal and Great Society, noting that over the past half century, the real value of the minimum wage stagnated, the welfare safety net was assailed, and a finally realized national health care program was attacked even before the ink on the president's signature was dry. These analyses usually begin by noting how far we have come in striking down formal political exclusions, but suggest that even as the dragons of segregation and suffrage restrictions were slain, inequalities of class continued to stand in the way of full democratic progress.

We strongly concur that the above are worrisome challenges to democratic inclusion in America today and firmly agree that access to civil and political rights is significantly stymied by festering social inequalities and flagging state commitment to the nation's less well off. But over and above the unequal distribution of individual resources and the state's failure to ameliorate it, we argue that democracy in America is challenged by another development: A large and growing swath of citizens has been made members of a pariah class by the policies and practices of the carceral state.

Some of these custodial citizens are defined by the choices they made to break the law. However, as we detail at length in chapter 2, most of this group are demarcated by experiences of having been stopped or arrested by police, or adjudicated in a court of law, but were not found guilty of any crime. Thus, where previous social cleavages have been identifiable by the characteristics of the targeted population—their gender, race, or relative wealth—custodial citizenship is defined by its relationship to the state. That is to say, the custodial citizen is described by practices and policies of criminal justice, not exclusively or in some cases even primarily by the individual behavior of criminal offending. Thus, the carceral state has not only accentuated social divisions based on prior divisions by race, gender, and class; it has also created a new division, a cleavage of durable political marginalization. Our book locates this new dimension of citizenship—not solely racial, social, or economic, but custodial.

This line of inquiry aims to strengthen a growing stream of scholarship in American political science that is attentive to the role of policies and institutions in shaping the attitudes and behavior of various social groups. But it is also important because the creation of a custodial citizenry has direct consequences for the central subjects of concern to American political scientists: political participation and representation. As we show in chapter 8, contact with criminal justice affects whether and how citizens engage with or withdraw from civic life. The story we tell here therefore serves not only to expand our notion of what role public policies play in how citizenship is understood, but also informs and clarifies our understanding of participation in the electoral process and of whose voices are heard or silent in the public square.

Exploring Complexities of Race and Criminal Justice

It is now common in scholarship, the news, and even congressional debates to note the overrepresentation of blacks in criminal justice. We add our voice to this growing group who contend that America's modern criminal justice policies have stymied the gains of the civil rights movement. As Bruce Western notes, "We can read the story of mass imprisonment as part of the evolution of African American citizenship. Each piece of this story—pervasive incarceration, unemployment, family instability—shows how mass imprisonment has created a novel social experience for disadvantaged blacks that is wholly outside of the mainstream of social life."[67] By exacerbating inequalities in income and education, criminal justice has kept many blacks from taking part in the American Dream.

Research on racial inequality paints a bleak portrait of the state of black America. Blacks have lower education levels, worse wages, higher rates of unemployment, and worse health outcomes. Even in times of economic prosperity, black poverty continues to be passed from one generation to the next. Just as important, however, is that a majority of blacks in America today still feel like second-class citizens. That is, it is not just that criminal justice keeps a large and disproportionately black segment of the population mired in poverty. In addition to cementing racialized economic stratification, criminal justice has also helped to maintain a racialized *civic* stratification, separating huge proportions of black citizens from the democratic process, its rich civic traditions, and its promise of full and equal citizenship. Our account of the carceral state is not only about economic marginality, but also about a deeply entrenched civic and political marginality that falls along racial lines. The criminal justice system is not only a site of continued racial disparity; it is instrumental in developing a unique racial experience of American democracy.

That criminal justice helps to "make" or "construct" race in America is not a new idea. In recent years, several scholars have argued that crime policy offers a way to control disadvantaged segments of the labor force and preserve white racial dominance. Extreme racial disparities in punishment are, as this argument goes, simply a modern manifestation of racial and social control. These scholars draw implicitly or explicitly on Foucault's idea that prisons spring from state efforts to control the citizenry. For instance, Loïc Wacquant argues that there is a functional

equivalence between slavery, Jim Crow, the ghetto, and the prison as systems of race control that replaced each other chronologically.[68] As blacks
were liberated from Jim Crow, "the prison abruptly returned to the fore-
front of American society and offered itself as the universal and simple solution to all manners of social problems." According to Wacquant,
prison was also a response to the collapse of the urban ghetto: "As the
ghetto lost its economic function and proved unable to ensure ethno-
racial closure, the prison was called upon to help contain a population
widely viewed as deviant, destitute, and dangerous."[69] Michael Tonry advances a similar thesis: "Contemporary drug and crime control policies
are in large part products of unconscious efforts by the white majority to
maintain political, social, and economic dominance over blacks."[70] And
in her high-profile book, *The New Jim Crow*, Michelle Alexander argues that imprisonment represents a new racial caste system. She writes:
"Rather than rely on race, we use our criminal justice system to label
people of color 'criminals' and then engage in all the practices we supposedly left behind. . . . We have not ended racial caste in America; we
have merely redesigned it."[71]

Our story adds additional complexities to the account of race and
criminal justice as it is most frequently understood. First, we suggest
that because custodial status hinges on social characteristics that are
connected to but separable from race—including class status, neighborhood, and other markers like hairstyle and dress—criminal justice
"teaches" race in more subtle and complex ways than previous regimes.
Many of those we interviewed spoke not about race as an isolated factor
but instead drew on multiple examples of intersectional disadvantage.
For them, race was just one element among several intersectional identities that constrained their chances; race combined with other minority statuses—being poor, being a convicted felon, having dark skin color,
living in a "bad" neighborhood. Criminal justice was not, then, an isolated domain where racial barriers and discrimination were rampant. Instead, some proffered quite complex descriptions of how the whole system functioned to keep them back. They spoke of criminal justice in the
larger context of how their neighborhoods had been allowed to decline,
and how the crack epidemic was located in an urban economy lacking
jobs and opportunities, seducing and destroying a generation of young
blacks.

More critically, though, we argue here that modern racial inequality
is not simply a continuation of historical inequalities or even a legacy

of past political injustices; instead, the design of criminal justice institutions differs in important ways from previous race-making institutions. Specifically, the pervasive "postracial" and "colorblind" messages that black Americans receive from modern political culture broadly—as well as from criminal justice agents and institutions specifically—helps to obscure the role of racial bias in the operation of crime control. This leads to a substantial disconnect between the obvious racial disproportionality that custodial citizens see firsthand in criminal justice, and the social narratives that are available to help them make sense of it; in essence, blacks were left without a coherent framework to explain persistent racial inequality. Moreover, as the "colorblind" approach came to dominate the legal framework of modern crime control, a personal responsibility narrative helped to fill that void. The result, we find, is that blacks as a whole are nearly as likely to turn to failings of black culture in order to explain the role of race in criminal justice as they are to consider explanations that hinge on black segregation, racialized poverty, and intentional discrimination.

The result is that criminal justice exists in a gray area between intentional discrimination and its proxies: personal responsibility, moral degradation, and the culture of poverty. This new and more complex racial regime is the modern threat to a racially equal democracy, which presents challenges that are far more intractable than in previous eras. In particular, the use of individual choice to explain black overrepresentation in criminal justice—whether the choice to commit crimes is seen as stemming from a lack of moral values or rooted in the trappings of poverty—is particularly pernicious, because it taps into another core value of liberal democracy, the idea of individual liberty. By using the language of personal choice to justify racial inequality, we effectively allow one democratic norm (liberty) to justify the subversion of another (equality).[72]

Our aim is therefore not to equate criminal justice to earlier racial caste systems, as scholars such as Alexander and Wacquant have done, however tempting it may be to remark on the continuities between criminal justice and previous political institutions (e.g., slavery and Jim Crow) that helped to maintain racial stratification. In fact, our point is exactly that criminal justice is *distinct* from earlier forms of racial organization in ways that matter for how blacks learn and understand their racial position in America. As James Forman Jr. aptly notes, "In Mississippi in 1950, the totalizing nature of Jim Crow ensured that to be black meant to be second class; there were no blacks free of its strictures. But mass incarceration is much less totalizing. In 2011, *no* institution can define what it 'means to be black' in the way that Jim Crow or slavery once did."[73] Thus, by saying that criminal justice contact helps to organize racial knowledge, we do not mean to analogize it with former systems of racial control and domination. In fact, we believe that it is only through identifying the ways that custodial status departs from past totalizing and formalized systems of racial oppression that its consequences can be fully understood.

Expanding Conceptions of Politics and Citizenship

Our final contribution is the expansion of current notions of citizenship, which have come to dominate studies of politics in America. In recent decades, scholars of American political science have focused on nearly every aspect of the relationship between citizens and their elected representatives. They have documented the significance of campaigns and examined returns to spending, the effects of going negative, and the role of campaign advertisements as sources of political information; they have assessed the responsiveness of congressmen to the needs and interests of their constituents and the ways that some group interests are advantaged over others; they have written on the causes and consequences of underrepresentation of racial minorities and women in the halls of power; and they have described and explained declining voter turnout, predictors of vote choice, and the effects of organized efforts to "Get Out the Vote."

Yet, as Jacob Hacker and Paul Pierson noted recently, the dominant lines of inquiry have little to say about the extent to which the electorate helps to shape policymaking through activities that are not centered on Election Day. In contrast to standard political studies that focus on the politician-voter connection, which Hacker and Pierson term "politics as electoral spectacle," their account tells a story of "politics as organized combat," in which organized groups put sustained pressure on elected officials through activities "taking place in the trenches of American politics on a daily basis."[74]

The work of Hacker, Pierson, and others places considerably less emphasis on elections, but is still primarily concerned with the relationship between the electorate and its democratic representatives. In studying political lobbying and organizing, the dominant questions are still "who gets what, when and how," which groups have influence over policymaking, and to whom the costs and benefits are distributed.[75] These are important questions, and responsiveness and representation are rightly central to the study of American politics. However, much of the most meaningful activity of democratic life—especially in the lives of individual citizens—happens outside the narrow bounds of elections and falls outside the scope of even formal law and policy, occurring in the regular contacts people have with the administrative state. Suzanne Mettler reminds us that "these seemingly mundane experiences are likely to be more instructive about citizens' relationship to government and their status within the polity than are their far less frequent visits to the voting booth, almost nonexistent encounters with elected officials, and impersonal sound bites of political advertising."[76]

This is not to say that there have been no serious studies of the American bureaucracy by modern political scientists. In particular, the vast expansion of public programs and institutions over the past century led to a host of studies expressing concern about political accountability and discussing the appropriate balance in the principal-agent relationship between discretion and control.[77] In these accounts, it was not only the burgeoning size of these institutions that was cause for consternation, but the extent to which they were shielded from oversight and allowed to make independent decisions. Indeed, in recent years, a number of studies have argued that America has developed a vast and unaccountable administrative state, a "new leviathan" of "government by expert."[78] As James Q. Wilson writes:

> The number of administrative agencies and employees grew slowly but steadily during the 19th and early 20th centuries and then increased explosively on the occasion of World War I, the Depression and World War II. It is difficult to say at what point in this process the administrative system became a distinct locus of power or an independent source of political initiatives and problems. What is clear is that the emphasis on the sheer size of the administrative establishment—conventional in many treatments of the subject—is misleading.[79]

Our concern here is related, but distinct. Studying public bureaucracy is not only important because it is a "synonym for . . . undemocratic authority," potentially uncontrolled by elected officials and unresponsive to the public good.[80] It is also important because bureaucratic design and culture matter for what citizens learn about democracy and citizenship in America; we take a broader view of democratic politics to examine the direct experience that citizens have with their governing institutions. Our book therefore leaves the halls of Washington and the confines of the statehouse to examine the agents and institutions of American public bureaucracy, where—as the national Commission on the State and Local Public Service argues—"the actual delivery of the most basic and essential services take place."[81] In so doing, *Arresting Citizenship* directs attention beyond democracy as primarily campaigns and elections, or even as the "organized combat" that takes place in the domain of civil society and interest group organizing. Instead, ours is an inquiry into the administrative institutions that comprise the everyday machinery of our modern democracy and the meaning of those institutions for the citizens who encounter them.

By focusing on the carceral state and its consequences, we emphasize that custodial citizenship is not only about exclusion from certain rights or benefits, but about the active construction of a different citizenship. Ours is a story of the ways that citizens directly experience democracy; that is, a *politics as lived experience.*[82] The majority of those we describe in this book maintain the rights and responsibilities of full and equal citizens. They are entitled to register and vote, and they are formally equal before the law. However, because of their race, their income, and the characteristics of the neighborhoods in which they live, these individuals are systematically more likely to be exposed to public institutions that deny them voice, treat them as suspect, do not respond to their needs, and are unaccountable to their complaints.

We join others who suggest that criminal justice delimits citizenship, its meaning and its practice. Alec Ewald, Michael Owens, Mary Katzenstein, and others have described how post-punishment policies, public opinion, and the media construct a different, and more limited, citizenship for those deemed offenders or felons. In particular, the ongoing debate over felon disenfranchisement has centered on its formally antidemocratic outcomes, how it prevents citizens from having a say in their government and choice of representatives. But by documenting the voices of custodial citizens themselves, we shed light on the broader way that individuals themselves come to conceptualize and understand the democracy they inhabit and their role within it.

Thus, our central contribution is to emphasize that citizenship is not only about formal standing, rights, and incorporation; it is also about the ways in which citizens are socialized to understand the democracy in which they live and their place in it. Sharon Krause describes free-dom as an affective or dispositional state (are we, in fact, free if we are made to feel that our rights are systematically circumscribed?) and ar-gues that freedom is "made real" to citizens by enabling human agency and reorienting self-understanding. She suggests that freedom must be understood to be as much about domination on the part of the oppres-sor as about self-realization on the part of the oppressed.[83] This more ex-pansive notion of citizenship makes room for a new dimension of eth-nographic citizenship. Citizenship and democratic political standing are most appropriately measured not only by the laws on the books, but also by how citizens conceptualize the state and their position in it.

We make these contributions on the shoulders of several pioneering scholars whose work should remind students of American politics that punishment is political; it both reflects and shapes our political context, culture, and institutions. These scholars show us that crime control and punishment are a central part of what our government does and has been doing for a very long time. They push us to recognize that—despite the shallow analysis it has generally received within political science—pun-ishment and crime policymaking are fundamentally a political exercise, "a universal attribute of regimes," and that what defines the state, at its core, is its monopoly on the legitimate use of force.[84] Punishment there-fore says something important about the character of our state, its gov-erning ideologies, and how it defines the boundaries of citizenship in the eyes of its citizens. While our book differs from existing works in several respects, it builds on this small but solid foundation of scholarship with the hope that the recent, but still underdeveloped, attention to the poli-tics of punishment continues to bloom.

CHAPTER TWO

Thinking about Crime
and the Custodial Citizen

Some readers might object that any damage that America's criminal justice system has done to citizens' democratic capacities is largely confined. Perhaps custodial citizens—those who the criminal justice system has touched—are the exception, not the rule, and thus the fundamental promise of democratic citizenship, that citizens can voice their opinions and are treated equally and fairly by their governing institutions, is not breached. Others might suggest that custodial citizens may be a large and growing group, but they are purposefully excluded from the law-abiding polity. By committing a crime, these individuals have proven themselves to be unworthy of equal citizenship and standing. We address these important concerns in the following sections, where we provide two distinct rejoinders.

First, we argue that the size of the carceral state and the proportion of citizens it affects have surpassed what any serious scholar of American politics can consider to be marginal. Most prominently, America has continuously swelled its prisons for the better part of five decades. Scholarship and journalism regularly discuss our growing prison populations and note how far we have stepped outside the cross-national norms of other rich democracies. However, while rising incarceration rates are important, focusing on imprisonment alone actually understates the reach of the carceral state. In fact, most people who have contact with criminal justice institutions in the twenty-first century are not confined to prisons. They are stopped by foot patrols as they make their way to jobs and homes. They are brought to court for failing to make their child-support payments. They are given citations for trespassing in public parks. They are taken to local jails for a range of behaviors, from public intoxication to loitering, from which no bodily harm to others results. Once we account for this far larger group of people, we see that the growth of criminal justice contact has depended only in part on the increasing use of prisons.

The total share of the population encountering criminal justice has grown substantially, as data on the experiences of young adults reveals. In the 1979 cohort of the National Longitudinal Study of Youth (NLSY), which surveyed a representative sample of eighteen- to twenty-three-year-olds in 1980, 11 percent had been arrested, 8 percent had been convicted of a crime, and 2 percent had spent time in prison or jail. The proportions reporting criminal justice contact had shifted by the time the 1997 cohort of the NLSY was eighteen to twenty-three years old, in 2002. In that year, fully 24 percent had been arrested, 12 percent had been convicted of a crime, and 5 percent had been incarcerated. Meanwhile, crime rates actually decreased significantly over this period. According to the FBI's Uniform Crime Report, the violent crime rate in 1980 was 597 crimes per 100,000 people, with 5,353 property crimes per 100,000. In 2002, the violent crime rate had decreased roughly 17 percent to 494 per 100,000 and the property crime rate dropped by nearly a third to 3,631.[1]

Moreover, zeroing in on imprisonment in isolation (rather than all criminal justice encounters) makes it easier to dismiss potential damages to citizenship as being earned and deserved, because it narrows our gaze to those most likely to be non–law-abiding and serious offenders. Criminal justice then appears less perilous for the democratic markers of voice, equality, and accountability. But the citizenship damages we explore in the remainder of this book have both a wider and more imprecise target. Custodial citizenship has become a defining position for a large and varied swath of individuals. For this group, being in the orbit of criminal justice now rivals other mainstays of citizen-state interaction, such as receiving welfare and being contacted by politicians.

Thus, a second rejoinder we would offer to those who downplay the damage of the carceral state to American democracy is this: once we broaden our gaze beyond solely those in prison and jail, we see that much of the contact citizens have with the criminal justice system never results in their being found guilty of committing a crime in a court of law. As a result, belonging to the custodial citizenry is actually only weakly correlated with being in the so-called criminal class. We therefore differentiate here between the "criminal" and the "custodial citizen." The designation "criminal" is conferred on individuals as a result of that individual engaging in illegal behavior. In contrast, the custodial citizen is defined by his or her relationship to the state, predicated on individual behavior (both legal and illegal), but also on the government's activities related to crime control. In this chapter, we provide evidence that the increasingly large disconnection between individual behavior and state interactions has real consequences for the composition of custodial citizens. If criminal behavior alone determined criminal justice contact, we would likely see fewer custodial citizens overall, and a different distribution by race and socioeconomic status.

In the following sections, we aim to document how large the custodial citizenry is and also to disaggregate it. The data we present in this chapter make clear that American criminal justice policies have done three things: (1) increased the number of citizens who are represented in the custodial population but have never been found guilty of a crime; (2) increased the share of minor offenders, who would not have been sentenced to prison in prior decades but are now confined in prisons and jails; and (3) resulted in a growing disconnect between those who engage in criminal behavior and those who encounter criminal justice. In short, custodial interactions are no longer confined primarily to offenders and prison is no longer targeted predominantly to serious offenders. The result is that sizable numbers of non-offenders and minor offenders, along with more serious offenders, bear firsthand witness to the antidemocratic face of American government. The lessons conveyed to citizens by the criminal justice system—which we describe in the following chapter—are therefore not anomalous and minimal diversions from democratic life, imparted to only a small or depraved group of criminals. They must be considered central to how a growing number of citizens understand and experience democracy in America today.

America's Modern Democratic Contraction

Policing and punishment are elementary functions of government. From the invention of the penitentiary to the opening of America's first supermax prison, the United States has monitored, policed, punished, and sometimes killed to enforce the boundaries of citizen behavior. Never before in our history, however, has American government and the polity exhibited so strong an urge to punish, so vast a network of institutions dedicated to controlling, confining, and supervising citizens, or a criminal justice system so targeted toward certain segments of the citizenry. Criminal justice institutions dot our geographic landscape, police and correctional interest groups populate our political landscape, and an elaborate web of state and federal laws define increasingly punitive punishments for decreasingly serious offenses. As one scholar recently observed "the power of the U.S. government to regulate, study, order, discipline, and punish its citizens—as well as other nations' citizens—has never been greater."[2]

This was not always the case. Crime policy barely registered as an item on state and local government agendas, and decades passed without the federal government revising its criminal code or passing crime legislation because it was reluctant to involve itself in what was seen as the province of states. It was not until the 1960s that crime policy began to appear as a larger part of the legislative agenda (as fig. 2.1 shows). By the 1980s, crime had surpassed attention to social welfare as a proportion of congressional activity. Crime also took up more attention in state

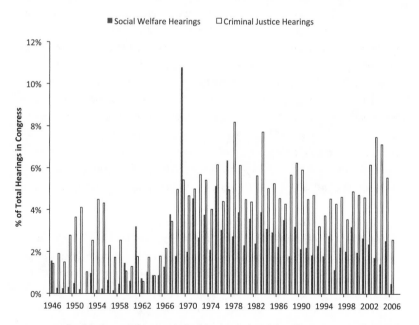

FIGURE 2.1. Legislative activity on criminal justice and social welfare, 1947–2006. *Source*: Policy Agendas Project. www.policyagendas.org.

legislatures, which in the latter period considered hundreds of new provisions and passed an enormous amount of legislation reforming state criminal codes.

In waging its consecutive wars on crime and drugs, the federal government began a decades-long program of financial support to the states for crime control, instituting policies that provided billions of dollars for prison construction and police professionalization. This influx of money greatly improved parochial law enforcement by increasing its manpower and capacities to arrest, convict, and confine, and to measure crime. It also incentivized states to move toward a more punitive approach to crime control. For instance, the national government urged states to incarcerate offenders for longer stretches by making imprisonment cheaper through truth-in-sentencing grants. In response, American states widened their nets of surveillance and punishment to include more people and new social groups, fortified these nets through more intrusive and intensive forms of state intervention, and created new nets as agents and agencies of punitive state control changed their tactics and developed additional infrastructure.[3]

Other segments of the criminal justice system were transformed in countless other ways. Early release from prisons was largely abolished, mandatory minimum penalties were passed for a wide array of offenses, youth were tried and incarcerated as adults, and states enacted criminal code reforms that increased the severity of sentences and added draconian sentence enhancements for the presence of certain factors in the commission of a crime, such as guns or drugs. This marked a radical break with history; in the past, confinement was reserved for the most violent and prison stays lasting over five years were rare. In sum, by most conceivable measures and by a wide margin, we live in a more punitive society now than fifty years ago. In the realm of criminal justice, the nation "embarked on one of the largest public policy experiments in our history."[4]

Many studies have focused on this rise in punishment, particularly as it pertains to the massive growth of the prison system. This is important, but it is not our primary focus. Our emphasis here is instead on a loosening over time in the relationship between having contact with the carceral state on the one hand, and engaging in criminal behavior on the other. Figures on the growth in policing and incarceration are by now well known, but a somewhat less obvious result of America's modern crime control policies is that a greater proportion of the nation's custodial citizens are non-serious offenders or even non-offenders. That is: the relationship between criminal behavior and contact with criminal justice, we argue, is increasingly tenuous.

To make this point, we must carefully distinguish between the custodial citizen and the criminal class through a systematic disaggregation of these overlapping but distinguishable social groups. In decoupling criminality from custodial status, we thus conceptualize the custodial citizenry as comprised of three distinct and non–mutually exclusive categories: the criminal suspect, the arrestee/misdemeanant, and the incarcerated offender. Criminal suspects include those who have experienced criminal justice contact, but have never been found guilty of a crime by a court of law. This encompasses the large numbers of individuals who are stopped and questioned by police but never arrested, those who are arrested but never formally adjudicated, and those who are adjudicated and ultimately found to be innocent of criminal wrongdoing. As we describe in detail in the following section, the likelihood of criminal justice contact resulting in suspect status has increased substantially over time, such that in many large, urban localities it is now the most likely category into which a custodial individual will fall.

The category of the arrestee/misdemeanant includes the growing group of individuals successfully prosecuted for so-called quality of life crimes, such as loitering, public drunkenness, and graffiti. These individuals are convicted of minor crimes that in previous eras might have gone unprosecuted, but that are now prosecuted criminally and often accompanied by large fines or stints behind bars. As we detail in the sections that follow, the growth of this group was aided in particular by the phenomenal rise of plea bargaining, which made it easier for the criminal justice system to dispose of large numbers of low-level offenders without investing the time and resources required for a trial. As William Stuntz explains:

> The combination of these two related trends—expanding criminal liability and a rising number of guilty pleas—meant that, as the *quantity* of criminal punishment grew, its *quality* declined. Thanks to broader criminal liability rules, the status of convicted felon no longer means what it once did: offenders acquire that status having committed offenses much less severe than the ones that traditionally led to felony convictions and prison terms. Thanks to

more easily induced guilty pleas, criminal litigation does a worse job than it once did of separating those who have committed the crimes charged from those who haven't.[5]

Finally, the category of convicted offender includes those individuals who are prosecuted and convicted of a "serious" crime. However, even within this category, only a minority has been convicted of a crime that involves serious bodily harm, such as rape, murder, or assault. The larger share has been convicted of a crime that does not involve the infliction of physical harm, such as drug offenses or property crimes. In a previous era, many of these individuals might have been sent to drug treatment, given noncustodial sentences, or imprisoned for a relatively short time. Many now serve long sentences in prison.

In the following sections, we review these three distinct classes of custodial citizens in greater detail.

The Criminal Suspect

The growing disconnection between the criminal and the custodial citizen is most obvious in the area of policing. In large cities across the country, police forces since the 1970s have adopted increasingly forceful tactics targeting a wider range of crimes, including low-level but high-visibility offenses, such as graffiti and public intoxication, following the logic that this led to more and more serious crime. The widely invoked moniker of a "war on crime and drugs" accurately typified street-level policing during this period, particularly in the inner-city, as many police departments and officers took a "warrior" approach to crime control, seeing themselves as the "detached, aloof crime-fighter who daily battles the hostile enemy—the public."[6] This approach was later transformed in many cities into a "professional model" of policing that employed new technologies, relied heavily on patrols by car rather than on foot, and "emphasize[d] crime-fighting with minimal contact with the public."[7]

Being stopped by police is now the most commonly reported form of citizen contact with criminal justice, but the least systematically measured; we know of no representative, national longitudinal data on pedestrian police stops. What we can piece together through cross-sectional surveys and city-specific reports, though, reveals that stop-and-frisk practices have surged in recent years. In New York City from 2002 to 2011, police stops increased by a whopping 603 percent to almost

700,000 people per year. In Philadelphia from 2005 to 2009, stops increased 148 percent to approximately 250,000.[8]

As stops have mushroomed, their quality has declined dramatically in netting criminal offenders. It is difficult to get an accurate measure of how frequently police stops result in an arrest, given the variance in police practices and data compilation methodologies across localities. However, estimates suggest that hit rates, or arrests resulting from police stops, are in some places as low as 5–6 percent.[9] For example, figure 2.2 shows the increase in stops over time in New York City; the vast majority of stops are of people not found to be doing anything wrong. In 2011, only 12 percent of the more than half a million police stops in New York City resulted in a formal arrest charge or summons. In Philadelphia, just under 6 percent of stops led to an arrest for wrongdoing.[10] Arrest rates are higher in Los Angeles and have increased over time as a proportion of overall stops, but an arrest in the City of Angels is still the outcome in only a minority of cases. In 2008, 34 percent of pedestrian stops in that city (up from 16% in 2002) resulted in an arrest.[11] The result is that hundreds of thousands of citizens who are not actually engaged in criminal

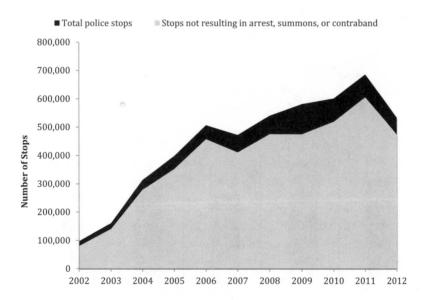

FIGURE 2.2. Incidence of police stops in New York City, 2002–2012. *Source*: http://www .nyclu.org/content/stop-and-frisk-data.

activity, or where there is little evidence of criminal wrongdoing, now have contact—sometimes repeatedly—with state authorities who treat them with suspicion.

In addition, the majority of individuals arrested by police are not found guilty. In fact, many arrests do not even lead to formal charges. This is particularly true for misdemeanor arrests. As Peter Moskos and others who have studied urban police practices argue, "the point of loitering arrests is not to convict people of the misdemeanor. . . . These lockups are used by the police to assert authority or get criminals off the street."[12] Even a large portion of cases that are prosecuted do not result in convictions (fig. 2.3). Data on a random sample of court cases from large urban counties show that about a third of all felony defendants ultimately are not convicted of a crime, and just over 40 percent are not convicted of a felony. The percentage of individuals found not guilty varies somewhat by the type of accused crime; it is somewhat higher among those accused of a violent crime (38%) and lower among those accused of a property or public-order offense (28%). Drug offenses fall somewhere in between: About 33 percent of felony drug defendants are not convicted and 41 percent are not convicted of a felony crime. However, for no type of crime does the conviction rate reach 50 percent. In other words, even among custodial citizens who are arrested and brought to

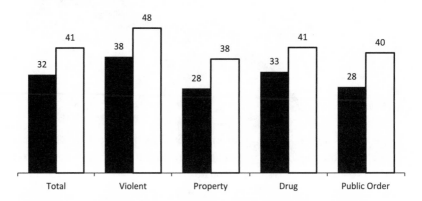

FIGURE 2.3. Adjudication outcome for felony defendants in large urban counties. *Source*: 2004 State Court Processing Statistics Program, Bureau of Justice Statistics.

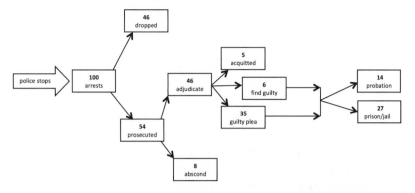

FIGURE 2.4. Outcomes in the criminal justice process for adults, for 100 typical cases. *Source*: Authors' calculations from data provided by Todd R. Clear, Michael D. Reisig, and George F. Cole, *American Corrections* (Belmont, CA: Wadsworth Publishing, 2011), 134.

trial, the majority are determined by the court not to have broken any law. It is likely that at least some of these individuals did commit a crime but are released due to insufficient evidence. It is clear, though, that neither police stops nor arrests implicate exclusively lawbreakers.

To get a better sense of these various points of contact, figure 2.4 details the outcome of 100 typical adult arrests.[13] As the figure shows, about one-half of all arrested adults are never processed by a criminal court; 46 percent are dropped before adjudication, most often for lack of sufficient evidence. An additional 8 percent of cases that are adjudicated fail to reach a verdict because the suspect absconds rather than appearing in court. Of the 46 percent that proceed, 5 percent end in acquittal. Thus, out of every 100 adults arrested, fewer than half end up with a criminal conviction, 35 through plea agreements and 6 through trial.[14]

It is not unlikely that some substantial minority of those who are stopped by police but not arrested, who are arrested and released, or who are adjudicated but found not guilty actually committed the crimes of which they were suspected. These individuals, despite their crimes, go unpunished. There is no way to know for sure the extent to which this is the case, but we can be reasonably sure that it sometimes occurs. As early scholars of criminal law noted:

> Our system does not guarantee either the conviction of the guilty or the acquittal of the innocent. Certain safeguards are erected which make it more

difficult to convict the innocent than to acquit the guilty, but all that our
system guarantees is a fair trial. It is a price which every member of a civilized community must pay for the erection and maintenance of machinery
for administering justice, that he may become the victim of its imperfect
functioning.[15]

We can be equally confident, however, that the reverse is even more
often the case: those who are cleared of criminal wrongdoing are more
often not guilty of their alleged crime. Our reasoning here is simple:
While certainly flawed, the American criminal court system is sure to
have more successes than failures. Most important, we know for sure that
all of these individuals have not been *proven* guilty of their crime by a
court of law, which is the standard by which we should judge their appropriate legal and social standing. Additionally, these figures still may not
accurately measure the extent to which arrests are correlated with law
breaking, because at least some suspects are likely encouraged to plead
guilty to charges of which they may be innocent in order to avoid the risk
of lengthy prison sentences. We return to this issue at some length in the
following section.[16]

Even more troubling than the growing number of citizens who fall in
the criminal suspect class are the factors that predict the likelihood of
this type of criminal justice contact. Blacks and Latinos undergo involuntary police encounters at much higher rates than whites, sometimes
on the order of thirty and forty percentage points. One analysis found
that controlling for delinquency, black preteens were more likely to have
police intervention by eighth grade and twice as likely as whites by the
tenth grade.[17] Qualitative studies of urban youth also document a substantial difference in minority surveillance: "more than half of the young
men in our sample with no history of serious offending nonetheless reported negative experiences with the police."[18] According to the work
of Jeffrey Fagan and others, many innocent blacks will not make it to
their mid-twenties without being stopped by police at some point.[19] This
would be unfathomable in the middle-class suburban neighborhoods in
which their white peers are more likely to reside.

As we have already noted, the rate of stop-and-frisk activity in New
York City and Philadelphia has increased substantially over time.[20]
Among blacks and Latinos in New York City, though, the stop rate in
the 2005–6 period was 131 and 64, respectively (per 1,000 in the population), compared to just 18 per 1,000 for whites in New York City.[21] To-

gether, blacks and Latinos comprised 80 percent of all stops from 2005 to 2008, although they represent about half of New York City's population.[22] Scholars estimate that the probability that a black male eighteen or nineteen years of age will be stopped by police in that city at least once during the year is 92 percent. The probability for a Latino male of the same age group is 50 percent. For a young white man, it is 20 percent.[23] Put another way, a young black man walking through New York City is virtually guaranteed to be stopped by police and a Latino young man would have the same chance as getting heads in a coin toss.

Police stops in Philadelphia and Los Angeles mirror the patterns for New York. In Philadelphia, blacks and Latinos were three-quarters of those stopped in the first two quarters of 2012 in a city where they comprise 56 percent of the population.[24] In Los Angeles police stops of pedestrians doubled from 2002 to 2008, and blacks accounted for 36 percent of stops while representing 11 percent of the city population. Los Angeles police stops were also geographically concentrated, such that residents of certain neighborhoods were much more likely to be stopped, and there was a great disparity across neighborhoods in how frequently stops led to an arrest.[25] Areas with the highest increases in stops were also the places with the least increase in hit rates. Stops were so high in two areas—Central LA and Hollywood—that there "were more stops of African Americans [there] in one year than there were African American residents."[26]

Other data suggest that New York, Philadelphia, and Los Angeles are not unique. In cities across the country, black and Latino youth are significantly more likely than other groups to have contact with police. In Chicago, over 70 percent of young black men reported being stopped by the police in a single year, compared to only 20 percent for the city as a whole.[27] In Washington, DC, 61 percent of young black men reported that they had been stopped by police, either as motorists or pedestrians—fully three times the rate for young white males in that city.[28]

These data provide compelling evidence that, despite prohibitions on race-based policing, police continue to disproportionately stop and search racial minorities. As we describe in chapter 7, though, locating the role of race and racism in the modern criminal justice is a complex task. Nor can we fully consider the wide array of new tactics that police have at their disposal, which has contributed to racial and economic disproportionality in the custodial class; space does not permit. However, arguably the most significant factor in the growth of racially disparate policing is the way that police in major American cities have increasingly employed Terry stops. This practice is named for John Terry, the litigant in *Terry v. Ohio*, a landmark 1968 US Supreme Court case. The court ruled in *Terry* that police were not violating the Fourth Amendment when they stopped and frisked an individual without probable cause. Instead, police needed only "reasonable suspicion" that the individual was engaged in criminal activity to initiate contact. Such encounters, based not on probable cause but on reasonable suspicion, "essentially allow the police to approach and investigate people for any reason, or for practically no reason at all; the officer's discretion is largely unregulated."[29] For instance, in NYPD data cataloguing all stop-and-frisk activity from 2010–11, 51 percent of all stops were justified at least in part by an individual's "furtive movements," 16 percent because an individual fit a suspect description, and 5 percent because an individual wore clothes commonly used in a crime. Additional circumstances contributing to a stop or questioning included evasive behavior, such as changing direction at the sight of an officer (25%) or evasive responses to questioning (20%), walking in a high-crime area (59%), or being around at a time of day that fits crime incidence (41%).[30] In Philadelphia during 2011, about 43–47 percent of pedestrian stops were made without reasonable suspicion.[31]

In general, the courts have defined two factors as providing reasonable suspicion: being in a high crime area and moving away from police. In essence, this means that anyone walking through a high-crime area might reasonably draw police attention; this is exactly what has happened. Jeffrey Fagan and his colleagues found that the sharply increasing rate of police stops in the mid-2000s was largely due to "extreme increases" in a very few neighborhoods where black and Latino residents dwell, including Mott Haven, Brownsville, East New York, and Harlem, among others.[32] As one legal scholar observes, "every person who works or lives in a high crime area and who avoids the police is subject to automatic seizure, and to automatic search." Given that minorities are more likely to reside in such areas and be suspicious of police harassment, these two court-defined conditions make them much more likely to have a police encounter. "Location plus evasion" has become a proxy for race.[33] Thus, despite formal restrictions against racialized policing, *Terry* has resulted in wide variation in both the discretion to stop and in the success, or hit rates, of those stops.

Most important, this has meant that blacks and Latinos are confronted by police at substantially higher rates than their share of criminal offenses. As Alexandra Natopoff argues, "much of urban policing consists of arrests made for purposes of street control, and the system has only weak post-arrest mechanisms for checking whether such offenses are actually based on evidence of crime."[34] Blacks and Latinos in New York City during 1998 and the first part of 1999 were three times more likely to be stopped for suspicion of weapons and violent offenses than their actual commission of these crimes.[35] In an excellent study, Jeffrey Fagan and his colleagues examine whether police stops in New York could be explained by higher minority offending or greater neighborhood disorder. They find that racial disparities remain robust after accounting for both crime rates and disorder, concluding that a concentration of blacks and Latinos is just as predictive as local crime conditions in explaining police stop activity.[36] The same is true in Los Angeles. After controlling for neighborhood crime and disadvantage—single parents, property ownership, poverty, and unemployment—blacks were stopped at a rate 340 times higher (per 1,000 population) and Latinos 36 times higher than whites.[37]

As a result, stops of minorities are much less likely to lead to arrest or summonses. Fagan and Davies show that 95 percent of the time blacks are stopped, police fail to find sufficient evidence of criminal wrongdoing. Moreover, in examining the motivation of police stops, These authors found that not only were two-thirds of stops unconstitutional in that they failed to meet a reasonable suspicion standard, but that stops of blacks were the most likely to be unwarranted. Thus, the residents of these areas are more likely to undergo a stop and because the standards used to justify stops are lower in such places, "stop and frisk strategies have departed from their original Broken Windows underpinnings, and more closely resemble policing of poor people in poor places."[38]

Along with Terry stops, another mechanism that has expanded the group of people with criminal justice contact without explicit regard to criminality is vertical patrols. In New York, the police department instituted a policy of vertical sweeps through public housing under which they could stop virtually anyone in the building and ask for identification. The frequency of police stops in public housing in New York increased by 50 percent from 2004 to 2008.[39] More than 59,000 people were stopped in public housing in New York City in 2010 alone—fewer than 9,000 of these found reason to make an arrest for trespass—prompting the National Association for the Advancement of Colored People Legal Defense Fund to file a class-action lawsuit asserting that city police were making unlawful stops and arrests of building residents, as well as their families and friends who had come to visit.[40] The city tenants' organization reported that the vertical patrols had led to "growing concern and perception among the residents [of public housing] that we are living in penal colonies instead of public housing communities."[41]

Notably, these types of police sweeps have gone beyond public housing projects. Thousands of private apartment buildings in New York City now fall under the NYPD's Operation Clean Halls program, which has been in effect since 1991 and allows the police to conduct vertical sweeps inside private apartment buildings in high-crime areas. As in public housing, even people who live in these buildings can be stopped and asked for identification.[42] According to a class-action lawsuit that seeks to enjoin the NYPD from conducting suspicion-less sweeps, the tactic has resulted in widespread harassment of tenants and their associates, as well as wrongful trespass arrests that are thrown out of court. According to the New York Civil Liberties Union executive director:

> For residents of Clean Halls buildings, taking the garbage out or checking the mail can result in being thrown against the wall and humiliated by police. Untold numbers of people have been wrongly arrested for trespassing because they had the audacity to leave their apartments without IDs or visit friends and family who live in Clean Halls buildings.

Again, residents of Clean Halls buildings are primarily people of color and trespass stops are heavily concentrated in low-income neighborhoods. In some predominantly minority neighborhoods, nearly all the private buildings come under the program. As with police stops more generally, trespass stops rarely result in either arrest (only 7.5%) or summons (5%).

Finally, it is worth noting that minorities also experience systematically different treatment in their encounters with police. A study by the Center for Constitutional Rights found that blacks and Latinos in New York City were not only much more likely to have contact with police, but were more likely to be frisked and subjected to the use of force; once stopped, half of blacks and Latinos but only 34 percent of whites were frisked, and 24 percent of Latinos and blacks had force used on them in these encounters, compared to 17 percent of whites. Almost 90 percent of encounters where the police used force did not result in the person being arrested for wrongdoing.[43] National numbers paint a similar picture:

Blacks who had police contact were three times as likely as whites to report having experienced threats or the use of force against them during the interaction.[44]

Police maintain that their tactics enhance crime control, and sometimes this may be the case. However, there are important collateral consequences of such aggressive policing, which we uncover in the chapters that follow. For millions of citizens across the country, criminal justice contact holds real meaning for their lived experience of American government. As a *New York Times* editorial opined, "if the number of stops keeps going up—and officers begin to be seen as acting recklessly and unfairly—the department will risk permanently alienating an entire generation of people in the very neighborhoods where trust in the law is most needed."[45] As we show, these effects may not be confined to public perceptions of police departments, but may carry over to beliefs about the democratic system as a whole.

The Arrestee/Misdemeanant

Popular and political discourses have frequently concentrated exclusively on the serious felony offender, but felons are by far the smallest group of convicted custodial citizens. Each year, approximately 10 million criminal cases are nontraffic misdemeanors, which account for 80 percent of state court caseloads and five times the felony docket.

In particular, a focus on quality-of-life policing in major cities led to increased police attention to and sentences for low-level offenders. In 2011 police made over 1.25 million drug possession arrests, almost 534,000 public drunkenness arrests, 582,000 disorderly conduct arrests, 238,000 vandalism arrests, 29,000 vagrancy arrests, and 78,000 loitering or curfew arrests.[46] In New York City, which undertook arguably the most aggressive campaign of broken windows policing in the nation, arrests increased by over 800 percent.[47] In that city, policing focused on quality-of-life offending, such as farebeating, under the logic that these minor offenses were at the root of more serious disorder and violence. One of the targets of this campaign was smoking marijuana in public view, or MPV. In 1990, police made less than 1,000 of these arrests; a decade later, they made 51,000.[48] Arrests for this low-level charge, which had traditionally been dealt with by citation, rose so quickly that by 2000 it constituted 15 percent of all adult arrests in the city.

Recent studies suggest that individuals picked up by police for MPV and other misdemeanor offenses rarely go to trial, and many have little access to counsel. Exploring the world of misdemeanor justice, Alexandra Natapoff exposes a separate and slippery system that is short on due process protections, yet churns out convictions en masse. Natapoff describes the criminal justice system as a pyramid. At the top of the pyramid are more serious felony offenses, which are the small minority of cases. Here, prosecutors and police must clear higher bars of procedural safeguards; in this arena, "convictions are indeed strong indicia of individual culpability." In contrast, those charged with misdemeanors occupy the much broader bottom of the pyramid. Here, police discretion to arrest is much more influential in determining who is ultimately convicted of petty offenses. At the bottom of the pyramid:

> Arrests can easily occur without probable cause. Prosecutors fail to screen and instead charge arrestees based solely on allegations in police reports. Defense counsel may never be appointed or, if they are, they lack time and resources to evaluate and litigate cases, while judges pressure defendants into pleading guilty in order to clear crowded dockets. Lacking evidentiary rigor and adversarial testing, it is a world in which a police officer's bare decision to arrest can lead inexorably, and with little scrutiny, to a guilty plea. It is, in other words, a world . . . in which the risk of wrongful conviction is high.[49]

As Natapoff points out, "the reduced penalties associated with misdemeanors exempt them from the structural integrity demands triggered by felonies."[50] Thus, prosecutors almost always move forward to charge—only about 2 percent of these cases do not proceed, though one study suggests that charges against whites are less likely to be prosecuted.[51] In response, arrestee/misdemeanants almost always accept a plea arrangement—only about 5–10 percent of cases fail to "plead out."[52] However, there is some evidence suggesting that custodial citizens may choose to plead guilty not only or even primarily because they are guilty, but instead because the pressures of bail, time spent waiting in jail for the case to get to court, the risk of conviction to a heavier charge, and a lack of available, affordable, and competent counsel all combine to make pleading to lower penalties and fines more attractive than insisting on further adjudication of innocence.

The result is that misdemeanor convictions are "largely a function of being selected for arrest" and convictions are obtained based on the "thinnest possible bases." According to Natapoff, the criminal justice system has a high tolerance for convicting misdemeanants based on arrest, rather than evidence of guilt, conferring criminal records on people who may not have violated the law: "In these high-volume, low scrutiny arenas, therefore, some non-negligible percentage of the hundreds of thousands of arrestees are likely innocent."[53]

Like policing patterns more broadly, this type of misdemeanor justice has been concentrated in certain neighborhoods and among certain social groups. Returning to the study of MPV arrests, in the first few years of New York's quality-of-life policing, most of these arrests occurred in business districts. However, around the middle of the 1990s and since then, police started making most MPV arrests in neighborhoods that were home to poor minorities. Over half of those arrested on this charge were black and, once charged with MPV, blacks were much more likely to be detained (by two and a half times), to be convicted, and to serve additional jail time. This disparity remains even after accounting for prior arrests and background. Blacks with a single prior arrest were three times more likely than whites with one prior arrest to get jail time for their MPV charge.[54] The result is that outcomes for the arrestee/misdemeanant have become further disassociated from evidence of wrongdoing and instead increasingly linked to being poor and vulnerable. As Natapoff writes:

> where procedural testing is weak, as it is for the bulk of poor underrepresented misdemeanants, the fact of arrest can determine the result. . . . When selection displaces evidence, racially driven selection decisions are not only discriminatory, they are also more likely to generate wrongful convictions. In other words, not only do bulk arrest practices discriminate against minorities, they potentially fill the system with innocent people of color who are then wrongly labeled "criminal." . . . the petty offense process is permitted to distribute criminal liability based on race and social vulnerability rather than individual fault.[55]

Scholars and journalists routinely overlook low-level misdemeanors—a slap on the wrist for a petty offender—without acknowledging that these convictions entail substantial costs to custodial citizens. They can result in many of the same denials experienced by convicted felons, of housing, franchise, employment, and education. They often result in at least some jail time, as an individual waits for processing. And once an individual has a criminal record, the likelihood of subsequent arrest rises, resulting in longer sentences for a later conviction.

The Incarcerated Offender

The rise of broken windows policing that we have just described coincided with a renewed focus on prosecuting the use and abuse of illicit substances. As the war on drugs gained steam, the nation's most populous cities saw a drastic increase in law enforcement activity, adding 31 million drug arrests since 1980. From 1980 to 2000, arrests for drug offenses nearly tripled, and a larger proportion of drug arrests were for marijuana, most for possession rather than trafficking and sale.[56]

Policing practices combined with shifts in sentencing policies have meant that a greater number of citizens face correctional supervision and confinement for drug possession, where they would previously have been dealt with through probation, fines, rehabilitation, or citation. Thus, state prison inmates serving time for drugs increased from 16,000 in 1979 to 266,000 by 2006, a seventeen-fold increase, even though the prevalence of drug abuse had not substantially increased.[57] The majority of these individuals were not "major dealers engaged in a lucrative economic undertaking," but "low-level actors in the drug trade and using or selling drugs due to their own addiction."[58] A 2002 study found that fully 58 percent of people serving time for drug offenses in state prisons had no history of violent crime or high-level drug involvement.[59] In addition to drug-related offenders, large prison populations are now sustained by the expanding number of ex-offenders readmitted for parole violations. In fact, more than a third of all state prison admissions in 2006 were individuals being returned to prison as a result of parole violations, rather than for new criminal convictions.[60]

Because they serve longer sentences, violent offenders still make up a large share of prison inmates at any given time. However, that has shifted over time. In 1980 nonviolent drug offenders accounted for less than 10 percent of the prison and jail population. By 2010 they comprised roughly a quarter, with nonviolent offenders overall making up more than 60 percent of the incarcerated. While there were only about 3 percent more violent crimes in 2008 than in 1980 and about 20 percent fewer property crimes, the total prison and jail population grew during this period by more than 350 percent.[61] As John Schmitt and colleagues note, "If incarceration rates had tracked violent crime rates . . . the incarceration rate would have peaked at 317 per 100,000 in 1992, and fallen to 227 per 100,000 by 2008—less than one third of the actual 2008 level and about the same level as in 1980."[62]

The disproportionate arrest of blacks for drug-related offenses, particularly marijuana possession, helps to explain a substantial part of this increase.[63] Despite blacks already being twice as likely to be arrested for drugs as whites in the late 1970s and early 1980s, drug arrests for blacks in the nation's largest cities increased by 225 percent from 1980 to 2003, compared to just 70 percent for whites. In certain cities, the arrest rate for blacks saw an even steeper increase. In a study of forty-three of the nation's largest cities, the black drug arrest rate increased by over 500 percent in eleven of them. In twenty-one cities, the racial disparity between black and white arrests more than doubled.[64] Seen from a different angle, such increases came to represent a sizable portion of the citizenry. In some states, a not insignificant portion of black adult residents had been arrested on a drug charge: over 3 percent of blacks in five states (California, Illinois, Minnesota, Nebraska, and Oregon).[65] In New York City alone, over 350,000 residents were arrested for marijuana possession from 2002 to 2010, and 80 percent were minorities.[66]

As figure 2.5 documents, blacks' drug-arrest rate climbed to unprecedented levels during the Reagan era; at its peak, the increase in the drug-arrest rate for blacks was six times as large as the increase for whites. In 1980 blacks were just 27 percent of people arrested on drug charges, still higher than their presence in the general population. Nine years later, they were 40 percent of all drug arrestees. At the height of the drug war, black people were arrested over five times as often as whites for drugs.[67] The spike in blacks' drug arrests has attenuated slightly in recent years, but has not returned to its 1980 level. In 2006 blacks made up 49 percent of those charged with drug crimes in large urban courts and 59 percent of those charged with trafficking.[68] The rate of arrest is reflected in the hue of the incarcerated; blacks were 38 percent of those admitted to state prisons for drug offenses and 45 percent of those held in state facilities in 2003 and 2006, respectively. Relative to their portion of the population, they were ten times as likely as whites to serve prison time for drug offenses.[69]

Important to note is that blacks are not arrested and confined in higher numbers for drug offenses because they tend to use and sell drugs at greater rates than whites; based on ongoing national surveys, for every

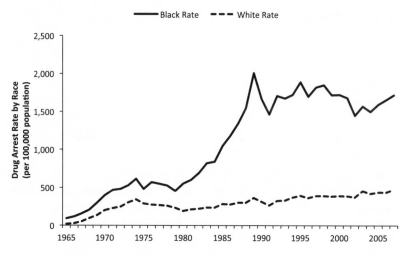

FIGURE 2.5. Drug arrests by race, 1965–2007. Before 1980, black is actually nonwhites and includes all arrests (including under eighteen). *Sources*: For the years 1965–79: "Age-Specific Arrest Rates and Race-Specific Arrest Rates for Selected Offenses, 1965–1992," US Department of Justice, FBI. Uniform Crime Reporting Program, Washington, DC, June 1998. For 1980 and after: Human Rights Watch, "Decades of Disparity: Arrests and Race in the United States," Human Rights Watch Press, 2009, http://www.hrw.org/sites/default/files/reports/us0309web_1.pdf. See also http://www.fbi.gov/about-us/cjis/ucr/additional-ucr-publications/age_race_arrest93-01.pdf and http://www.albany.edu/sourcebook/pdf/t410 2009.pdf.

drug with the exception of crack cocaine, whites report using drugs at higher rates than blacks.[70] In 2008, 51 percent of whites and 46 percent of blacks reported ever using an illicit drug. National surveys also confirm slightly lower rates of trafficking among blacks than whites. Some of the most compelling evidence comes from Katherine Beckett and her colleagues, gathered by closely observing Seattle drug markets. They found that the majority of drug use and trafficking in that city was done by whites; blacks, who made up less than a tenth of the population, were an overwhelming 64 percent of drug arrestees, largely due to the city police force's emphasis on making arrests for the only drug blacks use and sell more—crack—while purposefully overlooking prominent open-air drug markets populated by whites trafficking heroin and other drugs.[71]

It is not the case that violence has nothing to do with these developments, however. Rather, the sentencing of drug offenders was in some ways a reaction to violence. The late legal scholar William Stuntz argued that harsh drug sentencing laws were passed with violent offenders in mind, which led to an explosion of imprisonment of nonviolent drug offenders. The authors of these laws meant to punish violent drug offenders indirectly for their violence, when direct punishment was impossible due to evidentiary standards. In practice, however, a large group of drug offenders who were not suspected of violent acts were implicated, amounting to what he called "a sentencing enhancement, and a dramatic one at that, for black drug crime." Stuntz shows the spillover effect of trying to punish violence for nonviolent (but not innocent) offenders: "So non-violent drug offenders were, in effect, punished both for the crimes they committed and for the violence of the drug markets in which they participated. Because poor city neighborhoods had the most violent drug markets, residents of those neighborhoods received the most severe drug sentences."[72]

We cannot know what proportion of all custodial citizens—those who have had any type of contact with criminal justice authorities—were convicted of nonviolent offenses, because we do not have accurate national data on the total size of the custodial population. However, we can arrive at a very rough estimate based on a few straightforward assumptions. Across the nation, we know that police made 10,472,432 arrests in 2006. Let us assume that for every one person that was arrested, four were stopped by police but not arrested. This is a fairly conservative estimate given what we know about the relation between stops and arrests from New York, Philadelphia, and Los Angeles. With this assumption, police would have made 41,889,728 stops in 2006. We know from Add Health data that about half of youth who are arrested have had this experience more than once, and we assume this is also likely to be true of those who are stopped by police. We therefore consider just a third of the number of stops, to provide a conservative approximation of the total custodial population in one year.

What proportion of that population was convicted of a violent offense in state and district courts? According to recent data, 206,140 people were convicted in 2006 of violent crimes in state courts and another 2,685 were convicted in district courts. If we take these as a proportion of all custodial citizens, we see that they represent only 1.5 percent of all custodial citizens. Put simply, only 3 out of every 200 people who come into contact with criminal justice authorities are convicted of violent crimes.

A Further Comment on Crime and Violence

Our focus throughout this book is on the custodial citizen, a group that is empirically and substantively distinct, though overlapping, with those who have engaged in criminal behavior. In so doing, however, we do not mean to trivialize legitimate concerns about crime and violence. In particular, we would note that in the three decades since 1960, Americans witnessed a truly extreme crime cycle. The murder rate doubled and violent crime climbed rapidly and by a factor of four before swiftly subsiding—and violence rose even as many other threats to public health declined and people lived longer, more healthy lives.[73] At its peak, 24,703 people were murdered in 1991.[74] And while serious violence is rare as a share of all crime—and plummeted in the 1990s in all cities and states—it is still much more common here than in peer nations, and never returned to mid-century levels after its long-term decline; rates of death and serious injury from crime are four to eighteen times higher in America than in other developed democracies. More important, its effects are grievous. Around 15,000 people lose their lives to homicide each year.[75] Almost 6 million are victims of violent crimes and almost 700,000 are exposed to serious injury. Families lose children and businesses abandon communities for safer prospects.

Rates of violent victimization for blacks are particularly catastrophic.[76] Overall, blacks are victims of homicide at rates six times higher than those for whites, and they are half of all homicide victims, making murder the primary cause of death for black men between the ages of fifteen and thirty-four and the second leading cause among young Latino men.[77] During the 1980s, black homicides jumped 150 percent and, despite steady declines in overall homicide recently across the nation and for white men, young black men continued to die at increasing rates.[78] In 1980 young black men (aged 14–24) constituted 9 percent of all homicide victims. From 1995 until 2008, however, they were 16 percent, despite comprising roughly 1 percent of the population.[79] Unlike virtually every other demographic group, young black men now have a better chance of living another day inside prison than outside.[80]

The role of predatory violence in predominantly white areas thus bears little resemblance to the centrality of violence in poor, predominantly black neighborhoods. Ruth Peterson and Lauren Krivo's study of almost a hundred large cities found that violence was five times as common in the average black neighborhood (70% or more black residents) and about three times as common in typical Latino neighborhoods as the average white neighborhood. Only a minority (20%) of black neighborhoods could claim the levels of safety that 90 percent of white areas enjoy.[81] To take one of many examples, Hyde Park in Chicago had 3 murders per 100,000 residents, compared to Washington Park, its poorer, blacker neighbor, which had 78 per 100,000.[82] High rates of violence among black youth persist partly because, although the national homicide rate has declined considerably in recent years, gang-related homicides increased from 1 percent of all homicides to 6 percent, and blacks remained the majority of drug-related murder victims (61%).[83] However, even black middle-class communities are at greater risk of violence given their proximity to areas where violence is prevalent.[84]

As a result, black children will bear witness to more violence by adolescence than most whites see in a lifetime; in a national longitudinal survey of youth, 21 percent of blacks, 12 percent of Latinos, and 6 percent of whites had witnessed someone being shot firsthand.[85] In recent years, 45 percent of kids killed by gun-related violence were black, even though they make up only 15 percent of all kids.[86] Minorities register this heightened violence in their higher fear of crime, greater expectation of being victimized, and stronger emphasis on the need for safer streets. In our own survey analyses, we find that few white young people believe that drugs, violence, gangs, and crime are a big problem (9%) or even a moderately significant problem in their communities (20%). By comparison, about a quarter of Latino youth believed crime and violence to be a big or somewhat big problem, respectively, while nearly a third of black youth registered them as primary concerns (33 and 27% saying big or somewhat big problem, respectively).[87] In another survey, fully a third of young black men were "very worried" about being the victim of a violent crime and 23 percent were "somewhat worried," compared to 11 and 16 percent for young white men.[88] Rucker Johnson demonstrates that one of the effects of the rise in drug-related murders during the 1980s was a noticeably large downward shift in expectations for the future among black youth.[89]

When we talk about victimization and criminal justice contact, then, we actually refer to substantially overlapping demographic groups—those who are poor, nonwhite, and living in highly disadvantaged places. In other words, those most at risk for concentrated violence also became those most exposed to state punitive control.[90] This group was thus doubly punished for living around crime; in the words of legal scholar Randall Kennedy, they suffered a "racial tax," first as victims and second as targets of police intervention.[91] At the same time, these groups would not necessarily benefit from more punitive policies in the long-term because higher police resources do not mean more or better attention to black victims; in fact, police are actually less responsive to victims where victimization is higher. In high-crime communities, police may not have the resources to focus on each victim, reserving special attention for more serious offenses.[92] As Lisa Miller points out, "problems of under-protection from violence have historically been at least as problematic as over-enforcement of the law."[93]

Moreover, violence begets violence; in poor communities, the same people who perpetrate injury to others often also have legitimate concerns about their own safety. They may have been brought up with the "code of the street," leading them to rely on violence to establish status and to protect themselves in a context where they do not feel they can rely on police or informal social controls.[94] As James Forman Jr. notes in working with teens who had been involved with the juvenile justice system, "their acts of violence, we came to understand, had often been closely connected to being in an environment that felt unsafe." He describes one youngster named Bobby, who, after witnessing his close friend murdered, says, "Why can't I do that to anybody else, to anybody else, and not care about it?"[95] Bobby's experience is the norm for young black men. In a national survey, two-thirds of young black men reported having had a close friend or relative murdered, compared to only a quarter of young white men.[96]

The data in our surveys likewise reveal that the risk of experiencing criminal violence is tightly coupled with experiencing criminal justice interventions. In the Washington Post/Kaiser Family Foundation/Harvard African-American Men Survey (AAMS), only 12 percent of people who had not been arrested or jailed reported violent victimization; to compare, 29 percent of those who had been arrested, and fully half of those who had been to prison, had been the victim of a violent crime. In other words, 68 percent of the *victims* of violent crime had also had an encounter with criminal justice where they were suspected of criminality. The results among young people in the Black Youth Project (BYP) data are similar. Victimization was relatively rare among those who reported having had no contact with the criminal justice system (15%). It was higher for youth who had been stopped by police (34%) and a modal event for those who had been arrested (52%). Three-fourths (73%) of those who had been convicted reported having been the victim of a crime.[97] We learned from our qualitative data, too, that living around crime was a central roadblock to the lives of custodial citizens. For example, asked if some people had an easier chance in America, Michael told us: "Yeah, if they grew up around, in the right places or around the right people. Like where it's not drug-infested or not gang-infested, where we don't have to worry about walkin' outside looking around."

There is no question that the state has a crucial responsibility to protect citizens from crime and to punish those who undermine public safety. As Lisa Miller notes, "security from violence is arguably the essence of statehood." Yet custodial citizens, like so many of the nation's poor, face what Miller calls a security gap. They are made powerless by predatory violence and again by repressive state strategies to control their communities, both because they cannot challenge the state's punitive reach in their communities, and because they are unable to "hold the state accountable for security."[98] To think of victims as one population and criminals as another is therefore to obscure an important reality: Those who are most vulnerable to crime are also those most directly affected by state efforts to constrain it.

The Custodial Citizen, Not the Criminal Class

We have argued in this chapter that the number of custodial citizens grew even as crime rates dropped and that prison admissions of serious violent offenders were supplemented by nonviolent, order maintenance, and drug offenses. It is therefore safe to say that as the custodial population increased, the proportion of so-called hardened criminals among them substantially diminished. Moreover, it is not just that a greater number of nonoffender or low-level criminals have joined the ranks of those with criminal justice experience; it is also that state institutions and activities of surveillance and punishment have become increasingly concentrated in certain communities and among some populations. One group of citizens—largely white, middle class, and nonurban—does not encounter the police in their daily lives, does not attend schools with probation and police officers walking the halls, does not fear or experience being stopped and frisked, and will likely never know the inside of a cell. The other group of citizens is mostly black and Latino, and is far more likely to live in the segregated pockets of disadvantaged neighborhoods of the urban core, in neighborhoods that are ecologically unmatched in blight, concentrated poverty, and violence. They move through their daily lives with the expectation and experience of police contact, see the institutions of criminal justice on a routine basis, and will experience firsthand being a suspect, convict, inmate, or offender. The result is two sets of citizens: those (primarily poor and black) individuals for whom criminal justice contact is a nearly expected part of life, and those (largely white and middle-class) individuals for whom criminal justice contact remains a fairly uncommon occurrence.

Most crucially, contact with criminal justice now has as much to do with selection based on extralegal factors than with criminality; the custodial citizen is no longer synonymous with the criminal class, if indeed it ever was. Rather, the types of punitive contact that citizens experience with the state are increasingly dictated by the actions of the state, structured by political choices and policies related to crime control. A substantial share of custodial citizens have been convicted of a petty or nonviolent offense, but many are never convicted of a crime at all.

In scholarly and public discussions about the custodial population in the United States, this more expansive conception of the custodial citizenry is often overlooked, in part because the majority does not end up doing hard time. Yet citizens who undergo repeated and unwanted attention from police may still learn negative lessons about state power and their standing in the larger community. When they are stopped by police while going about their daily business, they are reminded that they are at the mercy of discretion-wielding authorities. They may be patted down, asked invasive questions about their whereabouts, and detained for long periods of time. If they appear to be uncooperative, they may face arrest or bodily harm. In the remainder of this book, we show that even being stopped and questioned by police can lead custodial citizens to withdraw from civic society and political life, at great cost to their communities.

Our purpose in disaggregating the custodial from the criminal population is not to reify such categorical divisions; we are not trying to identify the "real" bad guys or suggest that those who are violent offenders deserve to be exposed to institutions that deny voice, accountability, and equality. Rather, we seek to show that the custodial population goes well beyond violent offenders. If the evident effects were limited to this group, many would reasonably argue that the collateral cost is necessary to assure the maintenance of law and order. But the relative benefits of

America's criminal justice system are far harder to justify if growth in the custodial population has been primarily concentrated among suspects and arrestees/misdemeanants, particularly after accounting for rising racial disproportionality in these groups over time. It is among these individuals, whose crimes have incurred no physical harm or who have not been convicted of crimes at all, that the costs to democracy and citizenship we detail in the coming chapters are primarily borne.

CHAPTER THREE

Democratic Ideals and Institutional Design

In his classic tome *Democracy and Its Critics*, Robert Dahl conceptualizes the model democracy as "a political system in which the members regard one another as political equals, are collectively sovereign, and possess all the capacities, resources, and institutions they need in order to govern themselves."[1] Our objective in this chapter is to consider this ideal character of democracy in contrast with the policies and practices of modern criminal justice institutions. Specifically, in the sections that follow, we assess the role of criminal justice institutions in enabling or constraining the democratic imperatives of citizen political voice and institutional responsiveness.

Our review is far from comprehensive. Rather, we focus here on just a few key examples of how citizen voice and democratic responsiveness are curtailed within institutions of criminal justice, describing them in some detail. In so doing, we are likely to miss a host of other democratic indignities, both formal and informal, to which custodial citizens are exposed. Some administrative rules that we review, such as limitations on the political materials available to prison inmates, represent relatively minor departures from the democratic ideal. However, they arguably become more significant when viewed as part of the broader pattern we uncover. Other rules, such as laws and precedents that effectively deter litigation in cases where citizens have been injured by police or prosecutors, are more potent examples of how criminal justice policies and practices embody what we refer to here as antidemocratic norms. Our aim is to give the reader a sense of the experiences that custodial citizens have as they move through institutions of the carceral state and the political socialization that these institutions convey.

Let us be clear: We are not suggesting here that government has no enduring or legitimate interest in effectively combating crime, or that there is never a rational or moral basis for subjugating democratic virtues for the public good. There is obvious value in granting criminal justice personnel enough power to ensure the safety of all citizens. Nor are we arguing that the due process revolution of the 1960s did not substantially expand the rights of the accused or better conditions in America's houses of confinement. It did. However, in many important ways, institutions of surveillance and punishment remain far less responsive and participatory than what democratic institutions require, even as they have grown to ensnare a larger body of the law-abiding population. Perhaps most critically, we find reason to contend that many of these subjugations of democratic ideals are not essential to the successful control of crime.

Democratic Ideals and Institutions

Democracy is both an "idea, and practices embodying it," argues Robert Dahl.[2] A nation can hold up political equality, responsiveness, and citizen participation as ideals, but that is not the same as creating democratic institutions that are in concert with these principles—institutions that allow citizens to voice their opinions and be responded to equally and fairly, have a say over who represents them and how, and contribute meaningfully to the institutions that govern their lives. Our concern lies in just how far the ideals of American democracy fall short of the practices within it.

So, what features characterize an ideal democracy? By what standards can we judge how well our democratic ideals are inscribed within our national institutions? There are nearly as many answers to these questions as there are books and articles on the subject, and wading into the contentious debate over how best to define and measure democracy is not our primary focus. However, in reviewing the literature, we find it safe to say that the basic principles of liberal democratic theory are fairly uncontroversial. Critics of this core set of civic virtues most often cite sins of omission rather than commission.

Perhaps the most important precondition to a legitimate democracy is political equality. Other democratic "virtues," Sidney Verba argues, "are either fostered by or foster equal political voice."[3] Equality, "the extent to which citizens have an equal voice over governmental decisions . . . expressed in such principles as one-person/one-vote, equality before the law, and equal rights of free speech," is "intrinsically valuable and valuable as the key to equality in other realms."[4] Essential features of this democratic principle include full rights to suffrage and other channels for effective participation—such as the freedoms to organize as well as to assemble and demonstrate—as well as fair and free elections and freedom of the press. Citizens must also have equal capacity to take part in democratic life and the government that rules them; equality in political expression must be perceived and experienced by its citizens, not exist merely as a matter of written rule.[5]

Democracy further requires that institutions and political authorities be accountable to the people and represent their preferences and interests; these are "both the source and the limits of government power."[6] Underlying the democratic norm of popular accountability is the idea that the decisions and procedures of governing bodies should be transparent, that is, visible and open to scrutiny by citizens. When decisions are opaque and there are few checks on state power, democratic rule is called into question. As Eric Luna writes, "Inaccessible, unresponsive, and unaccountable authority may satisfy the desires of the official, but not the will of the people; this is autocratic government, rather than popular rule."[7] After all, having equal voice in politics means little if one's voice is not heard or if public officials are not responsive to the public will. Thus, democracy entails what the government does—its responsiveness to citizen preferences and its regard for them as political equals—as well as what individual citizens must possess—that is, the franchise and the right to free speech and association.

It is the design of political institutions that translates these democratic benchmarks into practice. Political institutions are the means through which we formalize and make real the character of democracy, reflecting our democratic ideals through the way they are organized and their internal rules of operation. Institutions can be claimed as democratic when they are marked by the free and fair election of leaders, channels for transmitting citizen preferences to political officials, deliberation between authorities and citizens, visibility of decisions and procedures to the public, and checks on arbitrary action.[8] Conversely, institutions within a democratic system may embody antidemocratic values. They may constrain freedom of speech, limit association, and offer few channels for citizens to express their preferences and organize around shared interests. They also may demand little accountability to public preferences, provide low transparency, and contain few checks on the discretionary decisions of political elites. It is within this theoretical framework that we consider the design of criminal justice institutions.

Unfortunately, there is no more consensus among penal theorists about the criteria that make a criminal justice system more or less democratic than there is among democratic theorists about what features characterize an ideal democratic state. We therefore start from the premise that a democratic criminal justice institution must effectively balance the goals of coercion and responsiveness, providing political agents with the tools they need to effectively address crime and ensure public safety while still maintaining the core conditions of democracy. Nicola Lacey defines criminal justice similarly, considering it to be in line with democratic ambitions when it has the "capacity to respond effectively and even-handedly to the harms and rights violations represented by criminal conduct without resorting to measures which in effect negate the democratic membership and entitlements of offenders."[9] In practice, this means that a democratic criminal justice system should combat crime with as few violations as possible to the fundamental promises of democratic citizenship, and without relieving democratic institutions and officials of their responsibilities regarding democratic accountability.

Rather than resorting to broad claims about the punitive or antidemocratic character of the American criminal justice regime, we therefore offer specific evidence of antidemocratic practices within criminal justice institutions, given the constraints and countervailing goals of the system as a whole. Specifically, we assess America's criminal justice institutions by the extent to which their practices unnecessarily violate the democratic imperatives of voice, responsiveness, and accountability. Thus, we do not discuss due process rights, inhumane punishment, the presumption of innocence, or budgetary tradeoffs, though they are clearly important in evaluating systems of justice and rightfully occupy other debates. Instead, we are interested in the characteristics of state crime-control institutions as part of the broader political system and the extent to which the American criminal justice system reflects the normative values of the wider democratic project.

Criminal Justice: Improving Procedure, Not Democracy

Devoting substantial time to assessing the character of criminal justice institutions today may be a curious choice in view of the tremendous improvement in the conditions of prisons and the treatment of people accused of crimes since mid-century. For most of the nation's history, prison inmates were largely considered to have surrendered their constitutional protections; as the court in *Ruffin v. Commonwealth* held, they were "for the time being the slave of the state."[10] Prisons were virtually unregulated and their conditions were abysmal; inmate deaths were common, some prisoners toiled in the fields from dawn to dusk with little food, water, or medical care, and floggings, lashings, and torture were regular practice. For example, in *Talley v. Stephens* (1965) a lower court ruled that "whether an inmate is to be whipped and how much he is to be whipped are matters resting within the sole discretion of the prison employee administering the punishment . . . [as long as] the blows administered for a single offense shall not exceed ten."[11] Inmates were almost entirely at the mercy of the state institutions that held them.

This changed in the 1960s and 1970s, as the prisoner rights movement helped expose deplorable conditions within these institutions and the Court ruled in *Wolff v. MacDonnell* (1974) that "there is no iron curtain drawn between the Constitution and the prisons of this country."[12] Prison inmates were not alone in witnessing the resulting improvements. The Warren Court of the 1960s sparked a broad revolution in procedural rights that promised system-wide reforms in the criminal justice system. Major decisions such as *Miranda v. Arizona* (1966), *Mapp v. Ohio* (1961), *Escobedo v. Illinois* (1964), and *Gideon v. Wainwright* (1963), along with others, established, broadened, and institutionalized the rights of the accused. Almost overnight, it appeared that fidelity to the procedural rules promised by the constitution would come to pass. This history is well known and rightly celebrated.

However, we argue that procedural protections and court oversight of prisons vastly improved conditions *but did little to expand democratic operations within prisons and police departments*; as Suzanne Mettler points out, "the creation of democratic procedures does not necessarily translate into democratic practice."[13] The new procedural safeguards, while giving the appearance of democratic expansion, did not impugn the basic antidemocratic practices within police agencies and prisons.

Not only did the focus on and expansion of procedural rights effectively make an end-run around thicker democratic reforms leaving antidemocratic practices intact, it invited new developments that further scaled back responsiveness, accountability, and voice. Below we trace the emergence of several such reforms, which reduced the responsiveness of criminal justice institutions and diminished channels for citizen voice even as the prisoners' rights movement and due process revolution codified procedures for fairness and equality.

Our point here is not that due process did not make gains but, rather, that it roundly failed at bringing about a substantive commitment to democratic ideals; these due process reforms prioritized procedure over substance. Moreover, the notion that prisoners, parolees, and suspects deserve due process (and implicitly nothing more) undercuts our ability to see the bruises to democracy that go beyond prison conditions and poor interrogation techniques. Accepted wisdom now dictates that, so long as you were read your Miranda rights and were given a public defender, the nation has upheld its democratic duties. That you travel through institutions that do not enable democratic citizenship is beside the point because "you had your day in court." The result, as we show in the latter half of the book, is that institutions that in many ways became procedurally more fair and began to operate more humanely continue to be *experienced* by custodial citizens as unaccountable and capricious, where they are not rights-bearing citizens but subjects with little voice into the institutions that control almost every aspect of their existence.

Our argument is that procedural fairness and due process protections—negative rights—should not stand in for the substantive democratic values of equality, voice, and representation; these are not substitutes. If the metric is humane treatment, the developments we discuss below may well be minor compared to the flagrant abuses within prisons and police interrogation rooms of prior decades; but if the standard is the substance of democracy—voice, responsiveness, and accountability—then they are quite large indeed.

Democratic Responsiveness and Accountability

The principles of accountability and responsiveness—that political authorities, while wielding power to govern, will ultimately be answerable to the people—is a key part of what distinguishes a democracy from an authoritarian regime. As Eric Luna writes, democratic rule requires "that discretionary judgments and actions be open to the electorate . . . and subject to democratic mechanisms for change [so that] harmful abuses of discretion can be dealt with through legal and political recourse."[14] Institutions that allow individuals' grievances, preferences, and claims to be heard and responded to help ensure that public officials, whether elected or appointed, govern responsibly. When officials are allowed to act instead with impunity or without accountability, they violate a core component of the democratic pact.

In our systematic review, we find several features of the criminal justice system that stand in marked contrast to the democratic responsiveness ideal. Institutions of punishment and surveillance provide few channels through which citizens can express their grievances and concerns, and criminal justice authorities are often not held accountable to their constituencies or the broader public. In the following sections, we describe a number of ways in which actors within the architecture of criminal justice—prisons, police, prosecutors, and parole boards—have become increasingly insulated from accountability over time.

Police

As we discussed in chapter 2, police have wide-ranging authority and discretion to approach and stop people on the street. In addition, custodial citizens often have limited recourse to check abuses by police, protest or prevent unwarranted stops and racial profiling, or change police practices. Indeed, citizens have almost no recourse whatsoever to challenge a pedestrian stop-question-and frisk or pretextual traffic stop unless they can prove that the stop was unreasonable—a difficult thing to establish—or that they were stopped due to their race. Because the majority of Terry stops do not result in arrest or criminal prosecution, in most cases because the stop-and-frisk fails to turn up sufficient evidence that the individual was doing anything unlawful, those stopped have virtually no opportunity to raise claims of unfair treatment.[15]

More broadly, citizens' power to hold police officers and departments accountable has been substantially eroded over the past few decades by a variety of court-erected hurdles, even when police have inflicted physical harm on an individual. The case of *Los Angeles v. Lyons* (1983) provides a telling example. In *Lyons*, police searched a black man for weapons during a routine traffic stop for a broken taillight. When Adolph Lyons lowered his arms after the search had turned up nothing, "an officer slammed his hands onto his head, and when Lyons complained of pain, the officer applied a chokehold which rendered Lyons unconscious." When he awoke, "he was lying face down on the ground, choking, gasping for air, and spitting up blood and dirt" and sprawled in his own defecation.[16]

Lyons sued the city, seeking to stop LAPD officers from using chokeholds unless they feared for their lives.[17] At the time, Los Angeles police used them not infrequently; 975 instances were recorded from 1975 to 1980.[18] By the time the case had been brought to court, over two dozen people in Los Angeles had died from being placed in them.[19] Of those who had died from LAPD chokeholds, 75 percent were black in a city where fewer than one-fifth of residents were black.

Lyons ultimately received damages for his injuries. However, the court also ruled that because the plaintiff could not prove with "substantial certainty" that he would be a future victim of a police chokehold, Lyons did not have standing to sue for an injunction. The court maintained that to have standing, Lyons had to show that enjoining the LAPD from using the technique would provide relief to him personally, and not just to other citizens, directly in the future. Courts have used similar logic in numerous other cases involving police abuse. For instance, *Rizzo v. Goode* (1976) overturned a district court's injunction on the Philadelphia police department for widespread violations of citizens' constitutional rights because the court ruled that the plaintiffs lacked standing, having failed to demonstrate that past violations and injuries were likely to recur in the future.[20] Moreover, the *Lyons* decision created an incredibly high hurdle to citizens seeking remedy for misconduct, brutality, or excessive force: Not only did Lyons have to show that he would be victim to another incident of being choked by police, but he was also required "to make the incredible assertion . . . that *all* police officers in Los Angeles *always* choke *any* citizen with whom they happen to have an encounter."[21]

These precedents effectively slammed the door on private citizens who were the target of injurious police actions. In the aftermath of *Lyons*, one scholar analyzed cases in which a private citizen sought injunctive relief against a police practice, finding that the vast majority (1,158 out of 1,200 cases) failed because they could not establish standing.[22] The result is that victims of police brutality may be able to get compensation for their suffering (if they survive, as Lyons did), but are largely left powerless to curtail the police practices that led to their injuries. Moreover, as legal scholar Myriam Gilles points out, the strict standing test is unique to police misconduct and brutality cases. If other landmark cases seeking to enjoin government practices had been forced to meet the same standard as in *Lyons—Brown v. Board*, for instance—the practices they ended would most likely have continued unchecked.

In California and other states, individual officers are also rarely held financially accountable for professional wrongdoing. Even when a jury finds malicious misconduct by police officers, cities may retain discretion to effectively overrule the decision and decide that the officer acted in good faith.[23] In that event, the city pays the punitive damages the officer owes out of city coffers. In some cities, officers are indemnified from paying damages at all, unless they are punitive damages.[24] The implications for accountability and responsiveness are clear: Even when officers are found guilty and damages are awarded, they may not be held personally responsible for their behavior. They may also escape further sanction; Human Rights Watch found that even when a plaintiff recovers damages in a civil suit, most officers were not investigated by internal affairs and many were not disciplined. One analysis examined the outcomes of 185 police officers who had been involved in a hundred civil lawsuits from 1986 to 1991, all cases that found for the plaintiffs in damages of at least $100,000; of the 185 officers named in lawsuits totaling $92 million in punitive damages, a mere 8 were disciplined by the police departments they worked for, 160 faced no action at all, and 17 received promotions.[25] The Christopher Commission found largely the same trend in its report, detailing even higher rates of promotion following human rights violations by police. Similarly, in 561 citizen claims of police abuse in Los Angeles, "the department did not sustain a single allegation of misconduct against a sworn employee."[26]

Limitations on redress through courts are particularly important because police departments' internal grievance processes are often neither independent nor transparent. One article sums it up this way:

> In most police departments throughout the United States, citizen complaints are investigated by the internal affairs division or by a body composed of police and civilians, with ultimate control resting with the police department. This is often the sole method of investigating excessive force complaints. The division is located within the police department—the investigators are police officers, and the entire process is concealed from the public. The only infor-

mation a complainant receives is the final outcome: whether the complaint was dismissed or sustained. Details such as the discipline imposed on the officer are completely confidential. . . . This lack of public access has created a procedure prone to abuse. In some cases the sole aim of the internal process is to establish the innocence of the officer.[27]

Citizens filing complaints against police often face barriers, hostility, and sometimes outright intimidation. In an interview, one police officer described how the process of filing a grievance may dissuade people, saying that it is "common practice" in such situations to first see if the complainer has any outstanding warrants and make an arrest if they do.[28] For instance, Rodney King's brother attempted to file a complaint after King's beating by police officers and "the sergeant on duty treated him skeptically, asked him whether he had ever been in trouble, and never filled out a complaint form."[29] Police in New York City similarly failed to file a complaint in the case of Abner Louima, despite substantial evidence showing that he had been beaten and forcibly sodomized by city officers in a precinct bathroom after being brought in on a routine arrest.[30]

States including Minnesota, Nevada, Ohio, and Wisconsin have even passed legislation that effectively discourages citizens from pursuing action against police officers by imposing criminal penalties for false complaints. A 1995 California statute, for example, makes it a misdemeanor crime to file a false complaint of police misconduct and requires complainants to sign a disclaimer stating that "it is against the law to make a complaint that you know to be false. If you make a complaint against an officer knowing that it is false, you can be prosecuted on a misdemeanor charge."[31] Notably, the statute is vague about how "knowingly false" accusations against police are to be judged and applies only to individual complaints against peace officers and not allegations against other governmental officials. This explicit threat of prosecution has likely deterred many citizens from submitting complaints against police through departments' formal channels.[32]

Police officers have another resource to protect themselves against a citizen seeking redress: the qualified immunity defense, which allows police to claim that their actions were undertaken in good faith. This defense is intended to protect officers acting where the law is unclear or the legal standard is undeveloped such that an official could reasonably believe his behavior was lawful. In practice, however, qualified immunity has been employed to deny victims damages for even extreme violations of their rights that courts have not explicitly proscribed.[33] For instance, in *Robles v. Prince George's County*, the court extended qualified immunity to police officers who chained an arrestee to a pole "in the middle of a deserted shopping center parking lot at 3 a.m." because he was wanted for arrest in another county. The officers left him there to be picked up by officers in another jurisdiction. The court in *Robles* reasoned that the conduct was indeed a violation, but granted the officers immunity because judicial precedent did not explicitly prohibit leaving a person chained to a pole. Other cases have similarly sided with officers who have used excessive force by ruling that they acted reasonably (even if mistakenly) in believing that the situation called for more force than was actually needed. One scholar notes that officers are well aware of the qualified immunity doctrine, giving them incentives to act on a "sub-constitutional level."[34] Another notes that under this standard, "only the most flagrant, shocking conduct—not just inept actions—will defeat qualified immunity."[35]

Police officers can still face criminal prosecution for their behavior. However, only certain unconstitutional violations are eligible for criminal procedure. Actions that do not involve unwarranted seizures, excessive force, or coercion in interrogation are excluded. In addition, citizens often face great difficulty and expense in pressing their claims in court. District attorneys are reluctant to prosecute, lawyers are reluctant to represent plaintiffs with criminal histories, juries are reluctant to hold police accountable, and cities mount aggressive defenses in cases against their police forces.[36] Often, even when the evidence of misconduct and abuse is egregious, cities will opt to take the case to trial instead of settling. The individual victim then faces a city attorney's office that has "virtually unlimited resources" and a court case that normally takes several years and thousands of dollars to reach its conclusion. As many citizens and their attorneys balk at the prospect of such a long and expensive battle, many prosecutable cases are ultimately dropped.[37] Even when a department settles, it rarely acknowledges wrongdoing.[38]

Cases that do proceed often face substantial hurdles. In many places, the only way for a prosecutor to learn of allegations of misconduct is if the police department itself reveals the situation to the prosecutor; few prosecutors' offices have systematic means by which they can become aware of citizen complaints directly.[39] Prosecutors and elected districted attorneys that take on cases against police may also fear retaliation from powerful police labor unions.[40] These issues are likely to mean that citizens seeking recourse through criminal prosecutions have many reasons to doubt their likelihood of success:

> Police misconduct, therefore, often is immune to successful criminal prosecution. . . . Law enforcement officers account for almost all the acquittals in cases prosecuted by the Civil Rights Division. When officers are prosecuted, but subsequently acquitted, they almost always avoid any further discipline or they get their jobs back through arbitration. Firing even the most violent officers can be "nearly impossible." When convicted, officers spend little or no time incarcerated. In New York City, in fact, officers responsible for substantiated complaints of misconduct are more likely to be promoted than dismissed, and the police department awards medals to officers at the same time that those officers are receiving civilian complaints.[41]

Clearly, police officers must have the freedom and authority to do what is a dangerous job without constant concern that they will be prosecuted for every misstep. However, the end result of these growing protections is that police departments are too often insulated from legitimate citizen challenges. Individuals face a number of constraints to filing claims in court. When they meet the requirements, they face additional barriers to successful resolution. With the expansions of the qualified immunity defense, restrictions on injunctions, and legislation criminalizing false grievances, citizens are denied effective mechanisms for ensuring that police are held accountable. In a 2000 law review article, Myriam Gilles questions whether citizens can use the courts at all any longer to reform prisons and police departments, given the substantial procedural hurdles and lack of regulation. She writes:

> The question takes on particular poignancy in the area of police misconduct litigation . . . where the federal government lacks the sort of regulatory presence that it has in such other areas as education, voting, housing, and employment. And yet, the most critical and incendiary civil rights issues of today are not being played out in the schools, voting booths, housing markets, or workplaces; they are being played out in the relations between local law enforcement agencies and the communities they police.[42]

Prosecutors

While the qualified immunity defense shields police from custodial citizens' claims, prosecutors—who have been described as having "more
control over life, liberty, and reputation than any other person in America"—have an even more powerful tool when acting in their role as advocates at trial: absolute immunity.[43] As investigators or administrators,
they receive only qualified immunity; under absolute immunity, prosecutors are protected from civil suits even when they intentionally violate the Constitution and act maliciously to secure a conviction. In some
cases, prosecutors have received absolute immunity for perjury, fabrica-
tion of evidence, suppression of exculpatory evidence, giving false testimony, coercing witnesses, and other violations.[44] As one expert notes
in discussing the extensive case law related to prosecutorial immunity,
"the misconduct at issue does not involve gray areas of controversy over
which reasonable minds might differ. The cases involve blatant and often criminal misconduct—manufacturing evidence, tampering with witnesses, suborning perjury." Prosecutors in these cases have not been
held culpable even when police would be.[45]

Even under qualified immunity, the lesser protection that prosecutors enjoy when investigating a case, citizens still face high thresholds
before they can seek remedy. Like those pursuing civil actions against
the police for abuses, citizens must show that the prosecutor "violated
clearly established constitutional law"; if a legal standard is undeveloped
or blurry, or even if the conduct was objectively unreasonable, prosecutors enjoy qualified immunity. Citizens must also show that the prosecutor acted "with a culpable state of mind," a requirement that is difficult to prove. Perhaps the most significant barrier to seeking remedies
for prosecutorial misconduct is that, unlike noncustodial citizens seeking civil remedies in court, custodial citizens must first navigate the ar-
duous process of having their criminal convictions overturned. In other
words, for custodial citizens to pursue a claim, they must first demonstrate that their conviction has been reversed through appeal, expunged,
or that they have been given a writ of habeas corpus.[46] In practice, this
is extremely difficult. Even when prosecutors have engaged in egregious
misconduct, it is difficult to overturn a conviction due to both the harmless error doctrine and recent limitations on federal habeas corpus.

Under the harmless error doctrine, if a prosecutor has exculpatory
evidence and does not produce it, courts have ruled that the evidence

has to be material.[47] It is therefore not enough for a person to show misconduct; he must also demonstrate that the misconduct had a prejudicial effect and that the outcome of the original trial would probably not have led to his conviction had the evidence been produced. Unsurprisingly, many misconduct cases thus do not result in reversed convictions. One study found that of nearly 11,500 allegations of prosecutorial misconduct, the court ruled a majority of cases (8,709) to fall under the harmless error standard.[48]

Citizens face additional constraints in overturning their convictions in federal courts. The Supreme Court has ruled that federal courts should not hear constitutionality claims related to state prosecutions (*Younger v. Harris*). More important, the Antiterrorism and Effective Death Penalty Act (AEDPA), which Congress passed in 1996, limited citizens' ability to have federal courts review their convictions; federal courts must now defer to state court decisions in cases in which a sentenced person alleges unconstitutional error. Thus, in seeking to have a conviction overturned through habeas corpus, petitioners must navigate a "procedural minefield." If they manage to have a federal review of a state conviction, the court can still find that the constitutional error was harmless so long as it did not substantially influence the jury's ultimate verdict. This, along with qualified immunity and the good faith exception, mean that citizens are prevented from remedies across a range of cases.[49]

The motivation for according prosecutors absolute immunity is to deter disgruntled citizens from harassing prosecutors through lawsuits, following the reasonable logic that prosecutors fearing reprisal do not vigorously pursue their cases. In *Imbler v. Pachtman*, the Supreme Court noted that its decision would leave the wrongly convicted without a channel for redress, but nevertheless decided that it was "better to leave unredressed the wrongs done by dishonest officers than to subject those who try to do their duty to the constant dread of retaliation."[50] Courts have also reasoned that there are mechanisms other than a civil remedy that can check prosecutorial misconduct.

The practical result of such limitations, however, is to leave custodial citizens with few institutional checks on all but the most egregious prosecutorial abuses, denying accountability to custodial citizens even when they spend years or even decades behind bars for offenses of which they were wrongfully convicted. And prosecutorial misconduct is far from a rare occurrence. Reporters from the *Chicago Tribune* investigating prosecutorial misconduct found an alarming pattern of cases: "[Prosecutors] have prosecuted black men, hiding evidence the real killers were white. They have prosecuted a wife, hiding evidence her husband committed suicide. They have prosecuted parents, hiding evidence their daughter was killed by wild dogs."[51] In a few cases, prosecutors put away people for homicide even when the victim was later found alive. In one particularly high-profile case, prosecutors aggressively pursued the conviction and imprisonment of thirty-nine people in Tulia, Texas, on false drug distribution charges; those charged constituted fully 10 percent of Tulia's black population. In that case, an aggressive prosecutor suppressed evidence that the individuals were innocent and relied on false testimony from a sheriff. After being sentenced to a combined total of 750 years in prison, and only after some had already served a significant amount of time in prison, their convictions were reversed. The defendants in Tulia recovered $6 million in damages, but the prosecutor was held to be immune from civil liability.

Tulia is far from unique. Several empirical studies have shown frequent misconduct among prosecutors and demonstrated that it is instrumental in wrongful convictions. Between 1970 and 2003, prosecutorial misconduct led to dismissed charges, overturned convictions, and reduced sentences in over 2,000 criminal cases. A nontrivial number of the cases were for very serious charges that could have resulted in execution.[52] Many other cases found serious prosecutorial conduct, but did not reverse convictions. Finally, the actual incidence of misconduct may be obscured. Because over 90 percent of federal sentences result from plea bargains and do not go to trial, the prosecutor's conduct is hidden from view; plea bargains require little in the way of official records, so failing to produce exculpatory evidence and other types of misconduct "is often an undocumented event."[53]

Studies also show that prosecutors who have engaged in serious misconduct are rarely disciplined or face criminal sentences. In the study of 2,000 reversals for prosecutorial misconduct described above, prosecutors faced discipline in only forty-four cases, and none were brought up on criminal charges.[54] Another study found that of 381 cases across thirty-six years in which a conviction was reversed due to the prosecutor withholding or falsifying evidence—a serious type of misconduct—only two prosecutors were criminally prosecuted, and in both cases, charges were dismissed.[55] In the twentieth century, only six prosecutors were criminally convicted.

Jails and Prisons

Police and prosecutors are not the only criminal justice agents that have become less democratically responsive and accountable over time. Prisoners have long been made subject to the whims of authorities who exercise nearly complete control over them. Erving Goffman described prisons as "total institutions" precisely because they entail totalizing supervision, regulation, and control.[56] Democratic voice, responsiveness, and accountability are scarce or nonexistent commodities in prison, where "most of the methods by which we, as a polity, foster government accountability and equality among citizens are unavailable or at least not currently practiced."[57] Despite this long-acknowledged truth, however, two aspects remain worthy of mention. First, even the limited responsiveness of prisons has varied over time, widening briefly in the middle of the twentieth century in response to the activism of prisoners and reformers and then quickly retrenching in more recent decades. And second, it is not only those who have been sentenced to prison who are subject to the lack of accountability and responsiveness of correctional institutions. So, too, are individuals who are held in pretrial detention before having been adjudicated in a court of law.

Prison inmates for most of American history stood largely outside constitutional protection. As late as 1951, a federal circuit court suggested that legal protections were appropriately abrogated in many ways during a period of punishment: "We think it well settled that it is not the function of the courts to superintend the treatment and discipline of persons in penitentiaries, but only to deliver from imprisonment those who are illegally confined."[58] The legal environment in which prisons operated did not begin to change until the 1960s and 1970s, as inmates organized behind prison walls and activists successfully sought court action on their behalf.[59] Courts subsequently gave greater scrutiny to conditions behind prison walls, expanded inmate habeas corpus, and intervened on behalf of inmates' rights under the Eighth Amendment.

For prisoners, who are both formally and informally cut off from many other mainstream channels through which they might express their voices and have government respond—voting, donating money, volunteering on a campaign—newly granted access to courts carried great significance. Indeed, the Court recognized the particular importance of prisoner access to courts in *McCarthy v. Madigan* (1992): "Because a prisoner ordinarily is divested of the privilege to vote, the right to file a court action might be said to be his remaining most fundamental political right, because preservative of all rights."[60]

The promise of greater responsiveness to those serving time in prison and jail, sparked by prison activism that swept the nation's jails and prisons during the late 1960s, disappeared abruptly with several court decisions and legislative reforms that expanded deference to prison managers and limited the scope of prisoners' grievances that courts would hear.[61] The nail in the coffin of prisoners' recourse was the Prison Litigation Reform Act (PLRA), which Congress passed in 1996 as a rider to a budget reconciliation bill. The PLRA was motivated by a desire to curb court costs from frivolous prisoner litigation and it passed easily amid a prevailing tough-on-crime sentiment among legislators. Indeed, it received only one congressional hearing and very little congressional debate and was only twelve pages long. However, the consequences of the PLRA cannot be exaggerated in their scope.[62] Before the PLRA, inmates and advocates could force correctional institutions to respond to legitimate grievances by bringing federal civil suits before the courts. And they did: The expansion of rights in the 1960s and 1970s led to a surge of class-action suits concerning prison conditions and other correctional abuses.[63]

The PLRA immediately collapsed this access to the courts. The core of the PLRA was a set of rules that imposed extremely high barriers before a federal court would hear an inmate's claims of unconstitutional treatment in a state or federal correctional facility (through Section 1983, part of the Civil Rights Act of 1871).[64] Custodial citizens, for whom the courts were the primary point of institutional leverage, would now have to clear a series of hurdles—hurdles that do not apply to noncustodial citizens—before the court would hear their cases. Moreover, PLRA provisions applied not only to those convicted and sentenced to confinement, but also to those held in jails or awaiting trial, individuals whose guilt or innocence had not yet been decided.[65] This population is by no means small; local jails, which largely hold misdemeanants awaiting processing—many for low-level public order offenses—hold 11 million people suspected of breaking the law in a given year.[66]

The PLRA implemented a number of new restrictions that together reduced prisoners' recourse in claiming mistreatment by the state. First, it removed standards requirements for state prison and jail grievance systems. Under the legal status quo before the PLRA, a court could order an inmate to go through a prison's grievance procedure only if the attorney general had officially certified that process as compliant with "minimum acceptable standards" requiring them to be "plain, speedy, and effective."[67] In this regard, the previous standard had outlined maximum time limits for a prison to respond to an inmates' grievance, allowed for emergency grievances to be processed quickly, created safeguards to prevent reprisals against inmates who filed grievances, and provided for independent review of the resolution of a grievance.[68]

Virtually overnight, the PLRA undid these requirements. In addition, one central provision of the PLRA was the so-called exhaustion provision, which prevented inmates from filing federal suit if they had not already navigated all available grievance procedures in the prison or jail, irrespective of the quality of the internal process. Through this new provision, potentially meritorious claims of unconstitutional abuse or excessive punishment could be thrown out because an inmate had not negotiated a complex or unreasonable prison bureaucracy. A single misstep in the grievance procedure by an inmate could result in the custodial citizen permanently forfeiting his right to seek redress through the courts.[69] One legal scholar noted that "applied to the mostly uneducated, unsophisticated, and legally uncounselled population of the prisons," the effect of this provision was to scuttle the constitutional rights of inmates through procedural and technical error.[70] Under the PLRA, thousands of custodial citizens were turned away from the courts; one study found that in cases where the exhaustion issue was raised, fully 70 percent of inmates' claims were dismissed because they had failed to exhaust the administrative grievance procedure.[71] Courts have ruled that failure to exhaust may still result in denial of a hearing even when extenuating circumstances prevented a prisoner from meeting the prison's technical requirements for submitting a grievance.[72]

As Human Rights Watch notes, deference to internal prison grievance systems, combined with limited restrictions on how internal grievance processes must be structured, "creates obvious incentives for prison officials to design grievance systems with short deadlines, multiple steps, and numerous technical requirements"—in short, a "procedural minefield" that prison administrators can use to shield their institutions against judicial scrutiny of abuse.[73] Courts have ruled in favor of prisons in several cases related to complex and unclear grievance procedures, suggesting that there are virtually no limits to the type of grievance procedures a prison can now adopt. *Jones v. Bock* and *Woodford* gave "prison officials *carte blanche* to design complicated procedural barriers to prisoners' court access."[74]

Even more problematic is the lack of independence between the grievance process and the implicated institution.[75] Under the PLRA, the jail or prison sets the rules for submitting grievances and appealing decisions, completely controlling the mechanisms through which custodial citizens seek redress. As one scholar notes, "in effect, the defendant is judge."[76] The prison grievance system is therefore not an independent arbitration of disputes.[77] Rather, the process is inherently biased towards those with a stake in the institutions: "A dispute resolution process in which the State defines the rules of the process and then becomes both a party in the dispute and the adjudicator violates basic notions of procedural fairness. Complaint handlers have a patent stake in resolving complaints with the interests of their employer in mind."[78] Even those who believe they are in imminent danger or who fear retaliation from their abusers still must clear procedural hurdles. A sexually abused prisoner may have to hand his grievance to the same sheriff or correctional officer that he is claiming has abused him.

It is not difficult to see that many inmates faced with this requirement opt to stay silent. Inmates may fear that filing a grievance will result in losing good time credits or affect the outcome of a parole hearing.[79] Yet a court held in *Garcia v. Glover* that fear of retaliation from prison authorities does not exempt an inmate from the exhaustion provision; the court dismissed Garcia's case against five jail authorities who allegedly abused him and then threatened him with further beatings if he reported the attack.[80] Arguably, this provision "subjects prisoners' right to sue over unconstitutional conduct to the considerable power of prison staff to retaliate against and intimidate prisoners and to manipulate the operation of grievance systems."[81] Stories of guards not providing the requested forms, "losing" the filed claim, failing to respond to filed claims, or retaliating against inmates abound.[82]

Finally, the PLRA includes several provisions that are particularly likely to discourage indigent prisoners from submitting their claims for legal remedy. First, a three-strikes provision prevents the filing of *in forma pauperis* claims, regardless of the merit, from poor inmates who have brought three prior claims in federal court that were deemed frivolous, malicious, or that failed to state a claim, even if those claims occurred before the PLRA's passage.[83] This provision applies only to indigent inmates and does not account for an inmate's length of incarceration or any successful claims they may have filed previously. John Boston notes that these third-strike litigants are "composed of the most oppressed people in the prison system, those held in administrative and disciplinary segregation units, frequently the locus of the worst abuses and harshest conditions in the prison system." Some inmates thus become "walking rights-free zones."[84] Second, under the PLRA, indigent inmates must pay a fee to file in federal court that is billed in installments over time; no other indigent person filing claims in federal court must pay this type of fee. The effect for inmates, who most often have little or no income, is to substantially diminish their ability to seek redress.[85] Other fiscal PLRA provisions seem designed to discourage any prisoners, even those with financial resources, from seeking recourse through the courts. For instance, for prisoners who manage to win claims in federal court, the PLRA also limited attorney compensation to 150 percent of the finding; as much as 25 percent of this can be paid from the inmate's recovery.[86] Given these potential returns, it is not hard to imagine that lawyers would become much less likely to represent inmate cases.[87]

In effect, the PLRA curtailed the ability of prisoners to petition the government for redress, a fundamental constitutional right and long-standing democratic principle. While custodial citizens can still press their claims in state court, this avenue for redress has been hollowed out, too, as states have followed the federal government's lead and enacted similar legislation limiting inmate litigation.[88] In the aftermath of the PLRA, action on behalf of inmates almost immediately dropped. In the first two years after the PLRA's enactment, inmate filings in court fell by one-third. By 2001 they had fallen by 43 percent, and by 2006 they had dropped by 60 percent. Moreover, critics of the PRLA contend that its heightened requirements prevent inmates from raising legitimate claims of constitutional violations, such "that rather than filtering out meritless lawsuits, the PLRA has simply tilted the playing field against prisoners across the board."[89] If the PLRA was successfully "reduc[ing] the quantity and improv[ing] the quality of prisoner suits," as its supporters intended, one would expect the dramatic decline in filings to be accompanied by a concomitant increase in plaintiffs' success rates. The evidence is quite the contrary. The shrunken inmate docket is less successful than before the PLRA's enactment; more cases are dismissed, and fewer settle.[90]

Democratic Participation, Citizen Voice, and Equality

A second core democratic value with which we are concerned is citizen voice, expressed through suffrage, speech, and association. Normative democratic theory is predicated on the idea that citizens should be actively involved in the agencies that govern their lives: They should have a say in how government functions, through institutional channels that allow them to express their preferences and organize with others around shared interests. Individual rights, such as freedoms of expression and association, provide the means and opportunity for citizen participation. Through freedom of speech, individuals contribute to the marketplace of ideas, expressing their thoughts, ideas, and beliefs. Through free association, citizens with similar attitudes and preferences can combine their political voices and organize around common goals.

Citizen participation is also a necessary condition for representation. When citizens participate, they can express their preferences and grievances and organize in their collective interests. To the extent that citizens can vote and participate politically, they can seek to constrain state action so that what the state does reflects the needs and demands of the citizenry. For both early modern theorists (e.g., John Locke) and more contemporary social scientists (e.g., Robert Dahl), participation both affirms the value of one's political voice and offers a tool for ensuring state legitimacy. Despite the importance of citizen voice to the health of democracy, however, modern criminal justice policies and institutions regularly and actively preclude citizen participation. By limiting direct participation through voting, as well as restricting freedoms of speech and association, criminal justice formally denies individuals the opportunity to engage in civic life.

The Freedom of Association

Commenting on the character of American democracy, Alexis de Tocqueville noted that "nothing, in my view, deserves more attention than the intellectual and moral associations in America."[91] In his view, association allowed people to view their own interests as inextricably tied to the good of the many; voluntary associations help build "habits of cooperation and public-spiritedness" among citizens and allow citizens to collaborate on issues of shared concern.[92] Freedom of association likewise benefits the democratic system as a whole. Justice Harlan, writing in *NAACP v. Alabama ex rel. Patterson*, argued that "effective advocacy of both public and private points of view, particularly controversial ones, is undeniably enhanced by group association."[93]

Custodial citizens, however, experience limitations on association at nearly every phase of criminal surveillance, adjudication, and punishment. One notable example is that, since the beginning of the 1980s, a growing number of cities have employed civil injunctions to fight gang-related crime. Injunctions arise from civil lawsuits filed by city or district attorneys and target particular individual and group behavior within defined geographic areas. In 1997 the California Supreme Court ruled in *People ex rel. Gallo v. Acuna* that police and prosecutors in Los Angeles could enforce a civil injunction against suspected gang members, which prohibited them from already illegal activities, such as selling drugs, but also certain otherwise legal activities, including associating with certain individuals.[94] Specifically, the injunction "bars 38 named members of a Latino gang from 'standing, sitting, walking, driving, gathering or appearing anywhere in public view with any other defendant . . . or with any other known [gang] member.'"[95] According to recent data from its city attorney's office, Los Angeles has forty-four permanent gang injunctions of this kind, involving seventy-two street gangs.[96] Localities from San Francisco to Fort Worth have mounted similar efforts to bar suspected gang members from a range of legal activities such as "loitering at schools, carrying pagers and riding bicycles"; suspected gang members who do so "face arrest."[97] And while cities' early efforts to employ these types of injunctions were scaled back after courts deemed them to be overly broad, recent injunctions that are more narrowly tailored have so far largely withstood judicial scrutiny.

Police call injunctions a "silver bullet," citing data that suggest injunctions can cut overall gang crime by half.[98] Those who defend injunctions argue that they are necessary to reduce the prevalence of gang activity by limiting the otherwise legal activities in which individuals engage during the organization and commission of gang-related criminal activities, such as having a beeper or standing on a rooftop. Yet whether or not gang injunctions effectively combat the devastating effects of gang violence, they pose a serious challenge to the freedom of association. This is particularly concerning because injunctions can be applied to individuals who have never been formally convicted of any crime, in some cases on mere suspicion of criminal activity. Moreover, because gang members are often all of a single race, injunctions are frequently accused of being racially discriminatory.[99] The lone dissenting judge in California's landmark *People ex rel. Gallo v. Acuna* case, Stanley Mosk, described the decision as one "that does not enhance liberty but deprives a number of simple rights to a group of Latino youths who have not been convicted of a crime."[100]

In addition, prosecutors seeking injunctions need not meet particularly rigorous evidentiary standards concerning alleged gang involvement. In making their case that certain individuals are responsible for creating a "public nuisance," prosecutors can rely almost exclusively on witness testimony from residents of a particular area, or from police officers or informants. In some cases the court strikes one or more defendants from a complaint or modifies the terms of the injunction, but "at most hearings, the court [issues] the injunction largely as requested."[101] Nor are those ultimately prosecuted for violating the terms of an injunction generally provided the protections of due process.[102] Violations can be prosecuted in either civil or criminal court and penalties under injunctions can vary widely.

Civil injunctions are just one of the ways in which the freedom to associate is limited for custodial citizens. Equally significant are laws that seek to permanently exclude custodial citizens from particular geographic areas, ranging from relatively small parts of a particular city to the large majority of a state. In *Banished: The New Social Control in Urban America*, Katherine Beckett and Steve Herbert suggest that city police forces increasingly use three mechanisms—off-limits orders, parks exclusion orders, and trespass admonishments—to banish undesirable (usually poor and black) people from public spaces. Through these mechanisms, police have wide discretion to ban people from large areas of cities, even if they have not committed a criminal offense. For example, an individual may be given a trespass admonishment or exclusion order for sleeping on a park bench, prohibiting him from entering that park again. If that individual then violates the order—which studies show often occurs, as individuals can find themselves restricted from geographic areas where they work, live, and socialize and are therefore difficult for them to avoid—the order then triggers a criminal offense for which the person can be arrested, facing the prospect of jail time and a criminal record. In this way, civil code restrictions sidestep the criminal process, while at the same time increasing some citizens' "vulnerability to criminal sanctions." By making it a crime "for some people simply to be in certain places," the orders target the poor, the homeless, and youth of color who may be law abiding but are deemed to be "out of place."[103] Scholars have shown that exclusion orders and trespass admonishments have grown tremendously over time. Beckett and Herbert estimate that in four months in 2005, Seattle alone issued up to 10,000 trespass admonishments and park exclusion orders.[104] Again, there is a marked racial bent to these practices: in 2005, blacks were 40 percent of those given trespass admonishments in Seattle, despite comprising under 10 percent of the population.

While these restrictions do not by definition limit association for political purposes, the practices broadly limit where custodial citizens can congregate. In addition, like gang injunctions, many forms of banishment are governed by civil rather than criminal procedures, so targets do not receive due process protections when they are imposed. Thus, as Beckett and Herbert note, "banishment is practiced in Seattle in a way that resists contestation by its targets."[105] By the time of their writing, only two appeals of thousands of parks exclusion orders had been successful.

Beckett and Herbert note several disturbing aspects of geographic banishment: the practices have reinforced spatial segregation; enhanced the power of police to stop, search, and arrest; and brought many new recruits into entanglement with criminal justice. They are most concerned, however, that these exclusion zones reduce access to "jobs, services, or social connections people need" and thereby increase "social marginality." These place-based restrictions also limit the freedom to associate, as people subjected to these restrictions find they are separated from local political communities, networks, and places they might otherwise assemble. In interviews with those who had undergone some form of geographic exclusion, individuals described "their social and spatial marginalization in sharp terms, not just as a complication in their everyday lives but an expulsion from the body politic."[106]

Freedom of Association during Incarceration

The United Nations recognizes "the right to freedom of peaceful assembly and association with others" to be a fundamental human right.[107] Yet, despite their centrality to citizens' democratic voice, First Amendment rights of peaceable assembly are also substantially restricted during incarceration. In several cases, courts have affirmed that inmates do not have the right to free association with friends or family, presenting significant difficulties for those seeking to maintain close emotional ties to prisoners with long sentences.[108] More troubling from a democratic perspective, however, are restrictions against association through participation in social, economic and civic organizations.

Aside from litigating in the courts, one of the primary ways that custodial citizens might participate politically, express their opinions, protest treatment within the institutions that hold them, and petition the government is through inmate organizations, councils, and prison unions. Such inmate political organizations flourished during the 1960s and 1970s and while prison conditions were often their target, reformers and activists also envisioned a more democratic and responsive institution, and encouraged the idea of inmate participation through elected inmate councils. The idea was not new; mutual aid leagues and inmate councils developed in the early twentieth century in the United States, organized by reformers such as Thomas Mott Osborne and Reverend E. M. Wells, who envisioned inmates as able to effectively self-govern. Several brief experiments in inmate self-government during this period involved inmates meting out discipline, formulating education programs, and managing inmate labor. The idea reemerged after prison disturbances made the logic of the authoritarian prison regime increasingly untenable.[109] As one scholar notes, "Attica brought into stark relief the contradictions that existed between the use of imprisonment with its closed, often brutal and controlling hierarchical system and democratic ideals like egalitarianism, liberty and transparency that supposedly informed American government."[110] Yet despite at least some suggestive evidence that inmate councils could improve prisons, encourage good citizens, and lead to greater self-esteem among inmates, at many institutions they either failed to take hold or declined in practice over time.[111]

Like inmate self-government organizations, prison labor unions emerged in the aftermath of Attica and other violent prison revolts and, for a brief time, enjoyed widespread support from reformers and the inmates who joined their ranks. The first inmate union developed at Soledad Prison in California and quickly spread to Folsom Prison, where 2,000 workers participated in a strike in 1970 that lasted seventeen days.[112] The inmates, who received anywhere from two to sixteen cents an hour, were protesting for a minimum wage and worker's compensation benefits.[113] The strike resulted in the establishment of the United Prisoner's Union in California, whose members numbered over 3,000, and to a

"Bill of Rights of the Convicted Class." Other unions soon formed in California and many other states followed.[114] By the mid-1970s, the Prisoner's Union had been established in prison systems across the country and counted nearly 23,000 members.[115] Some even carried affiliations with local unions outside the prison and the National Prisoners' Reform Association began calling for a national coalition of inmate unions.[116]

The purpose of inmate unions—like labor unions generally—was to communicate citizens' desire for specific policy reforms, such as a desire for higher wages and better working conditions. However, the inmate union was also designed to bring inmates into the political process inside the prison. Unions were advocacy groups for those confined: "prisoners, through unionization, sought a participatory role in the operation of the institution and greater control over the decisions that affected their lives."[117] Unions also represented the voice of prisoners in an institution where they had historically had little input into prison governance or limited access to external representatives. While "the driving force behind prisoners' unionization related to prison conditions," their purpose was broader, "grounded in [prisoners'] desire for political participation and recognition as democratic citizens."[118]

Yet, again, despite their potential, inmate organizing in American prisons was halted almost as soon as it began. The Supreme Court effectively abolished inmate unions in *Jones v. North Carolina Prisoner Union* in 1977. In deciding the case, the court formally acknowledged that the right to associate can be "curtailed whenever the institution's officials, in the exercise of their informed discretion, reasonably conclude that such associations . . . possess the likelihood of disruption to prison order or stability, or otherwise interfere with the legitimate penological objectives of the prison environment."[119] This decision effectively curtailed the ability of confined citizens to organize and associate. At the same time, it reflected the idea that "there are segments of our society which, due to a seemingly justified need for stricter governmental supervision, will not enjoy as broad first amendment protections as the rest of society."[120] In their dissent, Justices Thurgood Marshall and William Brennan were prescient in appreciating what would become of inmates' rights in the wake of the decision.[121] "After all, if the courts refused to analyze the positive capabilities of a carefully structured prison organization, and only considered the alleged security threat which unions may pose, then the first amendment rights of inmates would lose out to the 'governmental interest' every time."[122] While some lower courts continued to provide protections to unions, *Jones* ultimately "sounded the death knell" for prison unionization across the country.[123]

Democratic Voice through Suffrage and the Jury Pool

In addition to the rights to associate and organize, democratic theory describes the model state as one that affords each citizen equal chance to express his or her civic voice. The right to vote thus lies at the core of democratic citizenship; it is "the pivotal right."[124] Through the vote, citizens communicate their preferences to their political leaders, develop democratic habits, and become active participants in the structures by which they are governed. The principle of "one citizen, one vote" also provides for democratic legitimacy. As Sidney Verba notes, "Democracies are sounder when the reason why some lose does not rest on the fact that they are invisible to those who make decisions."[125]

Arguably the greatest distortion of democratic values in the modern carceral state, then, is that many custodial citizens lose the right to vote in democratic elections, expelling them from equal civic membership. As one federal judge argued:

> Disenfranchisement is the harshest civil sanction imposed by a democratic society. When brought beneath its axe, the disenfranchised is severed from the body politic and condemned to the lowest form of citizenship, where voiceless at the ballot box . . . the disinherited must sit idly by while others elect his civic leaders and while others choose the fiscal and governmental policies which will govern him and his family. Such a shadowy form of citizenship must not be imposed lightly.[126]

Some states have eased voting restrictions for felons in recent years, but court challenges to felony disenfranchisement writ large have largely failed. In the precedent-setting *Richardson v. Ramirez*, the US Supreme Court upheld California's prohibition on ex-felons voting, ruling that it did not violate the Fourteenth Amendment's Equal Protection Clause.[127] This firmly established the constitutionality of felon disenfranchisement laws, closing off further challenges of this kind.

One aspect of disenfranchisement policies that has received particular attention from scholars and reformers is their racial effect. Under current felon disenfranchisement laws, an estimated 13 percent of black men nationally are denied the right to vote, with nearly one in four unable to vote in states that maintain the most restrictive disenfranchisement laws.[128] For many blacks, felon disenfranchisement bears the reminder of the nation's sordid history of disenfranchising blacks through other long discredited mechanisms, such as literacy tests and poll taxes.[129]

Some custodial citizens experience other forms of political exclusion, too, including a restriction on jury participation. The framers of the Constitution, as well as early democratic theorists, believed jury service to be "one of the fundamental prerequisites to majoritarian self-government."[130] For them, jury service was analogous to voting, as they believed both to be key avenues by which citizens "participate in the workings of government in America."[131] In de Tocqueville's view, democratic voice in the judicial arena must be considered as important as in the legislative arena because they "are both equally powerful means of making the majority prevail."[132] Jury lists were thus tied to voter rolls; the logic was that the electorate should also make up the jury, and that citizens should have a say in judicial proceedings for the same reasons that they have a say in selecting representatives. The importance of serving on juries for democracy was no less important to later observers; as Justice Kennedy argued in an opinion, "with the exception of voting, for most citizens the honor and privilege of jury duty is their most significant opportunity to participate in the democratic process."[133] In this respect, statutes preventing those with a felony conviction from serving on a jury "creat[e] a class of outsiders, forced to watch democracy move forward with only limited opportunities to influence its direction."[134]

Yet felon jury exclusion is a more widespread practice than bans on felon voting: The majority of states and the federal government permanently exclude people with a felony conviction from serving on juries. Scholars have estimated that, as a result, 13 million citizens can never participate in a jury and an unknown number of others are excluded for some period of time. As with felon disenfranchisement, the practice combines with the skewed racial demographics of the custodial population to diminish the democratic voice of blacks in particular. While only about 6.5 percent of all adults are purged from jury service, an astounding 37 percent of black men are deemed ineligible to participate in this way (before other exclusions, like peremptory strikes).[135] In a dissertation on felon jury exclusion, Darren Wheelock found that several counties in the state of Georgia excluded over half of black men from appearing on juries. In one county in that state, 70 percent of black men had a felony conviction and were therefore disqualified for life from serving.[136] Even though black people on trial in those areas will not be tried by a jury of their peers, at least as it is racially construed, challenges to the practice of lifetime disqualification have so far not prevailed on equal protection or other constitutional grounds.

Democratic Voice through Free Speech and Information

Felon disenfranchisement laws and jury exclusions are two threads in a broader set of laws and policies that limit the voice and power of custodial citizens. Others, such as restrictions on free speech and information, are also pernicious but have received far less scholarly scrutiny. Because adequate data do not exist on jail and prison practices that limit free speech and association, we largely rely on court challenges where prisoners sought to express, and prisons suppressed, their political voice. In many of these cases, the courts have ruled that correctional institutions can drastically constrain the ability of inmates to express themselves and upheld the right of prisons and jails to restrict prisoners' access to political information while confined.

While the courts have not granted prisons an unfettered ability to violate inmates' rights to free speech, they have generally argued that "the fact of confinement and the needs of the penal institution impose limitations on constitutional rights, including those derived from the First Amendment."[137] Again, it is important to note that these restrictions have been applied not only to inmates and offenders who have been found guilty of a crime in a court of law. Many of these practices are routinely employed in jails where individuals are awaiting disposition of their cases, and all are applied to the large population of nonviolent individuals serving increasingly lengthy sentences behind bars.

A prominent example of how courts have limited the free speech of convicted offenders and those awaiting trial is in the restriction of prison writing. Since the first prison newspaper was founded in a debtors' prison in the 1800s, inmates have a long history of expressing their opinions, contesting mistreatment, and connecting with the outside world through prison publications. Prison newspapers had their heyday in the 1960s, when there were an estimated 250 prison publications, some of which were published weekly, with a circulation of readers both inside and outside the prison that numbered 2 million. Some prison newspapers became highly acclaimed and wildly successful, even winning major journalism and poetry awards, as they became increasingly critical in the movement to reform the brutal and largely invisible conditions inmates faced. For instance, the *Angolite*, the newspaper of the prison farm at the Louisiana State Penitentiary, was perhaps the first to garner attention to the problem of prison rape and the tolerance of correctional staff to chronic sexual violence, for which it won the George Polk Award.[138]

Yet just as active as prison publications during this period were correctional officials' efforts to stymie their operation. As inmate newspapers began to challenge prison practices in the 1960s and 1970s, they and their authors increasingly came under fire. Some had to clear their issues with wardens before being printed, copies were destroyed before distribution, and administrators pulled stories if they cast a negative light on the administration. Paper editors were fired and newspaper offices were locked.[139]

It was not long before freedom of the prison press came before the courts. These cases initially supported the free speech of inmates through prison writing. However, the initial precedent was largely replaced in 1974 in *Pell v. Procunier*, after which courts began to allow censorship of prison newspaper articles that correctional administrators deemed to be either potentially inflammatory or to challenge the rehabilitative purpose of the prison.[140] For example, the state of Virginia prevented the distribution of *FYSK* (Facts You Should Know), a prison newspaper at the state penitentiary in Richmond, after one story shed light on the death of a sick prisoner whom guards had ignored and other articles similarly painted a poor image of prison officials. In deciding that case, the courts ruled that the prison's security interests trumped the free speech rights of inmates. More significantly, a Ninth Circuit court ruled in 2007 that a prison could keep inmates from publishing a prison newspaper at all because internal communications between inmates do "not present the type of atypical significant deprivation in which a State might conceivably create a liberty interest."[141]

The result of this more recent jurisprudence is that prison newspapers have moved toward extinction. By the 1990s, almost all of California's once-vibrant prison newspapers were defunct, and in the nation, only one of the top ten prison newspapers listed in the 1963 *Saturday Review* still operated. The rapid decline of prison newspapers marked not just the end of a once-important piece of prison culture, but also of one of the central mechanisms of free speech and democratic voice behind prison walls.[142] As one expert on the history of prison journalism noted, prison newspapers "serve as a means for redress for a disenfranchised segment of our citizenry. For most inmates, there will be no media acting as watchdogs in their community unless there is a prison newspaper. . . . With the end of a viable prison press, freedom of speech will become an increasingly distant concept to inmates."[143]

Other avenues of political communication have fared similarly. In general, the court has ruled that unpopular political views are protected speech for inmates, just as they are among the general public.[144] However, the courts have given wide latitude to prison administrators to determine through a "conscientious review" what constitutes appropriate content.[145] Michael Mushlin describes the case of *Malik v. Coughlin* (1990), in which the court ruled that prison officials had not violated the Constitution in censoring an issue of *Freedom Press* because it contained an article accusing prison officials of conspiring to commit "mass genocide" on black and Hispanic prisoners through medical experimentation. Mushlin notes that the court "characterized the article as 'clearly intended to incite disobedience to prison personnel and possibly hysteria and violence.' The court failed to explain, however, in what way this article which was undoubtedly critical of prison practices incited unlawful disobedience to prison authority."[146]

The particular article in question was surely little more than conspiracy theory. However, the censorship in this particular case takes on special significance in light of America's extensive history of medical experimentation on prisoners. In a review of "horrific US medical experiments," the Associated Press found more than forty studies in which doctors had intentionally exposed disabled people and prison inmates to diseases ranging from gonorrhea to pandemic flu virus to malaria. In congressional hearings on the subject of medical experimentation, representatives of the pharmaceutical industry admitted to relying on inmates for testing because they "were cheaper than chimpanzees."[147] In this context, the court's holding in *Malik v. Coughlin*—which involved speech that would be clearly protected among the general public—takes on a more troubling hue.

Nor do free speech restrictions affect only the extent of information available to the incarcerated; they have secondary consequences for the information available to the broader public. In *Pell v. Procunier*, prison inmates and journalists also challenged a regulation of the California Department of Corrections that stipulated that "press and other media interviews with specific individual inmates will not be permitted."

The logic of this particular restriction, according to the department, was that freely allowing members of the press to conduct face-to-face interviews with prisoners had "resulted in a relatively small number of inmates gaining disproportionate notoriety and influence among their fellow inmates."[148] The *Pell* decision found the regulation to be constitutional, arguing that the media ban was not overly restrictive because prisoners could always use alternative means of communication, such as phone calls or mail.

In so concluding, the court drew a stark line between custodial and noncustodial citizens, noting explicitly that it "would find the availability of such alternatives unimpressive if they were submitted as justification for governmental restriction of personal communication among members of the general public." They held, however, that the relationship of the inmate to the state is inherently different, in that it is "far more intimate than that of a State and a private citizen." In a footnote to the majority opinion, the court acknowledged the potential issue the decision might raise for democratic accountability, recognizing "that the conditions in this Nation's prisons are a matter that is both newsworthy and of great public importance" and that prisoners might be in a unique position to see and publicize these important and newsworthy concerns.[149] Yet the court maintained its position that correctional administrators were not infringing on constitutionally protected rights and thus allowed the regulations to stand.

Conclusion

It has long been asserted that the character of a nation's criminal justice system is "a key index of the state of a democracy."[150] Alexis de Tocqueville long ago surmised that our nation's progress toward democratic government was stalled by criminal justice: "The progress of mankind from physical force to the substitution of moral power in the art and science of government in general, is but very slow, but in none of its branches has this progress, which alone affords the standard by which we can judge of the civil development of a society, been more retarded than in the organization and discipline of prisons."[151]

That this remains true is at least in part attributable to the fact that, in contrast to other policy domains and their attendant institutions, criminal justice poses special difficulties to the everyday practice of our democratic virtues. It is hard to deny a fundamental tension between a view of government defined as "the will of the people" and consent of the governed and systems of criminal control that are inherently designed to monitor and control citizens' behavior. Scholars have often noted (and been uncomfortable with) the fact that criminal justice is both "a major support and a major threat to democratic society"; the agents of criminal justice are "charged with using undemocratic means to obtain democratic ends."[152]

It is not the case, however, that police, courts, and prisons must necessarily function as nondemocratic regimes within democratic republics. Rather, many a democracy abroad has explicitly constructed correctional institutions to be in concert with their broader democratic ideologies. For example, inmate unions have continuously operated in democratic countries abroad; Denmark and Sweden have longstanding and very effective unions, known as KRIM and KRUM, respectively, with large memberships and coherent political goals. As Marie Gottschalk describes the Swedish system:

> Prisoners in Sweden did not need to mobilize to secure basic rights, for they retain all civil rights while incarcerated, including the right to vote. They were not subject to tight censorship of their mail and were able to maintain wide contacts with the outside through extensive use of furloughs and unsupervised visits in prison. Swedish offenders also had rights to redress from the government that have deep institutional and historical roots. Established in 1809 when the constitution was adopted, the Office of the Parliamentary Ombudsman gives Parliament authority to appoint a judicial ombudsman. This position has been an important avenue for addressing complaints lodged against the police, prosecutors, or corrections officials.[153]

America's restrictions on democratic voice within the criminal justice sphere are likewise exceptional. We know of no comprehensive comparative study of felon disenfranchisement laws, but most evidence suggests that the United States is the lone democracy to permanently bar felons from voting after completing their sentence.[154] Indeed, many European countries have no restrictions on felon voting, even for those serving time in prison; in a 2001 survey of sixty-three democracies, 25 percent allowed prisoners to continue to vote behind bars.[155] Moreover, a number of countries, including Israel, Canada, and South Africa, have in recent years moved toward fewer restrictions, leading one scholar to conclude that "an identifiable global trajectory has emerged towards the expansion of felon suffrage."[156] In striking down legislation to curb prisoner franchise, Canada's high court argued that it did not serve any legitimate state objective. The court's rationale hinged on the importance of democratic voice: "If we accept that governmental power in a democracy flows from the citizens, it is difficult to see how that power can be used to disenfranchise the very citizens from whom the government's power flows."[157] Similarly, the European Court of Human Rights overturned a ban on inmate voting in the United Kingdom in *Hirst v. United Kingdom*, ruling that it violated the Convention for the Protection of Human Rights and Fundamental Freedoms.

Some scholars have countered that the very design of America's criminal justice institutions and their attendant limitations on democratic practices are themselves a function of the popular will. Certainly, many of our most punitive policy choices in criminal justice stem from an electorate that generally supports the death penalty, limitations on prisoners' rights, and the ability of police to stop citizens.[158] That the will of the majority always should—or will—win out over other democratic principles seems to us to be a troublingly thin basis to describe a democratic state. Indeed, the pragmatist John Dewey warned against collapsing majoritarianism as a democratic end in itself. We know now that many of our most antidemocratic moments were supported by the will of the people.

In the chapters that follow, we assess the question of whether the antidemocratic features of the state to which custodial citizens are exposed have downstream consequences for how they come to understand citizenship and democracy in America today. As custodial citizens interact with some of our most central and expanding institutions in America—those governing how to punish citizens and control crime—they see a system at odds with the principles of democracy. To calculate the full costs of the growing carceral state, we must contend not only with its sizable economic, social, and health effects, but also with the ways in which they promote a specific civic learning that may stand at odds with the ideals of democracy itself.

CHAPTER FOUR

Assessing the Effects
of Criminal Justice

Even if we acknowledge that more citizens travel through criminal justice institutions than ever before, and that the institutions to which they are exposed are failing to conform to democratic ideals, how might this matter for citizenship and democracy? For our argument to be persuasive, it also has to be the case that these interventions are politically consequential. That is, we must ask: How does the character of these institutions shape what custodial citizens come to learn about government and their place in the political order? And, consequently, does it change how much they trust the system and the extent to which they feel they have a say in what their elected representatives do?

The main way criminal justice promotes political learning has already been described in great detail in the last chapter; it partakes of a different, and antidemocratic, set of practices. Because these institutions differ in their character from other domains of the American state—they are less responsive, allow citizens fewer avenues for agency and voice, and reflect a more deeply racialized inequality (a feature to which we return in chapter 7)—they provide a counterpoint to the formal civic education received in public schools and a contrasting set of lessons than are provided by institutions whose purpose is more centrally distributive. But there are other characteristics of these encounters that make it a salient site of political socialization. Custodial interactions exhibit at least six exceptional features that promote a different, more encompassing, and likely more durable form of political learning.

First, criminal justice interactions are often involuntary. Hierarchical institutions where agents hold power over citizens and have a large degree of discretion will impart very different lessons than those institutions where citizens are "customers" and can voice complaints, exit easily, and have a degree of power relative to the institution. Staffan Kumlin has found that institutions that empower citizens have great consequences for how citizens experience their government; how much an institution empowers citizens depends, in his formulation, on how institutional design affects the power balance between the agency and the citizen. Institutions that are organized in such a way that bureaucrats maintain a large degree of discretion and where there are few "exit options" (the ability of citizens to "turn their backs" on the agency when discontented) available to citizens were disempowering.[1] Criminal justice interventions are defined by very limited citizen agency, few exit options, and involve powerful agents who wield vast amounts of discretion in who to stop, charge, and how much to punish.

Second, and related, encounters with criminal justice engage a direct and obvious connection between criminal justice authorities and government. Much of the redistributive side of government takes place in the "submerged state"; because many of today's social programs and benefits occur through tax breaks, private benefits, and government-sponsored initiatives that obscure the role of government and exaggerate the role of the market, citizens often fail to recognize the role of the state in their lives.[2] Moreover, it may also be that social benefits are less visible to citizens because they often occur through the mail, rather than through personal contact with government agencies or officials, making it easier to disconnect social benefits from government and the political system. As Kumlin writes in explaining why some social service experiences are less "salient and emotionally charged in citizens' memories": "universal insurances involve less direct personal contact with public employees and actual physical institutions; these institutions do not have a very visible interface. Experiences are often reduced to the reception of an anticipated sum of money."[3]

In criminal justice, the role of the state is clearly on display. Unlike other interactions where the role of government is more camouflaged (i.e., a Social Security check arriving in the mail), these interactions prominently feature visible state power. Where schoolteachers and welfare workers provide few visual cues to their position as public employees, criminal justice workers are distinguished by uniforms, badges, and official transport vehicles, all of which bear their government titles and locate their institutional authority. Even in the most visible welfare-state

interactions, whereby a client must have face-to-face contact with a welfare caseworker, the role of the state is not as expansive as in the criminal justice domain. Thus, where participants in distributive programs
may be less likely to experience civic and political socialization through
their contact with government, because the government's role is not immediately obvious, or in some cases is camouflaged, criminal justice contact results in political learning because it so clearly displays the role of
government.

Third, and perhaps most important, these interactions can be totalizing and stigmatizing. Particularly for those who spend time in prison or
jail, the state assumes responsibility for nearly every social, economic,
and political function: "For state prisoners, eating, sleeping, dressing,
washing, working and playing are all done under the watchful eye of the
State. . . . What for a private citizen would be a dispute with his landlord,
with his employer, with his tailor, with his neighbor, or with his banker
becomes, for the prisoner, a dispute with the state."[4]

Likewise, criminal justice experiences can systematically shape other
encounters with the state and redefine one's future interactions with
other state agents. Soss shows that interactions in the welfare domain
shape individuals' views of the broader political system, so that subsequent encounters with government are fed through the cognitive filter of
the welfare system they know best and interact with most. By contrast,
in criminal justice, a single encounter can *directly* shape subsequent encounters with the state. Contact with criminal justice can often become
a critical juncture that determines the nature of future citizenship and
relationship to the state; long after their initial contact with criminal justice, custodial citizens continue to occupy "semi-citizenship."[5] Through
formal and informal exclusion from many important political and social
rights of citizenship, including the right to serve on a jury, the ability to
pursue many public sector jobs, and access to the social safety net, felons undergo a form of "civil death."[6] They have variously been described
as "diminished citizens," "civic outsiders," "internal exiles," and "partial citizens."[7] The bedrock of this impaired citizenship is losing the right
to vote in democratic elections. The vote is central to civic membership,
and without it they are illegitimate actors in our political process and
democratic procedures. Indeed, through encounters with criminal justice, custodial citizens experience a process we might think of as political *denaturalization*. Rather than gaining access to greater rights and incorporation, as is experienced by new immigrants who are ushered into

the body politic, custodial citizens experience a gradual or abrupt expulsion from the democratic polity.

These exclusions from the political rights and responsibilities of citizenship are joined by countless other legal, economic, and social handicaps. For instance, convicts are barred from public sector jobs and many private sector occupations. Employers routinely make hiring and firing decisions based on an arrest record (even those that did not result in conviction), leaving offenders and even once-suspected persons as the last group that can be legally discriminated against.[8] In an audit study, employers were twice as likely to reject a job application if the applicant had a criminal record.[9]

Criminal justice policies likewise limit the ability of custodial populations to partake of America's social welfare state: convicts are denied veterans' and disability benefits and, under the 1996 welfare overhaul, people convicted of a felony drug offense are prohibited for life from ever accessing two central antipoverty programs, welfare and food stamps (TANF and SNAP), as well as federal financial aid for college.[10] Housing authorities can exclude those with a single arrest from receiving public housing or Section 8 vouchers and, under recent one-strike provisions, can evict residents without due process if they even suspect criminal wrongdoing.[11]

In addition to altering the state/citizen relationship, encounters with criminal justice authorities are often dramatic "crisis" events that involve the humiliation of being searched in public, being physically handled and experiences of trauma and loss—losing homes, jobs, family members, and legal rights. This is likely to make them highly emotional, salient, and durable memories of state contact.[12] Studies have shown that police-citizen encounters routinely feature derogatory remarks, bodily contact, and citizens being made to do humiliating things, and an arrest involves invasive and dehumanizing searches of one's person and property.[13] These and other practices—mandatory drug tests as a provision of parole, evictions from housing based on suspicion of crime alone, having one's person searched in a roadside traffic stop—all make virtually certain that custodial populations will "have an occasional brush with public humiliation," and serve to regularly underscore their otherness and exclusion.[14]

Moreover, while remaining citizens formally, offenders are perceived as "undeserving of public and civic regard."[15] They are relegated to a hyperstigmatized social status, sent consistent symbolic messages through the media, public discourse, and, indeed, through the institutions of criminal justice themselves that they are not worthy of equal citizenship. Treating those with a felony conviction as democratic pariahs, criminal justice policies serve to stigmatize through both formal and informal processes of degradation and political exclusion. Custodial populations internalize these ideas, inheriting a "stigma consciousness" that makes them less likely to think they can make legitimate demands of government and see those demands met.[16]

These first three features of criminal justice describe ways in which policies and institutions within this domain are distinct from other state activities. We might also consider three other features of custodial interactions, which make custodial citizens uniquely positioned to experience a substantial socializing impact of the carceral state.

First, contact with criminal justice is often experienced for the first time at an early age, imprinting political ideas before individuals have formed other firm and stable preferences and beliefs that will help shape their adult political behavior.[17] Indeed, many of our interviewees had been stopped by police, searched, questioned, and even incarcerated before they had reached voting age, could file a tax return, or apply for a driver's license. A few of the people we spoke with had their first encounter under twelve years old, while they were still in primary school and one fellow was so young that he did not distinguish between being in an institution for orphaned youngsters as a young child and the institution for juvenile delinquents that he moved to early in his adolescence. More systematically, data from a nationally representative sample of inmates in state and federal correctional institutions suggest that the median age at which state prisoners were first arrested is seventeen, and 75 percent of inmates in state prisons experienced their first arrest by age twenty-one.[18] Imprisonment is also likely to be experienced early in the lifecycle. The risk of experiencing a first incarceration is highest for men ages twenty to thirty and declines substantially after age thirty-five.[19] In 2010, about 53 percent of inmates held in state or federal prison or local jail were under age thirty-five.[20] Thus for many young people, surveillance and incarceration is part of the fabric of adolescence. Describing her experience doing ethnographic work in a Philadelphia ghetto, the sociologist Alice Goffman writes:

> Children learn at an early age to watch out for the police and to prepare to run. The first week I spent on 6th Street, I saw two boys, 5 and 7 years old,

play a game of chase in which one assumed the role of the cop who must run after the other. When the "cop" caught up to the other child, he pushed him down and cuffed him with imaginary handcuffs. He patted the other child down and felt in his pockets, asking if he had warrants or was carrying a gun or any drugs. The child then took a quarter out of the other child's pocket, laughing and yelling, "I'm seizing that!" In the following months, I saw children give up running and simply stick their hands behind their backs, as if in handcuffs, or push their bodies up against a car, or lie flat on the ground and put their hands over their head. The children yelled, "I'm going to lock you up! I'm going to lock you up, and you ain't never coming home." I once saw a 6-year-old child pull another child's pants down and try to do a "cavity search."[21]

Even more important, encounters with criminal justice occur most frequently among those who lack other sources of political influence. For some individuals in poor communities, the most visible and direct contact with government may be with a police officer rather than a welfare counselor, in a police station rather than on a military base.[22] Indeed, Jennifer Lawless and Richard Fox, in their study of poor, inner-city residents of the South Bronx area of New York, report one of their respondents noting in passing that "in cities like this . . . most people have their only real contact with government in hostile confrontations with the police."[23] To provide a more systematic measure, we examined citizen reports of salient government interactions. In a nationally representative survey of Americans ages 24–32, contact with institutions of surveillance, adjudication, and punishment were a major nexus between the citizen and the state (see fig. 4.1). In that survey, respondents were nearly as likely to say that they had been arrested (30%) as to have ever received welfare (36%). Other types of contact with the state have been similarly outpaced. Only 7 percent of those surveyed reported having spent time in the military, and 2 percent had spent time in foster care. In 2007, when America was engaged in two wars overseas, there were more Americans serving time in prison than were serving active duty in the military.[24] In short, the importance of criminal justice institutions to Americans' political socialization has likely grown over time, rivaling traditional sites of state activity with which previous scholars have been concerned.

Second, because criminal justice contact is concentrated in certain groups and neighborhoods, its effects are both direct and secondary. Individuals learn from their personal experiences, cultivating their ideas

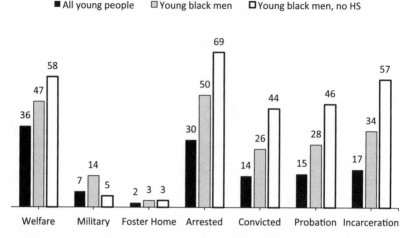

FIGURE 4.1. Share of Americans with different types of government contact, ages 24–32. Incarceration includes people who have ever been to jail, regardless of conviction. *Source*: National Longitudinal Study of Adolescent Health, Wave III.

about democracy and citizenship through their own interactions with the carceral state. At the same time, however, custodial citizens tend to be embedded in neighborhoods and networks where criminal justice contact is routine. For example, most of our interview subjects revealed that among their neighbors, friends, family, and church, over half had criminal justice exposure. One young woman we spoke with, Patrice, mentioned during the interview that she was the "only one that hasn't been fingerprinted.... On both sides of the family. My mom's been to jail, my dad's been to jail, my grandma's been to jail, my grandfather's been to jail." More systematically, according to data from the Bureau of Justice Statistics, 46 percent of jail inmates in 1996 and 37 percent of inmates in state prison in 1991 had a family member who had been incarcerated.[25] Similarly, nearly half (43%) of respondents to a nationally representative survey of Americans who had themselves spent time in prison or jail also reported having a close friend or family member who had been incarcerated.[26] Thus, rather than being an isolated incident experienced by an individual, these encounters teach lessons that tend to be reinforced by social contacts and existing community narratives.

And finally, for custodial citizens, criminal justice contact is often a frequent and sustained event in their lives. Table 4.1 details the proportion of custodial citizens in a national survey for whom contact with

TABLE 4.1. **Frequency of contact among custodial citizens ages 24–32**

	Total	Black men	Black men, no high school diploma
Of those who have been arrested more than once	51.2%	68.7%	79.1%
Of those who have been convicted more than once	37.7%	40.5%	48.9%
Of those who have been incarcerated more than once	47.5%	57.1%	64.4%
Of those who have been incarcerated			
Total months served before age 18	7.5	11.5	14.7
Total months served after age 18	7.2	16.9	25.2
Total months served	21.3	38.3	47.3

Source: National Longitudinal Study of Adolescent Health, Wave III.

criminal justice is recurrent. Among Americans ages 24–32, more than half of those who have ever been arrested report having had multiple arrests. The same is true for more intense contact: more than a third of individuals who have been convicted and nearly half of those who have been incarcerated report having had this type of interaction with criminal justice more than once. Certain entire social groups are now living large segments of their lives under correctional jurisdiction. On average, custodial citizens will log nearly two years behind bars by the time they reach young adulthood. For black men, the average time spent in prison or jail by ages 24–32 is over three years, and black men without a high school diploma lose nearly four years to incarceration before reaching this age range.

For each of these reasons, passage through institutions of criminal justice is likely to be a salient source of political learning relative to contacts with government that are voluntary, infrequent, do not occur through physical institutions, do not result in harmful effects, are less stigmatizing, or where the role of the state is "submerged," like much of contemporary social provision.

Documenting Criminal Justice and Political Learning

So what political "lessons" does criminal justice contact provide? Our basic premise is that criminal justice contact matters to political life. Through encounters with criminal justice agents and institutions, custodial citizens form particular views of democracy and citizenship in America today. Having now provided a detailed background of the char-

acter of criminal justice institutions and the process by which they socialize citizens, we turn our attention in the remainder of this book to
the lessons that criminal justice contacts impart.

Connecting political socialization with criminal justice experiences
is a surprisingly complex task, however. Despite the pervasiveness of
citizen contact with crime control and penal institutions, we know little about how custodial interactions influence perceptions of government and participatory habits. The voices of custodial citizens have been
mostly absent in studies of policy and politics, largely because they are
underrepresented or unidentifiable in the majority of social surveys.[27]
The typical data analyzed in studies of American political behavior
come from large-n surveys conducted via face-to-face or phone interviews designed to be representative of the American public through random sampling and weighting. However, with few exceptions, these surveys do not include interviews with individuals in prisons or jails, and
since inmates are restricted in their access to phones, phone surveys exclude them as well. Thus, the probability of an incarcerated person being
included in a public opinion survey sample is often zero. Individuals who
were formerly incarcerated are likewise difficult to include in a survey
because they are less likely than never-incarcerated citizens to remain
in one household for a long period of time, are more likely to be homeless, and are less likely to be the primary occupant of a household. When
these citizens are systematically underrepresented in random sampling
designs, their views are also underrepresented.

Additionally, even where existing surveys do include samples of custodial citizens, they normally do not query respondents about their experiences with criminal justice, leaving us no way to know who has had contact with police or been incarcerated. Large surveys such as the Current
Population Survey and Panel Study of Income Dynamics do not measure
contact with the criminal justice system, nor do mainstream political science and social surveys such as the General Social Survey, American
National Election Studies, and Social Capital Community Benchmark
Survey. Meanwhile, Bureau of Justice Statistics surveys of inmates and
ex-offenders do not query custodial populations about their political beliefs and engagement. We also lack good qualitative material on custodial populations. A handful of urban ethnographers have conducted
in-depth studies of low-income neighborhoods and the role of criminal
justice in their lives, but only one study that we know of has been explicitly concerned with examining the political experiences of felons and

former felons—in particular, how losing the right to vote affected their ideas about government.[28] In the coming chapters, we therefore combine systematic analyses of large sample, quantitative data on custodial and noncustodial populations with intensive interviews with a smaller sample of people —both custodial and noncustodial citizens—in three cities. These two data sources are intended to be complementary.

Quantitative Survey Data

We rely on several unusual quantitative sources that fulfill three necessary and sufficient conditions: an adequate number of people in the sample who have experienced police contact or confinement, detailed measures of involvement with criminal justice, and items related to subsequent political behavior and attitudes. These data allow us to undertake an analysis that would otherwise be impossible. We employ six quantitative surveys in this book, which are described in appendix A.

Because our surveys vary in their populations of interest, they also differ in the proportion of custodial citizens they represent. In the National Longitudinal Study of Adolescent Health (Add Health), although the vast majority of respondents had not had encounters with the police, courts, or corrections, about 20 percent of the sample had some contact with adult criminal justice agencies by their young adulthood. Of the Wave III sample, 20 percent reported being stopped by the police for questioning, 9 percent had been arrested as adults, 4 percent had been convicted in adult court, about 1 percent had been confined in an adult correctional facility, and 0.3 percent had served one year or more behind bars. In the National Longitudinal Study of Youth (NLSY79) 2006 young adult sample, 6 percent had been convicted of a crime and 3 percent had served in a correctional facility. In the 1997 NLSY cohort (NLSY97) 2002 sample, 24 percent had been arrested, 12 percent convicted, and 5 percent incarcerated.

In the surveys sampling disadvantaged youth or racial minorities, criminal justice contact was more extensive. Compared to the Add Health study, a much greater proportion of respondents in the Fragile Families and Child Wellbeing Study (Fragile Families) had exposure to criminal justice, and many more had actually served hard time. According to their self-reported custodial history, 61 percent of the fathers interviewed in the three-year follow-up had been stopped or questioned by police, 36 percent had been charged and arrested, 25 percent had been convicted of a crime in court, 22 percent had served time in a correctional facility, and 10 percent had been imprisoned for one year or more. Among black youth in the Black Youth Project Youth Culture Survey (BYP) data, contact with criminal justice was likewise extensive: 62 percent of black youth reported being stopped by police, 28 percent reported having been arrested, and 11 percent had been convicted of a crime. In the Washington Post/Kaiser Family Foundation/Harvard African-American Men Survey (AAMS), 28 percent of blacks (and 36 percent of black men) reported being arrested and 15 percent of blacks (and 19 percent of black men) reported being incarcerated.

In the quantitative analyses, we seek to isolate the effects of criminal justice interventions on subsequent political beliefs and behavior; using multivariate regression and nonparametric analysis, we are able to estimate the size of these effects and say something about how criminal justice contact shapes trust, efficacy, participation in the political process, and perceptions of racial equality. Because our analyses employ large, representative samples, we can generalize our results to the population as a whole and show that the effects of criminal justice encounters do not depend on region, age, race, or other characteristics. We can also estimate how the effect sizes we uncover compare to other government interventions or politically relevant characteristics, such as income and education.

Qualitative Interview Data

With our qualitative data, we hope to fill in the gaps where the quantitative analyses necessarily fall short. Our representative surveys allow us to probe the relationships between contact with different institutions of criminal justice and political outcomes among large samples of the American public. However, the large-*n* survey analyses obscure the deeper narratives people bring to bear when thinking about government and tell us little about the reasons these individuals opt out of the political process. We turned to qualitative tools because we wanted to get a sense not only of levels of trust and participation among the custodial population as compared to others, but also of citizens' broader interpretations of and orientations toward government—that is, their own understanding of the political world and their role in it.

To understand how individuals conceptualize and articulate their own experiences, we visited three cities in late 2010 and early 2011—Charlottesville, Virginia; New Orleans, Louisiana; and Trenton, New Jersey—where we sat down and spoke to over eighty individuals who had varying degrees of criminal justice contact. Some of the people we spoke to had spent years cycling back and forth to the "workhouse" or had spent much of their lives as inmates in correctional facilities. Others had no felony record but had experienced frequent encounters with police, while still others had only a single misdemeanor. Our interview subjects likewise varied in myriad other ways; they were black and white, young and old, middle class and impoverished. Throughout the text, we refer to our interview subjects using fictional names; a full listing of our interviewees and their age, race, gender, and location can be found in appendix B. We chose Charlottesville, Trenton, and New Orleans because these cities vary in size, political culture, racial composition, socioeconomic status, and prevalence of crime. The states they are in also vary along key policy indicators of criminal justice punitiveness. Additional details of these state differences and our qualitative data are also provided in appendix B.

Charlottesville, Virginia, our first interview site, is a small southern college town of about 41,000 population located in central Virginia. It is a predominantly white city with a population that is only 20 percent black, yet minorities make up the majority in the jail (51% black), which houses over 5,000 inmates a year. Most of the jail's inmates reside in the Belmont and Fifeville neighborhoods, where a majority of Charlottesville's black and poor residents live. The northern tip of wealthier and whiter neighborhoods contains few people who have gone to jail. Though they are a majority of those with criminal justice contacts, blacks made up just 12 percent of the city police force.

In Charlottesville, we worked with the Offender Aid and Restoration office, which serves people at every stage of the criminal justice process, from pretrial counseling to ex-inmate reentry. They distributed our fliers to their clients to recruit interview subjects. In addition, we solicited participants by going to the local Labor Ready, a day laborer temp agency that is one of the only places in town where ex-felons can find reliable work, and distributed our fliers at the Haven, a local day shelter that serves people in need, many of whom have had brushes with the law.

Trenton, New Jersey, the site of our second set of interviews, is a medium-sized, heavily black city with a population of 82,883 (51% black and 30% Latino). It has the hallmarks of a deindustrializing, riot-torn city. A high percentage of its residents are unemployed, in poverty, and did not graduate from high school. The city has a high crime rate and gang issues; a CQ Press survey in 2011–12 ranked it the fourth most dangerous city of its size.[29] A landmark in the center of the city is a large state prison—the state's only fully maximum-security facility—holding 1,944 inmates.[30]

We interviewed residents at two locations in Trenton: Helping Arms and Albert "Bo" Robinson Assessment and Treatment Center. Helping Arms is a nonprofit that provides transitional housing and other aid to ex-inmates to help them locate jobs, apply for benefits, and get substance abuse treatment and counseling. Bo Robinson is a parole center that houses 900 formerly incarcerated people returning from prison or parole. Instead of being returned to prison to serve out their original sentence, they are sent to Bo Robinson for a shorter duration. Though it is a parole center, it looks and operates much like a prison. Inmates confined there cannot leave the premises and must follow a strict daily routine.

Our final set of interviews was conducted in New Orleans, Louisiana. New Orleans is larger than Trenton or Charlottesville, with a population of 455,000 people, 68 percent of whom are black. The violent crime rate in New Orleans is not as high as it is in Trenton, with 1,131 violent offenses and 6,086 property crimes per 100,000 people. However, much like Trenton, a large share of its population—22 percent of families—lives in poverty. Eighteen percent have not received a high school diploma and 45 percent have a high school diploma or less. Like other cities, a large proportion of the black population is familiar with the police, courts, and imprisonment; the city has the highest incarceration rate in the state.

In New Orleans, we interviewed at the site of an AmeriCorps program for ex-offenders. The program provided people with a stipend where they worked doing community service and outreach until they located a more stable job. While there, we also interviewed a man who now runs VoteNola, a group that aims to encourage ex-felons to engage in politics, as well as a former local politician who had served time in prison for accepting a bribe while in office.

Each subject was offered a twenty-dollar incentive to take part in an hour-long interview. These individuals' narratives contextualize and deepen our empirical analyses, documenting the shared experiences of people, across boundaries of age, race, and location, who have spent some of their lives under criminal justice jurisdiction. Through their voices and in their own words, we can better understand what democratic citizenship means to this large and growing group of Americans. Especially important is that the qualitative data allow us to explore disagreement; especially in chapter 7, we use the interviews to draw out two conflicting narratives obscured by the aggregate trends we uncover in our survey data.

Had we interviewed only people who had contact with criminal justice, readers might rightly wonder whether the things they said were substantially different from what people might say who are black, poor, unemployed, and had not experienced adversarial contacts with criminal justice. Therefore, we also conducted a dozen interviews with people in Charlottesville who had no experience being stopped, arrested, convicted, or confined. These interviews further draw out contrasts and give us a baseline group for comparison. Just as our quantitative data include people without carceral contact who are similar on all other background characteristics, these interviews shed further light on whether it is criminal justice contact or its correlates that drives the results we show.

Most of our interview subjects were male (75%) and black (70% black, 27% white, 3% Latino), and the majority were in poverty. Many had not completed high school and most were unemployed or marginally employed at the time we interviewed them. Few owned their homes or made more than $30,000 a year. Only a few of our respondents could be called middle class and only a handful had obtained college degrees. Many had experienced homelessness, substance abuse, and mental health issues.

Our respondents also ran the gamut of correctional involvement, from those who had no personal experience being stopped and questioned by the police to those who had spent most of their lives in prison or jail. Based on their highest level of contact, 8 percent had been stopped by police, 5 percent had been arrested but nothing more, 15 percent had been convicted, 48 percent had been to prison or jail, and 25 percent had been imprisoned, serving a sentence of a year or more. Even among those who had been confined, there was wide variation in the nature and frequency of those experiences. Some had multiple stints in a "workhouse" but no prison time. Others had been in and out of state facilities most of their adult lives. Some had relatively minor offenses—cursing in public, public intoxication, or nonpayment of child support—while others were incarcerated for grand larceny, armed robbery, aggravated assault, and manslaughter. Some were still under supervision, and a few had been released from prison in the last month.

Also notable was that, though our respondents ranged in age—16 percent were 18–30 years old, 37 percent were 30–45, 33 percent were 45–55, and 14 percent were 55 or older—the vast majority had their first encounter with criminal justice institutions at a very early age. A number described being sent to a boy's home at age seven or eight, or having their first conviction under the age of 12. It was rare for someone to report having been involved with the criminal justice system for the first time after age 25. Most of our interviewees lived in neighborhoods where criminal justice contact was routine and some said that most or all of the people they knew—friends, family, neighbors—had been to prison.

Our interview data help us to deepen and extend the result of our quantitative data in a variety of ways. First, in the interviews, we are able to ask questions that the existing surveys did not ask, allow for open-ended responses, and engage in longer conversations with respondents about how they conceptualize citizenship and democracy. In all of our interviews, we guided respondents with a core set of semi-structured questions, but allowed them to elaborate on their experiences and ideas. Through this method, we uncovered more than the forced-choice survey items allowed for. We saw how interviewees understood the role of government, why they felt alienated, and how they connected their everyday experiences of government—a main part of which involved the criminal justice apparatus—to their feelings about politics and racial equality.

We read carefully through our transcribed interviews and pulled out common themes and tensions. Where we quote from the interviews, we select only material that represents themes consistently articulated across the interviews. We do not systematically code the interviews (e.g., what percentage said this or that) because our interviews did not proceed as a replicable survey, with each question being asked the same way and in the same order. That said, in each conversation we attempted to ask the same general questions and to bring each conversation back to the script as often as possible. We detail our core questions in appendix C.

Second, the interviews allow us to explore new and complex themes that emerge when custodial citizens are explicitly asked to consider their political citizenship. Our task was not only to examine opinions on a given issue, but we also sought to gain insight into underlying perceptions of democracy, government, and race in America. The informal structure of our in-depth interview sessions allowed us to ask questions in response to what individual interview subjects had to say and allowed respondents to raise topics that were important to them but not necessarily on our radar. Some ideas emerged that we did not expect, such as the avoidance behavior we discuss in chapter 8. Other ideas were expected, but quickly became far more central to the emerging narrative than we would have predicted in advance. In particular, our interviews helped us develop our theory in chapter 3 about the antidemocratic character of institutions. Our interview subjects spoke not just about their sentence lengths (the *punitiveness* of the system) but about the avenues closed to them to exhibit voice and hold officials accountable (the *character* of the system). For instance, Cordell spent a good deal of the time with us sharing his frustration at not being able to file his grievance in prison, leading us to think more critically about the democratic deficits of the institutions our conversation partners had experienced.

Finally, our interview data allow us to explore the mechanisms that explain the patterns we find in our quantitative analyses. Instead of simply letting us know whether someone trusts the government or not, the interviews provide a picture of *why* they distrust the government and how the government's role in their lives has shaped their perceptions. The interview data allow us to say something about how criminal justice figures into their resulting views, and how they see government in their own terms. Instead of simply knowing that people were stopped by police, we can gather information on how they felt they were treated during their police encounter and how it subsequently affected them.

In short, the quantitative data allow us to rigorously test the links between criminal justice contact and political attitudes and behavior, while the qualitative data allow people to articulate, in their own words, the connections they make between their criminal justice contact and their perceptions of government, racial equality, and citizenship. Together, the two analyses create a more complete picture of how criminal justice shapes citizens' distinct political lifeworlds.

A Note about Causality

We recognize that it may be impossible to perfectly isolate the effect of exposure to criminal justice; as we discuss later, these interactions both reflect and deepen existing disparities. Moreover, we note that this group is distinct; they come into contact with criminal justice for many reasons that should not necessarily be "controlled away" but are instead part and parcel of the experience of custodial citizenship. In technical terms, we might conceptualize this as being akin to the question of whether there is imbalance or a lack of complete overlap between custodial and noncustodial citizens; on some important dimensions that precede (and predict) contact with criminal justice, these two groups are simply not the same. This was made clear to us in the process of recruiting our qualitative interview subjects. Despite extensive outreach and field planning, finding people who were similarly situated to our custodial citizens in their racial, economic, and geographic profile, but who had never been stopped by police and questioned, was extraordinarily difficult. In fact, in some of the places in Charlottesville where custodial citizens were most heavily concentrated, we had great difficulty finding *anyone* who was black and poor but had not ever had an unwanted encounter with police.

Our approach throughout the book is to analyze the effect of criminal justice contact on each of several outcomes of interest. Clearly, the primary issue with which we must contend is selection. Because contact with the criminal justice system is not randomly distributed, custodial populations are systematically different from noncustodial citizens in a variety of respects. They are much more likely to be poor, less educated, more unstable in their family relationships and employment, and more likely to a member of a racial or ethnic minority group. Many of these factors make them less likely to engage in politics in the first place and are also important in predicting both their political attitudes and criminal justice contact. In all our data, selection bias thus may limit the conclusions that we can draw from statistically significant associations between political indicators and measures of custodial contact. A major hurdle for our analyses in the book, therefore, is to adequately dispel the possibility that any significant relationship between custodial status and political activity is due to respondents selecting into both criminal activity and lower levels of political engagement.

The gold standard for demonstrating causality can only be met through a randomly assigned experiment or some type of "as if" random quasi-experiment that treats some citizens to an intervention (being stopped by police, arrested, or confined) and leaves a comparable control group untouched. Only through random assignment can we assure that both observed and unobserved factors are balanced across the treatment and control groups. Such a design, while being the closest we could come to demonstrating causality, is unethical. However, in conducting our analyses we rely on three different empirical strategies to mitigate against the possibility that pre-existing differences across individuals, and not exposure to criminal justice, accounts for different levels of participation. We detail each of these strategies in appendix C.

None of these tests is by itself dispositive. Without a randomized or quasi-experiment, we cannot be sure that some important confounder has gone unaddressed. However, by incorporating these additional estimation procedures and modeling strategies into our analyses, we have navigated the tricky causal inference question to the best of our ability and believe we have strengthened the causal claims of the book.

CHAPTER FIVE

"Democracy don't get you a second chance"

(Un)Learning Citizenship

Having been under correctional supervision continuously since he was too young to vote, Darnell has never taken part in an election. He used to think he had some political power, though, and that he could play a positive role in changing his community. "I used to. Not anymore. It's like—we're different eras. My generation? We all in jail! So the younger generation that's out there right now, they just runnin' amok. So, it's hopeless." Darnell was just shy of his twenty-seventh birthday when we interviewed him in Trenton's parole facility, where he was sent due to a parole violation. Like many of those with whom we spoke, Darnell had gotten involved in the criminal justice system at a very early age, charged with possession of a controlled substance at age eighteen and serving a five-year prison term. (Later, he was awarded damages in a class action suit against the police for planting evidence on him.) Out only briefly, he wound up back in prison, this time for an offense he said "was on him."

After thinking for a moment about whether his experience with criminal justice had changed the way he looked at government, he replied:

> Yes it did. It changed it dramatically, actually. Dramatically. 'Cause I never thought it would turn out like that. I didn't. For me, growing up until me hitting 18, I never like, I never like—I thought everything was nice. I didn't *see*—you know how you don't see the other side of the fence? So, you walkin' around like "Yeah, this is nice, this is good" until one day, it happens and

now you see everything clearer. You see the whole picture now. . . . [When I was growing up,] I thought it was sweet. I did. I was like, yo, you have no worries, no cares. All you have to do is go to school, come home, go to after-school programs, go play basketball, go play football. But then I just started getting older and I just started noticing like, "Why everybody getting' beat up? I didn't know cops did that." Like, when you young, you don't pay attention to it, but when you get older you start seein' "Damn, they just jumped out on him, for what? He just came outta the house!" Like, they just leave you there, beat up! Yeah, it's serious.

In the previous chapter, we argued that there are several features of interactions with the punitive face of government that make it a particularly powerful site of socialization into citizenship. Indeed, we offer a host of reasons to think criminal justice contact rivals other more traditional politically socializing experiences and venues for civic education. Yet, the more important point we seek to make is that this socialization, unlike other interactions with government, cleaves custodial citizens from the broader democratic polity, and much like Darnell, they learn a different set of lessons about citizenship and state.

If custodial interactions structure beliefs about government and citizenship, what lessons are learned and what behaviors are adopted? In this chapter and the next, we argue that criminal justice promotes a political socialization that results in a fundamentally distinct lifeworld, comprised of two aspects. The first is socialization into *custodial citizenship*, by which we mean what they come to know and believe about their political standing, their worth, and their role in the democratic community. We argue in this chapter that, through interactions with criminal justice, custodial citizens observe how the state treats them and people like them. Custodial citizens are constituted not as participatory members of the democratic polity, but as disciplined subjects of the carceral state; they are "objectified and dependent rather than equal participant."[1] And rather than communicating that they are worthy and valued citizens, their experiences with criminal justice teach them that they have little voice and mark them as outside consideration.

The second and related aspect of the custodial lifeworld, the focus of chapter 6, is made up of what individuals come to learn about the state and how it operates. Rather than seeing a government that provides for the collective good, their experiences with criminal justice are defined by domination. As a result, custodial citizens' "sense of the state" is one of control, hierarchy, and arbitrary power. Both types of political learning have important consequences for how custodial citizens relate to the political system. Rather than instilling a sense of efficacy, custodial citizens feel that they are not full citizens, that their concerns are not heard by government, that elected officials are unwilling to respond to and help them, that they cannot trust government to act in their interests, and that taking part or trying to influence the political process is futile.

Custodial citizens often develop a distinct set of norms governing how best to move through the social world. Similar to the "code of the streets" that Elijah Anderson finds among blacks navigating lives in underclass ghettos, these rules and understandings are incorporated as common-sense wisdom, are taken largely as truth, and govern everything from how to interact with authorities to what they came to believe about the political system.[2] In fact, so embedded and accepted were these lessons that they often emerged matter-of-factly during our interviews, mentioned just in passing. In our many conversations with custodial citizens, respondents would often seem surprised that we did not understand this social education, which was so plain to them and formed the basis of subsequent judgments and decision making.

The end consequence of this process of political socialization is that criminal justice contact does not *only* reinforce existing political beliefs and behaviors that are associated with their demographic profiles — different levels of efficacy and trust, for example, that characterize low-income, low-educated, black citizens as a group — though this is a significant part of its function. In addition, it actively creates a *custodial lifeworld*. In this way, the custodial citizen becomes differentiated from those who have never had contact with the criminal justice system, socialized into particular ways of being and thinking about their state and their place within it. It is to the specifics of this lifeworld that we devote the rest of this chapter and those that follow.

Custodial Citizenship

What characterizes custodial citizenship? Many of the individuals with whom we spoke had developed an informal code for how to move through daily life, as well as a number of guidelines concerning how things "really" work in America for people like them. The first set of ideas, which we refer to as "the code of prohibitions," was made up of behaviors that were inadvisable because—combined with being black, poor, and from a high crime neighborhood—they might make one look suspicious and thereby invite the attention of police or probation officers. This set of lessons in custodial citizenship is about the *threat* of suspicion, arrest, and incarceration; the code concerns the background characteristics that make one a custodial citizen in the eyes of the state and society. Because of who they were—black, poor, young, without much schooling or job prospects—our interviewees describe to us how they were automatically seen as suspicious, and how the rights and freedoms they knew they had in theory were delimited in practice.

The second set of lessons in custodial citizenship is what we call the "the rules of the game." While the code referred to things that made one suspicious (the first step in custodial citizenship), the rules of the game were about what could be expected once one was formally designated a custodial citizen, that is, once one had been brought to court or had received the mark of a criminal record. This "real talk" about how things are—the taken-for-granted, common-sense reality—was contrasted with ideals of American nation and citizenship, or how things were *supposed* to be.

We describe each of these lessons in detail in the following sections. Notably, these narratives were not simply a community narrative, though some of the ideas are also evident in the wider communities to which custodial citizens belong. Nor do they represent simply a shared street culture, as Elijah Anderson and others describe. Instead, we find that custodial citizens saw a different *state* from those who had never had criminal justice contact, and in consequence adopted a distinct set of rules and norms.

Lessons in Custodial Citizenship: The Code of Prohibitions

What our interviewees learned through criminal justice was not simply about the punishment and surveillance they experienced; it was also about their social standing within the broader political community, and about the many behaviors that were off-limits to "people like them." Many knew that police needed probable cause in order to search them, but in their experience searches often took place what seemed to them like anytime, anywhere, and with little provocation. They were searched because they had a particular hairdo: "Everybody with chee wees [a type of hairdo, like very short dreadlocks] and they don't care who you are—

tall, short, black, ugly. . . . They won't take time, straight up. They want them chee wees. They don't care who did it. They want them chee wees." They were searched because of the people with whom they associated: "My godbrothers, all them are white. I can't even hang with, they can't even come to my house in the hood, because if they come and the police see them in my house, they either buying drugs. . . . They're going to stop and search, just make sure nothing ain't on us." They were searched simply for being outside, the assumption being: "If you're on the streets between 7:00 and 3:00 and you haven't got no job, you're selling drugs."

We were not surprised to learn that a set of norms existed for how to avoid unwanted contact with the state, or how often these ideas were learned through criminal justice encounters themselves. We were, however, surprised at the extensiveness of what was proscribed, which included a host of behaviors that seemed otherwise innocuous and mundane. In fact, many of our interviewees articulated an extensive list of attributes and behaviors that were precluded because they would surely result in the attention of law enforcement, a list that included everyday activities: wearing certain clothes, donning a certain hairstyle, driving a nice car, playing loud music, standing on the sidewalk texting, being in a group of young people, being with whites in a black neighborhood, being black in a white neighborhood, being with too many other blacks, being homeless, being in poor areas/being in rich areas. Willie, a young adult from Charlottesville, said matter-of-factly, "don't carry a bookbag." To others, simply being black and unemployed would likely provoke suspicion: "If a black man don't have a job, and they not productive, first thing they gonna say: he's selling dope." Conversely, if a black person displayed too much wealth or drove a luxury car, according to our interviewees, that might also prompt an inquiry about criminal involvement.

Felisha, also from Charlottesville, avoided having too many friends and family come to her house "because if you have so much company coming, they automatically think you dealin' drugs." Ray in Trenton, a man of few words, said plainly, "to me, all the experiences with the police is just all bad." When we pressed him to elaborate, he noted, "I mean, being stopped for no reason . . . especially if there's more than two." When we asked him to explain, he said that "more than two black people . . . in a car" was "pretty much . . . it's like it's forbidden." In his view, having more than two black people in a car would almost automatically result in being pulled over by police. Likewise, convening with people of different races or being "out of place" racially was prohibited. We heard from several respondents that police officers were likely to question white people who were seen *associating* with black people in high crime neighborhoods. As Marshall from Charlottesville explained:

> This officer in town, everybody knows him . . . and some of the neighborhoods that known for drug dealing, if there's a black guy and a white guy riding in an old beat-up car, they gonna get stopped. He think they goin' out buying drugs. They couldn't just be buddies catchin' a ride with someone or passing through . . . he thinks they're buying drugs. . . . "Them two don't fit together. This is a predominantly one color neighborhood. Why are these two people together in this neighborhood?"

In addition to one's associates, certain styles of dress were a commonly articulated part of the code of prohibitions. If someone wore a white T-shirt, he was assumed to be in a gang. Having "a mouthful of gold" and tattoos made police assume someone was a drug dealer. For Ronnie, a young woman from Charlottesville, wearing a do-rag on her head had generated police attention. Once, when she was walking down the street in a do-rag, an officer had pulled up next to her to ask, "Are you into something devious today?" Willie, another of our interviewees in Virginia, described his frustration at not being able to dress how he wanted or walk through his own neighborhood: "My problem with the Charlottesville Police department is, just because of the way I dress, don't assume that I sell drugs. I work hard for my money. Every day. Now if I walk into a certain part of the neighborhood, dressed like I am, he gonna pull up and want to search me." We asked him how he would have to dress to avoid getting stopped and he shrugged, saying he guessed the police would leave him alone if he wore a business suit or a University of Virginia sweatshirt. His uncle Lester, who was with him at the interview, chimed in: "they will stop you, and they say, 'where can I search you?' And you'll be like 'for what?' . . . 'Well, you can either let me search you here or I can take you downtown.'" "But so neither of them is a good choice," says his nephew.

More broadly, many of our black respondents described being stopped because they "fit a description" of a crime suspect. Most understood this as an easy excuse for police to stop anyone they wanted to question—"just to see who you are." Marshall was incarcerated for the first time at nineteen on a DUI. He had also been arrested and locked up briefly on a domestic violence charge and served twelve months for failing to pay child support. He works now with his father doing occasional landscaping jobs, but is finding it difficult to secure steady work. In the meantime, Marshall talks about police profiling as a fact of daily life in his community.

> There's a thing they call "fittin' the description" . . . just because you may have the same color clothes on, you fit the description, 'cause you black and you this height. You fit the description . . . [but] when you have everybody in the neighborhood wearing white t-shirts and blue jeans, of *course* you gonna fit the description. White t-shirts and blue jeans is not a crime. . . . Then they ask you if you got any weapons or drugs on you. They not really concerned whether you been in the area of the crime when it happened. They wanna know about weapons and drugs . . . just to see who you are, just to see if you got any warrants out on you, to lock you up, to get an arrest.

Given that such stops occurred with unpredictable regularity, another part of the code was to never, ever be outside without proper identification. An ID offered protection and could help one establish that he did not have outstanding warrants or was not a suspect in a crime. Willie and his Uncle Lester explained to us that:

> WILLIE: If you don't have an ID, they take you downtown.
> LESTER: Yeah, they'll put you in handcuffs off the top.
> WILLIE: So I try to keep two [IDs] on me. I got my work ID and got my ID in pocket.
> LESTER: Day, night, it doesn't matter . . . you have to have an ID on you at all times.

The importance of having documents to prove your identity was widely accepted in our interviews. Stanley from Trenton spoke forcefully about how secure he felt once he got his birth certificate, Social Security card, and his ID. When we asked why this was so significant to him, he said:

> You never know . . . what's going to happen . . . because you could be walking down the street and not doing anything and a police officer could stop you . . . and he could say, "Well, you got any ID?" "No, I don't have any ID." That's a reason for him right there, to you know, check you out, take you down to the police station, check you out because you don't have anything to show who you are. . . . It's really against the law not to walk around without ID.

In response to this code of prohibitions, many of our interview sub-jects adapted their behavior, going about their lives differently. This might mean something trivial, like altering how they dressed, but fre-quently imposed a greater imposition, such as going around the long way to get home or not visiting a friend or relative who lived in a certain area. Tom told us that he has adapted his behavior to police activities "because that's how it is, because they doing they job. I'll take the long way around, no shortcuts. There are drug areas all over the city, [so I] keep it moving. Get where I want to go. Soon as you stop and run off at the mouth, you get questioned." For Abe, whom we came across in New Orleans, this meant a self-imposed house arrest, avoiding public spaces altogether:

I used to like hanging out in the streets but I know one thing like, now when I get up for work, I got to get up and go straight home, walk my dog. You know, just walking or watch TV, that's the best shot I have to survive. That's the best shot. . . . Just stop and drink a beer, I'm asking for disaster. I can't even stop—I can't even get off and just ride with my car on the city, just enjoying the sight. I'm asking for disaster. So, my way to work with the government is to put myself in a . . . got me a big TV, I just like my house. I got to tell myself, I like my house more than I like the jail.

Some of our subjects, like Willie and Marshall, were obviously an-gered by what seemed to be constant attention from police. Others, par-ticularly many of the older individuals with whom we spoke, were more resigned. Donnie, who had just been released from a short imprisonment and was now homeless in Charlottesville, was calm and collected during our short interview of mainly one-word responses. He describes what goes on in a typical encounter: "Ask for my ID, 'do you have warrants?' 'What you doing,' in a certain area, 'what you doing?' Certain areas they see, certain time of night, they'll just stop you." Accepting the practice, he says: "I mean certain things happen in one area more than in others, so, it's just gotta be like that, I dunno." He breaks character and laughs aloud when we ask him how many times this happened, saying twenty or more, including one just a few weeks back. "It's just expected. It's no big deal. If I don't do nothing, I ain't have nothing to worry about."

Similarly, Rick, a black man from Trenton, did not believe police ra-cially profiled "because if you do something bad, I mean the cops got the right to lock you up . . . it's not your color or nothing like that." How-ever, he knew some things were plainly off-limits to him because he was poor and black. He described having been stopped by a police officer in a white neighborhood in New Jersey and the officer telling him plainly that he looked like a suspect. He explains matter-of-factly how police believe all blacks look the same: like criminals. And he reiterates that there are some things that black men simply cannot do: "Oh, yes, being in a white neighborhood and that somebody don't know you, that's a bad sign—when you're black anyway."

Lessons in Custodial Citizenship: The Rules of the Game

In addition to the Code of Prohibitions, our interview subjects also articulated a set of ideas about how things work in the United States, the "rules of the game" as they understood them. For instance, nearly all our subjects knew that criminal justice and other societal institutions were in theory colorblind, fair, and neutral. They were aware of legal protections against discrimination in housing, employment, and education. But in our conversations, custodial citizens consistently described a society and justice system that exposed them to a parallel set of rules, opportunities, and punishments. Race played a role in structuring this two-tiered citizenship, but it did so not always, or even usually, through unbridled racial discrimination but also through the pathways of class, neighborhood, and the mark of a criminal record. The first rule of the game was about the importance of resources, and how those who did not have money or other markers of status lacked any power and standing in the broader community. The second rule was related to being from the "wrong" neighborhood, and what this meant for how one could expect to be treated. The third rule concerned being "in the system." Once individuals had been marked by an arrest or a criminal record, they experienced a deep and enduring stigma, pushed out of the economic mainstream and viewed with suspicion by society, employers, and authorities. Together with the code, these three rules formed the custodial lifeworld, the backdrop against which custodial citizens' sense of equality rested.

RULE I: THE TECHNICALITIES OF FREEDOM—"YOU GOT TO PAY FOR THAT." The first "rule of the game" was about economic worth. In principle, each person had the same chance to pursue a comfortable middle-class existence if he or she was willing to work hard. The black and Latino men and women with whom we spoke were well aware of this widely shared tenet of the American Dream. Abe paraphrased the traditional logic, saying with not a little sarcasm, "Everybody has the same chance, the same opportunity, so all you got to do is go to school, graduate, go to college, get a degree." Most of our respondents articulated a different reality, though, whose rules stood starkly juxtaposed to this ideal. This natural way of things resulted in a plain and simple rule: your position in democratic society depended on the financial resources at your disposal and the background from which you hailed.

We often heard things like David telling us "if your parents ain't got money, or you ain't come from money, no opportunities up here for you, to make no living, man," and Xavier saying "If you haven't got money, down here in the South, you ain't going to succeed." Some referred to themselves as a group of "little people"—struggling to survive, getting by on selling their food stamps, and living on the streets. Likewise, one's fate at the hands of criminal justice depended on money, according to just about every one of our interview subjects. Nearly everyone knew that in principle the justice system should be a neutral arbiter whose outcomes were not contingent on individual wealth. However, the real rule of the game was that "there's justice if you got the right kind of money." Not a single one of our interviewees departed from this view: individual guilt was secondary to the command of resources. If one was fortunate to have money, one's innocence was secure. In contrast, if one was unlucky and without money, one was better off taking a plea bargain, even if he or she had not done anything wrong. Marshall described how plea bargains worked; the prosecutor would dangle the threat of several years of imprisonment and the public defender would advise taking a plea because "you're playing with a loaded deck and you're not going to win."

To many, this was a double bind. The justice an individual received was contingent on his economic situation, but one's presence before the justice system in the first instance had to do with how well positioned he was economically. Xavier explained that "democracy don't get you a second chance" but then he qualified this by saying that "if you got the money and to pay your way through it, you will." His friend Reggie immediately countered, reminding him that "but if you got the money to pay your way through, you wouldn't even be there!"

Here we see how race and class were overlapping. Class helped convey something also about race, even if it was not strictly about being black. Many, though not all, of our black and Latino interviewees had been appointed legal counsel because they lacked the resources to pay for a private attorney. Because whites were (accurately) seen as more likely to be able to afford private counsel,[3] they were generally thought to fare better throughout the process. Rick, a black man in Trenton who held mostly conservative views on personal responsibility and individualism, nonetheless described how you were at the mercy of the criminal justice system if you had no money:

> because they [the criminal justice system] can do anything, what they want to do to you. And if you don't got no money, they could do anything to you. You know what I mean? They can say anything they want to say . . . , In short, you're not nobody if you got no money. You know what I mean? So you got to follow their rules.

He struggled a bit, though, when we asked whether this had to do with race:

> Yes. I mean, yes, I don't think it's—in a way, yes. . . . Well, because like I said, when you don't have no money . . . like I said, I mean you don't have no money like a black man . . . I might got something, but I'm not rich.

He goes on:

> You got that money, you're going to get off. You know what I mean? That's how the world is.

Emmett, of New Orleans, agreed and explained that most of the people in prison were there not because they were guilty, but because they could not afford adequate representation to defend their innocence: "they don't have the ability to prove that they are not guilty. They don't have the funds. . . . The technicalities of freedom. You got to pay for that."

RULE 2: THE ROLE OF SPACE AND PLACE—"LIKE HERE, THEY DON'T CARE ABOUT YOU."   Similarly, one's value was closely tied to geography. Neighborhoods, it soon became clear, were not simply physical places where groups of people resided; they were places where different patterns, different "faces" of the state emerged. In our discussions, it was fairly common for people to refer to one neighborhood as "bad" and another as "good"—as Darcy from Charlottesville bluntly put it: "I don't go anywhere near the bad neighborhoods"—and for people to describe quite specific mental maps of which areas had what level of drugs or violence. Neighborhood conditions, which were not entirely distinct from race, defined one's chances in life.

Many also knew that the neighborhoods they called home were a source of stigma to the outside world. Xavier from New Orleans told us how he was having a difficult time getting a job even though he "ain't no convicted felon." When we asked why, he replied: "just where you live! You just tell 'em look, my address" and that made it impossible to find work. He gave us another example that came quickly to mind: "They got like, delivery pizza, Domino's. So like Domino's delivery . . . they won't deliver to certain addresses . . . Say I stay at [one address]. I can't get no pizza from Papa John's. But if I stayed [at another], it would be easy. . . . They don't want to come straight in the middle of the hood." Likewise, his friend Reggie argued that because of where he lives, "ain't no government official going to come into my neighborhood talking with me. Straight up."

Living in the "wrong" neighborhood could also mean being subject to particularly aggressive police oversight. Most believed their neighborhoods to be the places targeted for surveillance by authorities and many described extensive involvement of the police in their communities; Marshall pronounced that "the upper-class white neighborhoods, there's no police at all. In my neighborhood, it's police constantly." Some expected, and received, different treatment based on where they were from, like Renard: "I'm from Covington where all the drugs and everything. So that's when they're searching me down. . . . They weren't searching my friend because he said he was from Folsom and who his people was and all that. I'm telling them I ain't got no people. It's just me. I'm from Covington, born and raised there."

At the same time, somewhat ironically, the same neighborhoods were frequently described as *under*-served by police. Carlos, a Puerto Rican man who grew up in the projects in northern New Jersey, has "been locked up almost all my life. In and out. In and out," mostly for drug offenses. His brother is a police officer and he generally believes that most police are respectful. Still, he feels they could do more to address the rampant "stealing and robbing and killing" that plagues low-income neighborhoods like the one where he grew up, and where his ailing mother still lives. He contrasts his neighborhood to a wealthier suburb nearby, saying that if "[you call the police in that town,] "the police come right there, in 5 minutes. . . . In [my area], it's different. You call the police, an hour later, they come. Two hours later. . . . Depends what town you call the police. . . . like here, they don't care about you."

RULE 3: THE DURABLE MARK OF CRIMINALITY—"DEMOCRACY DON'T GET YOU A SECOND CHANCE."   When our interviewees described their experiences in police custody or jail, their stories were shot through with stigma and humiliation. They spoke of a total lack of privacy, regular and invasive strip searches, exposure to bugs and pestilence, and being derided and called derogatory names. Leila, a young black woman from New Orleans who had gone to college on a basketball scholarship, spent several days in jail as a teenager. She described the local jail system as "the worst" and described the food as "horrible." But what had been particularly difficult, she says, was how she was treated. "They feel like they can handle you and talk to you any kind of way. . . . I mean, they just feel like they have power over you." Trevor, a middle-aged black man who had served a substantial amount of time in prison, told us that even correctional counselors and other staff tasked with helping offenders get back on their feet "treat you like a piece of crap, like you less than them. I'm still a man. Regardless of what I did. . . . It's like, to them my life ain't worth nothing." An anecdote recounted by Theresa, a middle-aged white woman from Charlottesville, is similarly illustrative:

> I was put in a jumpsuit with no undergarments. Okay. And a jumpsuit, if you have to use the bathroom, you have to drop your whole jumpsuit down. Okay? The toilet is a—right here like this. You have a mirror, a two-way mirror where a correctional officer stands behind and watches there all the inmates, whatever and it's not always a woman. . . . I'm naked and you're watching me because you can't provide me with—and you aren't letting me keep my own undergarments.

Many others described how having even a single arrest had set them apart, consigning them to a class of people deserving of suspicion and oversight. In encounters with police, they would be instantly recognized by sight or from computer records as someone who had already had a brush with the law. We heard this view from Miles, a forty-seven-year-old black man who had been incarcerated for the first time at the relatively late age of thirty. Miles had been involved in criminal activity since his early twenties, however, using and selling drugs and eventually serving as the muscle for a high-level drug dealer. He went back and forth to prison six times over the ensuing sixteen years. Despite having cleaned himself up since then, he felt that he could never escape the stigma of his past:

> I've come to know that, now, instead of being judged by "Miles," especially when the police pull you over, the first thing they do is run your rap sheet. As soon as they run your ID, your rap sheet comes up. Especially in this day and age of the computer, there's nothing you can hide. So they see that, and they don't see Miles the person, they see: "this is his jacket, this is who he is." I don't blame them for that, because I created that mess. But until they get to speaking to me and learn, wait a minute. You know, it's not that you've got the wrong person. I did that. But I'm not that man anymore.

Once categorized as "offenders," Miles and others felt that they were then treated with suspicion even when they were doing nothing wrong. Lester told us, "They know your name. They see your face. All they have to do is go, 'Oh, shoot. This guy's got five felonies, three misdemeanors. . . . Let me stop him just to see what he up to.' . . . I mean, I'm not doin' anything. I'm just walkin.' You got no reason to stop and ask me anything. But they do."

This was true even for individuals who were in need of assistance. Tanya, a young black woman in Charlottesville who claimed no criminal history except for a few days in jail for cursing in public, recounted at length how she once called the police to get her boyfriend to leave her apartment after a fight. Though she called for help, she explained how the police arrived and immediately made her into the suspect. Her voice shaking, she described how they searched her home, threatened to take away her child if she did not cooperate, and accused her of hiding drugs on the property.

Many suspected that, to criminal justice authorities, once someone was in the system that person belonged there forever. Trevor explained: "When you go to leave out the door [of the prison], the first thing police tell you, 'I [will] see you when you get back.' . . . I ain't seen a place that don't do that yet!" Neal, an exonerated ex-inmate in New Orleans, described how even the legally innocent could not lay claim to innocence once they were in the system; among those who opposed legislation to award damages for the wrongfully convicted, the overwhelming sentiment was "if they ain't guilty of that, they're probably guilty of something." Innocence was a property that eluded them in dealings with authorities. When police were "called to the scene or whatever, they're automatically assuming [you did something wrong]. . . . You know, it's not that innocent until proven guilty. I mean, you're treated as though you're guilty even though, you know, you still haven't been, you know, charged or tried."

Criminal justice histories also shaped dealings with other arms of government, particularly social service agencies. Our interview subjects spoke of being stereotyped by welfare agencies, denied public housing, or being evicted from their homes because of a criminal record. Once they had a conviction, no matter how long ago, they could be denied other social benefits or treated with disdain by public service providers. Marcus, a middle-aged black man from Trenton who suffered from mental health issues, only had one conviction for which he had served seven months in jail. He is on parole now, and is finding that his status as a parolee affects his relationship with the caseworker who handles his disability insurance:

> It's the same building as unemployment; it's for the people with handicaps. . . .
> I'm also on their caseload and they're not doing anything for me. [*Why?*]
> 'Cause it's, I believe it's my caseworker, 'cause of the fact that I have a felony.
> She wanna overlook me, but wanna scold me from time to time.

Silas, a middle-aged black man from Trenton, also explained that his felony conviction followed him, affecting every aspect of his life, from a string of job application denials, to the difficulty he faced getting into public housing and receiving assistance, to his unsuccessful attempts to go back to school. Before his conviction, he "had a nice house, beautiful marriage, two lovely children," but as soon as his felony charge happened: "Zoom! I'm talking about a boulder that's weighing 500 pounds at an angle 90 degrees down. And it hasn't stopped." He notes:

> I can't even get a decent place to live because of this. You know, right now, they have areas of Trenton where people live called the projects. You know, I can't even get an apartment in the projects? These are some of the biggest drug areas in the city! I'm talking about drug dealers there. I can't get an apartment there, but the drug dealers can. Go figure that!

Likewise, Trevor described the immovability of his criminal record, and how he would never get away from it. Trevor had served seventeen years in prison and, despite having been out for nearly ten years, believed that his history would permanently define his relationship to government:

> Certain things . . . it's like this: because of my rap sheet, certain things the State ain't going to let me do no matter what. No matter who I know. No matter what I do.

Consequences of Custodial Citizenship

The importance of this socialization as custodial citizens is not just in that it cultivated a different set of beliefs about how criminal justice worked or what was possible and off-limits; rather, these lessons fueled feelings of diminished citizenship and influence in the political world around them. At this point, we move from specific aspects of custodial citizenship—the rules and the code embodied therein—to broader beliefs in equality, chances of success, and political efficacy. From their stigmatized, delegitimated position, custodial populations infer that they are not equal members of the polity and do not deserve to be equal participants in the political process. As Silas put it, the political system—and society as a whole—had "turned its back on any individual that have been convicted of a felony."

"You don't have no say-so": Stigma and Political Standing

The first consequence of these lessons in custodial citizenship is that, because custodial citizens learned they were suspicious in the eyes of law and society and were unworthy of social benefits or employment, they mostly abandoned a belief in equal citizenship and equal chances. In both our interviews and in the surveys we examined, those who had contact with criminal justice were much less likely to believe they carried equal citizenship and even less likely to believe they had an equal chance to succeed. Several lamented not being considered a citizen worthy of care and concern: "I love the United States, but I don't think the United States could care less about me."

Often, these broad beliefs were rooted in custodial status or criminal justice involvement. For example, one of our interview subjects spoke of the symbolic message his disenfranchisement carried: "We don't really consider you a citizen. You look like us. You talk like us. You bleed like us. But you're not really like us." While a few people believed everyone had equal chances to get ahead in life, most subscribed to a different set of beliefs, beliefs linked to experiences with criminal justice. After we asked Marshall whether criminal justice had changed what he thought about the world, he said: "I mean yeah, it definitely showed me the way the world works. How much money and who your family is and what color you are determines whether or not you go anywhere in life, whether or not you get a second chance. Whether or not you get any chances."

Nor was this stigmatized citizenship just confined to the legal prohibitions that custodial citizens face. Custodial citizens' stigmatized and separate status was constantly reinforced by the broader society in which they live, work, and reside. "Once they find out you gotta felony, a whole lotta people shy away from you," in the words of Carlton, an older black man in Charlottesville. Nor is he inaccurate in his assessment. In an era of widely held equality norms, offenders and suspects are still openly derided, discriminated against, and vilified in media and popular discourse. For example, in a recent survey, a majority of the public believed that felons were immoral, should not be treated as citizens, and could not be trusted; nearly half disagreed that felons who served their time should be returned as full citizens; and 45 percent thought convicted felons had too many rights already.[4] One study of employers found that they would prefer to hire high school dropouts and welfare recipients—two other highly stigmatized social groups—to those with criminal records.[5]

On this point, our subjects spoke in one collective voice, recounting that ex-felons (and even those with only an arrest record but no conviction) were the 'last hired, first fired.' Most of the people we interviewed had found obtaining employment after being released from prison or jail to be nearly impossible, whether at fast food restaurants or sweeping floors, in good economic times and bad; their experiences applying for jobs were wrought with shame and embarrassment. Even individuals with long and consistent work histories found that, after their arrest or conviction (often for a low-level offense), they might spend years trying unsuccessfully to obtain a job. Others were fired after their employer found out about their conviction in routine background checks. Carlton had worked for years before serving a stint behind bars for a drug offense and had since faced rejection after rejection at low-wage jobs; others had fared similarly:

Carlton (older black man, Charlottesville): It was a cleaning job and I have years experience. Man talked to me real nice and called me. He said "I want you to be the supervisor of this crew 'cause you qualified. But I have to do a background check on you." I said, "Man, I'm going to tell you I'm a felony." Click. Goodbye. . . . Even though I paid my debt to society, paid my court costs, did what they told me I had to do. It just never goes away, just never seems to go away.

Ronnie (young black woman, Charlottesville): Getting a job is, oh God, getting a job is awful. When they ask you that one question— have you ever been convicted—some of them have gotten to the point where it's a misdemeanor. And they want you to pretty much give them a brief summary of what the charge was and what happened and the resolution. . . . And if it had nothing to do with you working in a pie shop, you can't work there.

Linda (middle-aged white woman, Charlottesville): And people are very blunt with you. They'll tell you: "I'm not hiring you because of that." They will put on their little thing [application]: "This won't—if you tell us what you did, we won't hold it against you." But yet, that's the first thing they hold against you when they start talking to you.

Darnell (young black man, Trenton): No, you won't get hired. If you know somebody who works for that company that can assure 'em, even with the tax credit and the federal bonding, they still don't wanna take that risk, 'cause they like, "Oh he's a convicted felon, so he might come here and do the same thing . . ."

Marshall (young black man, Charlottesville): I tried to go to the Army and the Army wouldn't take me because of a misdemeanor. . . . I thought the Army would be the *best* place to go for a violent person.

Willie (young black man, Charlottesville): Me workin' is not the problem. It's me finding a job [with a felony conviction].

The embarrassment of being rejected after a criminal background check was a commonly articulated experience and the revelation of an arrest or conviction on job applications, in interviews, or background checks was a dreaded event. Theresa from Charlottesville spoke of feeling demeaned after being turned down for a job, even though she felt that the job for which she was applying was beneath her. Her felony conviction was not only an impediment to her employment, but a signal of her standing:

And then she actually said, "Well, here let me look at your application," and then asked if I had any kind of criminal—I put down DUI. It was a—I'm only applying for like maybe cashier/stock person. DUI has nothing to do with any of this. "Oh, oh my God, you have a DUI. Oh, I just don't think that's going to work." It was like I just got belittled in Family Dollar, a job that I would never even think about working at, but made me feel this big.

Not surprisingly, these lessons of shame, separate status, and unequal worth are internalized by custodial populations, who inherit what one scholar has termed a "stigma consciousness."[6] Custodial citizens come to see their political selves as locked into a deeply stigmatized and power-less class. In fact, the strength of the label of "felon," "suspect," or "convict" often overrides other relevant social categories and classifications, becoming a master status that confers "negative credentials."[7] Almost every person we interviewed viewed his or her criminal background—even a simple arrest—as a scarlet letter, a status that mattered to potential employees, friends, caseworkers, and neighbors more than any of their other qualities and no matter how distant in their past.[8] James, a middle-aged black man from Trenton, described his anguish about the permanent stigma of his criminal record:

I lay in bed every night, and I lay and I say if I could have only one wish, I wish I never had no criminal history. That's the biggest block that I always see. Everything is about criminal background. 'Cause I feel that I can do anything that I want to do, but when I really look at it I see that everything is background. Ain't no different than a job when you're doing a resume. What's your background? So every night I say if I could just have one wish, I wish my criminal history never existed . . . because I wouldn't have to worry about job situations that I wanted that paid decent. . . . My criminal justice history has affected my life, everything that I wanted to do that I can't do now.

To many, their criminal background became a marker that stuck permanently, no matter their positive credentials. Despite being a good parent, working in the community, or overcoming addiction and being a law-abiding member of society for years or even decades, their criminal history continued to serve as a badge of deep shame and exclusion. Silas noted that even his military service and the time he spent serving his country overseas was outweighed by his conviction:

All they recognize is "convicted felon." Nobody says "let me see your DD-214 [military service record]. Oh, you got a whole fruit salad on the stuff you done [in military service]." The state of New Jersey has turned its back on any individual that have been convicted of a felony.

Others reported similarly that the passage of time had failed to ameliorate the stigma they carried, no matter how much they felt they had changed:

Willie (young black man, Charlottesville): It's been nine years since I been in any trouble. But people don't see that. Once they see an "F" on your report card [a felony], that's what it is.

Silas (middle-aged black man, Trenton): I know that the record follows me. I really know that my record is going to follow me. I don't know about other states and that's what makes me want to jump from New Jersey to another state that may find me to be the person that I am now, not the person that they *assume* I was back twenty years ago. Judge me for who I am now. Check my character references now. Check the church that I'm a member of. Check the people that I live around. At least give me that much credit. That maybe this guy isn't a bad guy . . . And say to me, "[Silas], I know about your record, but what happened?" "Oh, well, this happened, this happened, this happened, but I'm not that person anymore."

Sarah (middle-aged black woman, Trenton): Oh, it's a major impact on my life, you know. It's something I will never be able to shake off. I wish I could, but, you know, I wish I could just wipe the slate clean, and you know, like restart my life. But that's not possible. It's something that's always gonna be with me.

Similarly, as figure 5.1 reveals, among those who have never been stopped by police, arrested, or convicted in the Black Youth Project survey (which includes white and Latino youth and young adults in addition to blacks), around three-quarters believed they were "a full and equal citizen in this country with all the rights and protections other people have." By comparison, this perception of full citizenship declined to under 60 percent for those who had experienced arrest and conviction. Similar to limited citizenship, 68 percent of all people without criminal justice involvement believed that in our nation, "everyone has an equal chance to succeed";

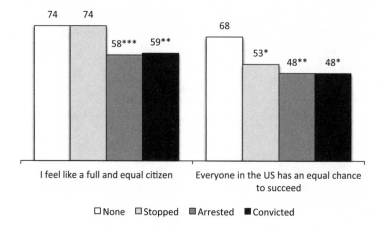

FIGURE 5.1. Percentage of people who believe that they are full and equal citizens and that people in the United States have an equal chance to succeed (% agree or strongly agree), by criminal justice contact. *$p < .05$; **$p < .01$; ***$p > .001$. *Source*: Cathy J. Cohen, "Black Youth Culture Survey," Black Youth Project, Chicago, IL, 2005, http://www.blackyouthproject.com.

only slightly over half of those who had been stopped by police (53%) and 48 percent of those who had been arrested or convicted believed in equality of chances.

Among this youthful population, these results remain strong and significant once we introduce controls.[9] Holding other variables at their mean values, the predicted probability of agreeing or strongly agreeing that one is a full and equal citizen diminishes from 76 percent for those who have never been involved with criminal justice to 72, 68, and 62 percent among those who have been stopped, arrested, or convicted, respectively. Similarly, the predicted probability of believing everyone has an equal chance to succeed diminishes from 63 percent among those without contact to 57, 50, and 44 percent for those who have been stopped, arrested, or convicted.

"You don't have no say-so": Efficacy and Agency

The second consequence of custodial citizenship is a diminished sense of agency, not just in dealing with employers and society, but in making claims on the state. Custodial citizens in large part did not believe they could influence representatives or government. They broadly acknowledged being powerless to affect political change or influence people in power. They did not believe their voice carried weight or that they could make a difference.

In some ways, this was a point of commonality between the views of custodial citizens about their citizenship and the views of our noncustodial sample with similar socioeconomic background. Nearly all of those with whom we spoke in our interviews, even those who had not had criminal justice contact, expressed their belief that those with few resources had little political power. For them, government often failed to pay attention to those in need, and most believed that "money talks" when it comes to politics.

Take Jerry, a fifty-eight-year-old black man from Trenton, whose first contact with police was at age twelve and who has since served at least a dozen stints for various misdemeanors, including drug possession and possession of stolen goods. Jerry struggles with drug addiction and partial paralysis of his hands, but he hardly takes a breath during our interview, speaking about everything from revitalizing Trenton, to the drug war, to the absence of black activism. He offers insightful ideas for what should be done about the nation's ills, and muses that he wants to get more involved in AIDS awareness. And while he describes waking up from the "fog" of his addiction a few years ago and being shocked at how his community had deteriorated, he feels no sense that those with political power might help. Describing why the governor of New Jersey ignores Trenton High School while beautifying the schools in richer townships, he says:

> I mean, it's no money coming out of Trenton to the state government or the federal government. So, there's no reason [for the government] to give back. And that's how the government look at it. If you don't scratch my back, why should I scratch yours?

James, another black man from Trenton agreed:

> I think government helps the people on the same level they're on. . . . "You help me, I help you" type thing. If you can do something for me, maybe I can do something for you. And I can't do nothing for 'em. So they can't help me. That's the way I look at it sometimes. And all I can do is keep trying . . . but I don't see them helping me. I don't.

The perception that government works on a reciprocal basis was a very prominent understanding of the system. Many of our interviewees saw the political system as one that works for a person only if that person has something to offer, much like a vending machine delivers a soda if a person puts in a coin. Nearly all of our interviewees, most of whom had little in the way of financial resources, felt they had nothing to give and so would be unlikely to get anything from government. Bert, a middle-aged black man from Charlottesville, described himself as having less than nothing; his bills had piled up, and even working was not making him enough money to dig out from under his debt. He turned to dealing cocaine for quick money, but says that he would have ended up in court even without the drug charge because his debt was persistently delinquent. Throughout our interview with him, Bert talked often and with passion about the need to help young people stay straight. His son was recently picked up for smoking marijuana. But like the others with whom we spoke, Bert does not have faith that he can do much to bring government to his aid:

> One hand washes the other. That's how I feel. If you do something for the government and help them, then they will help you. But if you don't have nothing to bring to the table, it's a dog eat dog world. If you went to a congressman and said your piece, he would listen to you and then once you'd gone, he would be like "That asshole."

He believed that the only way a congressperson would help someone is if that person could provide enough money to make it worth his while: "Well, if you got enough money—'take this hundred-thousand dollars and help me out.' 'Sure, I'll sign this bill.'" Charles Ray, a middle-aged white man from Charlottesville, accepted the situation:

> That's the way it is. So there's nothing I can do to change it. So just deal with it. I mean, they're not going to listen to me. Now if I were to become a millionaire or a billionaire or something like that, then they'll listen to me . . . that's the way it happens. People with all that money, they don't care. "Sorry about your life. Should have went to college."

Brandy, a middle-aged white woman from Charlottesville, agreed that "the small people" have less of a voice than others, saying that they were "not heard as much as they should be heard, as far as someone who's say a lawyer or a doctor. And we really need something else done. 'Cause we're being hurt."

The sense of powerlessness was pervasive throughout our interviews with the economically disadvantaged. Yet what differentiated the custodial citizens with whom we spoke from our other low-income interviewees was a sense that they also had been *formally* denied citizenship and inclusion. At the same time that they experienced the general feelings of powerlessness associated with being poor or a racial minority, their specific standing as *custodial* citizens in the polity had also been further and more directly diminished by political and legal practices that stripped them of rights, privileges, and numerous social supports. These policies directly conferred on them a dishonorable status, demarcating a clear boundary between the law-abiding and those branded as deviant offenders, deserving of opprobrium. Where many of our noncustodial interviewees spoke of poverty and education as resources that they lacked and that inhibited their political power, our custodial citizens spoke of their felony status as a durable constraint and marker of their citizenship. It was not only *what they did not have* that marked them as powerless; it was the totalizing experience of *who they were*.

Indeed, it was the rare person we came across in our sample of custodial citizens who was confident in the power of his or her opinion to influence the decision making of elected officials, or who believed that he or she could effect change. Most felt politicians would just brush them off, and that those with criminal convictions had virtually no political power. In response, many simply resigned themselves to "go it alone" even when faced with problems that begged for state attention. If an issue arose, many believed there was little to nothing they could do about it. Asked whether they felt they could influence politics, we received responses like:

Stanley (older black man, Trenton): No, actually I don't. I really don't. I just say "it is what it is" and you have to do right by yourself, you know what I mean? To get along in society, as long as you do that, I guess you'll be all right.

Trina (middle-aged black woman, Trenton): As far as my taxes go, they can do whatever they want with 'em. Because what say-so do I have? If I did have a say-so, yeah, I would want my money to go more to the have-nots than the haves.

Charles Ray (middle-aged white man, Charlottesville): There's some that go completely off the wall, they drive themselves insane, and THEN they find out they can't do anything about it.

Quinton (middle-aged black man, Trenton): I think whatever happens to me—I don't think nobody out here to help me. That's how I feel about the system. Nobody not here to help me. So I got to do it best by myself.

In addition to feeling they lacked influence because they had less wealth, education, and lived in poor neighborhoods, these individuals also directly connected their lack of voice to their stigmatized position as suspects, misdemeanants or felons. For Trevor and many others, his voice in the political process did not mean much precisely because of his custodial status: "Once you get into this system, you're always going to have that background, and to them that background means a whole lot. . . . Once you incarcerated, they might as well go get a big island and just put you on that island, 'cause you don't matter." A majority of our custodial interviewees expressed a view similar to the perspective articulated by Trevor. For example, Marshall, a thirty-one-year-old black man from Virginia, suggested that the experience of jail literally robbed him of any influence:

Basically jail is like a kidnapper. It takes you away and keeps you there 'till they're ready to release you or ready to kill you. It's like a robber. It robs you of everyday things that you take for granted . . . you get tagged as being a convicted felon and basically all you can do is work and take care of your family. You don't have no say-so in what's going on around you. You don't help put the right people there to make the right laws to make things any better for you. You just basically a slave working to pay public officials' salaries.

The three young men we spoke with in New Orleans, Xavier, Renard, and Reggie, were also not shy about cataloguing the problems in their community—from police harassment to the almost complete lack of jobs. But the political avenues for changing things were shut to them, because they were convicted felons with no meaningful voice:

XAVIER: Nobody want to put up the force to go fight against them because in the end, you know you're going to lose! [Why? Why do you know you're going to lose?] I don't know. You haven't got any help. Nobody . . .

RENARD: If you haven't got the money and the funds. You got the people. But you don't have the power or the money.

XAVIER: Nobody ain't trying to hear just a local dude. [Reggie sings lyrics, "Money, power, and respect . . . is the key to life."] I haven't got any name, nobody. Nobody is trying to hear me. They trying to figure out that, "oh, he just saying that because he's a convicted felon" and all that. Nobody is trying to hear you . . .

RENARD: You just another dude from a bad neighborhood.

XAVIER: If you haven't got any name, you aren't going to make it. If you haven't got no way where you can reach, it's all about—it's not what you know now. It's about who you know now. That back in the day, it was about what you know. Now, it's about who you know. If you don't know anybody, you don't get far in this world.

REGGIE: And that's like in the jail situation too. If you ain't know nobody in the jail, you shit outta luck. . . . You know what I'm saying?

Trevor, Marshall, Xavier, Reggie, Renard, and many others told us that they gave up trying to influence the system because they had received the message, clearly and consistently, that the status of arrestee or convict rendered them powerless. Politicians responded to those with "money, power, and respect," not the likes of them who were "just another dude from a bad neighborhood" or had been "tagged as a convicted felon." As was the case for Marshall, jail had "kidnapped" his status as a full and empowered citizen. Cordell, a young black man from Charlottesville, put it succinctly:

[In prison] you can't even file a proper grievance unless you go through the chain of command. . . . So your rights are stolen from you even on the inside. And when you out here? If you're a felon, you have no voice. And then you ask me how do I feel about the government? I can't protect my family because of a mistake I made when I was an adolescent.

Far from the cherished ideals of citizen voice and political equality, our interviewees painted a picture of their democratic citizenship as deeply stigmatized and wholly inefficacious. This was particularly true among our custodial citizen sample relative to those who had never had personal contact with criminal justice. Do these differences likewise appear in our quantitative data?

The BYP provides a number of questions that help us assess whether

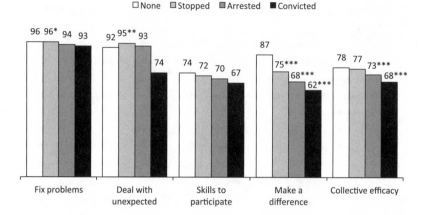

FIGURE 5.2. Percentage of respondents who agree or strongly agree with several measures of efficacy (%), by criminal justice contact. Items are: "I can fix problems," "I can deal with unexpected events," "I have the skills and knowledge to participate in politics," "I can make a difference by participating in politics," and "People working together in my neighborhood can solve our problems." *$p < .05$; **$p < .01$; ***$p > .001$. *Source*: Cathy J. Cohen, "Black Youth Culture Survey," Black Youth Project, Chicago, IL, 2005, http://www.blackyouthproject.com.

the feelings of political powerlessness expressed by our interview subjects can be generalized to custodial citizens more broadly. Somewhat surprisingly, these data show that the effects of criminal justice contact are concentrated on specific types of efficacy—those that are most closely associated with participation (see fig. 5.2). Criminal justice contact bears little relationship to a generalized sense of personal powerlessness. When a large and representative sample of young people was asked in the BYP survey whether they "can fix problems" or "deal with unexpected events," there was little significant effect of criminal justice contact. Custodial citizens, like the total sample of youth, overwhelmingly agree. (One notable and curious exception: having been stopped by police, the lowest degree of contact, does appear to increase agreement with these statements. However, the size of the effect is substantively small.) Similarly, experiences with criminal justice do not significantly shape beliefs about one's own capacity to engage with politics. Those who have been stopped by police, arrested, or convicted are also no less likely to agree that they "have the skills and knowledge necessary to participate in politics." Here as well, custodial citizens do not see themselves as lacking; internal political efficacy does not appear significantly affected by carceral contact.

Instead of adopting a general sense of incapacity in their own lives, custodial citizens become less likely to believe that they (and those like them) can change *the system*, a reduction in external efficacy. It is not the individual who comes up lacking; it is the government. About 87 percent of young people in the BYP without contact agreed or strongly agreed that "by participating in politics I can make a difference." By comparison, rates of agreement decline to 75 percent of those who have been stopped, 68 percent of those who have been arrested, and 62 percent of youth who have been convicted of a crime. We likewise find a negative relationship between criminal justice contact and perceptions of collective efficacy. Those who have been arrested or convicted are less likely to agree that "people working together in my neighborhood can solve many of our problems." As with attitudes toward political responsiveness, the effect of criminal justice contact on feelings of external and collective efficacy remain significant when we control for age, education, race, and gender. In multiple regressions, effects on collective efficacy are significant for conviction only.

Discussion

What does it mean to cultivate democratic citizens? Amy Gutmann describes the process of civic education as "the cultivation of the virtues, knowledge and skills necessary for political participation." The most deliberate way in which governments provide this political learning is through formal schooling.[10] However, political socialization is not confined to the schoolroom. Instead, political institutions are broadly implicated in the type of citizens government creates; the character of our citizenry is intrinsically tied to the nature of our government. When we change the "face" of government—creating criminal justice institutions that are decreasingly responsive, participatory, and accountable—we transform the type of civic education our political institutions provide. Rather than learning that they are full and equal citizens, that they deserve equal concern and respect, and that they can weigh in on issues and be heard by those in power, citizens learn that they are illegitimate actors, undeserving of social provision, employment, and political standing.

In this chapter, we have documented dimensions of the custodial life-world, a set of beliefs widely held by those who have had personal experiences with the criminal justice system. Our interviewees provide a powerful illustration of the euphemism that "where you stand depends on where you sit"; there is a strong connection between one's custodial status and his or her political perspectives, attitudes, and beliefs. Both our qualitative and quantitative data show the same results: moving through antidemocratic criminal justice institutions demonstrably restructures individuals' understanding of citizenship and empowerment writ large. In traversing state institutions of surveillance and punishment and interacting with agents of coercive control, citizens develop a host of norms and rules about what treatment they can expect, which in turn affects how they perceive citizenship and the ability to influence leaders. In sum, we argue here that socialization within the criminal justice system leads citizens to (un)learn citizenship.

These lessons learned would themselves be alarming. However, they form just the foundation of a deeper set of ideas concerning democracy and the state, racial equality, and the returns to democratic engagement. It is to these additional consequences of criminal justice that we turn in the chapters to come.

CHAPTER SIX

"You in their house now"

Learning about the State and Control

Government means different things to different people. To some, it is an organization of representatives who are the trustees of the people—elected to serve them, bring their districts funds and infrastructure, and defend their interests. To others, it may be a distant entity—a social security check arriving in the mail or news of a new law being passed. To custodial citizens, though, government is criminal justice. Across our conversations, one word was used more than any other to describe government: Control.

Albert, a middle-aged black man from Trenton, had a long history of crime and criminal justice contact. He was arrested for the first time at age eight on a misdemeanor, for which he was sent to a detention center. Charged with a felony at seventeen, he served his first (but not nearly his last) stint in prison. By age fifty, he had spent nearly thirty total years of his life in a cell. His regular passage back and forth through the criminal justice system had cost him the right to vote, access to public housing, his driver's license, and his welfare benefits. It was not surprising, then, that he spoke of a government that was not about providing for citizens, but about taking away rights and benefits. His was a state most concerned with "keeping them [citizens] in line." There is a "top dog, he call all the shots. You little dog, you gotta listen to him. . . . You don't speak till we tell you to." Rather than learning that governmental authority is a mechanism for achieving the collective good, Albert and the other custodial citizens with whom we spoke had come to conceptualize government as the manifestation of visible power and control. In Albert's words, government was "Somebody that runs the town. . . . What they say goes."

In the previous chapter, we explored the ways in which criminal justice contact recasts citizenship, imbuing individuals with a sense of stigma and reducing political efficacy. In addition to altering conceptions of one's own position in the polity, however, custodial citizenship is defined by a set of markedly distinct perceptions of the state. This set of beliefs is the focus of this chapter.

Few of those with whom we spoke, whether or not they had personal experience with criminal justice, saw government as responsive to their needs. Instead, most perceived those in power to have little understanding of their situations and circumstances. Elected officials and government agents were distant entities who exerted control over them without truly understanding them. However, interactions with the state through criminal justice had provided citizens with a particular framework for understanding government as whole. The result was a set of profound differences between the custodial citizens and others in our sample in how they conceptualized and understood American democracy.

Chief among these differences was that, for the custodial citizens with whom we spoke and in contrast to those who had not been exposed to criminal justice, many used police, courts, and institutions of confinement as their primary orientation for considering politics, a single lens through which the political system and its actors were viewed. For many custodial citizens, criminal justice *was* government; these individuals often failed to differentiate between this particular set of institutions and the political system writ large. In their interactions with criminal justice, they had been able to exert little authority; thus, government as a whole was perceived as a place where citizens have little control. American democracy, to them, was not fundamentally about representation at all. Instead, government in *practice* was often described as a semi-authoritarian body that inserted itself into their lives with the unwanted and overwhelming force of law. In this chapter, we explore these views of government in detail, and document its consequences for trust in governing authorities and perceptions of political responsiveness.

"Government can pretty much do as it please"

We started each of our interviews by asking subjects an open-ended question about what came to mind when they thought of government. Among those who had experienced criminal justice, in contrast to the rest of our sample, responses often directly referenced institutions and actors of crime control; even when our questions about government responsiveness and political trust did not have to do with criminal justice specifically, many responded by pointing to contact with police, courts, and prisons to explain why they felt the way they did. Respondents told us that when they thought of government what came to mind was "the criminal justice system," "what they doing in the criminal justice system, how they run they court system and all that," and that when they considered politics they "start from the police right on up" or "think from the president all down to the jail house people." This was not at all how government was described in our interviews with people who had not had involvement with criminal justice; in fact, none of the dozen individuals that we interviewed who had not had personal experience with the carceral state referenced criminal justice when thinking of government more generally.

That criminal justice is so central to their experience with the political system has consequences for how custodial citizens characterize the state. For these individuals, the characteristics of the carceral state serve as a reference point through which government is experienced and understood. Thus, criminal justice contact teaches citizens not simply how criminal justice operates, but how responsive and fair the political system is more broadly.

In describing their contact with the criminal justice system, custodial citizens portray a set of institutions that exerts near total control over them; as subjects of criminal justice, they had few institutional channels through which they could express their grievances or concerns. In the court system, they "just didn't have no control at all" and criminal justice authorities just "do what they wanna do"; in the jail, "you in their house now." Moreover, the control function of criminal justice and its repressive character was not seen as merely one isolated part of a larger whole. Instead, many conceptualized the political system in its entirety as authoritarian, hierarchical, and all-powerful. For the custodial citizens we talked to, government was construed not as a set of varied institutions with multiple and overlapping purposes, but as one all-subsuming force, or as one person put it: "a group of people who run my life. Every bit of it . . . they create the laws I go by and control my money, where I live."

Indeed, perhaps the most striking feature of our interviews with custodial citizens was that, despite many of our subjects having received some form of public assistance at one time or another—food stamps, disability, veterans benefits—few voiced a conceptualization of government as distributive. Though they recognized other agencies as part of the political system, and although many spoke of their experiences with welfare, unemployment, veterans' affairs, and disability offices, criminal justice carried a distinctive weight in their evaluations and in how they described their interactions with government. For instance, when asked to consider whether government does more to provide services or to ensure order, our interviewees overwhelmingly felt that the primary job of political authority was "keeping [people] in line, keeping them to their [government's] advantage."

To custodial citizens, the system was marked by extreme power asymmetry: ordinary people must fall in line or be at the mercy of the state. Those with whom we spoke did not see themselves as part of the give-and-take of a representative and responsive state. Instead, as Marcus, a young black man from Trenton, put it: "if you don't follow their rules or you know or the way that the rules are written, they figure that you're going against them, so they're going to make things harder." They described a government that had excessive power to control their lives and limit their choices. The view that government was not beneficent and was implacable was widely shared across our interviewees:

Bert (middle-aged black man, Charlottesville): When I think of government, I think of control . . . me not able to make the decisions I want to make because of being government and my decisions may not fit what the government wants. . . . Usually the outcome is the government takes over and I'm just stuck in a rut.

Abe (young black man, New Orleans): Power . . . They run everything. The government run everything.

Ray (older black man, Trention): Control. [*What makes you say that?*] This is where all the guidelines come from. So to me, that's control. Because, well I mean, boundaries should be set. I'm not saying control in a real negative way. More or less, that's how I think of government . . . controlling the people in the world.

Joachim (young Latino man, Trenton): Government is about strictness. Rules. Laws. And uh, something not to play with . . . take it very serious.

For most, these perceptions stemmed directly from criminal justice experiences. Many described feeling like police officials could stop and question them for anything, at any time. Reggie noted, "You got the right to freedom of speech at any time but when you're with them [police], when they're talking, you got to shut up. You aren't going to sit there and talk with them and have a conversation with them."

In stark contrast to the idea that the political system should "be for the people, by the people," contact with criminal justice institutions had taught them that government was a nefarious force that was mostly impervious to their will and could rarely be held accountable for its actions. When we asked Darnell what came to mind when he thought of government, he said grimly, "Something having to do with harsh, evil cruelty. Uh, lotta back-breaking pain. Yeah. 'Cause my run-in with it, that's how it's been. It's been a lotta heartache." Charles Ray of Charlottesville noted that "It's just all a big, I mean, once you get at their mercy you're screwed." Terrence cautioned that "the law around here, you've just got to stay out of the system if you can. 'Cause the system sucks. And they'll keep you in it as often as possible." Often these reactions referred to criminal justice specifically, but many custodial citizens saw criminal justice as synonymous with government. Thus, their brushes with the law presented them with powerful reminders of what government was really about and what it was capable of. From experience with criminal justice, custodial citizens learn, as Ray in Trenton put it, "that government is capable of pretty much anything . . . [that] government can pretty much do as it please. You know, whether it's good or bad." Custodial citizens learn that they do not have control over government; it has control over them.

"Put him in our shoes, how would he feel?"

Some of the conceptions of government voiced by custodial citizens were shared across our interviewees more broadly. Whether or not they had personal experience with criminal justice, our interviewees spoke with a clear and consistent voice: government does not walk in my shoes, so I cannot trust it. They felt they could not count on government because it was a very distant observer of their plight, a situation that included adversarial interactions with law enforcement and confinement but also the daily sense that their impoverished communities were ignored by those in power. Because government did not understand their situations and the challenges of daily life they faced, it could not be depended on to work in earnest for them or their community. Some were angry and frustrated about this, while others were calmly resigned to it as a fact of political life in America. But with few exceptions, those with whom we spoke felt that they could not entrust government with their concerns or count on politicians to be their trustees. They had few positive expectations of government at all.

Trina places little stock in the government or politicians because they "don't know what it's like to suffer." A middle-aged black woman from Trenton, Trina believes that elected representatives are not fair or faithful representatives of their communities—the poor, the down and out, and racial minorities. She would not count on the government to aid her or people like her "cause I don't believe in government—I don't trust government, let's put it that way. I don't trust the political system. 'Cause they all about themselves. Period." She strongly disagrees that government officials could represent her interests, because they do not have the faintest idea of what it means to live in poverty and have not experienced the suffering it entails:

> No. Absolutely not. They don't suffer. They don't know. They haven't been there. That's just like a blind man trying to lead a man with 20–20 vision. Come on. They don't care. . . . Him [a politician] and his family—they don't know what it's like to suffer. Just like in the 1920s or the 1930s with the crash, and all the people start jumping out of windows. You ain't see no black people jumping out of windows. I'm serious. Okay, we know what suffering is. So, when it crashed? We was already down there! They couldn't handle it. All the people with money couldn't handle it. And today, the same thing would happen. They couldn't handle being poor. And they know nothing about being poor. They look at it and they see it from the television. They see it on the computer. They don't deal with it. They don't know. They don't care.

This was a familiar refrain. When we asked whether politicians understood people in communities like theirs, the answers we received from nearly all of our interviewees consistently echoed Trina's beliefs: politicians could not understand their point of view because they had never had to wonder where their next meal would come from, or deal with the stress of locating a job that did not exist, or feel the sting of not being able to provide for their children. Sarah, a middle-aged black woman from Trenton, had been homeless for a while, but was now working part time and recently had found a place to live in transitional housing. Some of the social supports that had gotten her off the street—food stamps, transitional housing—were publicly provided. Yet when we asked her if government understood and could help with the needs and concerns of people in her communities, she told us that she did not think so:

> They really don't get the grip of what really goes on in places like this, I don't think so. They say experience is the best teacher. You can sit down, you can listen to somebody's story or you can see their pain or you can hear about things that you never would have thought that you would find yourself in that situation, but until you put yourself in that situation, and actually go through it, then you wouldn't understand it.

People told us again and again that politicians would have to "come into the area and stay a day or two," "live a day in our shoes," and "ride the bus for a week and eat at a soup kitchen" in order to understand the issues they faced. And because elected officials did not understand them, they did not adequately represent them. To Melvin, a young black man from Trenton, elected officials failed to provide meaningful support because they did not understand the problems he faced:

> People out there starving, struggling, living on the street, robbing, doing whatever they have to do to survive. I don't believe they actually had to experience what people like us or other people go through, or went through. They don't take it as serious as we do, that we are actually out there. They're like, "Ok, we give 'em a little bit of welfare . . . they be all right. I don't know what they went through, but I'm gonna hit 'em with this and that and they'll be fine." I don't think they actually been there to the bottom, to where they actually have to wear the same clothes every day. Have to beg and borrow and wonder how we gonna pay it back or how's my next day gonna be, how am I gonna eat or how I'm goin' . . . anything. I don't think they actually been through that.

Poverty, chronic unemployment, lack of schooling and decent wages, and homelessness had clearly played a role in shaping the views of Trina, Sarah, Melvin, and many others with whom we spoke. Yet, in addition, the custodial citizens in our sample felt that elected officials would not respond to their concerns because they did not understand the reality of the choices—or lack of choices—that many faced in their communities. This also meant that those in power did not understand why they or others might turn to drinking, drugs or crime. Among those we spoke to, there was a pervasive sense that politicians had never had to experience the struggle and the hustle that was required just to get by on a day-to-day basis and so did not understand the complex role of crime in their communities. For example, Andre, a young black man with whom we spoke in Trenton, described the situation like this:

> No, they [politicians] really can't relate to what we're going through as a minority. No, they can't relate. They can't relate. . . . Let me see. Birds of a feather flock together, so if his crew—if his surroundings is all wealthy, then yes, he can relate to that. But if you can just take him for a week, just take all his valuable belongings away from him for a week and put him in our shoes, how would he feel? Could he survive? Could he last just seven days of living like this—eating what we eat? Listening to somebody say, "you ain't never amount to nothing, you'll never be nothing, you ain't about nothing." Locked in. "No, you can't use the bathroom. No, you can't use the phone. I'm not giving you your mail."

In other words, Andre believes that politicians cannot relate because they do not understand what it is like to be locked up—a common experience where he is from—and could not handle being in prison, being told what to do, and being denied freedom of movement and communication with the outside world.

Others, like Dominic, believe that because government officials do not understand the lives of the "little people," they are interested only in locking people up, rather than addressing the poverty and educational deficits that many felt had led them to crime in the first place. Dominic, a young black man in Trenton we interviewed while he was transitioning back to the street from a parole violation, spoke particularly eloquently about the structural determinants of crime and the ways in which he believed criminal justice to be misguided:

> The vast majority of the people who come into the system today, it's drug related in some kind of way. There are very few people that are actually picking up a brick and throwing it through the post office window or mugging old women. Not saying that those things don't happen, not saying that people

aren't raped or murdered or anything like that because they do exist, obviously, in large numbers. But the vast majority of the crimes that occur, hence the number of people that populate this type of environment [in a halfway house], have to do with more interpersonal issues, problem solving skills, education in the form of having some type of vocational education. If I come in here and all I know is selling drugs, and there is no self-awareness that takes place, there's no training that takes place, I don't acquire any vocational skill, 9.9 out of 10 I'm going to go back out. Especially when the crunch comes and I got to eat or whatever, I'm going to go back to the same thing that I've done.

James, a middle-aged black man from Trenton, felt similarly. James had been "in and out of jail" and had served some time in prison. Like the others with whom we spoke, James believes that elected officials cannot understand poor people's needs because their experience is so distant: "I think if I did a survey, I would say that the higher officials who really have [power], not a lot of them come from poor communities. I can't honestly think of anybody who's really experienced that. And I think to do it you really have to live it." Yet, every time he talked about his mistrust of government, James referred not to perceptions of elected officials or to workers in welfare offices, but to criminal justice authorities and the lessons he had gleaned directly from his experience being locked up. When we asked him whether he trusted government, he brought up criminal justice out of the blue:

> No, I can't [say that I trust the government] cause it's like, going to court, you don't know what's going to be the outcome. I remember the first time I ever went to prison. The attorney I had, I was locked up like four months and he said you been locked up five months, they want to give you six months and that will give you time served. So plead to the six months and you'll get probation and go home. I went in there trusting him and I got six years. And when I looked up he was gone, and I'm standing up there with six years. So it's kind of hard trusting someone when your life is at stake. And that's the same thing you do with government. Your life is at stake.

However, James did not feel that all individuals received the same treatment at the hands of the justice system or were treated equally by the state at large. Rather, he was acutely aware of the ways that race and class combined to determine his treatment. When he tried to explain his general sense that the political system ignores the needs of the poor, he turned to his criminal justice experience as evidence, saying:

> It's like, when you're going through the system, it's not what you know, it's *who* you know. Who'll talk for you. Cause I've seen people with way worse records than I could ever have, and they go in and they get probation and go home.

Reggie, an energetic young black man we interviewed in New Orleans, had similarly come to view criminal justice as particularly unresponsive to people like him and, like James, felt that this was a fairly accurate characterization of the political system as a whole. We interviewed Reggie, along with his friends Xavier and Renard, in a Louisiana community center where they were participating in a city service program for ex-offenders. The three young men had seen their share of criminal justice contact, and they described their neighborhood as so infested with drugs that Domino's and Papa John's refused pizza delivery to their address. For them, trying to get the political system to respond to or assist them was like banging their heads against the wall. Xavier explained that he and his mom once went down to city hall to make a formal complaint about his being harassed by police, but nothing ever happened; no one ever contacted them and they never heard anything in response. Reggie chimed in:

> They can say, "Come down there and speak, come down there and speak," but when we get down there and speak, we ain't gonna have shit to say because they ain't even going to let us talk. You know what I'm saying? . . . City hall: "Get your complaints in." Yes, "Come down there and talk, come down there and talk." When we come down there and talk, what's that going to change? That ain't going to change shit.

How Does Criminal Justice Contact Affect Perceptions of Responsiveness and Trust?

Our interviewees spoke overwhelmingly of the political system as unresponsive to their needs and as untrustworthy advocates for their communities. Yet even over and above the generally high levels of political dissatisfaction that were evident among this impoverished and disadvantaged group, we saw a distinct pattern emerge among the custodial citizens with whom we spoke. For our interviewees who reported personal experience with criminal justice, it was not only that government did not provide adequate assistance or respond sufficiently to their needs. More often, the distributive side of the state was recognized as ineffective but seen as peripheral, wholly subsumed by government's more prominent law and order functions. Similary, while the sense that the state was unresponsive to "people like me" was widely held among this intersectionally disadvantaged population, custodial citizens seemed to feel this most acutely. For them, it was not only that government would not do enough to respond to their needs; government for them was designed as a top down imposition of authority that targeted them with a lesser justice.

In order to examine systematically the relationship between individual criminal justice contact and perceptions of political responsiveness and trust, we turn to nationally representative samples of young people from three surveys: the National Longitudinal Survey of Youth 1979 cohort (NLSY), the Black Youth Project (BYP), and the National Longitudinal Survey of Adolescent Health (Add Health). These data make clear that the perceptions described by our interviewees in Trenton, Charlottesville, and New Orleans—that government is not responsive to the will of citizens and that political authorities cannot be trusted—represent views widely held by the emerging generation of America's custodial citizens. In the NLSY, about 5,000 respondents were asked "how often does the federal government do what most Americans want." Overall, less than 10 percent of respondents gave the most efficacious views of "always" or "most of the time." However, perceptions of government as responsive were most clearly diminished among those who had experienced the carceral state firsthand. Among respondents to that survey, only 17 percent of those who had never been convicted or incarcerated said the federal government "never" did what Americans want; in contrast, 24 percent of those who had been convicted and 32 percent of those who had been imprisoned gave the most pessimistic response.

In our qualitative data, it is difficult to disentangle whether variation in individuals perceptions are truly related to criminal justice contact, or simply have to do with being a member of a systematically disadvantaged community, regardless of carceral experience. Certainly, many of our interviewees (and presumably those in the NLSY samples who had criminal justice contact) had experienced not just frequent attention from the police or being confined to jail or prison, but other challenges brought on by their social and economic standing: living in buildings "infested with bedbugs and rats," walking streets with broken windows and boarded-up buildings, and moving through neighborhoods marked by a dying economic infrastructure. Many also reported other negative contacts with government, outside the carceral state, including having struggled to obtain disability or public assistance, or feeling that the level of benefits provided by these programs were not sufficient to meet their often considerable needs.

Our survey data give us further purchase on whether the deeper sense of the state as unresponsive to Americans' preferences is specifically related to criminal justice contact, or whether these patterns instead reflect a more general orientation held by low-income citizens, racial minorities, or those with limited education. When we account for pre-existing differences between custodial citizens and those with no contact, including demographics, drug use, and measures of self-control, we find that the substantive relationship is unchanged (though conviction does not reach statistical significance). (Further details of regression analyses are presented in appendix C.) The expected value of this measure of government responsiveness is 3.67 for those with no convictions or incarceration, holding other factors constant at their mean values (scale is $1 =$ always to $5 =$ never); it rises to 3.73 and 3.78 for those convicted and incarcerated, respectively. The size of the effect is relatively small but the trend is clear: custodial citizens are less likely to believe that government works on behalf of most Americans.

These differences are even more pronounced in the BYP, where respondents are questioned not about whether government frequently fails to do what "most Americans" want, but rather about whether government is responsive to "people like me" and "people in my neighborhood" (see fig. 6.1) Compared to slightly more than a third of respondents with no criminal justice contact who agreed that "the leaders in government care very little about people like me," just more than half of those who had been stopped by police, nearly two-thirds of those who had been arrested, and about three-quarters of those who had been convicted of a crime concurred. The same pattern was true of beliefs that "people in my neighborhood are able to get the government to respond to our needs." Relative to those who had never had contact with police or the criminal courts, custodial citizens were significantly more likely to agree with the idea that government was not responsive to people in their neighborhood and, like other measures of political responsiveness,

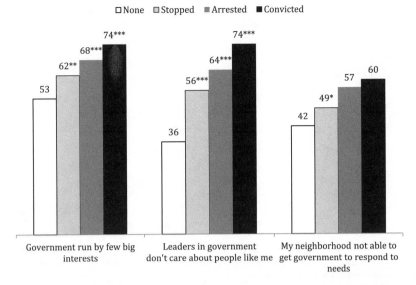

FIGURE 6.1. Perceptions of government responsiveness (% agree or strongly agree), by criminal justice contact. *$p < .05$; **$p < .01$; ***$p > .001$. *Source*: Cathy J. Cohen, "Black Youth Culture Survey," Black Youth Project, Chicago, IL, 2005, http://www.black youthproject.com.

these perceptions increased with each successive level of criminal justice contact. Finally, custodial citizens were also more likely to believe that "the government is pretty much run by a few big interests looking out for themselves and their friends." On this measure, 53 percent of those with no contact, 62 percent of those who had been stopped, 68 percent of those who had been arrested, and 74 percent of those who had been convicted expressed agreement.

Sample sizes in the BYP are relatively small at higher levels of criminal justice contact, precluding a multiple regression analysis with sufficiently comprehensive independent variables. However, like the responsiveness question from the NLSY, the sense that government is concerned with "people like me" remains significantly and negatively related to criminal justice contact even when we account for gender, age, education, and race.[1] The other two measures of perceived responsiveness are not significant once these controls are introduced.

As in our interviews, survey data show that experiences with criminal justice are also negatively associated with trust in government. For example, only 18 percent of respondents in the Add Health survey who

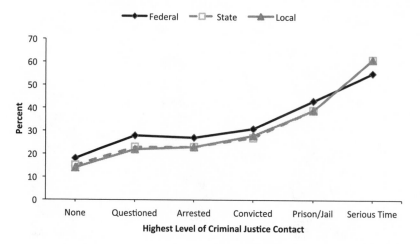

FIGURE 6.2. Distrust of government (% strongly disagreeing or disagreeing that they trust the government), by criminal justice contact. *Source*: National Longitudinal Study of Adolescent Health, Wave III.

had not encountered criminal justice in any form said they did not trust the federal government; this percent rises to 28 and 27 percent for those who were questioned or arrested, 31 for those who were convicted, 43 for those who had been incarcerated, and reaches a majority (55%) for those who had experienced imprisonment of over a year in duration. As figure 6.2 shows, the same is true for trust in state and local government. There is a precipitous and progressive increase in distrust of government at each level of criminal justice contact; as criminal justice interventions become more intensive, suspicions of government spread.

To again account for potential confounders, we regress trust in government on criminal justice contact as well as a host of relevant variables. When we combine trust in federal, state, and local government into a single index, we find that being stopped and questioned by the police is associated with a 3 percent decrease in trust in the government, being arrested is associated with a 2 percent decline, a court conviction is associated with a 4 percent decline in trust, being incarcerated is associated with a decline of 9 percent, and having been incarcerated for over a year was associated with a decline of 11 percent net of other factors. We present predicted values from this model in figure 6.3. As these results show, citizens who have directly experienced criminal justice interventions are sizably less trusting of the state, all else equal.

These analyses present substantial evidence that criminal justice is significantly correlated with attitudes toward government, even accounting for important potential confounders like race, education, and income. With the Add Health data, we are able to conduct further assessments of whether decreased trust is truly the result of criminal justice contact, or whether it is instead predicted by correlates of criminal justice experience, such as race or income. We describe these additional tests in greater detail in appendix C.

As a first robustness check of our results, we compare levels of political trust across four subgroups of the Add Health sample: respondents with no history of illegal drug use or criminal justice contact ($N = 6,266$), respondents with no history of illegal drug use but with custodial contact ($N = 628$), respondents with illegal drug use and no custodial contact ($N = 5,631$), and respondents with both illegal drug use and custodial contact ($N = 2,282$). This lets us account for potential biases stemming from differences between custodial citizens and noncustodial citizens in the likelihood of engaging in criminal behavior. Differences in trust in government across the four groups are highly significant (F test $p < .001$ for all tests). Specifically, those with both illegal drug use and custodial

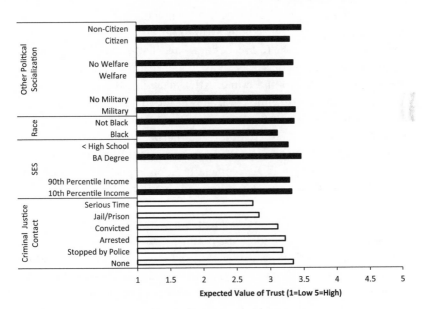

FIGURE 6.3. Expected value of trust in government, by criminal justice contact. *Source*: National Longitudinal Study of Adolescent Health, Wave III.

contact have the lowest levels of political trust of the four groups, significantly lower even than those who also report illegal drug use but have
had no criminal justice contact.

We then examine the effects of criminal justice contact among only
the subset of 7,913 Add Health respondents who self-report illegal drug
use. Limiting the sample to only those respondents who have taken part
in illegal drug activity helps confirm that the effects of criminal justice
contact are not solely the result of preexisting criminal tendencies. In
multiple regression models estimating effects of progressive contact
among only this subset, we find consistent effects; among illegal drug users, contact with the criminal justice system significantly decreases trust
and, as in the full sample analyses, the size of the effects increases as
contact becomes more intense. Specifically, among illegal drug users and
ceteris paribus, being questioned or arrested lowers trust by about 2 percent, being convicted by about 3 percent, serving time in prison or jail by
about 9 percent, and serving serious time lowers trust by roughly 11 percent. Substantively equivalent results are obtained from these models
when the sample is further restricted to include only serious illegal drug
users, excluding those who report using marijuana, steroids, or prescription drugs but nothing more.

We then use weights from genetic matching to create a matched set of
convicted and never-convicted drug users, ensuring that the two groups
are well balanced on the full set of covariates that we describe in the preceding parametric models, as well as on a propensity score that predicts
having been convicted of a crime. After matching, there are no significant differences on baseline covariates in the matched sample between
illegal drug users who have been convicted of a crime and those who
have not. However, there are differences between the two groups in the
outcomes of interest: Among self-reported drug users, having a criminal
conviction lowers trust in government by about 3 percent. We find similar effects of other types of contact, and again the effects are larger as
contact becomes more severe.

Taken together, these analyses help ameliorate the likelihood that it
is solely differences in underlying criminal propensities between those
who have had criminal justice contact and those who have not that explain our results, rather than the criminal justice contact itself. However,
even among illegal drug users, the probability of encountering a criminal sanction is still nonrandom. One particularly stark example of this
is reflected in the noncorresponding race gaps between drug use and

drug arrest, which we described in chapter 2. A recent Human Rights Watch report suggests that there are about six times more white than black drug users, but that African Americans constitute almost 53 percent of all drug offenders who enter state prison. As Katherine Beckett and colleagues point out, a number of explanations have been offered for these disparities.[2] Some scholars contend that racial minorities use serious drugs in higher numbers.[3] Others point to unequal probabilities in the likelihood that police apprehend black and white drug users.[4]

Our second cut at establishing causality thus follows a somewhat different logic. Whereas the previous analysis addressed potential differences in the "criminality" of the custodial and non-custodial samples, here we address differences in the likelihood of criminal justice contact itself. Again using Add Health, our strategy is to compare the political attitudes of respondents in Wave III who have experienced a criminal justice intervention against a demographically comparable group of Wave III respondents who have not yet experienced that type of contact, but who will have joined this segment of the custodial population by Wave IV. That is, we compare our treatment group (those who report a criminal contact by the third wave survey) with our control group (those who do not report that type of criminal contact by the third wave but do report one in the fourth wave) on political outcomes at Wave III. In bivariate analyses, those who have been convicted of a crime by Wave III, compared to those who have not yet but will have by Wave IV, have lower levels of political trust (F stat $= 103.21$, $p < .001$). In a multiple regression similar to those described previously, having a conviction at Wave III relative to those who do not have a conviction until Wave IV predicts a decrease in trust of 4 percent. In our matched sample, we again find a significant and negative effect of a criminal conviction on trust (3%).

As a final placebo test, we compare respondents who do not have a conviction in Wave III but will in Wave IV with those who do not report this type of carceral contact in either wave. As expected, we find that future convicts in Wave III, all else equal, have levels of political trust that are statistically indistinguishable from respondents who report no contact with criminal justice in either wave. Put simply, *future* criminal justice contact is not predictive of trust in government. This lends further support to our assertion that these differences reflect a treatment effect of contact with criminal justice that is independent of existing differences related to the probability of criminal offending.

Conclusion

In this chapter, we have assessed the role of criminal justice contact in shaping custodial citizens' views of government. We find that contact with the carceral state shapes beliefs about government responsiveness and trustworthiness in important ways. Most of those with whom we spoke exhibited overwhelming distrust of politicians. They did not feel that elected officials understood their problems or concerns and generally believed that politicians would not listen to them or work on their behalf. These attitudes reflect ideas widely held by Americans, particularly racial minorities and the poor. Indeed, scholars have documented historically low levels of political trust among the American public as a whole and have tracked significant declines in public confidence in political institutions.[5] However, both our interviews and surveys made clear that the attitudes of custodial citizens were in some important ways distinct. For this group, government was not merely unresponsive, it was often repressive. For them, government was designed to control rather than serve.

Moreover, it is clear from our multivariate analyses that custodial citizens occupy a position of political alienation that is unique even relative to other struggling Americans. Despite accounting for income, age, education, and race, we still find that personal contact with criminal justice diminishes trust and increases perceptions of American government as unresponsive to its citizens. Thus, just as criminal justice has been shown to have important consequences for employment, families, health, and other social outcomes, the scope and character of the carceral state has profound importance for the political attitudes of individual Americans.

CHAPTER SEVEN

"We're free, but we're not *free*"

Black Custodial Citizenship and Complex Racial Narratives

Many young black men in America have their earliest and most sa-lient interaction with the state in an encounter with police. Indeed, much like blacks' lives have been defined by other formal and informal American institutions throughout the twentieth century—attending un-equal schools, confinement to grotesque city tenements, relegation to grueling work on fields and as domestic servants—the lives of an extraor-dinary number of blacks are now demarcated by the experiences of be-ing patted down by a city cop, being led away in handcuffs, and learning the isolation and segregation of prison life. For many, these interactions are pervaded by perceptions of racial bias, stigma, and humiliation.

It stands to reason, then, that in addition to shaping political action and thought generally, criminal justice may help organize racial knowl-edge and cultivate racial meaning. Along these lines, scholars have sug-gested that criminal justice is a "race-making institution"; beyond merely reflecting racial dynamics and social understandings in the wider soci-ety, it actively "shapes racial experience and conditions meaning," de-fines racial identities and membership, and positions racial groups.[1] For example, as I. Bennett Capers notes, racialized policing enforces ideas about who should be where, how they should look and act, and what con-stitutes "suspicious behavior" from individuals of different races. This points not only "to a flaw in how we police. It also sends an expressive message, from a representative of the state no less, about who belongs, and who does not."[2] When a black youth believes he has been frisked by police for doing little more than walking through a white neighborhood wearing a hoodie, or a black woman goes to court and feels the judge treats her with greater severity than whites, or a black man goes to prison and finds himself surrounded by other black and brown faces, these individuals may read these events through a racial lens and incorporate what they learn through these experiences into their sense of what it means to be a black man or woman in America. For just one example, Darnell explained to us that police would ride by whites standing on the corner; "But me? And my skin color? Stand on my block for just five minutes. . . . Put it this way—if you're darker, you're liable to get drugs put on you, beat the fuck up and go to jail."

We agree that criminal justice is an important site of racial socialization, a place where what it means to be black is conveyed and learned, mostly involuntarily. Black custodial citizens derive specific racial meanings from race-laden criminal justice institutions, which in turn help to inform how they perceive the position of their group in America; individual contact with the criminal justice system serves as an information 'shortcut' about the wellbeing and lived experience of the group. Interactions with the criminal justice system are instrumental, then, because such contact brings to mind a powerful script: that blacks are mistreated at the hands of the state. Capers notes that "the incident becomes an uncomfortable anecdote shared with other minorities, stories exchanged, almost therapeutically, about 'being black [or Hispanic, or Asian] in this country.'"[3]

However, unlike earlier institutions that "made race" in America by explicitly dividing citizens along racial lines and subjecting whites and blacks to different harms and opportunities, the explicit role of race in criminal justice is often times obscured. In this chapter, we argue that social norms and legal jurisprudence concerned with "colorblind" equality have undermined explicit, race-based discrimination within the operations of police, courts, and prisons. This was an important and positive development. As it became sanitized of intentional bigotry and malice, minorities navigated a justice system that was more racially fair on its face. And yet, the system remained deeply rooted in racial inequality and although individual treatment became formally equal, it remained racially inflected. At the same time, the overriding lesson of criminal justice to its wards was personal responsibility grounded in individual decisions; for example, penal institutions made release from confinement contingent on accepting individual guilt, teaching custodial citizens to "make better choices." This explicit message leaves little room for a meaningful discussion of structural inequalities as a cause of crime, or of the role of incarceration in perpetuating durable social and economic disadvantage.

In both our surveys and in the perceptions of the custodial citizens we interviewed, we find evidence that criminal justice encounters do promote racial learning. Most blacks—whether or not they have had criminal justice contact—see race as a guiding factor in their lives, register high levels of discrimination, and have serious misgivings about the extent of equality in the United States. Criminal justice encounters amplify these already bleak racial views. In our quantitative data, we find that being stopped by police, arrested, and incarcerated is associated with a diminished faith in equality and greater discontent with government treatment. Yet, in contrast to what we would expect from an overtly "race-making institution" and diverging from the political learning we detailed in previous chapters, the differences between custodial and non-custodial citizens are often modest and sometimes insignificant. While the broad story of racial learning is evident, it is much less powerful than we expected and far weaker than the political learning we find elsewhere in this book.

Clues to why this is so lie in our interview data, where a much more complex story emerges. For the black custodial citizens in our sample, criminal justice experiences (and the resultant lessons that were derived) came largely through things tied up with, but not directly subsumed by, race. People experienced the criminal justice system as unequal but not obviously *racially* unequal; instead, they found it difficult to identify where and how race mattered. Recall from chapter 5 that many minority respondents had developed a code of prohibitions, which offered them powerful intuitions about what was off-limits to them and people like them without explicitly putting race on display. Because this learning was only indirectly about race and was bound up with other statuses like class and neighborhood, race was difficult to locate. As a result, black custodial citizens struggled to arrive at a straightforward explanation for the experiences they had and the opportunities they lacked. In our interviews, we found many had difficulty making sense of their experiences, which often featured unequal treatment but was not in the main because of race and which often resulted from their own choices, even if those choices were made in contexts offering few viable alternative pathways.

In fact, not only do our interviews fail to show a unified racial message learned and adopted from criminal justice encounters, they show much the opposite—respondents often disagreed about the abiding role of race in their lives, communities, and nation. Moreover, they voiced contrasting accounts of what or who was to blame. For some of our black respondents, race was central to the barriers they faced and defined their custodial status. This group saw criminal justice as just another in a long line of state sanctioned segregation made possible by a new but familiar set of discriminatory institutions. This view, which we call a racial oppression narrative, attributes the situation of blacks to concerted efforts to disempower and disenfranchise blacks through criminal justice and beyond. In this telling, criminal justice was just the new incarnation of a long line of oppressive racial institutions, a "gentler kind of genocide" as Trina, one of our interviewees, told us.

For others, like Sarah, race is a scapegoat: "it's only what you make it. It's on the individual . . . doesn't matter what color you are." This second view, which we call the personal responsibility narrative, emphasizes reasons indigenous to black culture and individual choice in explaining racial disproportionalities in criminal justice contact. From this perspective, blacks had only themselves to blame for their overrepresentation in America's courtrooms, prisons, and jails, and should accept responsibility for their own poor decision making. Here, it was not America that had failed black citizens; black citizens had failed themselves.

In the pages to follow, we document these two racial "transcripts," or stories, from our interviewees about why blacks have fewer prospects than whites in America. These divergent narratives are rooted, we argue, in the counterposed messages of the criminal justice system itself. These institutions display vast racial inequality, producing well-documented disparities in treatment and outcome and regularly engaging particular citizens because they "fit the description" of an alleged criminal (read: are young, poor, and black). At the same time, though, custodial citizens are overtly taught the principles of individual agency, that one should take ownership of and make restitution for one's crimes, that one is being punished for individual (not societal) mistakes. These two transcripts thereby reflected the dual education of the criminal justice system, which engages a population mired in poverty and structural defects yet emphasizes an extreme form of personal responsibility. The result is that a gap has developed between what custodial citizens see and experience, on the one hand, and the narratives available to help them make sense of it, on the other. Ironically, criminal justice reforms made it more difficult for blacks and others to "see" racial bias and to develop a collective account of its operation from which to counter it, even as racial inequality in criminal justice ballooned.

Though these two sets of views draw on distinct ideological traditions and present very different causal stories and prescriptions, they are not as distinct as they might first appear. Both were ways that black citizens attempted to make sense of their experiences, developing an explanation of the world around them and a compelling narrative for their and their community's plight. Otherwise confusing and disempowering events outside their control could be made legible within these frameworks. Some made sense of their marginality by describing a system steeped in racial hierarchy where blacks had little power. Others made sense of their situation through a doctrine of individual choices, self-empowerment, and faith in God.

In addition, for most of those we interviewed, these dual narratives were not mutually exclusive. We mostly avoid an explanation of why some clung more to one transcript or the other because, as we emphasize below, while some consistently put forward one story, more often it was the case that people offered some of each at different points in the same interview, struggling for fluency in one consistent narrative.

And finally, even among those who held fast to one or the other narrative, most agreed on one point: government had turned its back on their communities. Adherents of both views pointed to disintegrating job prospects, urban decline, inescapable poverty, and the crack epidemic as ways that government neglected the black poor in the inner city. Blacks involved in crime and drugs made bad choices, as this argument goes, but these were often rational adaptations to situations largely out of their control. The result was that both narratives led people to believe that they had little agency beyond themselves. Those who held tightly to a personal responsibility narrative and believed "it's up to you to make good choices" were just as likely as those who clung to an oppression narrative to believe they had little influence and should "go it alone"; both groups believed "you have to help yourself" because the state would do little to assist, in the best case, and would do substantial harm, in the worst. The result of these conflicting narratives was that a mobilized consciousness among black custodial citizens failed to develop.

The Obscuring of Race in Criminal Justice and the Rise of Blame and Personal Responsibility

Over the past half century, the trajectory of the modern criminal justice system has been characterized by a complex set of forces, which have simultaneously entrenched and masked the forces that produce racial inequalities. In particular, we suggest that a narrowing legal and social conceptualization of racism—which focused primarily on overt acts of discrimination on the part of racist individuals—complicated custodial citizens' ability to see, articulate, and challenge the role of race in shaping their own experiences. This sociolegal development was not confined to criminal justice, but was instead part of a larger reorganization of racial norms and practices in the nation. For instance, one of the crucial legacies of *Brown v. Board of Education* was that it gave rise to a powerful new ideology of racial equality—what Lani Guinier calls "racial liberalism"—which "emphasized the corrosive effect of individual prejudice and the importance of interracial contact in promoting tolerance."[4] The underlying assumption of racial liberalism was that ending overt discrimination would quickly kill racial inequality.

This compromise came with significant costs. By defining racial inequality narrowly and as stemming only from isolated, irrational, and individual prejudice (and leading only to "psychological damage") the Court's decision in *Brown* "cast a long doctrinal shadow, allowing subsequent courts to limit constitutional relief to remedying acts of *intentional* discrimination by local entities or individuals."[5] "Formal equality and nothing more" became the law of the land, concentrating remedial efforts on individual perpetrators rather than historically informed and embedded inequalities. Owing to its emphasis on episodic and intentional racism, as opposed to structural racism, this legal development collapsed attempts to address racial inequality that could not be traced to individual bigots but which derived instead from more complex historical processes. As Cedric Powell writes:

> Literal equality, without regard to context or history, is the unifying principle of the Court's race jurisprudence. . . . "The similarly situated" must be treated the same, so the rhetoric of neutrality becomes especially appealing. Because everyone is the "same," or similarly situated, history can be ignored (or submerged) in the name of colorblindness (history is neutral); race can be

decontextualized so that it becomes an institutional value rather than a complex social construct.[6]

Furthermore, by focusing on formal rather than substantive equality—essentially prioritizing overt treatment over the results of multiple processes of disadvantage—the Court in *Brown* tacitly approved the consequences of racialized poverty; it did little to significantly remedy historically rooted disparities in resources, power, and opportunity across racial groups. Instead, broader systems of inequality could continue so long as they were not directly implicated in Jim Crow–style racism. The racial equality discourse thus made it difficult to confront lasting inequalities based on race; structural problems receded from the court's view while remaining vivid within most domains of life. Inequalities not attributable to visible, intentional bias were left to "incubate" and the role of race in American political, economic, and social life was "transformed but not overcome."[7]

A similar framework of colorblind jurisprudence prevailed within criminal justice. Just as it had in the educational arena, this emerging racial ideology emphasized the need to eliminate overt, intentional and individual racial biases in order to secure a "colorblind" society.[8] However, by failing to account for persistent disparities of outcome that stemmed from facially race-neutral policies, continuing implicit biases, and durable racial inequalities, it had the unintended but substantial consequence of permitting racial disparities within criminal justice to flourish.[9] Without specific evidence that police, juries, judges, or prison guards had acted with intentional racial animus, festering racial inequalities within criminal justice did not violate equal protection and were not justiciable.

In addition to supposedly race-neutral policies that have been shown to have racially disparate outcomes, racial liberalism failed to account for racial bias that does not stem from intentional discrimination. A host of new studies underscores the central role of implicit bias, or those racial attitudes subconsciously held and mostly resistant to conscious control, in criminal justice decision making. In one study of sworn law enforcement, police subjects were more likely to shoot unarmed black men in a simulated "shooter" exercise.[10] Police officers were also more likely to look at a black face than a white one when "primed to think about violent crime" and more likely to identify black faces, particularly of dark skin color and other stereotypic features, as more criminal.[11] Implicit bias is also evident in other stages of the criminal justice system. A recent study found that judges exhibit antiblack bias on a traditional implicit association test.[12] More important, these negative associations had a strong effect on judicial decision making.[13]

Yet despite a growing understanding of the enduring role of race, legal doctrines of colorblindness and intentionality virtually guaranteed that once-robust challenges against systemic racial inequality in criminal justice would wither on the vine. Most damningly, even claims of explicit racial discrimination now "provide a weak basis" for confronting enduring racial disparities in criminal justice, because locating and proving racial motives is often next to impossible when direct motivation has been concealed, or when disparities arise from "race-neutral" institutional practices and policies rather than overt discrimination.[14]

The effects of colorblindness are particularly clear in jurisprudence concerning felon disenfranchisement laws. Most recently, the case of *Farrakhan v. Gregoire* tested the question of whether the disparate racial effects of felon disenfranchisement laws violate section 2 of the 1965 Voting Rights Act, which prohibits voting practices and procedures that have a discriminatory result. The case, brought by a group of racial minorities incarcerated in the state of Washington, examined whether pervasive racial bias in the state's criminal justice system was germane to felon disenfranchisement law. Essentially, the plaintiffs argued that because the criminal justice system was itself discriminatory—a Washington task force in 2011 itself concluded that race affects "outcomes in the criminal justice system and matter(s) in ways that are not fair, that do not advance legitimate public safety objectives, and that undermine public confidence in our criminal justice system"—the resulting disproportionate number of disenfranchised blacks must also be considered a result of racial bias.

Lower courts initially accepted the plaintiff's arguments. However, four months after ruling that the state law violated the constitution, the Ninth Circuit decided *sua sponte* to rehear the case. In its new ruling against the discrimination claims of the Washington inmates, the court relied on "an unprecedented and nearly insurmountable 'intentional discrimination' standard."[15] Under this standard, it was not enough to show that the state's criminal justice system suffered from severe racial disparities. Instead, the plaintiffs had to show, at a minimum, first that the criminal justice system in general was "infected by *intentional* discrimination," and second that the denial of voting rights specifically was enacted with racial intent. The statistical racial disparities the plaintiffs presented to the court were not enough; "because plaintiffs presented no evidence of intentional discrimination in the operation of Washington's criminal justice system," they had not shown that the state was indeed in violation under the VRA. In addition, the court relied on the strength of due process protections to justify denying custodial citizens the right to vote; it ruled against the plaintiffs in part because it concluded that voting rights are restricted only after an individual has been found to be a felon by a court of law, a decision "made by the criminal justice system, which has its own unique safeguards and remedies against arbitrary, invidious or mistaken conviction."[16]

Despite disenfranchisement being bound up in the nation's inglorious racial history, courts have consistently refused to overturn felon exclusion statutes. This can be traced in many ways to the fact that, unlike explicitly racial policies of old, such policies can be justified using the logic of morality and personal responsibility. Because exclusion from the franchise is not explicitly based on race or gender, excluding categories of felons is seen as legitimate; it is considered "a matter of choices made, not burdens inherited."[17] Meanwhile, a growing group of blacks occupy a "shadowy form of citizenship," denied the central right of democracy and the primary mechanism through which they can express their political voice and wield their political power.[18]

The US Supreme Court's decision in *McCleskey v. Kemp* (1986) provides another landmark example of the way that racial liberalism has been expressed in criminal justice, though there are many others. In *McClesky*, the Court considered the case of a black man who had been convicted of murdering a white police officer and been sentenced to death. In his writ of habeas corpus, McClesky argued that the death penalty was administered by the state in a way that was racially biased, violating the Eighth and Fourteenth amendments. The now-famous study that McClesky's case was based on found that the race of the victim was associated with the likelihood that a death sentence would be imposed. Specifically, a capital punishment was handed down in 22 percent of cases involving black defendants and white victims, compared to eight percent of cases involving white defendants and white victims; one percent of cases with a black defendant and black victim; and three percent of cases involving white defendants and black victims.[19] As Justice Brennan noted in his dissenting opinion, the state of Georgia had a criminal code that gave different sentences to crimes depending on whether they had been committed by a black person or white person and depending on the race of the victim, "distinctions whose lineage traced back to the time of slavery."[20]

If there was a case that documented the role of race in the criminal justice system, this was it. In deciding the case, however, the Court started from the position that an equal protection violation must prove "the existence of *purposeful* discrimination" (emphasis added). Because McClesky could not show that racially disparate outcomes emerged from a *concerted* effort by the Georgia legislature to administer the death sentencing disproportionately based on race, the study did not "contribute anything of value" to his equal protection claims.

On this basis, colorblindness and the intent doctrine left untouched many punitive policy reforms that had a disproportionate impact on minorities—gang injunctions as we have already described; habitual offender laws that affect blacks disproportionately because blacks are more likely to have a prior record regardless of offending; drug zone laws that guaranteed more minorities would be triggered given that their urban locales were almost always near schools; stop-and-frisk practices that engaged in "location plus evasion" stops that were proxies for race. As legal scholar Ian Haney Lopez explains, "In the law enforcement context, colorblindness serves as more of a shield than a sword."[21] Indeed, policymakers designed policies that would pass the limited colorblind test while remaining willfully blind to their clearly racialized effects; numerous scholars have bemoaned the implications of "sentencing and related criminal justice policies that are ostensibly 'race neutral' [but] have in fact been seen over many years to have clear racial effects that could have been anticipated by legislators prior to enactment."[22]

With the racial liberalism ideology firmly institutionalized in legal, political, and social discourse, blacks and their allies had no language left to understand and challenge persistent and sometimes new inequalities tied to race. As Lani Guinier argues, because it "positioned the peculiarly American race 'problem' as a psychological and interpersonal challenge," racial liberalism rendered durable racial inequalities unintelligible in popular and legal discourse. And as we will see in the pages below, it also hurt custodial citizens' "capacity to decipher" the role of race within criminal justice.[23]

Without a robust alternative to the colorblind equality discourse, extreme racial disparities in contact with criminal justice are decoupled

from their complex social and economic foundations and therefore become attributable to higher black offending alone. The resulting "culture of denial about the continuing salience of race" created an opening
into which revised narratives around black inequality surfaced; lacking a
language of structural disparities, a powerful vocabulary of personal responsibility was able to take root.[24]

The black culture narrative and its prescriptive cousin, personal responsibility, have been used throughout modern history to explain persistent inequalities in schooling, employment, income, and other outcomes. Even among black elites, black youth are often depicted as having
squandered the gains made by the civil rights generation. According to
John McWhorter, Bill Cosby, Juan Williams, and others promoting the
"politics of respectability," blacks need to stop speaking ebonics, pull
their pants up, keep their noses clean, stay in school, and learn to be self-
reliant. Alluding to the disproportionate share of blacks behind bars,
Bill Cosby wonders aloud about the failure of black parenting: "I am
talking about these people who cry when their son is standing there in
an orange [prison] suit. Where were you when he was two? Where were
you when he was twelve? Where were you when he was eighteen, and
how come you didn't know that he had a pistol? In all of this work, we
cannot blame white people."[25]

In addition, Cosby and other promoters of the narrative of personal
responsibility and moral failures traded on the fact that residents in low-
income minority communities were more likely than other citizens to
be victimized by crime. In a recent survey by the Pew Research Center,
49 percent of blacks and Hispanics, relative to only 21 percent of whites,
reported that crime was a big problem in their local community.[26] Pointing to the fact that blacks themselves wanted aggressive policing in order to live in crime-free communities, preachers of the personal responsibility narrative gained cultural cover to discuss the problem of black
crime without appearing to denigrate blacks. Those espousing this ideology could enjoy legitimacy, in short, because blacks themselves ostensibly approved of it. They failed to mention that black residents of high-
crime communities also wanted more afterschool programs, more job
opportunities, and investments in housing and schools; in the same Pew
survey described above, blacks cited a lack of jobs in the local community as topping their list of concerns. As Ian Haney-Lopez remarked in
discussing this dynamic: "forced into a 'choice' between governmental

neglect versus neglect combined with aggressive policing, it seems cruel to defend such policing on the grounds it is 'preferred' by those trapped in impoverished nonwhite neighborhoods."[27]

But what makes these developments important for our purposes is not the adoption of a new narrative—the personal responsibility narrative had deep roots—but what it meant for how blacks themselves would come to understand why the people being handcuffed on the streets and sent to prison and jail were so disproportionately black and poor. Combined with colorblind rhetoric and jurisprudence, a vigorous personal responsibility narrative made it increasingly difficult for custodial citizens to define and articulate the role of race in the growing carceral state.

This is in some ways attributable to the design of the modern criminal justice system itself. Indeed, there are a number of ways that institutions of criminal justice are explicitly concerned with inculcating a sense of personal responsibility—rather than an understanding of systemic or racialized injustice—among custodial citizens. For instance, self-help psychology programs abound in prisons throughout the country, which emphasize structured processes of behavioral change. At one of the parole facilities where we conducted interviews in Trenton, roughly eight-foot-high signs lined the walls of otherwise sparse corridors. In bold green letters, they communicated ideas directed at the inmates like "make better choices" and "take responsibility for your life." A man or woman incarcerated in such facilities would find it virtually impossible to ignore the omnipresent message: that they alone were responsible for their outcomes in life, including the mistakes that led to their confinement. And a crucial—and well-known—precursor to release by the parole board is showing contrition and taking "ownership" for one's crime. Rather than seeing themselves as part of a broader system of racial or economic inequality—even if they acknowledge making poor choices within these social constraints—custodial citizens are explicitly encouraged to adopt a sense of themselves as personally lacking. As John McKendy notes of his interviews with inmates in a Canadian prison,

> The fact of their incarceration provided presumptive evidence of their standing as fitting objects of punishment—which is to say: culpable, rational agents who might have acted differently. The subject-position into which they were forcibly confined was one magnified by their agency. They were enjoined to speak of themselves as authors of their own actions, even as their lived experiences were often marked by powerlessness and victimization.[28]

Moreover, at the same time that they were receiving this formal message of personal agency, another informal lesson was being communicated. In our interview with Trevor, a 48-year-old black man, he reported that individuals leaving Bo Robinson at the completion of their sentence would sometimes hear correctional guards wave and jest, "[We'll] See you when you get back!" Thus, on the one hand, individuals had to accept the reason for their confinement as theirs alone, based on their mistakes and inability to "make better choices." On the other hand, "we'll see you when you get back" communicated that they were not individuals with agency at all, but were in fact powerless to control their own outcomes—that the system could, in the words of one of our interviewees, "just grab you, just on its own." Even as they left, Bo Robinson awaited their return.

It follows, then, that black custodial citizens seeking to make sense of racially inflected institutions and experiences are left struggling for a clear framework that integrates the ideology of personal responsibility with their lived experiences of structural disadvantage and racialized poverty. The result, as we describe in the following sections, is that institutions of criminal justice do help build the narrative of race in America. However, unlike the practices of criminal justice institutions described in chapter 3, practices that formally diminish voice and accountability, criminal justice institutions are formally equal while in virtually every way they exhibit racial inequality.[29] Thus, we find that black custodial citizens—who have learned both the informal and formal lessons of criminal justice—reveal far more variation in their conceptions of black citizenship and group standing broadly, and the import of race within criminal justice specifically, than is commonly assumed.

Race-based Alienation, Within and Beyond Criminal Justice: Testing a Causal Story

A belief in equality and opportunity has never been in abundant supply among black citizens in America, and the work of previous scholars has found a wide gap between the attitudes of black and white Americans. For example, John Hagan and colleagues find that black youth perceive significantly more criminal injustice than whites or Latinos, even controlling for socioeconomic and other differences.[30] In fact, the racial gap in perceptions of the criminal justice system is so cavernous that two scholars recently concluded that blacks and whites "inhabit different perceptual worlds" when it comes to racial fairness in this domain.[31] Consistent with these findings, most black respondents in our quantitative surveys had substantially divergent views from their white counterparts. For instance, in the BYP, 79 percent of young blacks agreed that police discriminate much more against black youth than white youth, compared to 63 percent of whites who said the same.[32]

However, on balance, black custodial citizens were even more pessimistic about racial equality and more dispirited with their treatment by government than other blacks. The measures we examined in chapter 5—feeling like a full and equal citizen and believing in equal chances to succeed— do not explicitly raise the issue of race. Among blacks, however, the differences by criminal justice contact are significant and substantial. Around 30 percent of blacks without criminal justice experience did not feel like "a full and equal citizen in this country with all the rights and protections other people have." By comparison, the proportion expressing this sense of limited citizenship rose to 40 percent for blacks who had been arrested, and to fully half of black youth who had been convicted (results are significantly different from those with no criminal justice exposure for those who have been convicted). Of blacks who had not had involuntary contact with criminal justice, just under a third did not believe everyone had equal chances to succeed; there is a statistically significant increase in disagreement with equal chances for those who had been stopped by police, arrested, or convicted (45%, 53%, and 51%, respectively).

On measures explicitly asking about racial treatment, respondents with criminal justice experience expressed a heightened belief that government cared less about the plight of blacks than about its white citizens or immigrants from other countries. For example, in figure 7.1 we see large divides within the black population in the view that "government treats most immigrants better than it treats most black people born in this country." On this item, there is nearly a twenty-point gap between blacks who had not come into contact with the criminal justice system and those with an arrest or conviction. This view was perhaps best articulated by Silas, one of our interviewees from Trenton, who responded to our question about feeling "full and equal" by saying:

> Absolutely not. Are you kidding? I feel like anybody that come from another country is a better citizen in the United States than I am. And that's the truth.

I mean, they can just come here—you can come here from Haiti—and you can be a better citizen than me.

James from Trenton was similarly frustrated:

Yeah, 'cause to me, I used to think, how could Mexicans come over or West Indians or whatever and get loans and no taxes, and I'm struggling and trying to get a business together and I can't? So I think people are treated differently. Why can other people from other countries come here and get a better start, and you're here and you're trying?

In the eyes of many black custodial citizens, government also reserved special neglect for blacks relative to whites. In one survey, we find large proportions of young blacks who believe that black youth get a worse education than whites, and that government responds differently to disease if more whites are affected. However, again we find a distinction between custodial and noncustodial black respondents. Relative to young people who have never had criminal justice contact, 27 percent more of those who have been convicted of a crime agree or strongly agree that "black youth receive a poorer education than white youth" and this group is

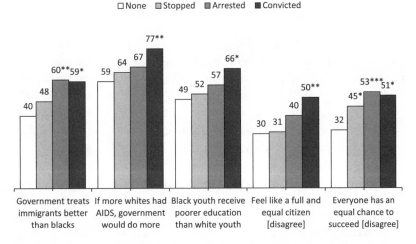

FIGURE 7.1. Blacks' perceptions of mistreatment by government (% agree or strongly agree) and full citizenship and equal chances (% disagree or strongly disagree), by criminal justice contact. Black respondents only. *$p < .05$; **$p < .01$; ***$p > .001$. *Source*: Cathy J. Cohen, "Black Youth Culture Survey," Black Youth Project, Chicago, IL, 2005, http://www.blackyouthproject.com.

fully 18 percent more likely to agree or strongly agree that "if more white people had AIDS, government would do more to find a cure."

That government neglected minorities came through just as clearly when speaking to custodial citizens directly; most believed that there were clear limits to the lengths to which government would go for their community. Joachim, a young Latino in Trenton, said simply that when it comes to whether minorities get treated equally by government, "It's a question that you and I already know. Of course not." To Abe, a young black man we interviewed in New Orleans, political officials viewed blacks as a group that was easily placated and dismissed. Discussing the Katrina disaster and how the government responded, Abe said:

> You got the whole rest of the world! And now you tell me they couldn't just get the government to come, save this one lost city? They could if they wanted to. They don't want. And I guess they don't have or they didn't want to be- cause if they have to, they would have did it. So, I'm guessing they didn't have to so they didn't. . . . They could've brought in the national guards, with just one little call. One little call. So why they didn't come? I don't know. Then, after the storm, they call this their help. . . . "Oh, we're just going to get ev- erybody some money and make them shut up, those black people, they like money. You give them money, make 'em shut up for a little while. Give them a couple of dollars, let 'em buy a new car, and they shut up."

Nor was Katrina the sole example. Blacks in our interviews detailed numerous instances where they believed government neglected or mis- treated black people. Cameron, a young West Indian man in Charlottes- ville, described his belief that black victims of crimes did not receive the same attention as murdered whites, drawing on the recent case of Mor- gan Harrington in Charlottesville, a young white woman who was kid- napped and later found dead:

> Because for instance a couple months, last year, they have a killing . . . with a little white dude and a black dude. The white dude had an AK47 and he go and shot this black dude. . . . They rallied like for two or three weeks and then it was gone. Then another instance in New York a couple years ago when the police shot up a young [black] dude on Empire Boulevard and they said that the young dude had a gun but when the police look there was no gun and they shot at the car and him and everything. And they rallied like for a couple

weeks and then it was gone. Now, the UVA instance with the [white] girl that went on for months and months and months and months. So different people get treated different way when it comes to certain things, and that ain't right because everybody, as the Constitution say, that everyone is created equal and should be treated equal regardless of race or gender and that is not how it is. It's really not.

Perceptions of this kind were not only about belonging to a marginalized racial group, but were often made in direct connection to subtle (and sometimes not so subtle) experiences within criminal justice. For example, Emmett reiterated Cameron's depiction of formal equality: "The law of the Constitution say you're supposed to be judged by your own peers." But in his experience, despite this formal grounding in equality, criminal justice didn't operate this way: "You're looking at the jury. There's no one up there who look like they grew up with me. . . . But these people are going to make a judgment on my life, it doesn't make sense to me."

Criminal justice contact also appears to heighten identification with one's disadvantaged racial group. Perceptions of exclusion and mistreatment often lead to a sense that one's fate in life is dependent on the chances of other blacks. When blacks' lives and chances are "overdetermined by the ascriptive feature of race," individual differences are submerged and perceived group interests serve as a proxy for one's own individual interests and chances.[33] Criminal justice exposure, we find, has a strong association with linked fate perceptions, the belief that one's individual opportunities are linked to the entire racial group. In both surveys, those who have had contact with the criminal justice system are more likely to believe that "what happens to black men in this country will have something to do with what happens in your own life" (AAMS) or "what happens to most black people in this country affects me" (BYP). In the AAMS, 52 percent of black respondents who have not experienced arrest or imprisonment concur. By comparison, 57 percent of those who have been arrested ($p < .05$) and 66 percent of those who have spent time in prison or jail believe this to be true ($p < .001$). Among the black young people in the BYP sample, 64 of those who reported no criminal justice interventions expressed linked fate compared to 81 percent of blacks who had been convicted ($p < .05$; linked fate among those who were stopped or arrested were not statistically significant).

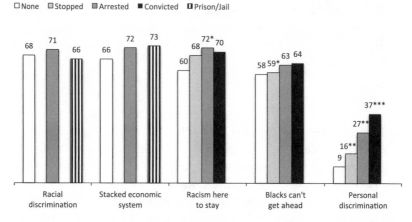

□None ▤Stopped ▥Arrested ■Convicted ▯Prison/Jail

FIGURE 7.2. Blacks' views of racial equality and discrimination (%), by criminal justice contact. Black respondents only. Items include: "Racial discrimination is a big problem for black men today," "America's economic system is stacked against blacks," "Racism will be eliminated during your lifetime" (never or not likely); "It is hard for young black people to get ahead because they face so much discrimination" (strongly agree or agree); and "how often you are discriminated against because of race" (often or very often). *$p < .05$; **$p < .01$; ***$p > .001$. Sources: Cathy J. Cohen, "Black Youth Culture Survey," Black Youth Project, Chicago, IL, 2005, http://www.blackyouthproject.com; "African American Men Survey," Washington Post/Kaiser Family Foundation/Harvard University, June 2006, http://www.kff.org/kaiserpolls/upload/7526.pdf.

Notably, however, we did not find equally robust differences between custodial and noncustodial citizens in more general perceptions of discrimination in America. Once we move beyond perceptions of poor treatment by government, equality of chances and citizenship, and linked fate, however, the distinctions between custodial and noncustodial blacks are less clear. The largest differences have to do with personal discrimination based on race. On this measure, custodial blacks are distinguished from those without personal criminal justice experiences (fig. 7.2). On many other measures, however, differences were few. Contact with criminal justice did not heighten agreement that "racial discrimination is a big problem for black men today," or "it is hard for young blacks to get ahead because they face so much discrimination," or the belief that "America's economic system is stacked against blacks." Though blacks who had been arrested were more likely to agree that "racism will never be or was not likely to be eliminated during my lifetime," most blacks (irrespective of custodial status) took a racially pessimistic view of the end of racism.

Unfortunately, the surveys we document here do not ask about illegal drug use or other criminal behavior. Nor do they include a panel akin to the Add Health survey. We are therefore precluded from conducting the causal analyses we provide in the previous chapter. We are, however, able to conduct a more straightforward assessment of whether the impact of criminal justice remains when we take other differences between custodial and noncustodial citizens into account, such as class background and gender.

In order to account for potentially confounding differences and to systematically parse out the relationship between criminal justice contact and racial beliefs, we again estimate a series of multiple regressions in which we control for relevant factors (see fig. 7.3).[34] These models provide some evidence that criminal justice contacts are associated with blacks' generalized beliefs about equality in America, the possibilities and limitations they faced, the standing of their group, and how responsive their government was to black needs. Respondents who have experienced coercive interventions from the state perceive government mistreatment to be a much more pressing problem for blacks as a whole, and they are significantly more pessimistic about equality in America. On balance, black custodial citizens thought and felt differently about the scope of equality in America than either whites or black citizens who had never felt the strong arm of the state. And yet, the differences are more modest than we expected and sometimes reveal insignificant differences. The perception that one's fate was linked to that of one's racial group was no longer significant once controls were introduced in the AAMS; however, in the BYP, blacks who had experienced a conviction remained more likely to express linked fate than those without criminal justice involvement after controls.

To explain these patterns, we return to our interview subjects. Throughout our interviews, issues of race were a recurrent thread. However, the narrative of race was often interwoven with other stories—those based on class, or geography, or other points of disadvantage. Similarly, many of our interviewees did not think explicit racism held them or their communities back. More than a few said being stopped by police regularly and with little cause was "not a profiling thing . . . this is the way it is, you living in a crime-ridden area." Others emphatically rejected the role of racism as an explanation for why the schools in their cities were of worse quality than the surrounding suburbs: "And you gonna hear a lotta people here say, it's the race thing. But as your money, your

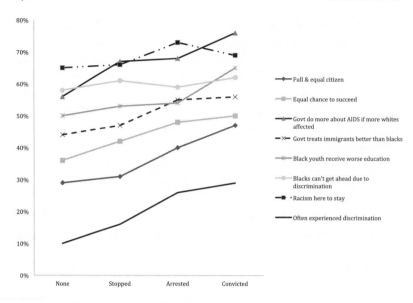

FIGURE 7.3. Blacks' perceptions of government mistreatment, racial equality, and discrimination, controlling for confounders. Blacks respondents only. Items include: "I feel like a full and equal citizen" (strongly disagree or disagree); "In the US, everyone has an equal chance to succeed" (strongly disagree or disagree); "If more whites had AIDS, government would do more to find a cure" (strongly agree or agree); "Government treats most immigrants better than it treats most black people" (strongly agree or agree); "Black youth receive a poorer education than white youth" (strongly agree or agree); "Racism will be eliminated during your lifetime" (never or not likely); "It is hard for young black people to get ahead because they face so much discrimination" (strongly agree or agree); and "how often you are discriminated against because of race" (often or very often). *Source*: Cathy J. Cohen, "Black Youth Culture Survey," Black Youth Project, Chicago, IL, 2005, http://www.blackyouthproject.com.

financial status increase, you'll be able to move your children out there, whether you're white, black, or Spanish. Into the suburbs and enter those schools . . . if you can afford it, come on all aboard . . . it's not a racist thing, it's about money."

In addition, the ways in which race was articulated and contextualized varied within our population. In our qualitative evidence, we uncover some important additional variation—two additional and opposing transcripts—which we believe explains the modest effects in the quantitative data. The interviews reveal divergent narratives that together likely "muddled" the results. The real story of racial learning emerges in these rich narratives, to which we now turn.

Intersections of Disadvantage

In contrast to the blunt questions available in our survey data, our interviews allowed us to uncover more complex relationships between criminal justice and racial learning. For most of our black and Latino interview subjects, the belief that blacks in America do not have equal status sprang from an admixture of race with place, poverty, and criminal record. In our interviews, references to race were often accompanied by references to being low-income, being from a certain part of town, being without a job or home, being "dark-skinned," or being from a family without a good name. Disadvantage based on any one of these things did not simply compound the others nor were they distinct; instead, it was the whole package that defined their citizenship. The intersection of these statuses thus did not merely condense their marginality; it created a new cleavage. As a result, our interviewees frequently expressed conflicting ideas about the role of race, and often lacked a coherent language for describing differences that were about race, but also beyond race. Thus, in many of our interviews, it became clear that disentangling views based solely on race from other features of custodial citizenship was complex, if not impossible. David asked one of us: "How come a person who looks like me can get all the bad things happen and a person who looks like you can open up doors for you with no problem?" When we asked David whether this had to do with race or gender or money, he replied, "a little of all, honestly."

We heard similar things from Cameron, a black man in his early thirties raised in Barbados and currently living in Charlottesville. He came to the States as a young adult and spent a decade in prison shortly after arriving. We spoke to him eight months after he was released, having served time in three different prisons. He was worried about his green card expiring and not being able to get it back because of his criminal history. During our interview, Cameron often drifted back and forth between describing the mark of his color and the mark of his criminal record, between his racial membership and being a custodial citizen. To him, being a custodial citizen owed in part to being black, but the criminal record (not being black per se) defined and furthered his proscribed chances. It was clear that to him, like many others with whom we spoke, his criminal record was a binding roadblock to a good and decent life—being able to support a family, having access to a green card, and being able to move freely without being "watched." At the same time, though, he felt that being black had limited his chances to avoid the drug trade in the first place and made him more likely to be seen as dangerous in the eyes of the state and society no matter what he did.

To Cameron, race and a criminal record are not separate pathways of disadvantage but inextricably entangled. He believes that, as a black man, society sees him as suspicious and dangerous: "We are drug addicts, dope dealers, baby killers, murderers and they [we] can't change. . . . So you know, they look at us as subhuman." But Cameron believes this perception is unfair not because it applies too broad a stereotype but be-cause, as a black man, his choices had been limited from the get-go. He went on to say that black men often faced limited economic prospects that made law breaking seem like the only option: "We surviving the only way we know how, in a sense. And I know a lot of black dudes that sell drugs because it is a way of fast cash or it is a way of they surviving the only way that they ever knew."

For Cameron, being a black man also makes the significance of his criminal record symbolically greater, by providing a constant and trou-bling reminder that society sees him as criminal. For instance, he de-scribed the short jaunt on public transportation he had taken on his way to our interview: "I just catch the trolley here and the whole back seat was open up [but] when white folks get in, they rather stand up than come back there. Miss, I ain't did you anything! . . . They just look at you like, 'Damn, he Black. I'm scared.'"

From Cameron's perspective, we saw clearly the multidimensional quality of marginality: being black made the world outside see him as dangerous; his status as a black man with limited opportunities had led him to sell drugs; as a custodial citizen, he had limited opportunities to get a decent job; and his criminal history continued to affect how he was perceived by society. All of these elements were at play, and each edge of his status was sharpened by the others.

The intersectional nature of being black, with a criminal record, and from a poor background often meant that respondents did not attribute their experiences to race alone; the role of race in their lives was difficult to pinpoint. However, we think an equally significant reason for these "muddled" results has to do with the conflicting messages that custo-dial citizens receive through criminal justice institutions themselves. On the one hand, these individuals saw clearly that those coming into invol-untary contact with criminal justice—those pursued by police, treated

as suspects, and confined—were mainly poor, minority men from similar circumstances. They were raised in communities where many had
hostile relationships with police, and where widely held community narratives instructed that they were targets of a punitive state and did not
share in equal opportunities extended to other social groups. And once
incarcerated, they received messages that they were not in control of
their fortunes. (As Cameron told us: "Now when I get out, [the prison
authorities are] going to tell the precinct that I am out so now the police there already know that I am coming out on this day so they already know to keep an eye out for me. So why are they keeping an eye
on me when I finish my time?") On the other hand, penal institutions
offered a steady stream of messages emphasizing individual culpability
and agency. For instance, some of our interview subjects described being required to take courses in anger management and accept personal
responsibility for their crime as a condition of parole. These counter-
posing messages—that criminal justice institutions targeted blacks and
that each individual is ultimately culpable for his or her rule-breaking
choices—meant that two often-conflicting narratives developed. Each of
these two racial narratives—the first relating to racial domination and
the second to personal responsibility—was voiced by a group of our respondents (and often within the same interview).

"A Gentler Kind of Genocide": Racial Domination and Criminal Justice

The first of the complex narratives we encountered was a racial-
domination perspective, centered on the view that racial inequalities of
the twenty-first century were rooted in intentional strategies to maintain white power and keep minorities down. In this view, racial progress was discounted and racial domination would continue even if some
things were allowed to change, as new systems were designed to achieve
the same ends (systematic racial oppression) through more sophisticated
means. The criminal justice system was a key part of this modern strategy of racial containment, targeted toward keeping blacks out of the
mainstream—from jobs, housing, and political influence.

This perspective was typified by Xavier, Reggie, and Renard, the
three young black men who we met in New Orleans. The three were close
friends who had grown up together in a small, mostly black Louisiana
town that had been disproportionately affected by aggressive policing

and the growth of incarceration. As they described it, nearly every person in their neighborhood had some sort of criminal record, mainly from drug offenses—they told us that "Come on Vacation, Leave on Probation" was the unofficial town slogan—and they themselves described being stopped by police "almost every other day." Renard had just been released from prison a month ago and had a felon record for possession of marijuana and a firearm; he was still under correctional supervision and referred to his situation as "They givin' you ten years to mess up" because in addition to the two and a half years in prison, he had to complete two and a half years of parole and after that five years of probation. Neither Reggie nor Xavier had a felony record, but they had both been stopped and searched many times, and both had spent time in the local jail. "We ain't no bad dudes," they told us. Though they felt frequently targeted by police, they were also involved in programs that help feed the homeless, and together formed a gospel rap group to spread a positive message about Christianity.

How did they see the role of race in the world around them? When we asked them about racial progress over the past fifty years, they acknowledged that, compared to a day in the life of their parents, opportunities for blacks in America had gotten a little better. They shouted and chanted "Obama!" and believed that his historic election stood as evidence that some things do change. As black men, they felt a sense of linked fate with the nation's first black president and with other blacks. They told us: "Every black man comes out the hood! I know Obama, he ain't like I was. But I know he came out the hood though. He probably came out the *sophisticated* hood. You feel what I'm saying? We all experience the same thing but different ways."

Yet, at the same time, they were quick to describe the current status of blacks in America as still deeply unequal, even systematically oppressed. In fact, throughout their conversation, the three drew on language that drew direct parallels to the historically subjugated position of black slaves in the American South:

> XAVIER: It's changing slowly, but at the same time, we still ain't too far from
>   where it was . . . because when we were reading my history how it was,
>   people couldn't really do nothing.
> RENARD: It's like we slaved in a different way. The prison system slave. It's a
>   way of being a good slavery.
> XAVIER: You a legal slave now, once you go to prison, 'cause you workin' for

free. Pickin' they crops, doing everything, cleaning up the highway. That's
what they were [doing]—that's what they were doing back in the day. . . .
RENARD: It might be—not be—might not be getting whipped physically, but
mentally you getting whipped.

Invoking the imagery of Angola, Louisiana's most infamous prison,
where the mode of prison farm still operated (mainly white prison
guards, called "overseers," rode on horseback watching over mainly
black prison inmates working in the field), they directly connected prison
to the history of slaves picking crops, referring to prison as little more
than a "good slavery."

How did Xavier and his friends arrive at this narrative, which stands
at such odds with the postracial narrative they celebrated in the wake of
Obama's electoral victory? The three youths had experienced two things
that provide essential context for understanding their perspective. First,
they perceived few true opportunities for advancement available to them
and to those like them. Reggie bristled with frustration that he and others in his neighborhood "can't get a job or nothing," and that not being
able to get a job is "what's killin' me." He explained that his mother did
not graduate from high school, and neither did he.

The second, and perhaps more important, context for this narrative
was the direct and unwanted experience that the three had had with
criminal justice authorities, particularly police, through which they
gleaned lessons about how the government valued and treated them. For
instance, Xavier described how one day he was walking up to his friend's
porch and all of a sudden the police said, "get him!" and jumped on him,
then charged him with disturbing the peace. When he contested the
charge, the officers who had tackled him to the ground did not show up
in court so the charge was dismissed. But he still had to pay court fines,
saying, "That's just a way to get money out of you the quick way." He ad-
amantly rejected the idea that he had some responsibility for the encounter and argued with his friend when he told him that he messed things up:
"How did I mess that up when I'm just walking by my cousin's house?!!
I ain't mess nothing up!" These and other experiences in their adolescence had taught them that some things were rigged. Recall Renard saying, "We're targets. We got that bull's eye on our back as soon as we're
born." They had very few examples within their own lives of being able
to take control over a situation or of being free to make choices that did
not ultimately all lead to the same (lousy) outcome.

In short, they had no evidence to help them conclude that the system was not there to hold them back. The attention their communities received from governing authorities always seemed to be from the criminal justice system rather than from the state's distributive hand (recall from the opening to this book how one of these young men noted that they don't know the good side of government), a system that just told them to stay silent ("when you're with them, you got to shut up") and treated them with little regard ("it's like they're hunting tigers or something"). Most of their friends would ultimately wind up with some sort of a record and would then see their economic prospects further diminished. From this starting point, they easily slid into the language of racial domination, explaining that the cycle of joblessness and criminal justice involvement is purposeful, functioning to limit black opportunities and co-opt black labor:

> XAVIER: They ain't givin' you no job, so you're going to sell drugs so we can convict you and throw away your whole life, throw away your whole life.
>
> REGGIE: What you're going to do? What you're going to do if you ain't got no job and every job you went to you got turned down? . . .
>
> XAVIER: You goin' to go the easy way and make money! They make you turn to drugs.
>
> RENARD: Like, brainwash you. So they can lock you up and make money off of you . . . from the prison standpoint and use your services.
>
> REGGIE: Basically, the police putting dope back in the hood. . . . That's how it is, though. That's how it is, though. It's one big circle. . . .
>
> RENARD: Instead of giving you that job while you're free, they're going to lock you up, and use your same time for free.
>
> XAVIER: The jobs used to be open, but most of the jobs are to the people who was in jail who [are in the] halfway house now where they can work and instead of paying them, give them that $7.25 minimum wage, they give them three or four dollars . . . three or four dollars when you ought to pay the full price. . . . They know you're going to work twice as hard as somebody who out here in the free world.
>
> REGGIE: I think the police put the dope back in the hood, personally. Basically, the government is the kingpin. . . . I wanna see where they putting all those drugs that they seizing.

The racial oppression narrative was not only articulated by our interviews with blacks in the South; the views of Trina and Silas in Trenton were guided by similar logics. In comparison to Xavier, Reggie, and Renard, these individuals did not hail from impoverished or drug-infested neighborhoods and had had comparatively fewer contacts with criminal justice. Trina was solidly middle class, with a college degree in psychology and a successful career in social work. She was forty-five years old before she was arrested and convicted for the first time after a personal catastrophe (her son's drowning accident) plunged her into drug addiction; she served sixteen days for a felony drug offense. Silas had a successful military career, having served in Bosnia and Panama, and had at one point been middle class with a stable marriage and a nice house. Like Trina, Silas had his first contact with criminal justice fairly late in life. In his case, he had taken a plea deal for five years of probation after a fight escalated and he pulled out a gun. Both Trina and Silas spoke with more confidence than many of our other interviewees about a range of topics, commenting on issues from city government to recent statistics on incarceration, and both had exhibited more agency in their dealings with government than most of our interview subjects (Silas had sought to get his record expunged and Trina successfully got her position as a social worker back after employing the help of her congressman).

Trina felt she had been treated fairly by police, many of whom she had known professionally prior to her arrest. Despite acknowledging that she had been engaging in illegal drug use, however, she reads her experience as part of a system designed to contain blacks; just seconds after describing her impartial treatment by police, she said: "This is the way that this system makes sure that every black person . . . this is the way they keep us down. They wanna make sure that every single one of us has some sort of record." She elaborated on that "system" when we asked her why she thinks black men have a higher chance of winding up in prison, saying confidently:

> That's the way the system wants it. It's just a more gentler form of genocide, to me. And you know, because that's what it is. It helps keep procreation down for the black race. . . . I think when it comes to black men, this country is threatened. I really do. I really believe that. 'Cause there's a lot of talent. There's a lot of intelligence in the black race and if these black men have had what any—well, what most other people who do well had had—if they had you know, if it wasn't like the broken families that we come from, and if it wasn't like a broken school system, then they would have excelled. And they would have been in places where they were feared to be. . . . I think this coun-

try fears black males. So you keep 'em corralled and you keep 'em locked up. You keep their spirits broken.

To Trina, racial progress is a fiction; she refused to say blacks' prospects had improved since the 1960s: "I don't think I would use the term 'better.' I say they just released or loosened the chains. They just loosened them up a little bit. The chains are still there. They're still there."

Silas echoed Trina's views, and was adamant that black involvement in criminal justice was part of a broader system of racial oppression that sought to extract cheap labor from blacks and to hoard economic and political opportunities for whites. Speaking of felony disenfranchisement as part of a larger scheme of racialized social control that operated through criminal justice, he said: "Legislators have figured out, 'Well this is how we hold the black people back. This is how we can keep 'em down. This is how we can hold the Spanish people back. This is how we keep 'em down. 'Cause white Americans deserve these jobs!'" The collateral consequences of a felony conviction—from felon disenfranchisement to exclusion from public housing to the difficulties of securing work following release from prison—were conceived of as an organized effort to limit the life chances of minorities:

> I can't [vote]. I cannot. That's a nice system. Because if there's more blacks
> and they all fall in the same system as me, that means if you run for governor,
> you don't have to worry about these blacks and the Spanish really voting for
> you, because they can't vote. "I already got that locked up. I already figured
> out that part of the system. I don't have to worry about the majority of blacks
> and Hispanics, because I already got them locked up." [*Why do you think that
> is?*] . . . "If we don't do something to control this plague or this outbreak . . .
> they gonna wind up taking over the United States. So before they end up tak-
> ing over, we gotta figure out a system, where they can't take over. A legal-
> ized system." And what better way to get control over voting than to come up
> with a system where you can't vote? What other way to control jobs than to
> come up with a system where you can't get a job because we can use your past
> against you? What other way to control housing than to say, "Hey, unfortu-
> nately, we can't take you in housing because you have a criminal record."

This sentiment, that whites use the criminal justice system to "corral" and contain minorities, was part of the racial narrative outlined by many of our respondents. In describing the logic behind the criminal justice system, respondents often attributed a motive of racial dominance:

> Patrice (young black woman, Charlottesville): Once you do something, they automatically want to fingerprint you. I'm not racist or nothing, but they say "this the white man's state." That's what a lot of people say. So once they see a black person doing something, they automatically getting fingerprinted. So if you do something or they think you did something, they can automatically get to you quick.

> Cordell (young black man, Charlottesville): Me, I call it. . . . Hmph, you don't want to know what I call it. . . . Population control. If you control a man, then you can control his family. If his kids grow up without a father, then his kids grow up with resentment and anger, then they have to learn. . . . And if they don't learn it fast enough, they end up in the system, and there go another male.

> David (black man, Charlottesville, referring to Obama's election): So the best way to keep the animals in they cages is to give them what they want. But don't give them everything they want 'cause see, the animal is thinking, and when I say animals, I'm talking about African Americans, I'm talking about the white people that are out there homeless on the street, I'm talking about everybody that don't have the means to survive day to day. And the best way to keep them animals under control is to give them what they want, but don't give them everything they want, just tell them what they want to hear.

"They fail they own self": Individualism, Personal Responsibility, and Choices

Despite the prevalence of the intentional discrimination narrative among a subset of our interviewees, there were many who voiced an entirely different set of transcripts. In addition to the racial oppression narrative, there was a second way that some black custodial citizens made sense of their devastated communities and personal misfortune. In contrast to the ideas of race-based oppression and control outlined in the previous section, some responded to limited prospects by turning inward and putting even more stock in control over their choices and their lives, believing they were the authors of their destinies. This perspective centered around the individual, personal responsibility, and God. A substantial few, while they were in the minority among our respondents, voiced their feeling that blacks, particularly young black men today, were "the first ones to cry, 'race, race, race,'" blaming their lot in life on discrimination. They were incredulous at the blacks who blamed the "system" and seemed not to want more out of life than stealing and robbing. Luke, a middle-aged black man from Trenton who had spent much of his youth in prison for armed robbery, described the blacks he knew as "always trying to . . . you know, affirmative action and shit like that. . . . When I was in prison, I always used to hear guys talking about the white man, 'you know, if the white man hadn't oppressed me, I wouldn't be in this position.' But 95 percent of black men [who] are in jail for murder, they did not kill a white man—they killed a black man. They always looking for a scapegoat." Luke believed that "If you need help, you gotta be willing to help yourself."

Those who held this view often recounted similar stories to those told by Xavier, Reggie, and Silas—of foster care, of growing up on the streets, and of lives marked by disappointments and unsteady work. However, rather than attributing their situation to a repressive state, they believed that blacks themselves played a significant role in their economic and political marginality, and they were not reluctant to point out the personal failings of black youth and black fathers. For example, Sarah, a black woman we interviewed in Trenton, did not think blacks had a harder time getting ahead in America: "It's only what you make it. It's on the individual, whether you black, white, blue, orange, or pink. You can make it if you put your foot forward and go." According to Sarah, blacks therefore had only themselves to blame for persistent inequality: "Black men are hard-headed. They hard-headed. They just don't get it. Some of 'em just don't get it. They like doing the same thing over and over and over and over and over." Darcy, a military veteran in his late forties whom we interviewed in Charlottesville, was especially critical of black youth, who he described as "a rough generation" that "don't want to work at all. . . . It's just a lot of these kids rather go make a thousand dollars a day and to risk their—put their life on the line—you know, spend the rest of their life in jail rather than go work a nine to five."

As we discuss in more detail below, this perspective was not always a straightforward "bootstraps" ideology, however; much of the time, it was accompanied by a very plain, and often times pain-filled, appreciation for the barriers faced by poor blacks in their communities. Thus, while adherents to this view often ridiculed people like Renard, Xavier, Trina, Reggie, and Silas for "crying race" and flatly rejected a race oppression narrative to explain the situation of blacks, there was significant overlap in the degree to which they believed that government had turned its back on their communities and agreement that "politicians don't care about the low income." Like Reggie and Silas, they too acknowledged that their communities were beset by evaporated job prospects and believed that government couldn't be relied on for help. In short, their alienation sprung from the same source, but rather than seeing inequality as part of a larger system of racial control, as Trina, Xavier, and Silas did, they believed that blacks themselves played a large role in furthering their already bleak situation, not working hard enough, and "loving the streets" too much. How they sought to resolve this sense of political alienation was to "go it alone," seek God, better oneself through education, or some combination.

Quinton was one of our most ardent defenders of the personal responsibility narrative. We spoke to Quinton, a recovering addict who is physically disabled, in Trenton. He dropped out of high school, but was trying to get his GED and had two adult daughters in college. After spending time in juvenile corrections, he went to the "workhouse" at eighteen, a world he described as very scary "'cause my mom couldn't come get me no more." By the time he was older, he estimates, 85 percent of the people he knew either were or had been locked up. Struggling with addiction for most of his life, he is now receiving treatment and is "done with the law" (not getting into trouble anymore) and he is proud to have voted for the first time in the Obama election. Despite describing the help he is getting from many government programs (Section 8, drug treatment, and welfare), though, he still expressed a feeling of being alone in the world: "I think whatever happens to me—I don't think nobody out here to help me. That's how I feel about the system. Nobody not here to help me. So I got to do it best by myself." This view stems from the sense—which we discussed in the last chapter—that government does not understand the problems of people like him, and he implores government to "live a day in our shoes and see how rough it is." He described how hard it is to find work, how opportunities to learn a trade have declined and "computers takin' over now," and that with fewer unskilled jobs, you "can't afford to feed your children." But he also implored black people to "be responsible" and believes they can get ahead "if they wanna work hard enough."

Quinton believes in individual choices and in his own culpability: "If I wasn't doin' it in the first place, it wouldn't have happened, so I got what

I deserved. You know. . . . And that's how the system work, you know. I
mean, you do something bad, you gotta pay for it. It been like that forever."
He believes that the ticket up and out is education: "If you got a good education, you can go anywhere you wanna go, do anything you wanna do.
Be anybody you wanna be." He frowns on people who refuse to accept responsibility or fall back on easy justifications for their behavior, describing a time in his youth when he had made these excuses himself:

> When I was out there doing all the bad things, I was always "the white man this,
> the white man that, that white man this" and it wasn't them, it was me. It was
> me doing what I was doing—always getting in trouble. I'm blaming them for
> what I'm doing. Now that my mind is clear, it's up to me—whatever I do, it's my
> fault. If I get into trouble, it's my fault. So I can't blame nobody for my action.

Carlton, an older black man who was born and raised in Charlottesville, held many of the same views as Quinton. He quickly turned pessimistic when he described being racially profiled, being turned down for
jobs sweeping floors or bagging groceries because of his criminal conviction, and experiencing a variety of other things he perceives as race-
based aggressions. He recalled in vivid detail how blacks were kept out
of the schools and university before civil rights, how black neighborhoods were torn down during urban renewal and blacks were scattered
to public housing, and how most whites "don't want black men fooling
with the white women. 'Why should my daughter fool with some low life
N—?'" For most of the interview, Carlton spoke of injustices he has seen
visited on the poor, the homeless, and minorities that make it a struggle to get affordable housing and decent wages, and he went on at length
about how blacks in his generation were not pushed in school and had
few opportunities to succeed. Yet, rather than seeing himself as part of a
broader system of racial inequality—even if he acknowledged structural
constraints—Carlton adopted a narrative of his own intrinsic failings and
the failings of other black men. For Carlton, like Quinton, Sarah, Darcy,
and others in our sample, each example of structural inequality or racial
profiling was followed by a vigorous commitment to ideas of personal
uplift: "You can't give up. It might not happen exactly the way you want
it to happen, but eventually it's gonna happen. You have to have hope
and faith." Even if much of what Carlton had seen and experienced went
against a belief in principles of individualism, his commitment to personal responsibility was undeterred.

When it comes to black men today, Carlton agreed with Silas and Reggie and Trina, saying black men are targeted and "labeled from the get-go" as drug dealers: "If you label people right from the get go—if you tell them they ain't no good from the get go—they start believing that." But here again, while Carlton recognized the code of prohibitions (discussed in chapter 5) that guided how black custodial citizens moved through their lives, he dealt with the resulting alienation by inscribing agency to black men, saying they just need to work harder, change their mindset, and accept responsibility if things do not work out:

> I think many of us black mens today make the wrong choices. Because we don't want to make that change. You have to make that change. A lot of black young men bring problems on themselves. It's not that the system failed. It's they fail they own self. They got the opportunity . . . if you asked me that question thirty years ago, it would be a totally different answer, because I would say the system failed them. But the system don't fail you no more. It's up to you to make something of youself these days, and if you don't? Oh, well. Then that's on you.

Between them, Carlton and Quinton had accrued several decades of incarceration, and neither was a stranger to desperate economic times. But they resisted faulting factors beyond themselves and believed that the answer was personal uplift and behavioral change.

Making Sense of Inequality and Personal Responsibility

While some of those we interviewed subscribed to one or the other narrative, most of our interview conversations were marked by a commitment to both. In one breath, the same individual would speak forcefully about the need for blacks to be accountable for their own choices and just a few minutes later detail how their communities had been kept down and out. When pressed on the possible contradiction, many would talk about the real social conditions they and other blacks faced—the lack of adequate jobs, decent housing, and poor and underfunded schools—which in turn structured the (often poor) choices that some blacks make. Even many of those who felt that individuals should take more personal responsibility for their crimes—and more broadly, for their successes and failures in life—would often also talk about feeling hemmed in by stagnant opportunity and describe racial discrimination as a salient feature in their lives. In fact, many were quick to point out that the two logics were not only compatible, but linked: blacks who broke the law had made poor choices, but often this was because the choices that were available to them were limited by few employment opportunities, minimum-wage jobs, inadequate education and training, and limited social supports. Many young blacks were getting involved in crime and turning to drugs to make ends meet or because "they don't know any other way of life" and "that's all they know."

Our interviews with Jerry, Michael, Miles, and Daryl exemplify how custodial citizens relied on strands of both narratives to help them to navigate their complex reality. Jerry, a fifty-eight-year-old black man, had been in near-constant custody since the age of twelve, when he was stopped by police for the first time. First arrested at thirteen, he had been convicted of ten misdemeanors and two felonies by the time we interviewed him and he had served multiple stints in jail, which he referred to as the "workhouse," though never prison. Like Quinton, Jerry suffered a serious disability and spent years struggling to overcome drug addiction. He had received little help to get back on his feet, having been released "like a bird into the wild" after serving time. Jerry described many of the black men he knew as prone to "brag about their experiences" to those around them, and as being quick to "cry the blues . . . you gonna hear a lot about, people hollering about, 'It's the white man's fault. It's the white man's fault' . . . and this is what they boo-hoo about. And I don't want to hear that. I don't wanna talk, have those type of conversations with nobody." He accepts that a racial order exists, but argues that outcomes are the result of personal choices: "Yes, white men, they are the powers that be; they did what they supposed to do to get where they are and that's just how it is. And I accept that."

At the same time, Jerry's focus on individual choice and educational uplift comfortably coexists with the knowledge that too many in his community never receive that message. Jerry described the poverty and joblessness that beset his community as primary causes of crime, much like Xavier and Reggie: "There's no jobs. If you had a job, where you worked every day and earned a decent paycheck, you wouldn't have to commit crimes. So they out there selling drugs, they out there robbing this and that to buy drugs. . . . You need jobs. There's nowhere to work around here, nowhere in Trenton." In fact, despite Jerry's assertion that blacks were simply "boo-hooing" about race, he bore witness to the desperate conditions faced by many, including those in his neighborhood. Jerry talked for some time about how Trenton's job market evaporated, the crack cocaine market emerged, how families and communities were destroyed by both, and the absence of any activism to confront the decimation that resulted:

> Trenton started deteriorating in the 80s. . . . Factories and shops started closing down, moving out, and then there was no jobs . . . and then this crack cocaine came in. . . . I looked around my community and it had totally deteriorated. It was consumed by drug abuse, gangs, poverty, and all this stuff. And there was nobody doing anything about this. There was nobody talking about how do we revitalize this and change this and make this happen. I'm like "Wow, what's going on here?"

Yet after he described in detail how his community began to slip, and eventually cascade, into what it is today, Jerry resolutely stated:

> [My] life per se turned out the way that it did because of my choices. . . . And I accept where I went wrong. . . . See, I can't blame the government, the police force, or whatever for whatever happened to me in my criminal life. That was on me. That was choices that I made; if I wouldn't have broke the law, I wouldn't never had no contact with the police.

Despite the multiple forces beyond his control that he sees as playing a role in his community and his own experiences, including chronic joblessness, addiction, marital dissolution, depression, and disability, Jerry came back to his own agency and responsibility, separating his situation from the larger context, the result of his choices alone. While he believes that crime is the result of complex conditions that go beyond immoral choices, he traces his own dealings with criminal justice back to his own poor decisions.

More generally, Jerry believes that blacks themselves ultimately play the primary role in determining where they end up: "But I really see that with a lot of people of low income, poverty, whatever—they have to understand that they play a part in their own misery, they really do." Even though he agrees that government neglects black people and their communities, describing at length how the governor in his state ignores inner-city schools while lavishing resources on suburban schools, he reserves his ire for blacks themselves, saying that many blacks just think "it is easier to be a junkie or a bum than it is to do the right thing."

Jerry's views describe a complex environment, one beset by both individual wrong turns and desperate conditions. The intermixing of these narratives, however, also reflect the lessons of criminal justice institu-

tions. Jerry and others directly echoed the explicit messages of penal institutions to "make better choices" but also drew on their less overt, but
no less obvious, messages: that the police stopped people who looked
like them for "fitting a description" and that prisons and jails confined
people for unlawful behavior but did so disproportionately for those who
hailed from their racial group.

In our interviews, many older blacks like Jerry would wax nostalgic
about programs that used to exist for adolescents in their communities
but that had been shelved and recall with lament how jobs that used to
offer decent wages had migrated out of their communities, leaving nothing for kids to do other than get involved in street life—the same street
life they now identified as being the downfall of their young people today. Miles, a middle-aged man we spoke with in Trenton, played semipro
football until an injury took him out of the minor leagues and he had to
"really live life." He talked at length about the way things have changed
since he was a kid, making things even harder for those coming up. When
we asked him why he thought so many black men were in prison, he de-
lineated the contours of what he saw as a nearly impossible set of choices
for young men in poor communities like his:

> When you have no jobs and things like that, people are going to embrace
> the one thing [crime]. No one's going to starve, so if you're going out there
> and people aren't hiring you because of the color of your skin or whatever,
> who wants to starve? Who wants to see their family without? . . . How can
> you tell a kid it's not good to sell drugs, when I can't get a job at McDonald's,
> working minimum wage? And I can stand on the corner and in fifteen min-
> utes make the same amount of money as what I can make at McDonalds?
> And they won't even *give* me a job at McDonalds! And these kids are really,
> they're looking at it like that. Society made that. It's about the haves and the
> have nots. And no one is going to go without.

Likewise, some younger blacks spoke of a culture in which crime becomes normalized, which was shaped and reinforced by an absence of legal jobs for black men. Daryl and Michael were part of the "rough generation" that Darcy described with scorn. But they did not see themselves
this way. Michael, a soft-spoken twenty-four-year-old from Trenton, enjoys
helping people and taking care of his sister and has plans to go to college.
He was about to enroll in his local community college when he came into
financial trouble and turned to selling drugs. He was sent to prison when

he was twenty years old for fifteen months and when we interviewed him, he was in the halfway back institution for ninety days on a technical parole violation. He explained to us why black men have a higher chance of winding up in jail: "Most black men follow the next one. They try to do one thing the good way, try to find a job, but then after a couple turn downs, that's when they go back to doin' what they do. It's like they try to say, 'It didn't work this way, so I know it'll work this way. It worked for him, it'll work for me.'" His statement was autobiographical: Michael had followed the path of two older brothers and two uncles, all of whom had been to prison. Michael, as we described in chapter 2, believed that he would have had a better shot in life if he had grown up in the right place, one that wasn't "gang-infested or drug-infested." Yet, while recognizing the circumstances in which individual choices to commit crimes were made and while acknowledging that government was unresponsive to him and his community ("they try to brush you off the first time, first couple times"), he is adamant that "you really gotta keep trying." He spends his time on the outside looking for work, which he finds more difficult after his conviction, and told us, "Once two of them [employers] turn you down, it doesn't mean the next three are gonna turn you down. You just gotta keep on trying. You just gotta want it. Like I tell certain people, 'it's going to be a lot of turn downs in life, you not always going to get yes but you supposed to still keep trying.'" That, at least, was the message of the classes and "house meeting" he participated in at the Bo Robinson parole center.

Darryl, also a native of Trenton and just a bit older than Michael, is less optimistic that if he only tried harder, his path would be different. He has never been outside the city of his birth. In fact, he has not gotten far from the impoverished urban neighborhood where he was raised. At the time of our interview with him, Darryl had recently violated the terms of his parole and was hoping to avoid going back to prison. He leaned back in his chair, aloof, with his legs stretched out in front of him. His arms folded guardedly across his chest, he described a sense of near total disempowerment. Though he acknowledged that he played a part in his imprisonment, he described his situation as being characterized not only by poor choices, but by a lack of choices:

> I feel as though I put myself here. But if I had to do it all over again, I don't think I would have changed it. I would have had to [do what I did]. I had no choice. I had no options. Because, I mean, I seen it coming. But by the time I seen it, it was too late. So I really had no choices: either here or in the box

[a coffin]. And I'd rather keep living and be able to—I'm not going to say make the same mistake twice—but the choices I made that led me up to where I am now were the only choices I had.

When we asked him whether he has been helped at all by government programs, he simply shook his head, as though the answer should be obvious. Is there no one in government, we asked, who is working to improve things in his community? "In my eyes, in my neighborhood," he told us, "it's out of control. . . . But as long as they don't bother me, I don't get involved. I'm just trying to stay under the radar." In fact, the only attention that he sees government paying to him and to those like him is when they target him with increasingly punitive criminal justice policies. "That's the only influence I seen people I'm surrounded around have on anything: creating new laws as far as putting you away for longer. Nothing that's beneficial to us! I've never seen it. Now maybe they did it, but I haven't seen it."

These coexistent narratives can be similarly found in our quantitative data; our large-scale surveys show that blacks as a whole often voice both structural and cultural explanations for black incarceration. In the AAMS survey, black respondents were prompted to consider why "young black men have a higher chance than most people of winding up in jail." As with our interview subjects, a sizable proportion of the AAMS black sample as a whole felt that a big reason why so many black men are in jail is that "black men are less likely to think committing crimes is wrong" (42%) and that "many black parents are not teaching their children right from wrong" (56%) (see fig. 7.4). By comparison, a somewhat larger proportion of black respondents to the AAMS also believed that structural inequities played a significant role in determining incarceration rates across racial groups: 68 percent said that black men growing up in poverty was a major contributor to their high incarceration rates, 60 percent believed that a dearth of job opportunities was a major cause, and 47 percent suggested that a big reason for the disproportionate incarceration of black men was failing schools. These answers were not mutually exclusive, however. In fact, many blacks who believed that culture played some role in racially disproportionate rates of incarceration (measured as agreement with one of the two questions described above) also agreed with at least one question concerning the structural deficits that contributed to black mass incarceration.

One question that might remain is whether the prevalence of involuntary contact with criminal justice in black communities mutes the effect

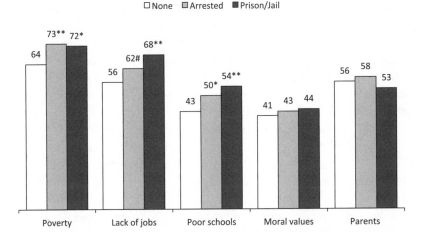

FIGURE 7.4. Blacks' explanations for higher incarceration rate of black men (%), by criminal justice contact. Percent of blacks who believe this is a "big reason" so many black men are in jail. Responses are: "more black men grow up in poverty," "fewer job opportunities," "schools are failing black men," "black men less likely to think crime is wrong," and "black parents not teaching children right from wrong." #p < .10; *p < .05; **p < .01; ***p > .001. *Source*: "African American Men Survey," Washington Post/Kaiser Family Foundation/ Harvard University, June 2006, http://www.kff.org/kaiserpolls/upload/7526.pdf.

of personal contact on blacks' perceptions. Data from the AAMS show that fewer than a third of white respondents had a close friend or family member who had been incarcerated. Among black respondents, this was true of well more than half (57 percent), and among black men ages 18– 29, 74 percent reported knowing someone who had served time. Even the most affluent and educated blacks are more likely than the least well-off whites to have a close personal contact who has been incarcerated.

The result of this intensive concentration among racial minorities— and the communal narratives that develop—may be that criminal justice contact has ceased to be a socializing experience for blacks. In fact, research by John Hagan and colleagues found that personal contact exerts a greater influence among Latinos and whites on perceptions of injustice; blacks, they argue, are less sensitive to these direct contacts given their "normal" nature.[35] Others have similarly found that among blacks, prior attitudes and negative vicarious experiences, not direct contact per se, exerted the greatest effects.[36]

Thus, criminal justice contact may not *change* attitudes, because the lessons learned through contact are already widely shared, part of a broader socialization about injustice and inequality in black communities. Not only are modern examples of police profiling and brutality "seared into the collective memory" of black communities, but Rodney King, Oscar Grant, and Abner Louima "join memories of official brutality and misconduct from the no-so-distant past—Bull Connor releasing his police dogs on civil rights activists, for example, or the wrongful conviction of Rubin 'Hurricane' Carter."[37]

We find strong evidence of such a dynamic. Among black respondents in the AAMS, those who have a close friend or family member who has served time in prison or jail are more likely to believe that the police are looking for any reason to give a black man a hard time, and to say that a big reason there are disproportionate numbers of black men in jail is that police target them and courts are more likely to convict them. However, social context is not entirely responsible for attitudinal differences between custodial and noncustodial blacks; in multiple regression models, personal experience with arrest or incarceration is positively and significantly related to perceptions of racial discrimination in criminal justice, even after accounting for vicarious contact and other factors.

We take this as preliminary evidence that the racial lessons of criminal justice go beyond existing and prevalent community narratives. And as with other political attitudes, such as perceptions of trust, efficacy, and responsiveness, we suspect that these ideas carry over into beliefs about America more broadly. Black custodial citizens may be less likely to interpret their personal contact with the criminal justice system as a solitary event—or if they perceive it as unfair, as an aberration in an otherwise fair system—but instead as racially directed treatment from a biased government and key to the lived experiences of the group. In this way, direct encounters with criminal justice may serve to amplify already negative views among blacks of racial equality in America, inculcating a belief that they are less than full citizens.

As a way of testing for this possibility, we reestimated our multiple regression models from the AAMS, including an additional control to account for whether respondents have a close friend or family member who has been to prison or jail. While we find that vicarious contact does diminish the effect of individual contact, it does so only slightly. Even after accounting for vicarious contact, we find that personal experience with both arrest ($p < .01$) and incarceration ($p < .05$) are still significantly associated with the belief that "America's economic system is stacked against black men."

A Mobilized Custodial Citizenry?: Criminal Justice and Linked Fate in the Post–Civil Rights Generation

The existence of these dual narratives among custodial citizens betrays an environment in which a political consciousness is unlikely to develop. Neither narrative provides a mobilizing understanding to black citizens about their plight. Neither could be called an "oppositional ideology" that "challenge[s] dominant systems of belief and provide[s] marginal group members with a different framework through which to assess their secondary position in society."[36] And neither, we speculate below, leads to the development of political resistance.

In the quantitative analyses we presented earlier, being stopped, arrested, convicted, or jailed significantly increased a sense that one's own plight hinged on the destiny of the larger racial group. In most existing work on the subject, a sense of racial group consciousness is believed to derive from perceptions of systemic racial inequality, mostly because discrimination "draw[s] attention to the collective aspects of black life."[37] Moreover, it is often viewed as politicized, leading its holders to be more active in political life and more likely to challenge their racial group's perceived mistreatment through group-based collective action.

But we speculate that a linked fate derived from criminal justice experiences is distinctly less politicized than a linked fate derived from Jim Crow racism. Linked fate itself is simply the belief among blacks that one's experiences have something to do with what befalls other blacks. Though it is often conflated with a *mobilized* racial consciousness—racial solidarity on the way to collective action—these survey measures are simply an assessment of linked prospects; it does not require its holders to be politically motivated towards the attainment of shared interests and goals ("what's good for the group is good for me"). While linked fate has the potential to lead to the development of an oppositional consciousness and the formation of resistance, such a development is not inevitable and thus, should not be assumed. Custodial citizens have a sense that their chances are linked, but as the two narratives show, not a unified perspective of why they are linked and who or what is to blame.

Moreover, it appears from our data that a custodial linked fate is not the building block of greater activism and a mobilized racial identity; instead, it is demobilizing. In contrast to linked fate developed from prior race-making institutions, these dual narratives emerged from the conflicting messages of the criminal justice system, institutions that obscure the role of race even as they regularly display inequality and engage in race-laden practices. The racial socialization of the criminal justice system holds little potential for resistance because it regularly conveys to its wards that their fates were due to their choices alone.

In fact, when we dig deeper in the quantitative data, criminal justice contact actually amplified the belief that "I have to look out for myself" by 11 percentage points. Criminal justice contact also led blacks to be less likely to engage in collective action or traditional methods of political participation. And despite what prior accounts of linked fate would lead one to believe, linked fate among custodial citizens is not generative of political action. Those custodial citizens high in linked fate were no more likely than those low in linked fate to be engaged in civic groups or participate in politics through voting and other means.

In sum, regardless of whether they read their experiences through a racialized lens or individual choices or some blend of the two, most custodial citizens we spoke to were closed off to politics. While the narratives of personal responsibility and racial domination seem polar opposites, they both resulted in strikingly similar responses; the rational response to each was to "go with the flow," "go it alone," and rely only on oneself rather than expect any assistance from government or coalesce with others to achieve collective goals. Emmett, an older black man in New Orleans, captured this withdrawal by explaining to us that "America is going to do what America does. They're going to do that and there's nothing—now whether it's right or whether it's wrong, I can't change it. I can't stop it." He explains to us that he has turned to himself: "But I can change me . . . and I start focusing on things I can change."

From the perspective of democratic equality, both transcripts that we recount from our interviews are therefore problematic. The racial oppression narrative robs blacks of agency and furthers their sense of alienation, just as the personal responsibility narrative exaggerates agency and obscures the structural conditions of life for minorities in America, divorcing the situation from its wider context and erasing the role of laws, institutions, and society. Both failed to give their believers what they could really have used—a way of understanding and challenging their diminished position, their custodial citizenship.

CHAPTER EIGHT

"I better stay below the radar"

Fear, Alienation, and Withdrawal

Citizen participation in the political process is a central tenet of a healthy democracy. As President Lyndon B. Johnson proclaimed in 1965 after signing the Voting Rights Act, "The vote is the most powerful instrument ever devised by man for breaking down injustice and destroying the terrible walls which imprison men because they are different from other men."[1] Yet in sad irony, since the decade in which Johnson commented on the power of voting to free metaphorically imprisoned men, the nation has vastly increased the share of its citizens in prison. In conjunction with the maintenance of felony disenfranchisement laws, this growth in the number of custodial citizens has resulted in a sizable swath of Americans, particularly black men, who are prohibited from taking part in democratic elections. Indeed, what was a figure of speech in 1965 has come to define the nation today, as mass black imprisonment gradually reverses the trend of suffrage expansion and reinstates formal exclusion.

We do not exaggerate when we say that many of the immediate gains of the Voting Rights Act have been dismantled. Consider some figures. In the United States today, 5.85 million Americans—about one in every forty voting age adults—are disenfranchised due to a criminal conviction. Of those, 45 percent have completed their sentences, including probation and parole.[2] To compare, about 383,000 black men in the states of the former confederacy were disenfranchised prior to the Fifteenth Amendment in 1870, an estimated 125,000 Native Americans were ineligible for suffrage without the Citizenship Act of 1924, and 10.8 million

Americans aged eighteen to twenty were excluded from the right to vote previous to the Twenty-sixth Amendment in 1971.[3]

And as was the case before the Voting Rights Act, blacks now constitute a large share of those excluded through legal voting restrictions. One in nine young black men celebrated the milestone election of Barack Obama from their prison and jail cells, and 13 percent of adult black men could not take part in his election by casting a vote, as they were disenfranchised due to a criminal record.[4] In states with particularly restrictive felon disenfranchisement laws, the proportion of minorities barred from voting is even higher; in these states, the proportion of the black voting age population denied suffrage hovers closer to one in four.[5] Widespread access to the vote in America, promised by the Voting Rights Act's goal of universal adult enfranchisement, can thus be seen as a brief experiment, lasting less than two decades.

Felon disenfranchisement has been the subject of substantial criticism from scholars, journalists, and advocates who argue that removing people from the democratic process, particularly after their punishment is complete, is antithetical to the American ethos of one citizen, one vote.[6] We strongly echo this critique. However, in this chapter we have another concern. In discussing the collateral consequences of criminal justice and their implications for democracy, scholars often implicitly assume that legal disenfranchisement is what keeps people from participating. But we argue here that a deeper instrument also diminishes participation, regardless of formal disenfranchisement: punishment and surveillance themselves activate a process of political withdrawal, alienation, and fear of government.

We devoted previous chapters to understanding the carceral lifeworlds of citizens who have had early, frequent, and adversarial encounters with authorities and institutions of criminal justice. Our results show that encounters with criminal justice have politically socializing effects on citizens, shaping their sense of the state and what they believe about government, as well as altering their beliefs about their own standing as citizens. This chapter provides the final link in the story: interactions with government shape not only our ideas about how government works and our own membership in the polity, but also our civic habits and behaviors. As custodial citizens learn that government is about control, that they carry a badge of shame that makes them unfit for citizenship, and that officials can wield seemingly unchecked power, they become (understandably) alienated from political life.

In the following sections, we explore custodial citizens' political behavior—the way they use the lessons they have learned. Through qualitative interviews and analyses of two large, nationally representative datasets, we show that citizens who have experienced the strong arm of the state mostly withdraw from civic life, removing themselves from virtually all avenues of political expression. They generally do not band together with others facing the same issues and needs in their communities, they do not turn to their representatives in office to resolve pressing political problems, and the majority abstain from voting even if they are legally able to do so.

A number of themes emerge from our data. The first viewpoint our interviewees expressed is encompassed by the statement made by one of our interviewees that "[I'll] never be a true American citizen again." Many custodial citizens who were legally allowed to vote encountered messages that discouraged them from doing so. Their loss of citizenship rights left a residue of stigma, shame, and discontent, and although many felt the right to vote was inalienable and important in a general sense, they decided to abstain personally because, having been stripped of their rights, they felt they no longer had a place at the table. What, then, was the point of voting?

This stigmatized status of the disenfranchised offender is arguably part of the underlying intent of felon exclusion policies. In the case of *Richardson v. Ramirez* (1974), the Supreme Court ruled that California had not violated the Equal Protection Clause of the Fourteenth Amendment, which mandates that states may not "deny to any person within its jurisdiction the equal protection of the laws," when the state excluded convicted felons from voting in state elections. In so ruling, the Supreme Court implicitly embraced the argument that the ex-felon is a special category of citizen who could be subject to permanent penalties, confirming the supposition embedded in lower court rulings that prohibiting ex-felons from voting protects the "purity of the ballot box."[7] As Brian Pinaire and colleagues argue, felon-disenfranchisement laws stem from the belief "not so much that a violation earns you time in the proverbial 'penalty box,' but rather that you no longer exude the qualities of a good and right 'team player,' and thus no longer deserve a spot on the roster."[8] Many remain disenfranchised, often for life, and for those who do see rights of citizenship returned, the stigma of having been deemed no longer "good and right" can have effects that linger long after voting rights are restored.

A second and related theme is that those who were formally excluded from voting felt stigmatized, and this sense of exclusion spilled over to affect other types of participation, such as joining clubs and advocacy groups or making claims on elected officials. Being banished from the voting booth created an overarching status of excluded citizenship that led them to withdraw from other viable avenues in which they could have legally participated; being formally disenfranchised therefore led to a broader demobilization from political and civic life.

Even more worrisome is that, in addition to lower voting rates among even re-enfranchised custodial citizens, we find evidence that echoes what Cathy Cohen has termed the "politics of invisibility," which is "an active strategy on the part of some black youth to make themselves invisible to government authorities whom they believe are interested only in identifying, regulating, controlling, and possibly incarcerating them."[9] For some custodial citizens, withdrawal is not simply a choice made because they do not believe politicians will listen or care or because they feel stigmatized. Rather, the choice is as much or more about staying below the radar. The government is something to be avoided, not participated in, and pressing one's claims results only in further difficulties, such as the loss of benefits, or worse, harassment and retribution. The only option is to stay low, out of sight, and beyond reach. Rather than being part of the "nation of joiners" or the "greatest civic generation," these citizens have substantially disengaged from the democratic project. The implication for participatory democracy in America is that some of the nation's most vulnerable citizens do not take part in a political system intended to represent all its people.

"They already stripped us": The Lingering Stigma of Disenfranchisement

Born and raised in New Orleans, Abe is a twenty-five-year-old man with a blue tear tattooed below his left eye and a ready smile. He was in jail during Hurricane Katrina and had also served a few years in the state penitentiary. At the time of his interview, Abe worked a government job where he tried to help others struggling as he had. While not at all muted about his negative views of government corruption, insincere politicians, and the handling of the Katrina and BP oil disasters—"I don't like the government" and "the government, they use and abuse the people"—

Abe felt passionately about voting and viewed exclusion from the voting booth as silencing his voice and ability to make demands of government officials. "Once you get convicted of a crime, you can't vote," he said. "So, people who vote, they control what the government do, right? So therefore, people who are convicted have no control. We don't have a word. We don't have a word." When we asked Abe a hypothetical question—what he would tell Barack Obama to help get people like him back into the political system—he proclaimed without qualification: "Let us vote. Let everybody have a chance to say who should be in the office."

For Abe, belief in the power of voting was as much about his status as a citizen as it was an instrumental need to see a particular candidate in office. Like many of those with whom we spoke, losing the fundamental right of democratic citizenship was a sharply negative moment, something recalled in great detail that had lasting effects on subsequent orientations toward government. For Abe and for others, the embarrassment associated with disenfranchisement had led to a more general alienation from government. Even after regaining the franchise, Abe told us, he declined to participate because of the civic stigma the initial loss caused:

> When they came to school, they were telling everybody to register their vote, but then I can't register the vote because I was a convicted offender. Like, after that . . . I never ever voted. . . . I still don't—and I should be able to vote today. I still don't. . . . Because they already stripped us. Because they already stripped us from the word go.

Even though Abe's voting rights were returned after he completed his sentence, the shame and frustration of felon disenfranchisement continued to affect his likelihood of political participation; long after his legal rights were restored, Abe chose to abstain because the state had "already stripped" him.

The experience of disenfranchisement sent a powerful signal to Abe about his limited citizenship and low status in the democratic community. Sarah expressed similar sentiments. She recalled that having been told she was disenfranchised when she had wanted to cast a vote was a deeply stigmatizing experience: "It makes me feel bad because I'm still a human being and I'm still a—I'm still somebody, and I should be allowed to vote. You know, 'cause people change. Because you're incarcerated doesn't mean you're any less than a person that's voting." Sarah was not sure whether she was allowed to vote or not. The rules, she said, had changed, "so I don't know. I haven't done it in a while." However, she hesitated to find out whether she was eligible because of the possibility of public embarrassment if she were denied: "A lotta places you go to fill out the card to vote and they ask you 'have you ever been convicted of a crime or have a felony' and as soon as you mark that box, they say you can't vote . . . the last time I voted, that happened. It discouraged me from even trying to vote."

Similarly, Carlton described how he had always voted, but lost the right due to a felony conviction in 2000. At election time, he was reminded of the stigma and felt "left out, because I don't have the opportunity other people have: I miss that. You talkin' about you goin' and vote; I can't vote because I have a felony. It's a downer." Silas felt this loss not only at election time, but more broadly. To him, it was a constant that signified his diminished standing in society: "I'll never be able to vote again. I'll never be a true American citizen again. I'll be living in America, I was born in America. But I'll never be that again."

In addition to the stigma of being previously or currently disenfranchised, many who had regained their political voice after being released from prison also felt that the exercise of suffrage was fundamentally useless because "my opinion didn't really matter"; the process was rigged and elected officials pursued their own agendas no matter what citizens had to say. Trevor, an older black man in Trenton who had served over seventeen years in prison, explained that he filled out a voter registration form, but decided against casting a ballot because he could not see the use: "I was going to vote but I changed my mind though. . . . Just nobody going to do anything for me. Why vote? I'm not going to lose nothing; I'm not going to gain nothing." David, a black man we interviewed in Charlottesville who had been recently paid to work on a campaign to reelect a Democratic congressman described voting as an irrational waste of time. Elected officials would not work for people like him in the end:

> They still put who they wanted to put in office anyway, don't they? See, that's what people don't realize. You could vote as much as you want, you know what I mean? But if the other person got the right people backing him up, it doesn't matter. . . . None of them are really gonna do nothing to help out where they really need to help out. . . . That's why it don't make sense to vote. They gonna do whatever they wanna do when they get in office. They gonna sit on TV and tell you whatever good thing they want you to hear and believe . . . [but] they only telling you what they think you wanna hear.

Others felt similarly, believing that participation was worthless because those in positions of authority did what they wanted regardless of constituents' opinions—putting in power who they wanted and giving the people only what they wanted them to have. As Charles, an older black man from Charlottesville, opined, "I look at it like this. The more you try to do, the less you get. You don't get anything over and above. You don't get anything at all. The only thing you get is what they want you to have." Samuel, a middle-aged white man from Trenton, agreed:

> Right now I think it would be completely worthless. 'Cause they're going to do what they want to do anyhow . . . even if they have all these people saying, we ought to do this, we ought to do that. "Oh sir, we'll take that into consideration." No they will not. . . . And that's basically why, and I'm sure I'm not the only one who feels like this, but you just throw your hands up and say oh well. It is what it is. What can I do about it? They're going to do what they want to do anyhow.

David, Samuel, and others like them had learned that political participation was a spectacle that yielded no meaningful result. For some, this was tied to their other dimensions of disadvantage, such as being black, not knowing the right people, or having few resources. For many, though, this was about being part of a custodial class that occupied a deeply—and often formally—stigmatized status.

"Them doors are shut": Stigma and Withdrawal beyond the Vote

For many of our interviewees, the stigma of exclusion from voting extended beyond the choice about whether to vote, affecting other forms of participation. Paul is a white man from Charlottesville who worked on and off as a welder, sometimes taking jobs from a local day labor operation, and at the time of his interview he was still struggling to get back on his feet. By the time Paul returned from a seventeen-year sentence in a Virginia penitentiary for grand larceny, his wife had left, his daughter had stopped contacting him, his parents and brothers had died, and the home he owned was long gone. He got a very heavy sentence by most standards—heavier relative to what he might have received in other states—and never had a chance at parole. Nonetheless, Paul told us that "the United States government is fair. . . . I can walk around, earn money, whatever." But he could not vote. For Paul and for several other people with whom we spoke, particularly in our Virginia sample, having a felony conviction meant lifetime exclusion from suffrage. In Virginia, before a new reform recently took effect to reenfranchise some nonviolent felons after they pay their court costs and restitution, about 378,000 people were disenfranchised for life, or 7 percent of the electorate, unless they navigated a complex process to have their vote restored. Paul said that if he were eligible, he would vote: "I would get back and more involved with it. . . . I hear 'em. It sounds good. I'd vote for you! But I can't. . . . [*So it would change things for you?*] Certainly. I'd get more involved in it if I could cast one vote."

Yet for Paul, it was not simply that he could not—and so did not—vote. Rather, this prohibition had led him to withdraw from politics altogether. "I can't vote or nothing like that. So that kind of politics, I just kind of got away from. I can't participate in it. I can gripe about it, but I got to live with it regardless." In contrast to many who believed that voting was meaningless because representatives did what they wanted anyway, Paul believed in the political process. However, because he was not allowed to be involved in the most central part of that process—casting a ballot for one's chosen representative—he withdrew from all of it. He avidly read the newspaper, kept abreast of world news, and "want[s] to be aware of what's happening in my government, but I'm not involved in it. Because I *can't* be involved in it, because I can't be an input to it. I can't carry it all the way." Like many of our interviewees, Paul saw his civic exclusion as so totalizing that participating in other ways did not seem to be an option. When we asked what would happen if he tried to write a letter to government or get involved in a campaign, he shrugged: "Them doors are shut. They shut 'em. You can't vote. And you ain't going to be able to participate in the manner you would, an unconvicted person would do. Then you get caught up in it, if you are in it, I think you're just setting yourself up for, 'cause you can't do anything about it."

Melvin, a twenty-nine-year-old black man from New Jersey who is legally disenfranchised, expressed views similar to Paul's. When we spoke to him, Melvin had just completed a fifteen-month prison term for multiple nonviolent offenses, including unpaid tickets and driving without a license. It was his first time behind bars, and he hoped it would be his last because "it's been a lesson learned." Not only was he separated from his wife and four young sons, but he missed the birth of his first daughter. Like Paul, he faced a host of problems. Finding a job was particularly tough, he said, "because they go by what's on your criminal record." He felt as though he could change things "if they would just listen" and he had voted a few years ago before serving time, but his conviction made him no longer eligible: "Now, they say now that I have a criminal record, I've been to prison, it's hard for me to vote, I can't vote. I don't believe that, but it's just the way the system is."

Melvin's frustration at being denied the vote was readily apparent. "I believe that everybody [should have] the right to vote," he said. "I really do. It don't matter. 'Cause that person that you vote for could be the one that could really change things. Or could be a mess-up [laughs]." Yet rather than turning to other forms of engagement, Melvin withdrew from political participation of all kinds. In light of this primary exclusion and the stigma of his criminal record, Melvin voiced hesitation about taking part in other types of civic participation, believing that it was unlikely to make a difference:

> I've thought about it, but I've never really did it, because I felt as though that they probably wouldn't listen. I think they wouldn't listen because they'd be like, "We got this guy writin' us, he's saying this, he's saying that" or "we got this group of people writin' us, they saying this, they saying that—we just gonna put it to the side. They don't mean nothin'." Like I said, once again, it's your background. . . . It's just my record. Because me myself, I have great potential. I have a wonderful personality. I'm not all thugged out and slouching like "I don't care about . . ." No, not me. I have a good head on my shoulders. I just made bad decisions. Wrong choices.

For Melvin and Paul and many of the others with whom we spoke, felon disenfranchisement was not only a formal barrier to voting; it erected an informal barrier to other forms of participation and civic engagement.

"We don't need more problems": Avoidance and Risks of Participating

We were not surprised to learn that many people with criminal justice experience had disengaged from the political process and held negative views of politics. What we did not expect to find was that many others had not only withdrawn from politics, but also actively avoided be-

ing involved with political institutions. In her book exploring the politics
of black youth, Cathy Cohen suggests a similar dynamic, pointing out
that some black youth who had encountered the surveillance and regulation of the state at very young ages had decided to disengage, "us[ing]
the limited agency available to them to stay under the radar."[10] She does
not test this idea empirically and does not focus primarily on incarceration and surveillance, but nevertheless sees punitive state interaction as
a central aspect of why avoidance behavior forms in black youth:

> Many of the young black Americans who told us their stories through sur-
> veys, in-depth interviews, and focus groups have grown up with police cars
> patrolling their streets to make the community safe from youth like them. . . .
> These young black people have watched friends and schoolmates get killed
> routinely, and the visible presence of police and metal detectors has come
> to define part of their school experience. . . . These young people have seen
> increasing numbers of family and friends arrested, sent to prisons and jails,
> and "domestically deported" out of their neighborhoods and their lives. Be-
> cause of such experiences, these young people have decided that their best
> survival strategy is to be invisible to state, community, and often family au-
> thorities. . . . These young people have chosen a politics of invisibility, dis-
> engaging from all forms of politics and trying to remain invisible to officials
> who possibly could provide assistance but were more likely to impose greater
> surveillance and regulations on their lives.[11]

Alice Goffman makes similar observations in her in-depth ethnography
of young men in a Philadelphia neighborhood, many of whom had outstanding warrants or previous negative experiences with police. In addition to avoiding "the hospital when their babies were born" or when they
were seriously injured, avoiding "places of employment" where "a man
with a warrant can get arrested on the job even if the police are not specifically searching for him," and avoiding "friends, family and romantic
partners [who] may pose a threat and thus have to be avoided or at least
carefully navigated," many men who had engaged in minor offenses actively avoided government. They made "tentative use of the police and
the courts" or ended up "simply staying away," even when they had been
the victim of a crime or were dealing with important legal matters, such
as those pertaining to custody of their children.[12]

Custodial citizens may also actively avoid engaging important social
services even when they need them desperately, for fear of surveillance

and arrest. This concern is not entirely off-base. Beginning in the late 1970s, some cities began requiring welfare recipients to pick up their checks at police stations and instituted fingerprinting and photographing of recipients.[13] This practice expanded to the point that one expert remarked that "applying for welfare is a lot like being booked by the police."[14] In the 1970s campaigns against welfare fraud, the state of Illinois hired police officers to locate people receiving public aid who were ineligible, and established hotlines for people to report on welfare recipients who exhibited suspicious behavior.[15] One of the stipulations of the 1996 welfare reform was that housing authorities and welfare agencies provide law enforcement with names, addresses, and photographs of public assistance recipients; more recently, proposals to fingerprint public housing residents have been advanced by mainstream politicians like Mayor Michael Bloomberg. Today, law enforcement officials use data on welfare recipients to locate them or members of their household for questioning.

A policy in the food stamp program has gone even further. Dubbed Operation Talon, this program not only shares data with police officers, but "transformed food stamp offices into the sites of sting operations for arresting aid recipients with outstanding arrest warrants."[16] Under this program, participants in the food stamp program who are wanted by police have been apprehended when they arrive to receive their benefits. The program has been instituted in cities nationwide and in under a decade led to almost 11,000 arrests.[17] In commending the program, then–vice president Al Gore remarked that "the National Food Stamp Program is designed to help decent, law-abiding citizens get back on their feet during times of need, not to help murderers and rapists stay on the streets."[18] Yet many of the arrests under Operation Talon have been for less serious offenses, such as outstanding debts. In Illinois, two-thirds of those caught under the program were for drug-related charges, while in California three-fourths of the outstanding warrants were for fraud-related violations, including welfare fraud.[19]

The likely result of this increased integration between social welfare and criminal justice is that people who have had interactions with the law may hesitate to apply for essential social programs. At potentially great cost to themselves and the families that depend on them, they may pass up food stamps or student loans, looking for a place to stay at a homeless shelter or public housing, or seeking out emergency aid. This is likely to be particularly true for those who have outstanding warrants or are engaged in even low-level forms of criminal behavior. However, avoidance behavior may seem prudent even to those who are not engaging in illegality. As Goffman notes:

> Young men worried that they would be picked up by the police and taken into custody even when they did not have a warrant out for their arrest. Those on probation or parole, on house arrest, and who were going through a trial expressed concern that they would soon be picked up and taken into custody for some violation that would "come up in the system." Even those with no pending legal action expressed concern that the police might "find some reason to hold them" because of what they had done, who or what they knew, or what they carried on their person.[20]

We found strikingly strong evidence of avoidance techniques among our interviewees who had had personal and adversarial contacts with the law—and not only among those who had experienced multiple or particularly severe negative encounters with criminal justice. For example, Silas was somewhat unique among our respondents for his relative lack of criminal justice involvement. Convicted of aggravated assault for a fight he had with his brother-in-law, Silas never spent time in prison, instead taking a plea bargain for five years of probation. He had not had any other contact with criminal justice before or since. Still, his criminal justice history defined his current relationship to government, more even than his years in the military, serving time in Bosnia, Panama, and Honduras. Like many of our interviewees, Silas knew a great deal about politics and had strong opinions about the way government works. Yet while he was upset about a host of social and political problems in his community and the nation—from racial inequality to unfair treatment of convicted felons—he had mostly withdrawn from political engagement, choosing to keep a low profile where matters of government were concerned:

> Have I ever tried to contact a senator or governor? No. I feel like they're not interested in what I have to say. I feel like if I contact a senator or governor, they'll probably want to put me in jail and leave me as a troublemaker. I'm serious. That's how I actually feel: "I better stay below the radar 'cause this guy's tryin' to start trouble." Now, again—keep in mind what I said—they have money and power. Who the hell am I? I am just a small peon at the bottom of the totem pole.

Many of our interviewees described long waits accessing their veterans' benefits or Social Security, unfair treatment by the housing authority, and long spells of unemployment, all of which deserved government attention and action. When we asked them whether they had tried to contact someone in government to resolve a problem or make a grievance, however, more than a few said that they could not for fear of repercussions or even retribution, such as the loss of important benefits or further interactions with the criminal justice system. Some laughed out loud at the idea of protesting their lot, while others simply asserted that if they spoke out, harm would be visited upon them. Not everyone held this view, but the number of times such sentiments were voiced in our interviews was strikingly high. Avoidance was a broadly shared tactic.

For instance, Brenda, who was homeless at the time we interviewed her, described how the police regularly harassed her and other transient people simply because they did not want them in a business area of Charlottesville where wealthier patrons strolled. She had been arrested many times for being drunk in public and tried to avoid the police and "move around as much as possible." When we asked whether she and other homeless people she knew had complained about being targeted by police, she shrugged: "There has been people who wanted to go down there and complain, but never actually did it because, I guess, we have too much going on already; we don't need more problems." When we asked Adele, an older white woman in Charlottesville, what she thought kept people like her from getting involved in politics and government, she said simply that "they are afraid of what's going to come down on them. They want to stay secret and quiet."

Others likewise were fearful of repercussions if they complained. They might get their assistance cut off, or worse. Marcus, a middle-aged black man we interviewed in Trenton who had a single conviction and was still on parole, described how "government do things . . . say, their way." Facing an uphill battle to find a job and get on his feet financially, he felt that he could not turn to public officials for help and did not think he had the power to make claims on government. A few times he thought about taking action regarding his problems, but had then reconsidered: "I don't wanna make things worse than it already is, even though I have this problem, I'm trying to work through it and hopefully, just say hopefully, things will get a little better." Nora, an older black woman from Trenton, agreed, noting that while she had thought about going to someone in government for help with a housing issue, she "got scared and didn't go" because she was fearful of what "they might say or do . . . tell me to get out, call security or something." Even as our interviewees faced a host of different problems—blighted neighborhoods, poor schools, limited access to jobs, homelessness—many felt they could not go to representatives or governing institutions because of a very real perception that if they complained, officials would make their lives more difficult. The political socialization of avoidance sprang from the lessons they imported directly from criminal justice. Some recounted how they had learned not to call police because, even when they called for help, they often ended up suspected of criminal activity or mistreated. Many of the people we interviewed believed that police could pick them up anytime, for anything. Simply walking down the street, they expected police to stop and ask about their business. Our interviewees therefore talked about their hesitation to call the police "unless there's a dire need. Then you have to call them. But other than that you avoid them at all costs." Similarly, when asked whether he avoided law enforcement, Trevor answered: "I stay away from them. I try to stay away from them the best I can. If something happens and I see it happen, they be like 'you see?' I'm like, 'I don't know what happened and I don't got nothing to do with it. Don't put me in it.' If you get treated unfairly by the police so many times, what do they expect?" Another way the avoidance strategy was cultivated by criminal justice stemmed more directly from the negative status of having been an offender. Cordell spoke bitterly of his treatment as a prison inmate and he believed that he had had time added to his sentence unfairly. But he angrily bit his tongue and swallowed the additional time because "when you do something about it, automatically, it's that light on you, and you're somebody that shouldn't be doing something like this. First of all, no wonder! You're a felon. Number two, I ain't got a voice anyway, what voice I got? I can't even vote."

A few believed that any attempt to directly challenge unfair police treatment would result in retribution. Xavier explained why people did not bring grievances when they had been subjected to unfair police targeting or use of force:

> If the police is seeing that you're trying to fight them, they're going to make it worse. They harass you. . . . They're going to try to lock you up. . . . Then once you in that jail cell, they can treat you however they want and they're going to get payback. 'Cause you in here now, we going to handle you.

Similarly, Darnell, a young black man in Trenton who was part of a class action lawsuit against the Camden police for planting drugs on innocent young people,[21] feared reprisals from the police and intended to leave the state:

> After I get my money [from the lawsuit], I'm leaving. 'Cause I know what they gonna do [laughs]. I know what they gonna do. They gonna try any and every little thing to try to get me on something. I know so. . . . They gonna try every little thing they can do to incriminate me or stop me from getting it or if I do get it, they gonna try to throw me back in jail.

Not surprisingly, Darnell and those who shared this view also refused to call the police, even when they needed help and had done nothing to warrant suspicion. One person we spoke to said he would refuse to call the police even if he was on his deathbed.

Many of our interviewees likewise expressed fears that they might be incarcerated again if they got too near the system. Bert had been released from prison two weeks before our interview, after serving nearly five years for a drug-dealing charge. He had been in the system most of his life; his first experience was being sent to a juvenile home for skipping school. Like so many others, he described government in one word: control. He described how his interaction in the court system left him feeling unjustly treated. Even though he had a job and was a long-term resident, he was denied bond. This led to the loss of his job, and he believed that his unemployment was a large part of why he landed in prison for so long. As a result of this negative experience, Bert came to fear further interactions with government:

> I try to stay away. . . . I'm trying to avoid from even going down there [the court building] and paying fines. I got fines I have to pay and I don't even want to go down there. I find a way of mailing it to 'em, talkin' over the phone, because I don't really want to be around them. Talking to them, personally . . . it just makes me feel like if I stay in here long enough, they might find something else on me to lock me up for.

His longtime girlfriend, Felisha, also avoided police and other institutions of criminal justice. "Having to deal with them . . . when I see them [police] I just want to go down the other way. Wasn't about doing anything wrong, or not, I just . . ." She went on to explain that she harbored a deep fear of being locked up again that was triggered by being in the presence of a correctional institution:

> The only thing about the government that I don't like, I don't like visiting people that's locked up. . . . Once I go start seeing somebody, I feel that I might get locked up. It's just, if I keep going to see them, I'm gonna end up over there. . . . Soon as I start going to visit somebody, it's like six months later and I'm over there too. I'll write, but I don't want to visit.

Our results suggest that people who have had adversarial encounters with the criminal justice system not only withdraw from, but also actively avoid, further interactions with government authorities of any kind. Their interactions with criminal justice had taught them that encountering authorities usually involved arbitrary and powerful control, and usually had very negative consequences. As a result, avoiding encounters with government of any kind came to be seen as the only way to steer clear of a system that seemed to be omnipresent in their lives, no matter how much they "kept their nose clean." As Terrence, a forty-year-old black man from Charlottesville, ruefully remarked, "I know this system [criminal justice] here fairly well now . . . and this system? You need to stay out of it as much as you can. And not even that. You need to keep your head low, because this system will grab you anyway, just on its own." Once he was labeled as a troublemaker, he felt he was caught in the "revolving door" of the system. "The more trouble you've got in, the more trouble you're going to get in."

Instead of engaging in the political process by seeking out elected representatives, they opt out. Their political isolation springs from a deep fear of interactions with political authorities and an abiding anxiety about a government that seems both all-powerful and primarily punitive. This form of disengagement—active avoidance—is troubling in a democracy, in which the root of political life is engaged citizen participation. As Sidney Verba reminds us, participation is important not only because "by being active people come to feel that they are members of the same polity," but also because "activity builds legitimacy. Voting in an election is an act of support for the political system."[22] Conversely, fearful avoidance is a mark of an antidemocratic system.

Our discussion of demobilization is not meant to imply that custodial citizens "lack a political life."[23] Their withdrawal from dealings with the state is itself a form of agency, a political decision in its own right. They choose daily to do something different, to avoid, "acts of nonconformity."[24] We were reminded of this by one of the succinct statements made in the course of our discussions: "the best way for me to influence this type of situation is to extricate myself from it."

Moreover, the daily politics practiced by custodial citizens may have a broader range than we allow. We heed the call of Cathy Cohen, James Scott, and Robin Kelley to look beyond politics as traditionally organized and "expand where we look for political acts."[25] For those whose "dealings with the state are often chosen and from an empowered position," it makes sense to examine traditional forms of political involvement, mobilization, and voice.[26] But for those who stand outside conventional politics and whose position vis-à-vis the state is as regulated subject, what constitutes political action may not only be found in "structured, coordinated, and seemingly purposeful acts" but in daily acts of oppositional behavior and defiance.[27] For example, scholars have found subversive tactics against courts in communities characterized by high incarceration. Specifically, many jurors in these areas have been found to engage in jury nullification, refusing to convict minor offenders even when they deemed them guilty of breaking the law on the facts of the case. As Paul Butler describes, these jurors act rationally when refusing to send away another black person for a first time drug offense. Because, to them, the nation devalues black lives, individuals may see nullification as a way of registering their opposition: "the juror makes a decision not to be a passive symbol of support for a system for which she has no respect."[28]

Thus, we might need to search harder for glimpses of agency, resistance, and voice, creative means of influence and a broader repertoire of political practices engaged in by this group. Engagement with the state could take on more subaltern forms which the limited focus on voting, contributing, and joining neighborhood clubs may conceal. Essentially, we need to leave open the "possibility of oppositional politics rooted outside of traditional or formal political institutions."[29]

Perhaps some custodial citizens choose a politics of avoidance to generate a space where they can be viable. Perhaps they "use the restricted agency available to them to create autonomous spaces absent the continuous stream of power *from* outside authorities."[30] And if these practices cumulate across individuals to create the space for a politics of resistance, a different set of norms and values and practices that are oppositional, they are potentially mobilizing. Cohen holds open the possibility that these individual, uncoordinated acts of avoidance and defiance could evolve into a collective politics.

While we find this possibility alluring, we think its potential is overstated. Custodial citizens practicing avoidance should not be confused with a mobilized collective consciousness, which could contain the possibility of recognition and action on their behalf. Our evidence makes clear that custodial citizens were not only disaffected from politics, they did not have a consciousness of being one group united against unwanted state intervention in their lives. As Cohen herself reminds us, "cumulative acts of individual agency are not the same as collective agency."[31]

Their choice to avoid was not entirely volitional either. In some cases, they believed it was a necessary action, that their very survival depended on keeping low. In other cases, like Abe and Bert, they desperately wanted to be seen and heard and recognized, but had *learned* that their best chance was to keep a low profile. Thus, avoidance was not a subversive act that was consciously intended to challenge and counter the status quo, to use what little agency they had to turn their backs on a state that they believed harmed them; instead, it was a survival mechanism. It was not an *unwillingness to adapt* to convention, a political act of nonadherence, but simply a way of adapting to the circumstances in which they found themselves.

Effects on Civic and Political Engagement

Our qualitative interviews suggest that contact with criminal justice is associated with diluted political engagement; despite often strong commitment to the idea that suffrage represents a basic right of democratic citizenship, citizens who have dealt with the supervisory, punitive side of the state voice deep alienation from government and the political process. For many individuals who have been denied the vote, their formal disenfranchisement is a sign of their limited standing in the polity, which in turn diminishes their interest in other forms of political participation. Among those who are permitted to vote, many prefer to disengage. In some cases, this results from a sense that those in power shun the political voices of those with felony convictions. For others, withdrawal from political life comes from a deep-rooted fear of the potential repercussions.

Do our interviewees' views represent a broader pattern of disengagement among custodial citizens? To answer that question, we turn to much larger samples drawn from two social surveys: Add Health, which contains over 15,000 respondents in its third wave, and the more than 3,000 male respondents from the third wave of the Fragile Families survey. What we find in our qualitative interviews is reinforced by strong quantitative evidence: namely, those who have experienced a punitive intervention are much less likely to take part in politics. Table 8.1 shows rates of participation for each level of criminal justice contact: being stopped and questioned by police, being arrested, being convicted, and serving time in jail or prison.[32] The data make clear that custodial citizens are less likely to vote, register, or join civic organizations than those who have never had contact with criminal justice.

However, in these data, the importance of custodial involvement is only somewhat evident in other types of political activities, such as contacting a government official or attending a march or rally. Compared to 6 percent of those with no criminal justice contact who have done at least one type of political activity in the past year, we find an increase to 10 percent among those who have been stopped and questioned by police and only a slight decline (to 3%) among those who have spent over a year in prison. On measures such as donating money to a campaign or party or running for office, we find no significant effect of criminal justice.

There is somewhat more variation between custodial and noncustodial citizens on measures of civic engagement. Those who experience punitive interventions, particularly those who have been convicted or spent time in prison or jail, are somewhat less likely to seek out civic society by participating in cultural, social, or political groups. Compared to about 34 percent of Fragile Families respondents who had no criminal justice experience, only about 28 percent of those who had been incarcerated and 29 percent of those who had spent serious time in prison reported being part of a church group. Similarly, 11 percent of respondents with no contact had been part of a service club in the past year, compared to 11 percent of those with a conviction, 6 percent of those who had served a short time in prison or jail, and 4 percent of those who had been incarcerated for a year or more.

These somewhat modest results may very likely be due to weak measures. Very few people actually reported having engaged in any political participation except voting in the past year; only 2.6 percent contacted an official, 1.8 percent contributed money to a party or candidate, and 3.3 percent reported participating in a political rally. Negligible

TABLE 8.1. **Criminal justice contact and political participation**

Survey	Voted		Registered		Political activities	Civic engagement	
	Add Health	Fragile families	Add Health	Fragile families	Add Health	Add Health	Fragile families
None	47%	65%	75%	88%	6%	28%	48%
Questioned	45	56	75	86	10	31	44
Arrested	38	53	74	82	6	27	47
Convicted	31	58	65	89	6	26	47
Prison/jail	22	39	53	81	5	21	38
Serious time	8	32	37	76	3	18	39
N	14,361	2,627	14,460	2,638	15,038	15,065	3,294
Chi squared	119.306	154.919	87.543	32.902	35.235	11.124	22.710
Sig	.000	.000	.000	.000	.000	.049	.000

Note: Voted and registered exclude noncitizens. In "Fragile families," those not eligible for other reasons are also excluded. Serious time includes those imprisoned for a year or more. "Political activities" includes at least one activity; "Civic engagement" includes at least one organization.

percentages of study respondents actually ran for a public or nonpublic office. This likely reflects the young age of the sample. This was not the case for participation in civic groups, which 28 percent of the sample reported having done in the past year. However, there are additional important reasons for the weak relationship here. It is possible that respondents who had had a disciplinary encounter were just as likely to do voluntary work with a group because they were court ordered to do so as a provision of their parole or probation. Unfortunately, we cannot further test this speculation because no measure of whether the community service was voluntary or court ordered is available.

By comparison, we find very strong evidence that criminal justice contact affects participation in democratic elections. Respondents who experienced criminal justice contact were significantly less likely to report having registered to vote or having voted in the last presidential election.[33] In addition, table 8.1 shows something we could not test in our qualitative data: as with effects on trust and efficacy described in the previous chapter, we find declining participation at every level of contact with criminal justice authorities. The gap in participation is largest for more serious encounters with criminal justice, such as incarceration. In the Add Health study, only 8 percent of respondents reported having voted if they had served a lengthy sentence behind bars, compared to 47 percent of those who had no experience with criminal justice. Even less intensive interventions are associated with a reduced likelihood of turning out in an election, though. Self-reported voter turnout was 45 percent among those who had experienced police contact, 38 percent among those who had ever been arrested, 31 percent among the convicted, and 22 percent among those who had served time in prison or jail.

In the Add Health study, it is likely that depressed participation results from both decreased turnout among the eligible and formal exclusion from exercising the franchise. By comparison, felon disenfranchisement is not the only reason for diminished voting among Fragile Families respondents because the measure of voting in that study specifically excludes those who were ineligible to vote. Thus, the differences in turnout evident in the data represent the gap in voting between custodial and noncustodial eligible voters. Here, as in our interviews, we see evidence of a broader effect of criminal justice that goes beyond legal disenfranchisement. Even among those who retain the legal right to vote, individuals who have had criminal justice experience look markedly different from those who have not.

These results are striking, but do they really indicate an effect of criminal justice contact? As emphasized in earlier chapters, experiences with the criminal justice system are not randomly distributed. Custodial populations are systematically different from noncustodial citizens, in that they are much more likely to be poor, less educated, more unstable in their family relationships and employment, and more likely to be members of a racial or ethnic minority group. These factors make them less likely to engage in politics in the first place. A major hurdle of this analysis is thus to adequately dispel the possibility that any positive relation between custodial status and political activity is due to other factors that encourage respondents to select into both criminal activity and lower levels of political participation.

To isolate the effect of custodial involvement on engagement, we must account for preexisting differences that predict different levels of participation, such as age, socioeconomic status, gender, race, region, and parental background. If the effect of punitive encounters is working through these other distinctive aspects of the carceral population, then the significant relations evident in table 8.1 should disappear when controls are introduced. Most important, as in the regressions in earlier chapters, we must control for criminality.[34] We likewise control for military service and past receipt of welfare benefits. (Additional details of the regression models are provided in appendix C.)

The relationship between contact with criminal justice and other means of participating in politics was mostly insignificant after accounting for other influences, and one significant association is not in the hypothesized direction (being questioned by the police was positively related to participation). Civic participation also did not exhibit a strong relationship to criminal justice contact; participation in civic groups was only significant for those who were incarcerated or imprisoned. The results for those who were stopped and arrested are not significant after including controls. This is not surprising, given the relatively weak correlation already described between criminal justice contact and these measures of civic engagement.

However, there is a substantial effect of custodial status on voting and registering to vote in both the Add Health and Fragile Families data, even after accounting for differences in socioeconomic status and demographic factors (fig. 8.1). In Add Health, we find that the likelihood of registering to vote declines by 8 percent for those who were convicted in adult court but did not serve time, 16 percent for those incarcerated

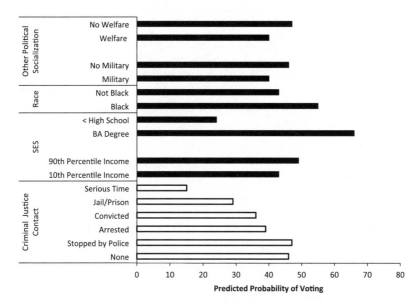

FIGURE 8.1. Predicted probability of voting, by criminal justice contact. *Source*: National Longitudinal Study of Adolescent Health, Wave III.

less than a year, and 29 percent for those who had been imprisoned for one year or more, holding other factors constant at their means.[35] Criminal justice involvement also lessened the likelihood of turning out to vote, and the magnitude of the effect was larger for more severe punitive encounters: Holding other factors constant at their means, being arrested reduced the likelihood of voting by 7 percent, being convicted reduced the odds of turning out by 10 percent, being sentenced to jail or prison reduced it further by 17 percent, and serving more than one year reduced the likelihood of voting by nearly one-third.

These effects are disturbingly large; to compare, being unemployed is associated with a decline of less than 3 percent in the predicted probability of voting, receiving welfare decreased the likelihood of voting by 7 percent, and the probability of voting increased by 6 percent moving from the tenth to ninetieth income percentile—similar in size to being arrested. The only factor that outdoes custodial contact in the size of its influence is having a college degree, associated with a 42 percent increase in voting.

Contact with the criminal justice system also influences political engagement in the Fragile Families study, replicating the pattern seen in

Add Health. These data, unlike those in Add Health, include only people who are eligible to vote; thus, the effects of criminal justice contact on turnout and registration are tapping into only informal barriers to voting, including voluntary withdrawal from political participation. As before, custodial involvement is associated with a significant decline in the likelihood of being registered to vote or voting in the last presidential election, independent of other influences, including poverty, education, and criminality.

In the Fragile Families data, among those who are legally eligible to vote, being arrested, incarcerated, and confined for more than one year is associated with a decrease of 5 percent, 6 percent, and 8 percent, respectively, in the probability of registering to vote (see fig. 8.2). The probability of voting declined by 8 percent for those who had been stopped and questioned by the police; by 16 percent for those with a history of being arrested; by 18 percent for those with a conviction; by 22 percent for those serving time in jail or prison; and, if their sentence was a year or more in duration, the probability of voting declined by an overwhelming 26 percent, holding other factors at their means. Again, these effects are quite large, given that the probability of voting only decreases by 11 percent when we move from the lowest to highest level of poverty (fig. 8.2). The effect of being incarcerated or imprisoned is also larger in size than having a college-educated parent, being in the military, receiving welfare, and being black. Like Add Health, only the effect of a college diploma is larger in size (increases voting probability by 31%).

To summarize, there is a large, negative effect of criminal justice contact for several aspects of political life, particularly registering to vote and turning out at election time, and more severe encounters are associated with a larger decline in political participation. These results are consistent across two very different samples—one of primarily unmarried parents from seriously disadvantaged circumstances in urban settings, the other of a young adult population that is more highly educated and nationally representative—and arise not simply because those in the custodial population come from disadvantaged backgrounds or are prevented from voting due to felon exclusions. The results point to a large, independent effect of punitive encounters that does not depend on preexisting characteristics and is not only the result of formal disenfranchisement. This echoes the stories we recount from our interview subjects. For them, formal disenfranchisement was just one factor limiting

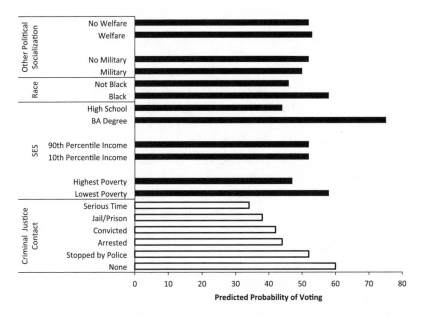

FIGURE 8.2. Predicted probability of voting, by criminal justice contact. *Source*: Fragile Families and Child Wellbeing Study, Wave III.

their political participation; their alienation and disengagement from the political process ran far deeper than not being allowed to go to the polls on Election Day.

Further Tests of Causality

Because an unobserved characteristic of offenders may predict the propensity for criminality, we again conduct a set of additional analyses. We first address potential biases that might result from differences between custodial and noncustodial citizens in criminal behavior. To do this, we limit our analysis to only those survey respondents who reported engaging in illegal drug use.[36] We then leverage the fact that some of these individuals have experienced criminal justice contact while others have not. We match respondents who have had carceral contact with respondents who have not had contact on a complete set of covariates, as well as on a propensity score that predicts criminal justice contact. This allows us to further parse the effect of contact from the effect of self-selection into crime. (Additional details of these analyses are provided in appendix C.)

Comparing political engagement across four subgroups—6,266 respondents with no history of illegal drug use or criminal justice contact, 628 respondents with no history of illegal drug use but with custodial contact, 5,631 respondents with illegal drug use and no custodial contact, and 2,282 respondents with both illegal drug use and custodial contact—helps us gain further insight into the extent to which preexisting criminality may be driving our results. We find that differences in voter turnout and registration across the four groups are small but highly significant: Those with both illegal drug use and custodial contact have the lowest levels of political participation on these measures (see fig. 8.3). About 47 percent of nondrug users with no contact reported having voted in the last election, as had 44 percent of drug users with no criminal justice experience. By comparison, 37 percent of drug users with some type of custodial contact turned out to vote. Likewise, while 72 percent of those with no drug use and no criminal justice experience and 73 percent of drug users with no contact reported voter registration, only 69 percent of drug users with criminal justice contact had registered to vote.

We then examine the effects of criminal justice contact among only the subset of 7,913 Add Health respondents who self-reported ille-

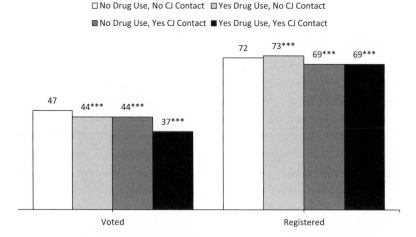

FIGURE 8.3. Voting and registration, by drug use and criminal justice contact. *Source*: National Longitudinal Study of Adolescent Health, Wave III.

gal drug use. In multiple regression models that estimate the effects of progressive contact among only this subset, we find consistent effects. Among illegal drug users, contact with the criminal justice system significantly lowers voter registration and turnout, and the size of the effects increases as contact becomes more intense. All else equal, among self-reported drug users, being convicted of a crime lowers the likelihood of voter registration by about 10 percent, incarceration by about 14 percent, and spending serious time in prison by 30 percent. Similarly, arrest lowers turnout by about 6 percent, conviction by about 11 percent, time in prison or jail by about 13 percent, and serving serious time lowers turnout by roughly 27 percent.[37] As in the full sample, there is no significant effect on our other measures of political and civic participation once we control for the full set of confounders. We interpret these nonsignificant results similarly to our previous discussion.

To account for a second potential source of bias, which stems from differences across our sample in the likelihood of being caught for illegal behavior, we conduct one further test. Here, rather than limiting variation in criminality, we focus on restricting our sample to only those who experience contact with criminal justice, but vary the time at which they experience it. While the third wave of the Add Health survey, conducted in 2001 and 2002, is the only panel that includes political measures, the fourth wave of that study, administered from 2008 to 2009, repeats questions that measure police contact, conviction, and incarceration. In the intervening years, about 1,079 respondents are added to the ranks of those who have experienced a criminal conviction, and 2,329 people are arrested for the first time. Being able to identify "future offenders" in the Wave III data allows us to compare the political attitudes and behaviors of individuals who have been exposed to a criminal justice intervention by 2001–2 with that of comparable individuals in those years who have not yet been exposed to criminal justice but who will experience this contact by 2008–9. We find significant differences in the political participation patterns of those who have been arrested by the third-wave survey compared to those who have not yet been arrested but will have experienced this type of contact by the next wave. For the Add Health data, having been arrested by the time of the survey predicts decreased rates of registration (70% relative to 60%) and voting (38% relative to 32%). The same is true for the previously relative to the future convicted. The data show that those who have been convicted of a crime by the third wave, compared to those who have not yet but will have by the fourth wave, are less likely to vote (47% compared to 34%) or to be registered (74% to 67%). In a multiple regression similar to those employed in our other analyses, having a conviction at Wave III relative to those who do not have a conviction until Wave IV predicts a decrease of 9 percent in the likelihood of registering to vote and 5 percent in the likelihood of voting. A past relative to future arrest likewise predicts a 4 percent gap in registration and 5 percent gap in turnout, controlling for other factors.

In addition, we use this setup to conduct a placebo test similar to that described in chapter 6, in which we match respondents who will have criminal justice contact by the survey's fourth wave but have not yet by the third wave with respondents who do not report criminal justice contact in either wave. We then estimate the effects on political attitudes and behaviors in the third wave. If our previous analysis is truly identifying a causal effect of contact with criminal justice, rather than reflecting underlying differences in the likelihood of experiencing contact, we expect that this analysis will fail to reject the null hypothesis of no difference across the two groups. Future convicts should be statistically indistinguishable from respondents who have no contact with criminal justice in either of the waves. Put simply, future criminal justice contact should not predict political behavior. Indeed, this is what we find.

A final way we attempt to test the sensitivity of our causal claim is by using the only data we know of that ask respondents about their political participation at two points in time. The 1997 National Longitudinal Survey of Youth (NLSY97) panel survey asks respondents whether they voted in both the 2004 and 2008 waves. We limit the sample to the 6,516 young adults who by 2004 had never been arrested, convicted, or incarcerated (2,467 of the original 1997 cohort in that year reported already having had contact with criminal justice), who were interviewed after the presidential election in 2004, were of voting age by that date, and were US citizens. Between that wave and the 2008–9 wave, 191 of these respondents had been arrested for the first time, 93 had been convicted for the first time, and 57 had been sentenced to prison for the first time. Using these data, we can analyze the effect of having a first-time encounter with criminal justice on voting in the 2008 election, controlling for whether a respondent voted in 2004. This allows us to treat individuals without criminal justice contact with an intervention and leverage the timing of the treatment to examine a change in political behavior (further details on this analysis are provided in appendix C).

The results are striking, especially given that we are only looking at change from one presidential election to the next. Holding participation in the 2004 election constant, as well as controlling for other demographic factors (e.g., race, age, gender, income, education, urbanicity, poverty, region, and marital status), we find that being newly arrested or incarcerated had a significant and negative effect on the probability of voting in 2008; a new conviction just misses statistical significance. Specifically, holding all other factors at their mean values, being arrested decreases the predicted probability of voting by 13 percentage points ($p = .05$) while being newly incarcerated decreases the likelihood of voting in 2008 by 52 percentage points ($p = .002$). Otherwise stated, only 19 percent of those who had been incarcerated and 58 percent of new arrestees voted in 2008, compared to 71 percent of those who remained free of criminal justice intervention. These effects are quite large; to compare, the predicted probability of voting in 2008 decreases by 35 percentage points if one had not voted in the earlier 2004 election.

Taken together, these analyses offer compelling evidence that the significant relationship between one's experience with criminal justice and his or her propensity to take part in the political process is not an artifact of preexisting characteristics or confounders. If criminal justice contact was not driving participatory habits, but was instead a stand-in for static factors, we would be unlikely to see a decrease over time in the likelihood of voting across survey waves based only on having been arrested or incarcerated. In other words, young adults became much less likely to take part in the political process once they had an adverse encounter with criminal justice. There is still the possibility that other changes during this period predict both criminal offending and voting. However, many of the most likely candidates, such as a change in employment or poverty status, are themselves a consequence of criminal justice contact.

Conclusion

Analyses of qualitative and quantitative data show that contact with criminal justice has deleterious effects on democratic citizenship, diminishing engagement in civic and political life and depressing political activism. Indeed, our empirical findings challenge a centerpiece of political participation orthodoxy: that individual resources such as time, knowledge, and money are the strongest predictors of participation. Instead, we find that direct experiences with the punitive state exert a strong effect on predilections for political engagement.

Our data suggest that the demobilizing effects of criminal justice involvement extend not only to those who are legally disenfranchised, but also to the large and growing numbers of citizens who experience direct contact with state agents of crime control. For these individuals, the choice to abstain from the political process comes not only from a loss of legal rights, but also from a deeply pervasive sense of alienation, stigma, and fear. In the best case, political representatives came to be seen as doing whatever they wanted regardless of the will of the people. In the worst, citizens actively feared and recoiled from the state.

One potential critique is that the results do not always reflect volitional choices about whether to engage in the political process by voting, but are often the outcome of limitations on the franchise for convicted felons. We offer two counterpoints. First, this could not explain why those who are newly arrested and not convicted or confined would be so much less likely to vote in a later election. Second, because we continue to find significant effects of criminal justice contact in the Fragile Families data, from which ineligible voters are excluded, we are confident that formal disenfranchisement is not solely responsible for the effects we find. Thus, we conclude that over and above the legal restrictions that withhold the franchise from millions of Americans is the de facto exclusion and voluntary withdrawal of many others. The evidence presented in this and previous chapters shows not only that custodial citizens vote less, but also that criminal justice has come to define their political lives and participatory experiences in ways that analyzing voting trends does not capture. In addition, it is certainly true that not all of our interview subjects had withdrawn from political life. Take Neal, whom we met in New Orleans. Neal had served most of his life behind the walls of Louisiana's Angola prison, where "overseers" would sit on horseback watching over inmates picking cotton and cutting cane on 18,000 acres of farmland. After serving nearly three decades on the prison farm, a judge overturned his sentence on the basis of new evidence clearing him of his crime.

Neal was obviously no stranger to unfair treatment and he echoed the deep distrust voiced by other interviewees. In our conversation with him, he described Louisiana police as "an octopus" that surrounds certain neighborhoods and targets certain citizens. However, unlike most of our respondents, Neal turned to political activism following his criminal justice experiences, determined to help ex-inmates like himself to have a bigger voice in politics. His résumé includes a long list of activist feats, including helping to reform the indigent defense system in New Orleans Parish; leading the charge to create an independent police monitor in New Orleans; building a coalition to depopulate the jail and gain agreements that no new beds would be built; and working for a spate of other criminal justice reforms, not least of which was a compensation bill for wrongly convicted people and helping to return eligibility for parole to those serving lengthy sentences. In addition, the nonprofit he founded and runs has registered 2,200 people in the jail to vote; he teaches a class on street law and paralegal training; and he is currently working on legislation to get the right to vote back to the 6,600 people on probation and parole.

In all that he had accomplished, Neal was certainly exceptional by any standard. However, there were others in our sample who had participated in more modest ways. Some mentioned having attended a community meeting at some point, or having gone to a political rally. What these individuals made clear, though—Neal included—was that the decision to participate had been made *in spite* of their experiences with criminal justice. What they described as the *result* of their custodial status echoes the broader trends we have focused on throughout this chapter.

The combined force of these results makes clear that the consequences of being a custodial citizen, even among those who are not permanently and formally excluded, affect the likelihood of engaging in political life, long after an encounter with criminal justice. In Abe and Sarah, we saw people who could vote but chose not to because of the shame of having been stripped of rights previously. In Paul, we saw that those who are formally excluded from the vote may choose to withdraw from politics entirely: Even though he could engage in other ways, he declined to. In Silas, Bert, and others, we found that many considered it wise to exclude themselves from political life, to avoid the gaze of a state that had so often been a source of substantial harm.

We often treat engagement in the political process as a democratic good because of its instrumental benefits, as a mechanism to transmit our desires, priorities, and beliefs to our trustees in office. But as participation scholars remind us, "participation itself is a value, conferring on the individual the dignity that comes with being a full member of the political community."[38] Voting and participation are central principles of democratic citizenship. Judith Shklar explains that voting is what distinguished citizens from chattel slaves. W.E.B. DuBois said the vote was "necessary to modern manhood."[39] The highest court in South Africa, in its decision to reinstate voting rights for inmates, called the vote a "badge of dignity. Quite literally, it says that everybody counts."[40] Participation also matters because individuals learn how to be good citizens; taking part in the political process imbues one with civic skills. Through the process of voting, citizens learn that they are part of a democratic community.

Custodial citizens, however, overwhelmingly described occupying a limited and stigmatized citizenship: "I'll never be a true American citizen again." We must therefore conclude that, more than simply punishing deviance, an overreaching carceral state has splintered the polity, deepening the divide between those who are heard and those who are silenced. The end result is a growing class of disempowered and alienated people who occupy both an *objectively* and *subjectively* subordinate position in the democratic community. And in a society founded on democratic inclusion and political equality ideals, this development is deeply troubling. As Joe Soss notes, "Flourishing democracies need citizens who are efficacious and engaged, aware of public issues, and conscious of collective interests—citizens who enjoy a modicum of dignity and security, who are not afraid to assert themselves, and who expect responsive action from government."[41] The significant number of citizens who feel excluded by their own liberal democracy has implications for our society as a whole, as engagement in the political process benefits "the community by cultivating democratic virtues and cooperation in the name of the common good."[42] It is to this broader damage to our democracy that we now turn.

CHAPTER NINE

Where We Go from Here

There are two Americas—separate, unequal, and no longer even acknowledging each other except on the barest cultural terms. In the one nation, new millionaires are minted every day. In the other, human beings no longer necessary to our economy, to our society, are being devalued and destroyed. — *David Simon* (2008)

What manner of democracy do we have? Democracy requires that government is responsive to citizens' preferences and concerns and that individuals have a "voice in the laws that govern them."[1] But as we argued at the start of this book, democracy is also constructed through the everyday experiences of citizens; it requires that the most vulnerable see democracy in their institutions, feel they can be seen and heard in communal life and are confident they can participate in the political process without retribution. Democracy means that the least powerful will still enter the contest, rather than choose to avoid it. When institutions embody practices that make citizens feel that they are unequal and unheard, we have reason to question the quality of our democracy.

The reforms that have characterized American criminal justice over the past half century—its growth to encompass a larger proportion of citizens, its persistent racial demography, and its decreasingly democratic character—have created a new form of second-class citizenship, *custodial citizenship*, a group that has withdrawn from participation in the political life of the nation. By inhibiting the development of civic skills, diverting citizens from having a say in their government and choice of representatives, and informing them that they are not worthy of "equal concern and respect," criminal justice has transformed the lived experience of citizenship in America today. As custodial citizens interact with some of our most basic and expanding institutions in America—those governing how to punish citizens and control crime—they see a system at odds with the principles of democracy.

Many of us would be troubled to know that a segment of our fellow citizens has been exiled from the democratic process, no matter what the justification. Many others, though, see it as an unfortunate but necessary compromise: A small minority must lose their right to a full and equal citizenship in order for the great majority to live in a safe and crime-free society. For those who believe this, as long as the former does not exceed the latter and as long as this justification holds true, there is no great need for alarm. Perhaps a group of citizens is left out and distrusts government, but ultimately, our democracy is strong. After all, the rest still enjoy a robust democratic citizenship and the democratic process generally works as it should.

We believe such a belief is patently wrong. It is convenient to see custodial citizens as a small group, insulated from the larger democratic project. This view is made even easier because some custodial citizens are not law abiding; they have stepped outside the bounds of legitimate behavior and are therefore easier to construe as morally suspect. But that should not distract us from seeing that the offense to democratic citizenship and equality affects us all. Indeed, custodial citizens are the canary in the mine, showing us that conditions in the polity are not well. "The community as a whole is harmed," one scholar argues, "when a substantial number of its citizens are subject to arbitrary treatment by the government without effective redress."[2] As past antidemocratic periods have shown us, the ugly effects of antidemocratic institutions rarely remain confined to their targets, even if they do not migrate outward in immediately apparent ways. In eras of sanctioned gender and racial inequality, it was certainly better to be a white male citizen. However, at those times, even the privileged lived in a society where the fullness of their rights could be felt only because they were calibrated against their fellow countrymen and countrywomen who were denied access to those same basic dignities. We may experience democratic citizenship, but if we do so in a system that denies it to others, then ours is not the full and equal democracy we claim it to be. The diminution of democratic citizenship for any group of Americans diminishes it for us all.

The socialization of democratic citizens is crucial, as "the development of a stable and effective democratic government depends upon the orientations that people have to the political process."[3] By not only actively excluding large groups of citizens from civil and political membership, but also failing to inculcate citizens with the fundamental notions of participatory citizenship, criminal justice substantially harms American democracy. The criminal justice system teaches custodial citizens to distrust government generally; it imparts the lesson that government does not understand or respond to their needs and shows them that dealings with the state should be avoided.

These individual-level effects of interactions with the punitive side of the state—the alienation, distrust, and avoidance—are not randomly distributed. Thus, there are two primary ways that these effects are likely to have broader repercussions: First, as these individuals have distinct political views, their withdrawal removes a unique perspective from democratic discussion. As scholars of political voice remind us, "what matters is not only the amount of civic activity but its distribution, not just how many people take part but who they are and what they say."[4] If the policy preferences and concerns of custodial citizens mirrored that of the voting population, we might worry somewhat less about their marginalization. Our intuition, though, is that this is not the case. Rather, we argue that criminal justice has created a concentrated group of citizens whose views are absent from the pluralist cacophony of American political life. Thus, criminal justice interventions that silence custodial citizens undermine the "equal protection of interests" so central to a healthy democracy in theory, which ultimately aggravates political inequality in practice.

Our surveys show a consistent divergence in opinions and priorities between individuals with carceral contact and those without, from their views on homosexuality to their patterns of church attendance.[5] The most striking differences between custodial citizens and others, however, are the concerns they express about their economic fortunes and their beliefs about the role of government in ensuring equal opportunity. Compared to those with no criminal justice contact, custodial citizens report higher levels of concern about their current situations and significantly greater pessimism about their future prospects. They are more likely to be very worried about losing their current job, sending their children to college, and paying their bills. They are less likely to believe that they will have a better life than their parents and report more frequently feeling that they are losing hope. And they are more likely to believe that the state should help them to overcome these substantial obstacles.[6] For example, the NLSY asked respondents whether it was a good or bad idea "if the federal government were to make sure that everyone has an equal opportunity to succeed in life." Respondents were more likely to say that it was an "extremely good idea" if they had been convicted (57%) or incarcerated (62%) than if they had not had these experiences (52%). These differences hold even when we control for other factors.

Through participation, citizens can convey their concerns, needs, and priorities to government and pressure officials to take action. This, at least in theory, influences what elected officials do, shaping the policies and laws that govern the nation. Yet because custodial citizens are so much less likely to participate, and in some cases are legally prohibited from doing so, their specific array of interests, needs, and points of view are less likely to be heard. Indeed, Howard Rosenthal and other scholars of political polarization suggest that, due to mass incarceration, the median voter has shifted over time, changing political debate and the constituencies to whom politicians cater.[7] This introduces a dynamic that America's founders were at pains to avoid, the tyranny of the majority, and threatens to continuously reinforce relations of subordination that, as our interviewees reported, seem nearly impossible to escape.

As legislators, parties, and advocacy groups have little incentive to promote their interests, custodial citizens' low levels of political activity make them peripheral to policymaking, their preferences receding from view even in important policy decisions that may disproportionately affect them, their families, and their communities. This is perhaps most starkly clear when it comes to criminal justice itself. Lisa Miller argues that, in the absence of high rates of crime, it is difficult for vulnerable populations to draw attention to the issue of violence, to say nothing of urban poverty and disadvantage. In principle, she argues, crime waves therefore provide unique opportunities for crime to become politicized and for disproportionately affected communities to mobilize widespread public concern. In these moments, in theory, residents of high-violence areas can "draw attention to the obligations of the state to remediate the criminogenic conditions in which they live."[8]

A broad range of policy responses might result from increased attention to the problems of crime and violence. In recent practice, however, the main responses when crime has become politicized in America have been primarily punitive: gang interventions, severe sentences for felony crimes, drug zones, habitual offender statutes, sentence enhancements, and enhanced stop and frisk. Mostly absent from the policy agenda were interventions that might have addressed the decimation of the urban economy, educational disparities across high- and low-income communities, or other social and economic insecurities that contribute to criminality. In essence, the focus has become the punishment of crime rather than the protection of citizens from it through the amelioration of its preconditions. This may be because custodial citizens are less likely to be heard in policy debates about violence.[9]

A second and related way in which our results are likely to have broader implications for American democracy is this: As custodial populations continue to grow, so too does political inequality. In other words, we should be concerned about the diminished engagement of custodial citizens because they are concentrated and their views are distinct, but also for the simple fact that their ranks are growing at breakneck speed. Now numbering over 2 million Americans, "if the incarcerated population could form its own state, it would qualify for five votes in the Electoral College."[10]

The political marginalization of custodial citizens is not the same as the inequality of voice that stems from economic disparities. Neither form of political disparity is insignificant, but in some ways the former should be even more troubling than the latter. As Sidney Verba says in summarizing an argument of Judith Shklar:

> Outcomes that derive from *human action* are more subject to moral evaluation than are acts of nature. Second, outcomes that derive from *intentional* actions of human actors are more subject to such evaluations than are outcomes that are unintended. Third, intended actions that affect *large populations* and affect them *differentially* are even more open to moral evaluation. And, lastly, such actions, when *carried out or endorsed by government* (the authorized actor) are most open to moral evaluations.[11] [italics original]

By this logic, criminal justice interventions that result in systematic disempowerment are most offensive because they are not an act of nature or oversight, but are instead the outcome of identifiable policy choices whose explicit intent is to remove people from the body politic. These intentional choices affect a large population that has grown substantially, they affect some groups systematically and leave others largely untouched, and they are formally sanctioned by government.

The damages to democracy that we have uncovered in this book are sizable. These effects, however, can be mitigated. In concluding this book, we turn our attention to a number of policy innovations that we believe can not only contract the carceral state but also bring it back in line with our nation's democratic ideals of voice, equality, and responsiveness. These prescriptions range from small programs to large philosophical transformations. However, we caution that the scale of the problem requires the political will to make real changes in the way we govern; first and foremost, it requires us to recognize that the domain of criminal justice is not an isolated set of policies and practices and institutions that affect just a narrow slice of the population, but rather that it is an integral part of our American state and central to our democracy writ large. Political decisions, rather than crime trends alone, drove the rise of the carceral state, and these choices had political effects. At the end of the day, it is political choices, too, that will ultimately determine whether we build a democracy that engages all citizens as equal and active participants, a nation whose institutions reflect the critical democratic values of equality, voice, and accountability.

Policy Recommendations

Agents of the carceral state must begin to take seriously the culture of their institutions. Real reform must be concerned with giving citizens voice in the process and providing channels that assure oversight, transparency, and responsiveness to citizens' complaints and concerns. For instance, community policing cannot only be about "officers playing basketball with kids in housing project and smiling at babies," but "requires that citizens, at the neighborhood level, meet regularly with police to jointly define neighborhood crime problems and set police priorities."[12] Only through this type of deep and fundamental shift in how criminal justice is practiced can we hope to walk back the substantial damage that the system has done to democracy over the past fifty years. It is to the practical application of a new and more democratic philosophy of crime control that we now turn our attention.

Our recommendations fall into three broad policy areas that should be simultaneously and energetically pursued: increasing democratic responsiveness and voice, increasing democratic accountability and transparency, and increasing racial equality. The policy agenda we outline below will not be easy or accomplished quickly, and some of our ideas have so far not been tried or tested. These three reforms will take more imagination from criminal justice scholars and policymakers because they demand not only that we scale back criminal justice, but that we also confront its antidemocratic features. To do that, we must begin to think of this not as a narrow issue about the political feasibility of downsizing the carceral state, but as a central issue for strengthening the democratic state and reasserting democratic principles within one of its central set of institutions.

More Democratic Institutions: Responsiveness and Voice

Over the past decade of increased financial strain, a number of states have reformed their criminal justice policies. Some repealed habitual offender laws, others widened parole eligibility, and still others made greater use of drug courts instead of harsh mandatory drug sentencing. We applaud these efforts. Scaling back incarceration will help ease overcrowding and myriad other issues that have plagued prisons; it may even help to reduce the number of minor offenders who are confined, which we discussed in chapter 2. However, there is a danger that such reforms will help mask the fact that few of these states have addressed the antidemocratic practices that have become standard operating procedure in their institutions. In our zeal to praise states for reducing their correctional populations, practices that are an offense to our democracy fly under the radar.

Reforming sentences and police practices alone is not enough; we must also be concerned with reforming the institutions themselves. In chapter 3 we showed that American criminal justice institutions have broken significantly with the democratic norms that govern most American institutions. Instead of embodying the commitments of a democratic republic—equality, responsiveness, and citizen voice—through the PLRA, immunity, intent doctrine, and other developments, institutions of criminal justice have been designed as places where citizens are not heard or responded to. To make really fundamental reforms, we must reinstate democratic principles into the everyday practices of these institutions.

Imagining policies that democratize police departments and prisons is, on its face, more difficult than designing policies that reduce prison populations, partly because there is an inherent tension between liberal democracy and institutions of surveillance and punishment. Prisoners are segregated from mainstream citizenship by virtue of their confine-

ment. How do we make democracy—open and participatory by definition—part of a closed world with a mission to confine, limit rights, and
control? How can we make criminal justice institutions serve the cause
of democracy?

The answer is more straightforward than it might initially seem, and
international models abound. First, through policy reforms and financial support for existing public and nonprofit initiatives, we should bring
custodial citizens back into the democratic project and make them full
members of the democratic community. Most obviously, we should end
political banishment. Giving custodial citizens a voice in the political
process through voting is the most crucial way to restore their political
standing. The right to vote is "the characteristic, the identifying feature
of democratic citizenship in America, not a means to other ends"; granting suffrage to custodial citizens allows them input into the choice of
policies and representatives but also communicates to them that they are
legitimate actors in the body politic, deserving of equal consideration of
their needs and preferences.[13] Their ability to take part in political discussion may lessen their invisibility to policymakers, prompting elected
officials to respond more attentively to communities of citizens who are
in dire need of resources and assistance. The vote would also help custodial citizens develop civic skills and habits that may have longer-term
benefits to themselves and their communities.[14] Some evidence even suggests that voting lowers recidivism; sociologists Jeffrey Manza and Chris
Uggen have found that former offenders who voted were less likely to be
rearrested, all else equal.[15]

Restoring the right to vote for most offenders is not politically infeasible. In fact, most Americans do not believe that felons should be ineligible to vote. A study based on a representative survey of Americans
found that just over half of the general public believed that "felons who
serve their time should return to society as full citizens, with full rights
and privileges." On the specific question of voting rights for felons, only
a small minority of people believed that felons should lose their right
to vote for the rest of their lives (16%); otherwise stated, a large majority (82%) disagreed with the policy of permanent political banishment
that some states still maintain. Most of those in the survey supported
much more lenient forms of disenfranchisement. About one-third believed that people should be denied the right to vote only for the duration of their incarceration.[16] Another survey of the Atlanta population
found even higher levels of support for full restoration (71%).[17] A similar

poll by the *Washington Post* in 2001 with a national adult sample showed that 61 percent of people favored returning the right to vote to ex-felons who had not committed a violent crime.[18]

In this area, the reform impulse has already begun to sweep the nation. After the 2000 election crisis in Florida, the country saw terrific mobilization on behalf of restoring the vote to ex-felons. As a result of these efforts, twenty-three states repealed or altered their laws, expanding vote eligibility to 800,000 citizens. Nine states with the most punitive laws lifted their permanent bans and eight others eased the vote restoration procedure.[19] Congress has recently considered legislation that would permit ex-felons, parolees, and probationers to vote in federal elections (the Democracy Restoration Act was introduced in July 2010).[20] However, thirty states continue to restrict those on parole or probation from voting, resulting in millions of custodial citizens still left out of democratic citizenship. Two states—Virginia and Kentucky—still bar at least some felons from voting for life. In those states, over 20 percent of blacks cannot vote.[21]

But will these citizens, made outsiders to political life in other ways, even want to vote? As in the public as a whole, our interviewees almost unanimously opposed felony disenfranchisement. Many expressed the belief that exclusion made them second-class citizens. Even while most of our participants were deeply disillusioned, and despite varying viewpoints on why they withdrew from political life, many also believed in the principle of democratic citizenship and the idea that every man and woman in America should be allowed access to the vote. Many of our respondents, even those who did not or could not vote, deeply desired the right to vote. For these individuals, suffrage was a keystone entitlement signifying citizenship and membership, and the loss of this fundamental right was deeply and negatively felt. As Carlton, a middle-aged black man from Charlottesville, put it, "I just feel that as being a citizen of the US, that is my right. To vote." Luke from Trenton agreed: "You can change the world with one vote. . . . Now I would appreciate the fact if I could vote. That would be something dear to me. If I could vote—oh my god—I'd vote."

Restoring citizenship through voting is an important first step toward the democratic reinclusion of custodial citizens, but it is a first step only. Many disagreed with Luke; given that even citizens who are legally permitted to vote often disengage, this is only the first step in undoing the damage of criminal justice.

As we made clear in chapter 8, withdrawal from voting and other forms of participation goes beyond formal exclusion. For many custodial citizens, it is an active withdrawal from civic life. It seems strange, then, that even with the increased public focus on reentry and reintegration in recent years, few models exist for returning custodial citizens not only to jobs and families, but also to neighborhoods, communities, and the political life of the nation. Employment preparation is the cornerstone of the reintegration agenda, and much prerelease programming is concerned with the job application process. However, policymakers and researchers have devoted considerably less attention to the process by which ex-offenders reconnect with civil society.

What might a program designed around reorienting prisoners to community and political life look like? In conducting our interviews, we came across two promising pilot programs that are working toward bringing ex-offenders back into civic life, and in the process, helping to rebuild their communities. In New Orleans, AmeriCorps has begun a program for ex-felons called the Cornerstone Builders. The program trains ex-offenders as AmeriCorps members who recruit, train, and manage teams of volunteers. The program is thus mutually beneficial to the individual and the community. Teams work in the community to develop food pantries, clean up vacant lots, develop community gardens and parks, organize neighborhood activities, and do community outreach. In return, the ex-offenders are given a stipend, job, housing assistance, and mentors. They also learn how to use computers, fill out resumes, and develop other transferable professional skills.

The second program we encountered was just getting off the ground during our research. The Community Volunteer Project is a program initiated by the Community Programs Division of the New Jersey State Parole Board. Recognizing that ex-offenders were having great difficulty finding work and becoming productive members of their communities, the Community Programs Division established the program to help ex-offenders acquire skills and work experience through volunteering. Social service organizations that have agreed to participate take on ex-offenders as volunteers. A certain amount of volunteer time then entitles ex-offenders to earn vouchers for furniture and clothing, as well as a certificate from the Department of Labor that shows they have completed community volunteer work. Most important, volunteering with an established organization potentially provides a source of referrals and recommendations for long-standing employment. Beyond the potential such programs have to link ex-offenders with later employment, we believe they have real potential to build community social capital and engage ex-offenders in pro-social civic work.

Civic reintegration is an idea whose time has come, and programs like the above should be rigorously evaluated as important complements to reentry initiatives that have so far focused primarily on individual needs like employment and drug treatment. However, civic reintegration should begin before the reentry phase; citizen voice and engagement are vital even during punishment. Prisons and jails often excessively limit free speech and citizen input. They can legally ban civic associations and inmate unions with little in the way of explanation, and prisoner-run newspapers likewise face discretionary control and censorship. These practices should be exposed to the highest levels of scrutiny and correctional administrators should be required to clearly articulate and defend their rationales in cases where they truly believe that allowing inmates to maintain free speech and association directly threatens institutional safety.

Infusing democratic principles into systems of punishment need not undermine punishment or crime control. As many scholars have argued previously, there is no legitimate penological rationale for felon disenfranchisement and it is similarly difficult to devise a compelling argument for how other forms of citizen expression threaten law and order.[22] Many prisons have retained numerous social and religious inmate organizations even as they have clamped down on inmate unions and councils. This makes the logic of denying association for reasons of safety untenable. Rather, many restrictions currently placed on the rights of custodial citizens are designed either to discourage criticism of authorities or to make life easier for criminal justice practitioners. Neither of these constitutes a legitimate rationale for limiting core democratic freedoms.

More Democratic Institutions: Transparency and Accountability

Assuring that political institutions are responsive to citizens' preferences and concerns is as important as securing citizens' voice in public life. As Sidney Verba notes, while citizen voice is the first prerequisite to political equality, "an unequal reception when equal political voices are raised may generate an even greater sense of unfairness than would the absence of equal expression."[23] Accountability to the citizenry is a central feature of a constitutional democracy, and accountability within the criminal justice system is perhaps even more crucial than in other institutions, precisely because of its unique power to apply force, detain, and deprive citizens of freedom. Eric Luna argues that correctional systems, because they entail so much discretion, pose specific and severe challenges to democratic accountability. "Nowhere is the . . . need for openness more urgent than in the execution of the penal code," he argues, because "the discretionary judgments of criminal law enforcement—to investigate, to arrest, to charge, to plea bargain, and so on— are among the most important decisions that any official can make. They are largely unreviewed or unreviewable by the other branches of government, thereby posing enormous potential for abuse."[24]

Yet, despite legal protections intended to preserve the rights of the accused, institutions governing punishment and surveillance in America are extremely closed off to outside scrutiny and often openly discourage accountability to inmates themselves. Luna argues that prisons and police in the United States are often governed by a "secret law" or "shadow code" that is concealed from the public: "Much law enforcement authority . . . is exercised covertly and without opportunity for electoral oversight. Below the radar of public scrutiny, certain groups are subjected to capricious policing, unauthorized displays of force, and unwritten codes of conduct."[25] Prisons in the United States are not the hidden gulags of North Korea, Russia, or China, but by international standards they still contain little in the way of oversight and accountability.

For those who think we exaggerate, consider how we would respond if any other of our nation's governing institutions refused to provide the media even minimal access to its operations, gave blanket immunity to officials who had engaged in misconduct or coercion, or let people submit claims of abuse but allowed the allegedly abusive officials to handle the claims themselves, and rarely punished the officials in question. Our criminal justice institutions in fact engage in such practices, wielding an inordinate amount of power over their subjects. They control their inmates' movement, speech, and contact with the outside world, and do so with few checks on their discretion.

National-level reform efforts that have sought to make various stages of the criminal justice process more transparent and accountable have so far been unsuccessful. Court challenges have failed and recent proposed legislation by Representative Robert Scott (D-VA), the Prison Abuse Remedies Act, died in committee.[26] The PARA was designed to amend some provisions of the PLRA in order to make it easier for individuals to successfully seek redress of legitimate claims regarding prison abuse. For instance, the PARA would have removed the physical injury requirement, which under current policy requires inmates to show they suffered physical injury in order to press a claim of abuse. Designed to deter frivolous claims, the physical injury requirement has been employed by the courts as the basis to exclude cases where inmates claimed they had been sodomized by a staff member, a prisoner was forced to stand naked for 10 hours, female prisoners were strip-searched by male guards—in these cases and others, the courts declined to hear that case because no physical injury was determined to have occurred. In the absence of a major federal reform, states must take the lead. State departments of corrections should immediately create independent oversight bodies that open up their systems' operations to outside scrutiny. These agencies can be positioned to recognize patterns of mistreatment. If individual incidents at one facility are shown to amount to systemic mistreatment, the agency should have the authority to mandate a reform plan. States should then outline reasonable rules to govern the submission of grievances and assure that there is an efficient procedure in place to appeal decisions.

Whatever form an independent agency takes, custodial citizens should not have to seek redress from the same institutions that mistreat them. A standard rule of operation in many other government institutions is that the complaint procedure and the target institution are independent. Other countries have independent agencies to oversee their prisons and jails. But in the United States, only three states—Hawaii, Iowa, and Nebraska—currently handle inmate claims through an independent ombudsman.[27] Other states need to follow their lead. There is no reason to believe that public safety will be compromised; rather, one would expect that a fairer process would lead to fewer eruptions of violence and insurgency within the prison. A growing body of literature suggests that when processes are seen as fair and legitimate, citizens are more satisfied irrespective of the outcome.[28]

Police accountability is also weak, and many departments still cloak their operations in relative secrecy. Chapter 3 discussed how custodial citizens have almost no power to hold police and departments accountable. Section 1983 claims are limited; citizens have trouble obtaining injunctions against police departments; doctrines such as the qualified immunity defense, good faith exception, and deliberate indifference standard conspire against citizens seeking to hold police to account;

and much like prison grievance procedures, citizen complaints are often handled by an internal affairs section of the police department, such that "the entire process is concealed from the public."[29] Powerful police unions and wary prosecutors only add to the obstacle course these citizens face. Not surprisingly, few individuals' complaints result in officer discipline or removal, and even fewer lead to large-scale reform of entire departments. As just one example from Los Angeles, the Rampart scandal ultimately revealed that police had engaged in the deliberate framing of innocent people, beatings, evidence planting, and cover-ups, all while prosecutors ignored evidence of serious police corruption and coercion and victims pled guilty to avoid life sentences. This and similar cases should make us very wary of entrusting police agencies with self-monitoring of abuse.

Motivated in part by such egregious cases, there has been some progress toward reform. Citizen oversight committees have been established in about 80 percent of large cities to monitor police agencies.[30] Yet, while they initially seemed to offer high hopes for instilling accountability and oversight, many of these agencies have come to face the same problems as previous prison grievance procedures. Many have no binding enforcement power over the departments they monitor. They can issue recommendations and review complaints, but they cannot directly change department policies or discipline officers and often have little contact with prosecutors. Furthermore, many are financially starved and understaffed, and others do little outreach in the community to encourage citizens to make use of them. One report referred to Atlanta's civilian review board as "one of the best-kept secrets in the city."[31] Worse, the oversight agencies can sometimes be coopted by the very groups that they are charged with monitoring; in seeking to get police cooperation, the committees often end up reflecting the views of the police department and deferring to officers rather than acting as an independent agency.[32] Police officials and associations sometimes even select the committees' governing boards.[33] Several oversight bodies have been deemed failures and decommissioned, such as in Washington, DC, where the backlog of citizen complaints eventually was handed back over to the police department.[34]

We believe civilian oversight agencies can be an important tool for police accountability, but only if they are well implemented. They must be kept independent from police agencies and maintained under civilian control, adequately funded, and allowed substantial authority to investigate allegations, make binding recommendations, require police cooperation, and take disciplinary action or forward actionable information to prosecutors. The agencies should also be required to make their findings and recommendations public, removing the secrecy and insulation many city police agencies currently enjoy.

But civilian review boards cannot be the sole source of accountability. Another aspect of police accountability is requiring police to keep and make public detailed data on their activities. These data, detailing who is stopped, why, and the outcome of citizen-police contact, should be monitored by an outside agency and become part of public record. It is simply unacceptable that with modern technology, many police departments are not given adequate resources to maintain computer databases tracking their stop patterns. It is even less acceptable that many police departments simply choose not to keep this information.

Similarly, we urge greater transparency and accountability in how law enforcement resources are concentrated; police should be required to disclose to the public where they are targeting their resources and enforcement. Katherine Beckett has found that in Seattle, police concentrated their drug enforcement tactics in minority areas and ignored white areas that had similar amounts of drug activity and open-air drug markets. The public was given no information on why law enforcement had decided to focus on certain areas and certain drugs, leaving others untouched. Without information, these discretionary decisions hurt police legitimacy in the wider community: "Minority citizens are generally left to draw their own conclusions regarding police motives; unsurprisingly, purposeful racial discrimination is a particularly popular interpretation in these neighborhoods."[35] When police fail to provide public rationales for their actions, black communities are left to connect the dots, constructing their own explanations for racially targeted policing.

We do not have all the answers yet, and many interventions that hold sizable promise have yet to be well implemented and rigorously evaluated. In part, this is because the democratic nature of criminal justice institutions has not been a topic of wide debate, even among prison activists and reformers concerned with mass incarceration. As mentioned above, calls for criminal justice reform still focus mainly on reducing prison populations and improving reentry programs. These are wholly worthwhile causes, but we should not ignore the larger and potentially more important debate on how we can design a criminal justice system that reflects our core democratic principles. When citizens lose faith in authorities' responsiveness and accountability, and when their voices and input into the institutions governing their lives are reduced to a whisper by design, we as a nation must be concerned and take action.

More Democratic Institutions: Racial Equality

It could be said that government in America has failed to secure the gains of civil rights by only weakly enforcing antidiscrimination policies. It could also be said that governmental policy has inadequately equalized schools and job opportunities and desegregated neighborhoods. It has failed to ameliorate racialized poverty through its withdrawal of welfare and other supports from poor blacks. But in addition, we have argued here that government has taken an active, even proactive, hand in maintaining the racial order in America through the criminal justice reforms of the last half-century, reforms that we discussed in chapter 2. At the same time, the equality discourse and its handmaiden, colorblind jurisprudence, which were the combined legacy of the civil rights era, have both masked and perpetuated racial disproportionality in criminal justice.

The criminal justice system is increasingly the primary point of contact between young black men and the state, and majorities of that group have had some type of criminal justice contact. To the extent that custodial citizens generally are unheard, then, the particular views and preferences of a large and distinctive subset of blacks in particular are underrepresented. The political effects of this reverberate through communities of color, as growing numbers of blacks are excluded or withdraw from civic and political life. The cumulative effects of criminal justice, particularly incarceration and post-punishment disenfranchisement, may marginalize the black community's political clout, jeopardize its political concerns, and "entrench black communities' political subordination."[36]

More broadly, the rise of the carceral state has effectively thwarted achievement of the rights, liberties, and political empowerment that black citizens were promised decades ago. Nearly 150 years after the Emancipation Proclamation, large segments of American blacks still live in sanctioned confinement for much of their lives. Nearly a half century after the Voting Rights Act, disproportionate numbers of blacks are still routinely denied access to suffrage or do not cast ballots because they fear the state. Decades after the passage of the Civil Rights Act, blacks are still disproportionately subject to a set of laws and institutions that limit their basic democratic rights and freedoms. It is in light of this historical context that the effects of criminal justice are particularly troubling. In 1963, Martin Luther King famously intoned that "one hundred years later [after the end of slavery], the Negro is still languished in the corners of American society and finds himself an exile in his own land."[37] His words ring true in many black communities today.

As we describe in chapter 7, courts have permitted policies to stand that have patently biased results, so long as the law is itself race neutral, and our national dialogue relies primarily on individual choices to explain massively disparate group outcomes, decoupling black crime from poverty. How, then, do we begin to confront racial inequality in criminal justice? Inscribing the fundamental democratic value of equality into our systems of crime control will take more than new laws and policies that prohibit overt discrimination, which already exist. Rather, it will require a shift in public consciousness and public priorities.

First we must tackle the proliferation of laws that have had disastrous racial effects, but have slid under the radar because they are formally colorblind. In undertaking broader criminal justice reforms, we should single out for special consideration those policies that feed racial disparities in custodial contact. This alone could do much to stem the overall growth in criminal justice, considering that if blacks and Latinos had the same incarceration rates as whites, the prison population would immediately be halved.[38] And again, the rollback of these policies need not undermine effective maintenance of law and order. As Marc Mauer of the Sentencing Project suggests, "Law enforcement and sentencing policies that exacerbate unwarranted racial disparities are generally also ineffective in contributing to public safety goals."[39]

Sentencing policies and policing practices that colonize black communities in the name of a war on drugs are a prime area for reform. Studies have found that even controlling for geographic differences between blacks and whites, blacks are much more likely to be arrested and convicted on a drug-free school zone offense.[40] But drug-related disparities are not the only area that demands attention. Habitual offender legislation has also contributed to racial disparities. Blacks make up 45 percent of three-strikers in California, compared to 29 percent of the prison population generally, and about 62 percent of those sentenced under Florida's 10–20-Life law.[41] A study of Minnesota's racial disparities, the highest in the nation, found that two-thirds of the disparity could be attributed to prior record; in other words, because blacks were more likely to have prior records, they were more likely to get longer sentences.[42] Numerous other policies that are ostensibly race neutral but that serve as shortcuts to racial disparities should be reevaluated or ended outright, including gang loitering ordinances, vertical patrols in public housing, and Terry stops that rely on location plus evasion—all of which have documented racially disparate effects.

Some states have already moved in this direction, peeling back policies that mandated excessive (and resulted in racially targeted) sentences. New York State has already reformed its Rockefeller drug laws, infamous for how drastically they escalated the black prison population and the number of incarcerated generally in that state, by eliminating mandatory minimum sentences for low-level nonviolent drug felonies. Michigan similarly repealed almost all of its mandatory minimums for drugs and removed the 650 Lifer law, which imposed a lifetime prison sentence without the possibility of parole for 650 grams of certain drugs. New Jersey reformed its drug-free zone laws, which had blanketed urban areas in that state and swept blacks into confinement for low-level drug offenses.

Equally important is proactively avoiding policies that disproportionately harm blacks. In many cases, the potential racial effects of new policies, easily discernible at the time they become laws, are not raised until after the fact. If a frank assessment and discussion had occurred before their adoption, legislators and experts might have been able to devise alternative policy options that would not have exponentially increased the number of young black men behind bars. Thus, in addition to undoing existing racially damaging laws, future criminal justice policies and practices should be evaluated before they are adopted to assess their potential for exacerbating racial disparities.

Such an approach is not infeasible. Racial impact statements—analyzing the racial repercussions of a policy before its adoption—could replicate environmental or fiscal impact statements that are now standard practice. These impact areas already require that policy proposals be accompanied by research documenting their potential budgetary impact or unintended environmental harms. Such statements regarding racial effects could therefore work in a similarly straightforward way. Research, usually from a legislative research agency, would provide projections of racial effects; if a policy was shown to potentially have deleterious effects on minorities, alternatives could be considered. Such impact statements could be used to evaluate whether the crime reduction benefits justified any predicted racially disparate consequences and to assess whether alternative solutions might exist that would accomplish similar ends without adversely increasing racial disparities. Impact statements could be applied to existing laws as well, and attached to policies that go beyond sentencing, such as parole revocation.

Moreover, there are already models from which to work. Iowa, Connecticut, Oregon, and Minnesota have adopted the practice of racial impact statements. Specific practices vary. In Minnesota the law does not require racial impact statements, but the sentencing commission in that state voluntarily produces the statements for legislators. As of July 2013, Oregon now requires racial impact statements for any changes to state criminal laws or criminal codes. Other states have adopted racial equity task forces that not only research the consequences of one policy, but also assess the function of the criminal justice system as a whole and identify the factors contributing to racial bias. The Justice Integrity Act, which was briefly considered in Congress, included a provision for data collection and analysis of current racial disparities at each level of criminal justice, and for then devising a plan in each district to address these disparities. While the legislation did not make it out of committee, its basic premise remains a sound starting point for further development.

Scholars Michael Tonry and Marc Mauer have been the most outspoken proponents of racial impact statements. Racial impact statements, argues Mauer, "would enable legislators and the public to anticipate any unwarranted racial disparities and to consider alternative policies that could accomplish the goals of the legislation without causing undue racial effects."[43] Tonry, in his book *Malign Neglect*, similarly argues that the negative consequences of war on drugs legislation could have been foreseen in advance and avoided. For instance, had crack offenders received equivalent sentences to cocaine offenders, rather than 100 times the sentence, it would have "averted a cumulative total of 24,000 prison years imposed, 90 percent of which would have benefitted African Americans."[44]

When unpredicted disparities become evident after the passage of a law—even soon after, as they did with the crack-to-cocaine sentencing disparity—the policy is harder to undo. It took well over two decades before the 100-to-1 ratio of crack to cocaine sentencing was reduced, despite a substantial body of evidence pointing to its disastrous racial effects. The racially disparate effects of Rockefeller drug laws, mandatory minimums like the 650 Lifer law, and drug zone laws took years to be mobilized against. Considering racial impact in the construction of a policy will make it easier to confront and *avoid* harm to blacks and Latinos. Certainly it is easier to avert adverse racial effects before a policy is enacted, funded, and put into practice.

In addition to addressing the racial effects of ostensibly colorblind policies, it is time to move beyond a singular focus on blatant, intentional, and episodic bias against blacks. Policymakers and practitioners increasingly recognize that subconscious biases operate in individual decision making in ways that create systematically disparate outcomes without overtly malicious intent. Police, prosecutors, judges, juries, and parole boards have an incredible amount of discretion in their routine decisions, many of which are made with little oversight or public awareness and are often not part of public record. Thus implicit bias may play an even greater, and disguised, role in criminal justice than in other domains.

Decisions that are influenced by people's implicit associations and unconscious stereotypes are not easily seen and, unlike overt discrimination, they usually do not carry identifiable markers (e.g., the use of racial epithets). Implicit bias is powerful because it can operate without the knowledge even of decision-makers themselves: "We tend to dismiss evidence of pervasive implicit bias as somehow inapplicable to ourselves. In other words, we assume that we are somehow exceptional and immune from the cognitive errors that others make."[45] More troubling, implicit bias in criminal justice can become self-reinforcing, leading not only to worse outcomes for blacks who commit crimes, but also to the appearance of higher black crime: "More frequent searches of black drivers will inevitably turn up higher rates of drug infractions, just as would be the case if white drivers were searched more frequently."[46] How can we mute the aggregated effect of implicit bias across the thousands, or hundreds of thousands, of discretionary decisions made every week about who to stop, search, and detain, who to judge guilty or innocent, and how long a sentence they deserve?

While legal scholars have begun to recognize and write about the role of implicit bias in the criminal justice arena, so far the evidence for what works in reducing implicit bias across the criminal justice arena is relatively scant.[47] Previous work, however, has posited that if individuals are informed about the possibility of implicit associations and are reminded of them upon making decisions, they might be able to better regulate their operation on decisions. In this vein, some have suggested that early and sustained training of police officers, prosecutors, judges, and other criminal justice administrators could ameliorate implicit bias by increasing awareness. This would not require the judge to call the prosecutor a racist. Rather, it only requires formal recognition that implicit biases abound: "If the Court were to emphasize the frequency with which stereotyping is unconscious, it would be much easier for a trial judge to cite that language in determining that race had influenced the exercise of a prosecutor's challenge, even though he or she may have been unaware of that influence."[48] The National Center for State Courts has undertaken a National Campaign to Ensure the Racial and Ethnic Fairness of America's State Courts, and one of their goals is to develop best practices for how to train judges regarding implicit bias.[49] To our knowledge, however, no analyses have been conducted on whether the training reduces implicit bias in criminal justice behavior and decision making. In addition, research outside the criminal justice arena warns of the potential for diversity or sensitivity training to have unwanted "backlash" effects.[50] Others suggest more aggressive approaches, such as blind jury selection, meaning that prosecutors could not see or know the race of the prospective juror.[51] Procedures for auditing the decisions of judges and prosecutors may also help in highlighting the role of implicit bias: "Jurisdictions could adopt a sort of peer-review process to evaluate decisions for effective impartiality and provide feedback."[52]

Other reforms may not have anything to do with criminal justice institutions at all. Jerry Kang provocatively endorses imposing limitations on the institutions most implicated in sustaining the powerful association between blacks and crime: news reporting on local media. He argues that local crime news overrepresents blacks as perpetrators and represents them in more criminal ways, through mugshots or pictures of blacks spread-eagle against a police cruiser. The density of negative imagery of blacks as suspects and criminals has the power to program our brains without our knowledge or endorsement. He writes:

> These newscasts also activate and strengthen linkages among certain racial categories, violent crime, and the fear and loathing such crime invokes. In this sense, the local news functions precisely like a Trojan Horse virus. We invite it into our homes, our dens, in through the gates of our minds, and accept it at face value, as an accurate representation of newsworthy events. But something lurks within those newscasts that programs our racial schemas in

ways we cannot notice but can, through scientific measurements, detect. And the viruses they harbor deliver a payload with consequences, affecting how we vote for "three strikes and you're out" laws, how awkwardly we interact with folks, and even how quickly we pull the trigger.[53]

Kang goes on to suggest that, as we would against a computer virus, we need to build a firewall against such negative media images through FCC regulations that would cap the amount and content of local crime news to which viewers are exposed. We would strongly oppose a government effort to censor the content of news broadcasts, as this replaces one anti-democratic practice with another. However, we would welcome serious conversation about Kang's other recommendation, a "disinfection" technique that would balance the effect of crime news on our subconscious through public service announcements, or in his words, "counter[ing] implicit fire with implicit fire."[54] This tactic, he suggests, would reduce the disassociation between our explicit commitments to racial equality and our implicit biases' constant pull against those commitments.

More broadly, we would urge policymakers to think creatively about public policy innovations that might address the presence of implicit racial biases in criminal justice and other domains. However, this would require thinking about the role of race in new terms, which befit the changes that have occurred in the modern era. Instead of talking about criminal justice solely as part of a historical legacy of racial discrimination, we must develop a new language to challenge criminal justice on racial grounds. As Michelle Alexander suggests, "a new civil rights movement cannot be organized around the relics of the earlier system of control if it is to address meaningfully the racial realities of our time. Any racial justice movement, to be successful, must vigorously challenge the public consensus that underlies the *prevailing* system of control."[55] Slavery was upheld as a normal and necessary part of the southern economic structure, legitimized by a view of blacks as biologically inferior. Jim Crow was held up as an appropriate segregation of the races, normalized by views of racial distinctiveness and black social inferiority. Criminal justice is built and sustained by the call for law and order, and premised on the argument that nothing short of the carceral state can hold back the tide of crime, violence, and "disorderly" communities.

As with past racial orders, strong ideologies legitimize the current order's effects on blacks; today, the language of personal responsibility and moral failing does this work. And because criminal justice "isn't about race," these ideologies are difficult to undo. Yet while criminal justice is markedly different from Jim Crow and a far cry from slavery, it poses no less of a threat to the health of American democracy because, like earlier racial regimes, it denies voice, accountability, and equality to a large and concentrated group of American citizens. Recognizing this fundamental parallel to past regimes of systematic inequity, *but also acknowledging the modern system's critical differences*, is the first step toward real racial progress.

More Responsible Crime Control

We agree with Bruce Western when he says that "ultimately, reversing mass imprisonment may depend less on embracing a rehabilitative philosophy of criminal punishment and more on promoting a viable legitimate economy in ghetto neighborhoods."[56] While we cannot detail the myriad interventions that would be needed to enact such a wholesale change in the nation's economic inequities—for that, we would need a much longer book—we can outline the ways we might direct the criminal justice system toward such change. If there is a recurring negative feedback loop from incarceration to communities to incarceration, we can also create positive feedback, one that reroutes incarcerated people and invests in their communities, and through these two mechanisms, interrupts the community-incarceration loop in the long run.

First, we would point toward the principles and practice of Justice Reinvestment. An idea pioneered by the Justice Mapping Institute and further elaborated by criminology professor Todd Clear, justice reinvestment is based on the logic that, at very high levels of concentration, incarceration actually promotes crime and destabilizes entire communities; that one of the largest correlates of crime and incarceration is economic disadvantage; and that many of those being held in prison could have been given a community-based sanction instead of confinement, without any sacrifice of public safety.

Justice reinvestment involves multiple steps. First, policy experts comprehensively analyze a state's criminal justice system to determine the reasons for high incarceration and where it is concentrated. They then employ these data to promote a plan for reducing prison admittance rates and recidivism. The state in question then implements the suggested policies. The important innovation of the justice reinvestment concept is that the money saved by reducing imprisonment then goes directly to the communities contributing the most to the prison population. Essentially, the plan calculates the budgetary savings to the state from reduced incarceration and reinvests the savings into efforts that will help revitalize the neighborhoods contributing to disorder and offending—efforts such as community services, job training, redevelopment of abandoned housing, business opportunities, and rehabilitating parks and playgrounds. By earmarking incarceration savings for investment in the very communities that have been devastated by the poverty-incarceration feedback loop, justice reinvestment not only has the potential to reduce imprisonment, but to directly counteract the conditions that led to high incarceration in the first place.

The most compelling plan for justice reinvestment that we have seen comes from Todd Clear at Rutgers University. Clear's strategy emphasizes community-based action and prioritizes diversion away from prison altogether, rather than focusing justice reinvestment initiatives on parole and probation. He proposes creating a voucher system, by which savings from early release or diversion from prison can be used by a community-based organization (CBO). The CBO would construct a detailed plan for how the savings will be used in the community and provide a plan for how a person diverted from prison will succeed in the community. So, for example, if the average cost of incarcerating someone in a given state is $40,000 a year and that person is diverted from three years of incarceration into community supervision, this amounts to a voucher of $120,000. The CBO can use the voucher to provide job training, employment, housing, or substance abuse treatment for the offender. It could also be directed toward subsidizing CBO efforts in the community, such as rehabilitating vacant property into transitional housing. The CBO has an incentive to facilitate the offender's successful employment, housing, and crime-free life; if the diverted offender gets a new conviction within a period of time, the CBO is assessed a failure fee.[57]

The justice reinvestment idea has begun to take off. The Council of State Governments now runs a justice reinvestment project in fifteen states, and the Criminal Justice Reinvestment Act was recently proposed to Congress, though it did not pass. Connecticut's justice reinvestment project showed a steep decrease in the prison population, leading to $30 million in savings, $13 million of which was reinvested in high criminal justice communities.[58] In North Carolina, state legislators passed House Bill 642, the Justice Reinvestment Act. It has been projected to save over $290 million in six years, with $4 million annually to be used for expanding community treatment programs for people under correctional supervision.[59] Texas, long regarded as one of the most punitive states in the country, has begun working toward reinvestment. According to the Justice Center, in May 2007 the Texas legislature enacted a package of criminal justice legislation that many policymakers consider to be the most expansive redirection in state corrections policy since the early 1990s: "The state re-invested $241 million, which would have otherwise been spent on prison construction and operation, to expand the capacity of in-prison and community-based treatment and diversion programs."[60]

In addition to the other gains that might flow from justice reinvestment, however, we see this process as a promising way to invest in the political capital of communities that have been damaged by incarceration. One of the elements missing from many justice reinvestment models is that they focus on handing out money to communities as a way to build infrastructure, which is then geared toward crime control and economic stability. Reducing poverty and expanding employment opportunities in disadvantaged neighborhoods, and thereby reducing crime, is a very good thing. However, these communities have also been depleted of political empowerment. Many of their members are barred from voting, they have few community groups, and they are the last places many politicians and political leaders visit. They are politically marginalized and civically deserted.

Our second recommendation, then, is that justice reinvestment can and should enhance democracy. We believe that a core component of the reinvestment model—one that would help reintegrate offenders and build community strength—should be to invest in political and civic empowerment. People diverted from prison or given early release through justice reinvestment initiatives should not only receive drug treatment and job training. The CBO should help them register to vote, provide them with information on the civic organizations and volunteer opportunities in their communities, and assist them in developing their political and civic skills. This might occur through models like the New Orleans Cornerstone Builders or the Civic Engagement Project in New Jersey, both discussed above, or it might be pursued through another model. Without helping communities ravaged by incarceration to build political power and civic capacity, we may improve them economically, but we will have failed to directly address the high levels of political alienation and marginalization that keep them from advocating for themselves.

Where We Go from Here

When scholars and practitioners talk about the urgent need to rein in the carceral state, they often do so with more than a little pessimism about the possibility of accomplishing this goal. Yet even as this book goes to press, we have witnessed remarkable shifts: for the first time in nearly three decades, the numbers of people admitted to prison began to fall. Sentencing reforms have swept the states, and the general direction of these reforms is away from mandatory minimums, strict time-served requirements, and drug zone laws, and toward diversion programs like HOPE, alternatives to incarceration for nonviolent offenders, and expanded parole release. Parole has been brought back to several states that had eliminated it, and other states have reduced their use of parole revocations. At least two dozen states are trying out Justice Reinvestment initiatives (even if much of the savings has landed in the hands of law enforcement and not communities). Prisons have been successfully closed in states like Texas and Florida where "lock 'em up" has long been the order of the day. The longstanding Rockefeller drug laws in New York were successfully ended, as were most mandatory minimum drug sentences in Michigan, and Kansas now diverts most drug offenders to treatment, capping years of high drug-related prison admissions.[61] Other states, like Kansas, cut their number of parole technical revocations in half by instituting graduated sanctions.[62] And in one of the most dramatic changes, California reduced the number of its state prison inmates by 25,000 from 2010 to 2012 in response to a court order to reduce overcrowded facilities. Early analyses of this "public safety realignment" indicate that inmates released after the change were not rearrested or reconvicted at higher rates than pre-realignment inmates.[63]

The national government has also begun a critical reexamination of the criminal justice system. In recent years, Congress passed landmark reforms like the Second Chance Act and the Fair Sentencing Act with broad support and with little political pushback about being "soft on crime." Attorney general Eric Holder, in a public announcement, said the Obama administration would look to end mandatory sentences for less serious drug offenders and instructed the states to do the same. He has also established a group to examine sentencing practices. Many experts and journalists credited this turn of events to several years of steadily declining crime rates and serious pressures on state budgets amid a worsening fiscal climate, as well as the emergence of an energetic bipartisan movement to get "smart on crime" instead of tough. Whatever the reason, for the first time since either of us began writing about criminal justice, indeed since we have been alive, it is clear that the nation has begun to seriously explore an alternative to crime politics as usual.

Much of our concern in chapter 2 focused also on stages in the criminal justice system that precede punishment; specifically, we addressed the voluminous numbers of citizens being stopped and frisked, given trespass admonishments, and saddled with court appearances for low-level misdemeanor arrests. Here too we see some evidence that a different future is possible. The stop-and-frisk policing regime that governed New York City life and neighborhoods for over a decade was dealt a fatal blow by a federal court in *Floyd v. City of New York*. In *Floyd*, the court ruled that the NYPD had violated the Fourth and Fourteenth Amendment rights of New Yorkers by stopping them without reasonable suspicion and in a racially discriminatory way, and it ordered the establishment of an independent federal monitor to oversee the police department. Police stops in this city had already started to plummet, in the wake of widespread criticism and legal action, going from 203,500 stops in the second quarter of 2012 to just 58,000 in the second quarter of 2013.[64] Our hope is that the proportion of police stops that do not lead to arrest will decline as well. Meanwhile, misdemeanor drug arrests have fallen after several states, including California, Connecticut, Maine, Massachusetts, Nebraska, and Rhode Island, reclassified low-level marijuana possession as a civil infraction that carries fines instead of criminal records. In California, for example, misdemeanor drug arrests fell by fifty percent from 2007 to 2012, and prosecutions for marijuana went from 61,000 to just 8,000.[65]

These major reforms provide substantial reason for optimism. However, future prospects are unclear. Some of the recent reductions in prison populations have been achieved by shifting the population to probation, so supervision overall may go unchanged. Moreover, while the number of people admitted to prisons for drug offenses has declined, the scale of drug prosecutions has not abated and the racial disparity in misdemeanor drug arrests has not appreciably diminished.[66] And while many of these recent reforms may well bring the association between custodial citizen and criminal offender more closely into sync, we are less optimistic about bringing the criminal justice system back into line with democratic values and practices. There has been some movement on this question—Virginia, one of only two states to have lifetime disenfranchisement, expanded the franchise to first-time, nonserious offenders—but this is a short step in a long journey; as we have emphasized, felon disenfranchisement is just the tip of a much bigger iceberg of policies and practices that stand at odds with our nation's democratic principles.

In addition, those who see little reason for optimism often point to the intractability of the problem to suggest that criminal justice reform remains a nonstarter in America today. In short, they argue that the problem is simply too large. We know that criminal justice is deeply embedded in the complex systems of race, class, and geography. Successful reforms that seek to do more than scratch the surface of the problem must therefore seriously address the complicated ways its deeper elements intertwine. They must consider the school-to-prison pipeline, the role of wealth inequality and economic instability in driving illegal economic activity and its attendant crime, and the role of race and racism in shaping criminal justice design and outcomes. This is a herculean task.

The problem of complexity is well illustrated in a story told by David Simon, the writer and producer of the HBO show *The Wire*, about a public lecture he once gave where he was discussing the interconnected problems of race, poverty, crime, and crime control in America. He recounts that "there came this point where a guy said, 'Well, what *is* the solution? Give me the paragraph; give me the lede. What's the solution, if not drug prohibition?" Simon replied:

> Look. For thirty-five years, you've systematically deindustrialized these cities. You've rendered them inhospitable to the working class, economically. You have marginalized a certain percentage of your population, most of them minority, and placed them in a situation where the only viable economic engine in their hypersegregated neighborhoods is the drug trade. Then you've alienated them further by fighting this draconian war in their neighborhoods, and not being able to distinguish between friend or foe and between that which is truly dangerous or that which is just illegal. And you want to sit across the table from me and say "What's the solution?" and get it in a paragraph? The solution is to undo the last thirty-five years, brick by brick. How long is that going to take? I don't know, but until you start it's only going to get worse.[67]

We agree wholeheartedly with Simon: the only way to improve the situation is to get started. We are not going to do away with criminal justice, nor would most reasonable people—ourselves firmly included—say that we should. Surveillance and punishment are critical parts of a democracy; without law and order, nothing else can be made possible. And criminal justice institutions will always be undemocratic to some degree. They have to limit liberty and freedom in some respects to accomplish their objectives. But they do not have to be antidemocratic.

Indeed, precisely because the pursuit of crime control is coercive, we need to be that much more careful about how we conduct ourselves in this domain. We have already outlined several reasons why, but they bear repeating here. First, the population that is most likely to encounter the criminal justice system is already lacking resources; they are our most powerless and most vulnerable. We should be especially worried that the group that arguably has the most to gain from being involved in politics is the most withdrawn and alienated. Second, criminal justice is, by definition, the strong arm of the state. That system has immense power over individuals' lives for some period, and has the authority to detain, search, and incarcerate, which are sizably more totalizing powers than other democratic institutions possess. They therefore will always pose a greater potential threat to democratic life. And finally, upholding democratic rights and principles matters most in criminal justice because of the problem's complexity, and because the affected population is suspect in the eyes of the public. It is easy to protect popular speech, just as it is easier to argue for redistribution in the name of sympathetic people. Protecting rights when they are most difficult to protect is the true mark of democratic strength.

Our motivation in writing this book is to recognize the threat to democratic values from our criminal justice system. We are cautiously optimistic that our nation can begin the process of democratic reform. However, the first step toward change is a full accounting of the damage that has already been done. That has been our primary goal here. When we take account of criminal justice and its attendant harm to citizenship, it becomes clear that the trajectory of state development in this domain has undermined the democracy we thought we had achieved. By silencing the political voice of a staggeringly large group of Americans who are heavily concentrated in the nation's most disadvantaged cities and towns, the criminal justice system has weakened the ability of communities to address problems of collective concern. By showing blacks that America is a land of disappointment and neglect, rather than equality and the

American Dream, we have walked back the gains of the civil rights era. By undermining citizens' political trust and efficacy and decreasing political engagement among substantial segments of society, the politics of punishment and the policies they have engendered have diminished democracy. In the past few decades, America has transformed its criminal justice system, but criminal justice has also transformed America.

Quantitative Data

Table A1 describes the sample size and sampling characteristics of each survey. As the table shows, each survey varies in its sample size, type of population targeted, and type of political and criminal justice measures included. Across these six diverse surveys, we have nationally representative samples, samples focused on the young or disadvantaged, and panel studies that allow us to leverage changes over time in criminal justice contact.

To examine broad views of government and engagement in political and civic life, we rely on four separate datasets. The first, the National Longitudinal Study of Adolescent Health (Add Health), follows youth over their lives to provide a nationally representative sample of school-age people in the United States.[1] Begun in 1994 with a sample of 20,745 adolescents from seventh to twelfth grade, the sample was derived by sampling 132 schools (80 high schools and 52 feeder middle schools) with an unequal probability of selection. The analyses presented in the chapters use data collected in the third wave of the study, in which a sample of 15,170 of the original adolescents were interviewed six years after the baseline survey from August 2001 to April 2002. By the third interview, respondents were young adults between the ages of eighteen and twenty-six.

Our second source of data, the Fragile Families and Child Wellbeing Study (Fragile Families), is a panel study that measures economic and social conditions for disadvantaged parents and their children. Mothers and fathers in 4,898 family units were interviewed in the hospital on their child's birth between 1998 and 2000, and subsequently interviewed one, three, and five years later.[2] Parents were interviewed in seventy-five hospitals in 22 US cities using a stratified random sample representative of

TABLE A1. **Survey size, content, and sample characteristics**

Survey	Year	Original sample size	Our focus	Survey focus	Political items	Criminal justice contact
National Longitudinal Study of Adolescent Health (AddHealth)	2001–2 (third wave)	20,745	15,170 young adults of all races aged 18–26 in third wave	National youth	Political participation, civic engagement, trust in government	Stopped, arrested, convicted, incarcerated, length of incarceration
Fragile Families and Child Wellbeing Study	2001–3 (third wave)	4,898	3,299 fathers of all races in third wave	Disadvantaged parents in cities of 200,000 or more	Political participation, civic engagement	Stopped, arrested, convicted, incarcerated, length of incarceration
National Longitudinal Survey of Youth 1979, 2006 Young Adult Survey	2006	5,844	3,421 young adults of all races that were asked political questions in 2006	Young adult children of original 1979 sample	Political efficacy	Convicted, incarcerated
National Longitudinal Survey of Youth 1997	2004 and 2008 waves	8,984	7,182 young adults of all races interviewed in round 8 after the 2004 election and 4,762 young adults interviewed in round 12 after the 2008 election	National youth	Political participation	Arrested, convicted, incarcerated
Black Youth Project	2006	1,589	634 black youth in chapter 7; full sample otherwise	Youth aged 15–25 with oversample of high black and Hispanic areas and Chicago sample	Perceptions of discrimination, racial equality, government treatment of blacks; government responsiveness; efficacy; linked fate; general equality perceptions	Stopped, arrested, convicted
African American Men Survey	2006	2,864 adults	1,328 black men and 507 black women	Adults of all races with black oversamples	Perceptions of racial bias; reasons for high black incarceration	Arrested, incarcerated

children born in large cities (more than 200,000 population).[3] Both Fragile Families and Add Health collected information about political attitudes, beliefs about government, and political activity in the third wave
of the panel studies.

We supplement these two primary studies with a third, the National Longitudinal Survey of Youth 1979 (NLSY), a nationally representative sample of 12,686 young people. This survey contained a supplement that interviewed the children of the original cohort of women
in the survey when they were young adults in 2006. There were 5,844
young adults (children of the original women who are over age fifteen).
Of these, 3,421 were twenty-one by 2006 and were asked the items of political relevance.

To test whether changes in criminal justice contact produce changes
in participation levels, we rely on a final survey in our analysis—the National Longitudinal Survey of Youth 1997—because it is the only survey that asks respondents about their political participation in more than
one wave of the survey. This survey is a nationally representative sample of 8,984 people aged twelve to sixteen in 1997. After the first round,
youth were interviewed each year after 1997. The NLSY 1997 includes
a cross-sectional sample as well as a supplemental sample aimed at representing the black and Hispanic population. Our analysis focuses on
the eighth and twelfth rounds (2004–5 and 2008–9), in which respondents were asked whether they participated in the presidential election.
In the eighth round, 7,182 respondents were asked about their vote in
2004 (they had been interviewed after the election) and in the twelfth
round, 4,762 respondents were asked about their vote in 2008 (also after
the election).

In addition to these surveys, we analyze data from two large-scale
surveys designed specifically to collect information on blacks: the Washington Post/Kaiser Family Foundation/Harvard African-American Men
Survey (AAMS) and the Black Youth Project Youth Culture Survey
(BYP).[4] The AAMS is a telephone-administered survey conducted in
2006 that includes a random sample of 2,864 US adults with a large oversample of 1,328 black men and 507 black women. The survey also over-
sampled young blacks. The BYP is a Random Digit Dial [RDD] survey
conducted in 2006 that includes a nationally representative sample with
an oversample of geographic areas that are 15 percent or higher Hispanic
or non-Hispanic black; it also contains a supplemental sample from the
city of Chicago. The survey includes only respondents ages fifteen to

twenty-five. The Chicago sample likewise screened for race, including only age-eligible black respondents. The total BYP sample is 1,589 respondents, including 634 blacks and 314 Hispanics. Because our analysis is concerned with how criminal justice shapes the racial lifeworlds of black Americans, we focus primarily on black respondents in these surveys.

Several important differences in the sample characteristics of each study bear mention, stemming from differences in their sampling design and focus. Add Health, BYP, and NLSY—both young adult and 1997—include a younger sample compared to Fragile Families and AAMS. Add Health respondents were, on average, twenty-two, having received an average of thirteen years of schooling. A slight majority were non-Hispanic whites. Fragile Families respondents were, on average, thirty-one years old, less likely to have received a high school education, and three times less likely to have a college-educated parent. A greater proportion were racial or ethnic minorities. Given the stated purpose of the sample design, it is not surprising that 26 percent of fathers in Fragile Families were under the federal poverty line, 61 percent were not married to the mothers of their children at the time of the survey, and the vast majority received some type of government assistance.

Criminal justice contact also varies significantly across the surveys. To capture the degree and severity of exposure to the criminal justice system, we rely on several similar items in each survey that tap criminal justice contact from the least to the most serious level of involvement: no encounters with the criminal justice system, stopped by police for questioning, charged or arrested for breaking the law, convicted (not including minor traffic offenses), served time in a correctional facility, and incarcerated for more than one year. Not all of the surveys included all degrees of contact. In the AAMS, the group indicated as having no contact could include those who have been stopped by police because that survey does not ask respondents about that particular type of encounter. Because the surveys only asked each successive question on criminal justice involvement of those who answered yes to the previous question, serving time in a correctional facility was necessarily due to being convicted of a crime and sentenced, rather than a night in jail for a bar fight or drunk driving that did not lead to charges. Our analyses focus only on the measures that deal with correctional involvement as an adult; juvenile offenders are excluded. The categories are mutually exclusive and represent the respondents' highest level of contact. Table A2 depicts the

TABLE A2. **Frequency of highest level of criminal justice contact in the surveys**

	Add Health	Fragile families[a]	BYP (blacks only)	AAMS (blacks only)	NLSY79 young adult
None	12,119 (80.4%)	1,296 (39.3%)	226 (33.9%)	1,040 (56.7%)	3,195 (93.8%)
Questioned	1,630 (10.8%)	810 (24.6%)	256 (38.4%)	–	–
Arrested	578 (3.8%)	356 (10.8%)	110 (16.5%)	512 (27.9%)	–
Convicted	582 (3.9%)	114 (3.5%)	75 (11.2%)	–	106 (3.1%)
Prison/jail	117 (0.8%)	392 (11.9%)	–	283 (15.4%)	104 (3.1%)
Serious time[b]	39 (0.3%)	331 (10.0%)	–	–	–
Total	15,065 (100%)	3,299 (100%)	667 (100%)	1,835 (100%)	3,405 (100%)

[a] Based on father's self-reports only.

[b] Serious time refers to those respondents who were sentenced to over a year of incarceration (imprisonment).

highest level of criminal justice contact across the surveys; these numbers differ from those above because they indicate the highest level of contact.

Panel Attrition

Several of the studies we employ are panel surveys. Although the Add Health, Fragile Families, and NLSY studies made substantial efforts to locate and conduct follow-up interviews with earlier respondents who were currently institutionalized, incarceration remains one of the primary factors associated with attrition in both studies. Both studies tried to obtain clearance to interview prison inmates, but this was not always allowed or the prisoner's security or privacy could not be assured.

Attrition of fathers is strongly correlated with custodial involvement in Fragile Families; 63 percent of fathers missing from the third-year interview had been incarcerated, based on mother and father combined reports, compared to only 44 percent of the fathers present for the third-year interview. Respondents differ on other key variables as well. When we compare the third-wave sample of respondents in Fragile Families to the baseline or second wave, there are significant differences between eligible and interviewed respondents. Fathers interviewed at baseline who dropped out in the third wave had much lower socioeconomic status (SES) and were more likely to be black or Hispanic than fathers interviewed in the third wave. It is thus possible that the third wave of both studies underrepresents fathers regarding incarceration and other relevant characteristics that predict participation, such as SES and race. Respondents in Add Health interviewed in the third wave differ from eligible respondents who were not interviewed in many of the same ways.

Although in both studies respondents with exposure to criminal justice were more likely to drop out of the sample by the third wave, we follow a weighting procedure that adjusts for nonresponse. In Add Health, analysis of potential bias due to nonresponse after including sampling weights indicates that on sixty-seven items, bias is less than 0.5 on most items (and only more than one percentage point on one item). For our purposes, there is some amount of bias remaining on substance abuse and violent and delinquent behaviors, but the bias is small: For ten of the fifteen items, bias was less than 0.5, and for the remaining five items it was between 0.5 and 1 percentage point. Scholars conducting bias tests concluded that "the Wave III sample adequately represents the same population as the Wave I sample when final sampling weights are used to compute population estimates."[5]

Self-Reported Criminal Justice Contact

A final aspect of our quantitative data that bears mention is that respondents may misrepresent their political participation and criminal behaviors. Participation scholars have demonstrated amply that vote misreporting is systematically related to respondent characteristics. Partisans, the highly educated, those with greater political interest and knowledge, and minorities exhibit a greater pattern of misreporting. Because we have no way of validating the self-reported measures with respondents' voting and registration records—the names and addresses of respondents are confidential and unavailable—we cannot be certain that some of our dependent variables do not contain measurement error. Given that our central hypothesis is that contact with criminal justice depresses turnout, we would be especially concerned if nonfelons were more likely than felons to exaggerate their turnout or if felons were more likely than nonfelons to underreport theirs. The latter possibility we can dismiss, given that underreporting is rare.[6] Although no studies have systematically tested the former possibility, studies have found that felons are much less likely to vote based on voting and registration records than indicated in surveys.[7] Thus, felons are much like nonfelons in this regard.

Similarly, our analysis follows a long line of criminal justice scholars who use self-reported data on delinquency; the primary sources of drug abuse and victimization trends in the United States often rely on such data, including the annual Monitoring the Future survey, the National Household Survey on Drug Abuse, the National Youth Survey, and the Youth Risk Behavior Survey. Studies have found that although underreporting is not insignificant, respondents were often quite willing to reveal their delinquent acts in self-administered interviews; self-reported measures of arrest and conviction have a high correlation with official records; and self-reported data, although not perfect, are both reliable and valid.[8] A review of multiple studies evaluating the effect of self-reported crime items has concluded that "self-reported delinquency responses are no less reliable than other social science measures."[9]

In addition, the survey design and our methodological approach help strengthen the validity of our results. Add Health was designed specifically to gather sensitive information on adolescent sexual behavior and risks. Both Add Health and Fragile Families use computer-assisted interviewing techniques (ACASI in Add Health, CATI in Fragile Families) for sensitive questions, which have been shown to reduce misreporting and item nonresponse and elicit 30 percent higher reports of risky or delinquent behaviors than when an interviewer is present.[10] Moreover, both surveys assured respondents of confidentiality, anonymity, and privacy, another design feature that has been shown to reduce misreporting. That the majority of the sample in both studies reported at least one illegal behavior gives us some confidence that respondents did not withhold information. Nonresponse to these items does not appear to be significantly larger than other items in the survey. Finally, the Fragile Families survey includes both mother and father reports of the father's criminal justice contact, which provides a fuller measure of contact. We focus on the relationship between custodial history and political behaviors for the 3,299 fathers in the three-year follow-up interview conducted between 2001 and 2003, who are much more likely to have had contact with the criminal justice system than mothers in the sample. However, we conducted analyses using the combination of mother and father reports, and the results do not substantially differ.

Qualitative Data

W e chose our interview sites because they provided diverse settings. As table B1 shows, Virginia, New Jersey, and Louisiana are relatively punitive, but each along a different dimension. Louisiana has the highest per capita incarceration rate in the country. New Jersey has a particularly high ratio of black relative to white citizens in prison. Virginia's particularly draconian felon disenfranchisement policies result in a high proportion of ineligible voters.

Virginia also boasts one of the highest incarceration rates in the nation; the incarceration rate in 2010 was 487 per 100,000. Sixty-two percent of these prisoners were black, compared to 20 percent of the population overall. The state eliminated parole so that offenders now must serve the maximum amount of their sentence before release and are given very little supervision after release. Its thirty-nine adult prisons, like so many southern states, are planted in the outer reaches of the rural landscape, where visitors at least until recently would report losing cell-phone service long before reaching their walls. Virginia is also distinctive among our interview sites in that it is one of only two states in the nation to permanently disenfranchise some convicted felons, meaning that it excluded 20 percent of its black residents from voting for life, nearing the top of the list for the nation.

At first blush, New Jersey is a relatively less punitive state than Virginia and Louisiana. It has a lower than average incarceration rate of only 297 per 100,000, half the rate of Virginia and one-fourth the rate in Louisiana. It did away with the death penalty in 2007 and few of its inmates are serving life sentences. However, the state is quite distinct in two respects. First, it incarcerates blacks at twelve times the rate of

TABLE B1. **State differences in incarceration, racial disparity, and disenfranchisement**

	Virginia	New Jersey	Louisiana
Incarceration rate	480	291	881
Black/white rate	6:1	12:1	5:1
Disenfranchised			
Total (%)	7	2	3
Black (%)	20	9	7

whites. While blacks and Latinos together are just over a quarter of the state population, blacks are 61 percent of inmates and Latinos are 16 percent.[1] As in other states, this racial disparity has much to do with the war on drugs: Over half of black admissions are for drug crimes. Not surprisingly, the state leads the nation in the proportion of its inmates that are serving time for drug offenses. Thirty-four percent of state prison inmates are serving for drug offenses—almost as many as violent offenders—and 48 percent of prison admissions are drug offenders, making New Jersey 80 percent over the national average. In addition, a large share of prisoners are serving mandatory minimum sentences, which have also increased dramatically over time. In 1982 just 11 percent of New Jersey inmates were serving mandatory sentences compared to 61 percent in 2001. The state is less punitive when it comes to giving felons the vote back. Felons can vote in the state as long as they have completed their prison, parole, or probation sentences. Still, an estimated 16 percent of blacks in the state cannot vote.[2]

With an incarceration rate of 881 per 100,000, Louisiana imprisons the greatest proportion of its population among the three states, double the rate of Virginia and four times the rate of New Jersey. The state also has some of the most draconian sentences in the nation. A large share of inmates are serving life without parole (LWOP), the harshest possible sentence outside of death. A person convicted under the state's serious habitual offender law automatically gets a strict sentence with no possibility of parole, and it is not used sparingly for the most violent offenders; some 11 percent of all prison inmates are on LWOP terms, 73 percent of whom are black.[3] Like New Jersey, a high proportion of offenders were convicted on drug charges (32%). Louisiana is not as harsh as Virginia, however, in its ex-offender voting rights. The state allows ex-felons to vote as long as they are off parole and probation, but this still excludes 7 percent of the black electorate.

Our intention in talking to residents of Charlottesville, Trenton, and New Orleans is not to focus on regional differences in how punitive interventions shape political action and thought, but instead to include custodial citizens from different political, racial, and cultural contexts so that we may say something broader about their lifeworlds. Given the diversity of the cities we examined, we are fairly confident that the results we find are not unique to these specific locations. While clearly not a representative sample, these cities are similar to many other US cities in their rates and concentration of unemployment, segregation, concentrated poverty, and crime. Likewise, our sample of interview subjects reflects the demographics of the nation's criminal justice population (table B2).

In general, respondents spoke with little reluctance about their experiences with criminal justice, often revealing quite detailed information about their personal histories. We interviewed people displaced by Hurricane Katrina, people struggling with AIDS, and people who had been wrongly convicted. Each of our interviews was semi-structured, but we asked all respondents essentially the following set of questions in this order (in addition to questions about their criminal justice experiences):

There are many things we mean when we say "government." What are the first things that come to your mind when you think about government?

Think about the past year or so; can you remember having contact with government in any way?

What, if anything, did you learn from these experiences about how government works?

Thinking over the course of your life, have you had any memorable experiences with government?

What are the two or three main ways you feel that government affects your life personally?

How would you describe your interactions with public officials or other government authorities?

Do you feel that in general government officials understand people in communities like yours?

Think about the major functions of government. Do you see government as primarily concerned with giving citizens services or keeping citizens in line?

Do you feel like you have much influence or power in dealing with government officials?

How much do public officials care what people like you think?

Do you feel like a full and equal citizen in this country?

Do you think people have an equal chance to succeed?

Do you feel that your concerns and the concerns of your community are heard by government or are invisible to government?

Have you ever voted in an election?

Have you ever personally gone to see, or spoken to, or written to—some member of local government or some other person of influence in the community about some needs or problems?

How interested are you in politics and national affairs?

Have you ever considered taking action about some need or problem, but decided not to?

TABLE B2. **Interview respondents (those with criminal justice contact only)**

City	Name	Sex	Race	Age
Charlottesville, VA	Alvin	M	White	58
	Bert	M	Black	47
	Blake	M	Black	61
	Bob	M	White	48
	Brandy	F	White	38
	Brenda	F	White	32
	Cameron	M	Black	33
	Carlton	M	Black	50
	Charles	M	Black	65
	Charles Ray	M	White	47
	Cordell	M	Black	35
	Darcy	M	Black	39
	David	M	Black	30
	Demonte	M	Black	Unknown
	Donny	M	Black	50
	Ebony	F	Black	27
	Ed	M	White	44
	Felisha	F	Black	40
	Jayda	F	Black	42
	Kareem	M	Black	26
	Lester	M	Black	50
	Linda	F	White	50
	Marshall	M	Black	31
	Martha	F	White	48
	Pat	F	White	41
	Patrice	F	Black	20
	Paul	M	White	55
	Reginald	M	Black	68
	Ronnie	F	Black	33
	Tanya	F	Black	30
	Terrence	M	Black	38
	Terry	M	White	60
	Theresa	F	White	50
	Willie	M	Black	32

City	Name	Sex	Race	Age
New Orleans, LA	Abe	M	Black	25
	Emmett	M	Black	59
	Evangeline	F	Black	Unknown
	Josh	M	Black	Unknown
	Leila	F	Black	Unknown
	Neal	M	Black	58
	Pearl	F	Black	33
	Reggie	M	Black	21
	Renard	M	Black	20
	Selena	F	White	55
	Vern	M	White	36
	Xavier	M	Black	20
Trenton, NJ	Adele	F	White	55
	Albert	M	Black	50
	Andre	M	Black	33
	Billy	M	White	34
	Carlos	M	Latino	32
	Cliff	M	White	45
	Darius	M	Black	31
	Darnell	M	Black	26
	Darryl	M	Black	28
	Dominic	M	Black	45
	James	M	Black	49
	Jerry	M	Black	58
	Joachim	M	Latino	24
	Julian	M	Black	69
	Keira	F	Black	45
	Luke	M	Black	40
	Malik	M	Black	25
	Marcus	M	Black	46
	Melvin	M	Black	29
	Michael	M	Black	24
	Miles	M	Black	47
	Nora	F	Black	58
	Norman	M	White	55
	Quinton	M	Black	47
	Ray	M	Black	58
	Rick	M	Black	44
	Samuel	M	Black	62
	Sarah	F	Black	44
	Silas	M	Black	47
	Stanley	M	Black	55
	Thomas	M	White	35
	Tom	M	Black	55
	Trevor	M	Black	48
	Trina	F	Black	46
	Victor	M	Black	29

Note: Names have been changed to preserve anonymity. Ages are in some cases approximate.

Three Strategies to Address Causality

Controlling for Potential Confounders

First, we use multivariate analyses to account for a wide variety of potential confounders. In our multivariate regression models, we use dummies for each level of contact and we include controls for age, education, sex, household income, employment, marital status, race and ethnicity, citizenship, region, poverty status and parental education. We also control for other types of contact with government (welfare, military service) and for measures of criminality (self-control, history of domestic violence, history of illicit drug use) that have been shown to predict criminal justice contact. If a predilection for criminality is driving our results rather than interactions with law enforcement and criminal justice, then including measures of individual propensity for offending will provide a rigorous test. In Add Health, we account for personality traits that predict criminal activity by including a scale of self-control items; research has established impulsivity to be one of the key determinants of violent offending.[1] We also include measures of self-reported violent and non-violent criminal activity over the past 12 months. In Fragile Families we use a similar index of self-control items, as well as history of domestic violence (as reported by the mother) and drug use. We control for these confounders in all multivariate models reported here. The introduction of controls helps to assure that these observables alone are not producing our outcomes. In fact, this provides a conservative test, given that most of our control variables are themselves consequences of criminal justice interventions.

Analysis of Subsets of the Population

In addition to controlling for potential predictors in multivariate models, we use subsets of the data in order to examine whether our causal claims hold. We subset the data in two ways. Because an unobserved characteristic of offenders may predict the propensity for criminality, we first limit our analysis to only those survey respondents who reported engaging in illegal drug use. We then leverage the fact that some of these individuals have experienced criminal justice contact while others have not. We match respondents who have had carceral contact with respondents who have not had contact on a complete set of covariates, as well as on a propensity score that predicts criminal justice contact. This allows us to further parse out the effect of contact from the effect of "self-selection" into crime.

First, we address the concern that individuals are "self-selecting" into criminal behavior due to some underlying predilection for breaking the law that is correlated with the outcomes we uncover, such as low levels of political trust, perceptions of political responsiveness, and reduced political participation. To assess this claim, we match respondents who had contact with criminal justice in Wave III of Add Health (the treatment group) to those who had not had contact at Wave III but will have contact with criminal justice by the next wave of the study (the control group) on all covariates and the propensity score. While Wave III is the only panel of Add Health that includes political measures, Wave IV of the study repeats questions from Wave III that measure criminal justice history. Between the two waves, about 1,079 respondents are added to the ranks of those who have experienced a criminal conviction. Being able to identify these "future offenders" in the Wave III data allows us to compare the political attitudes and behaviors of individuals who have been exposed to a criminal justice intervention by Wave III with a matched set of individuals in Wave III who have not yet been exposed to criminal justice but who will experience this contact by Wave IV. The logic here is that if criminal propensity is driving the results, and not criminal justice contact per se, then those respondents who will be involved with the criminal justice system in the future should exhibit higher levels of participation than those who have already experienced it. We then compare the political attitudes and behaviors of the treated and control groups at Wave III.

However, we are also concerned with the nonrandomness of criminal justice contact, even among those who self-report criminal behavior. As we discussed in detail in chapter 2, engaging in illegal activity is not a proxy for criminal justice contact and the "custodial citizen" is not synonymous with the "criminal class." In order to address this second issue, we conduct analyses on only those individuals who have self-reported engaging in illegal behavior. For example, in Add Health, approximately 54 percent of respondents reported having recently taken illegal drugs, including 16 percent who reported using "hard" drugs (excluding marijuana, steroids, and prescription medication without a doctor's order). However, crucial to our design is that only some of these individuals have experienced criminal justice contact; for instance, 71 percent of drug users and 58 percent of serious drug users in the Add Health, respectively, reported having no contact with police or criminal justice authorities. Thus, we can divide the roughly 15,000 person Add Health sample into four subgroups: 6,266 respondents with no history of illegal drug use or criminal justice contact, 628 respondents with no history of illegal drug use but with custodial contact, 5,631 respondents with illegal drug use and no custodial contact, and 2,282 respondents with both illegal drug use and custodial contact. Comparing across these groups gives us some leverage on this second complicating factor, addressing differences between custodial and noncustodial citizens in the likelihood of being stopped and arrested by police and convicted by the court.

In both of these analyses, we use a genetic matching algorithm to isolate the effects of criminal justice contact on our dependent variables without having to rely on the parametric assumptions of our multivariate models. In layman's terms, through the matching procedure we can identify a group of respondents who are statistically equivalent to our subsample of custodial citizens on all observable measures, but who differ in the nature of their contact with the carceral state.

We employ a nonparametric estimation method, Genetic Matching, to adjust for baseline covariates that differ across the two groups. Genetic Matching is a generalization of propensity score matching and Mahalanobis distance, which uses a genetic algorithm to maximize covariate balance between treated and control groups.[2] Cases are selected using the results of t-tests and bootstrapped Kolmogorov-Smirnov (KS) tests, a distribution free test of the equality of two cumulative distributions.[3] Genetic matching has been found to have better properties than alternative methods of matching, irrespective of whether the "equal percent bias reduction" property holds.[4]

Genetic matching can be used with or without a propensity score, but is significantly improved with the incorporation of a propensity score.[5] The propensity score is a unidimensional vector that estimates the conditional probability of receiving the treatment (here, criminal justice contact) given observed covariates.[6] In each of our matching analyses, we employ a logistic regression to estimate the propensity score. We then match on both the linear predictor, which has the benefit over the predicted probabilities of not compressing the propensity score near zero and one, and a set of covariates that have been orthogonalized to the propensity score.[7] We match on all covariates from the multiple regressions with the exception of employment and income, which are likely to be negatively affected by carceral contact.

In order to include an indicator of socioeconomic status without controlling for these posttreatment covariates, we proxy for these variables by matching on parents' income and employment, as well as parents' education, when these variables are available.[8] We employ one-to-one matching with replacement and allow GenMatch to break ties by including multiple matched weighted controls. We achieve excellent balance on the propensity score as well as individual predictors. Thus we are able to treat the two matched groups as if they are drawn from the same population and use the matched sample to estimate the effect of criminal justice contact on each of our dependent variables (the average treatment effect on the treated, or ATT) independent of potential confounding variables and without parametric assumptions.

Longitudinal Data with Multiple Waves Measuring Participation

A final way we attempt to test the sensitivity of our causal claim is by using the only data we know of that asks respondents about their political participation at two points in time. The NLSY97 panel survey asks respondents whether they voted in 2004 and 2008. We limit the sample to the 6,516 young adults who by 2004 had never been arrested, convicted, or incarcerated (2,467 of the original 1997 cohort had had contact with criminal justice). Between that wave and the 2008–9 wave, 191 respondents had been arrested for the first time, 93 had been convicted for the first time, and 57 had been sentenced to prison for the first time. Using

these data, we are able to analyze the impact of having a first-time criminal justice encounter on voting in the 2008 election, controlling for their
vote in 2004. This is the only test we have that can directly examine how
participation levels change as a result of changes in contact with criminal justice.

Notes

Chapter One

1. Based on authors' analysis of the National Longitudinal Survey of Youth 1997. The analysis is of the 2002 wave when respondents were 18–23 years old. Other analyses have found similar rates. See also Erica Goode, "Many in U.S. Are Arrested by Age 23, Study Finds," *New York Times*, December 19, 2011.

2. Sam Dillon, "Study Finds that about 10 Percent of Young Male Dropouts Are in Jail or Detention," *New York Times*, October 9, 2009.

3. John Hagan, Carla Shedd, and Monique R. Payne, "Race, Ethnicity, and Youth Perceptions of Criminal Injustice," *American Sociological Review* 70, no. 3 (2005): 381–407.

4. Christopher Uggen, Jeff Manza, and Melissa Thompson, "Citizenship, Democracy, and the Civic Reintegration of Criminal Offenders," *Annals of the American Academy of Political and Social Science* 605, no. 1 (2006): 190.

5. "Stop-and-Frisk Campaign: About the Issue," New York Civil Liberties Union, www.nyclu.org/issues/racial-justice/stop-and-frisk-practices.

6. Based on authors' analysis of the National Longitudinal Study of Adolescent Health wave III.

7. Robert D. Crutchfield, Martie L. Skinner, Kevin P. Haggerty, Anne Mc-Glynn, and Richard F. Catalano, "Racial Disparities in Early Criminal Justice Involvement," *Race and Social Problems* 1, no. 4 (2009): 218–30.

8. See, for example, Donald P. Green and Alan S. Gerber, *Get Out the Vote: How to Increase Voter Turnout* (Washington, DC: Brookings Institution, 2008); Sidney Verba, Kay Lehman Schlozman, and Henry Brady, *Voice and Equality: Civic Voluntarism in American Politics* (Cambridge, MA: Harvard University Press, 1995); Andrea Campbell, *How Policies Make Citizens: Senior Political Activism and the American Welfare State* (Princeton, NJ: Princeton University Press, 2003); Suzanne Mettler, *Soldiers to Citizens: The G.I. Bill and the Making of the Greatest Generation* (New York: Oxford University Press, 2007).

9. Jeff Manza and Christopher Uggen, *Locked Out: Felon Disenfranchisement and American Democracy* (New York: Oxford University Press, 2006).

10. Elizabeth Cohen, *Semi-Citizenship in Democratic Politics* (New York: Cambridge University Press, 2009).

11. Alexis de Tocqueville, *Democracy in America*, 3rd ed. (Cambridge: Seaver and Francis, 1863), 123.

12. Preamble to the US Constitution.

13. Barack Obama, "Speech on Race," Philadelphia, PA, March 18, 2008.

14. Suzanne Mettler, "The Development of Democratic Citizenship: Toward a New Research Agenda," in *Democratization in America: A Comparative-Historical Analysis*, ed. Desmond King, Robert C. Lieberman, Gretchen Ritter, and Laurence Whitehead (Baltimore: John Hopkins University Press, 2009); Desmond King and Robert C. Lieberman, "American Political Development as a Process of Democratization," in *Democratization in America*, ed. King et al., 4.

15. Robert Mickey, *Paths Out of Dixie: The Democratization of Authoritarian Enclaves in America's Deep South* (Princeton, NJ: Princeton University Press, 2012); Rogers Smith and Philip Klinkner, *The Unsteady March: The Rise and Decline of Racial Equality in America* (Chicago: University of Chicago Press, 1999).

16. Rogers Smith, *Civic Ideals: Conflicting Visions of Citizenship in U.S. History* (New Haven, CT: Yale University Press, 1997), 3; King and Lieberman, "American Political Development," 14.

17. T. H. Marshall, "Citizenship and Social Class" (1950), in *Citizenship and Social Class*, ed. T. H. Marshall and Tom Bottomore (London: Pluto Press, 1992).

18. Sidney Verba, "Fairness, Equality, and Democracy: Three Big Words," *Social Research: An International Quarterly* 73 (2006): 531.

19. Lawyers' Committee for Civil Rights under Law, "National Civil Rights Leaders Speak Out Against Voter Suppression Efforts: ID Bills, Attacks on Early Voting and Voter Registration Could Disenfranchise Millions of Minority Voters," press release, June 13, 2011.

20. King and Lieberman, "American Political Development," 4, 18.

21. Alec Ewald, "'Civil Death': The Ideological Paradox of Criminal Disenfranchisement Law in the United States," *Wisconsin Law Review* (2002): 1045–1132.

22. Michelle Natividad Rodriguez and Maurice Emsellem, "65 Million 'Need Not Apply': The Case for Reforming Criminal Background Checks for Employment," The National Employment Law Project, March. 2011, http://www.nelp.org/page/-/65_Million_Need_Not_Apply.pdf?nocdn=1.

23. Bureau of Justice Statistics, "One in 34 U.S. Adults under Correctional Supervision in 2011, Lowest Rate since 2000," http://www.bjs.gov/content/pub/press/cpus11ppus11pr.cfm.

24. Thomas P. Bonczar, "Prevalence of Imprisonment in the U.S. Population, 1974–2001," Bureau of Justice Statistics report, http://www.bjs.gov/index.cfm?ty=pbdetail&iid=836.

25. Jeffrey Fagan, Expert Report in *Floyd v. City of New York*, 08 Civ. 1034 (2008), http://ccrjustice.org/files/Expert_Report_JeffreyFagan.pdf.

26. These figures may actually be underestimated. See Alexandra Natapoff, "Misdemeanors," *Southern California Law Review* 85 (2012): 101–63.

27. Michael Tonry and Matthew Melewski, "The Malign Effects of Drug and Crime Control Policies on Black Americans," *Crime and Justice* 37, no. 1 (2008): 1–44; Jennifer Warren, Adam Gelb, Jake Horowitz, and Jessica Riordan, *One in 100: Behind Bars in America 2008* (Washington, DC: PEW Center on the States, 2008).

28. Bruce Western and Becky Pettit, "Incarceration and Social Inequality," *Daedalus* 139, no. 3 (2010): 11.

29. Michael Tonry, *Punishing Race: A Continuing American Dilemma* (New York: Oxford University Press, 2012), see 59–67 specifically. See also Jamie Fellner and P. Vinck, "Targeting Blacks: Drug Law Enforcement and Race in the United States," Human Rights Watch, 2008, http://www.hrw.org/sites/default/files/reports/uso508_1.pdf .

30. Katherine Beckett, Kris Nyrop, and Lori Pfingst, "Race, Drugs and Policing: Understanding Disparities in Drug Delivery Arrests," *Criminology* 44, no. 1 (2006): 105–38; Katherine Beckett, Kris Nyrop, Lori Pfingst, and Melissa Bowen, "Drug Use, Drug Possession Arrests, and the Question of Race: Lessons from Seattle," *Social Problems* 52, no. 3 (2005): 419–41.

31. Tonry, *Punishing Race*.

32. Michael Lipsky, *Street-level Bureaucracy* (New York: Russell Sage Foundation, 1980); Jennifer L. Lawless and Richard L. Fox, "Political Participation of the Urban Poor," *Social Problems* 48, no. 3 (2001): 362–85; Joe Soss, "Making Clients and Citizens: Welfare Policy as a Source of Status, Belief, and Action," in *Deserving and Entitled: Social Constructions and Public Policy*, ed. A. Schneider and H. Ingram (Albany: State University of New York Press, 2005).

33. Lipsky, *Street-level Bureaucracy*, 4.

34. Marc Landy, "Public Policy and Citizenship," in *Public Policy for Democracy* (Washington, DC: The Brookings Institute, 1993), 19.

35. Marshall, "Citizenship and Social Class."

36. Suzanne Mettler, "Bringing the State Back in to Civic Engagement: Policy Feedback Effects of the G.I. Bill for World War II Veterans," *American Political Science Review* 96, no. 2 (2002): 362.

37. Soss, "Making Clients and Citizens," 314.

38. Ibid., 309, 314.

39. Lawless and Fox, "Political Participation of the Urban Poor," 375.

40. Staffan Kumlin, "Institutions–Experiences–Preferences," in *Restructuring the Welfare State: Political Institutions and Policy Change*, ed. B. Rothstein and S. Steinmo (New York: Palgrave Macmillan, 2002), 20–50.

41. Mettler, *Soldiers to Citizens*, 13.

42. Ibid.

43. Anne Schneider and Helen Ingram, "Social Construction of Target Populations: Implications for Politics and Policy," *American Political Science Review* 87 (1993): 334–47.

44. Carole Pateman, *Participation and Democratic Theory* (Cambridge: Cambridge University Press, 1970), 64; Jane Mansbridge, "On the Idea that Participation Makes Better Citizens," in *Citizen Competence and Democratic Institutions*, ed. Stephen L. Elkin and Karol Edward Soltan (University Park: Pennsylvania State University Press, 1999).

45. Pierre Bourdieu, *Outline of a Theory of Practice* (Cambridge: Cambridge University Press, 1977).

46. Kumlin, "Institutions–Experiences–Preferences," 43.

47. Mettler, "Bringing the State Back in to Civic Engagement."

48. Soss, "Making Clients and Citizens."

49. Mansbridge, "On the Idea that Participation Makes Better Citizens."

50. Joe Soss, *Unwanted Claims: The Politics of Participation in the U.S. Welfare System* (Ann Arbor: University of Michigan Press, 2002), 169.

51. Jurgen Habermas, *Theory of Communicative Action*, vol. 2, *Lifeworld and System: A Critique of Functionalist Reason*, trans. Thomas A. McCarthy (Boston: Beacon Press, 1985).

52. Cathy J. Cohen, *Democracy Remixed: Black Youth and the Future of American Politics* (New York: Oxford University Press, 2010), 125.

53. As two scholars of criminal justice recently observed: "Criminologists and sociologists rarely make the political dimension of crime policy a principal concern, and political scientists almost never do." Franklin E. Zimring and David T. Johnson, "Public Opinion and the Governance of Punishment in Democratic Political Systems," *Annals of the American Academy of Political and Social Science* 605, no. 1 (2006): 267.

54. Loïc Wacquant, *Punishing the Poor: The Neoliberal Government of Social Insecurity* (Durham, NC: Duke University Press, 2009), 18.

55. Manza and Uggen, *Locked Out*.

56. Amanda Geller, Irwin Garfinkel, and Bruce Western, "Paternal Incarceration and Support for Children in Fragile Families," *Demography* 48, no. 1 (2011): 25–47; Bruce Western, Leonard M. Lopoo, and Sara McLanahan, "Incarceration and the Bonds among Parents in Fragile Families," in *Imprisoning America: The Social Effects of Mass Incarceration*, ed. Mary Pattillo, David Weiman, and Bruce Western (New York: Russell Sage, 2004); Michael Masso-

glia, "Incarceration, Health and Racial Disparities in Health," *Law and Society Review* 42 (2008): 2.

57. Brian Balogh, *A Government Out of Sight: The Mystery of National Authority in Nineteenth-century America* (New York: Cambridge University Press, 2009); Suzanne Mettler, *The Submerged State: How Invisible Government Policies Undermine American Democracy* (Chicago: University of Chicago Press, 2011). There are some important exceptions; several scholars are attentive to criminal justice as a central aspect of state development, including Marie Gottschalk, *The Prison and the Gallows: The Politics of Mass Incarceration in America* (Cambridge: Cambridge University Press, 2006); Lisa Miller, *The Perils of Federalism: Race, Poverty, and the Politics of Crime Control* (New York: Oxford University Press, 2008); Naomi Murakawa, "Origins of the Carceral Crisis: Racial Order as 'Law and Order' in Postwar American Politics," in *Race and American Political Development*, ed. Joseph Lowndes, Julie Novkov, and Dorian T. Warren (New York: Routledge, 2008); Stuart A. Scheingold, *The Politics of Street Crime: Criminal Process and Cultural Obsession* (Philadelphia: Temple University Press, 1991); Vanessa Barker, *Politics of Imprisonment: How the Democratic Process Shapes the Way America Punishes Offenders* (New York: Oxford University Press, 2009).

Several other scholars outside of the political science discipline have also been attentive to the historical and political development of the carceral state, including Katherine Beckett, *Making Crime Pay: Law and Order in Contemporary American Politic* (New York: Oxford University Press, 1999); David Garland, *The Culture of Control: Crime and Social Order in Contemporary Society* (Chicago: University of Chicago Press, 2002); Jonathan Simon, *Governing through Crime: How the War on Crime Transformed American Democracy and Created a Culture of Fear* (New York: Oxford University Press, 2007); Rebecca M. McLennan, *The Crisis of Imprisonment: Protest, Politics, and the Making of the American Penal State, 1776–1941* (New York: Cambridge University Press, 2008); Diana R. Gordon, *Justice Juggernaut: Fighting Street Crime, Controlling Citizens* (New Brunswick, NJ: Rutgers University Press, 1990); Ted Gest, *Crime and Politics: Big Government's Erratic Campaign for Law and Order* (New York: Cambridge University Press, 2003).

58. Paul Pierson, "The Rise and Reconfiguration of Activist Government," in *The Transformation of American Politics: Activist Government and the Rise of Conservatism*, ed. Paul Pierson and Theda Skocpol (Princeton, NJ: Princeton University Press, 2007), 19.

59. Gottschalk, *Prison and the Gallows*.

60. Jonathan Simon, "Rise of the Carceral State," *Social Research: An International Quarterly* 74, no. 2 (2007): 496.

61. Wacquant, *Punishing the Poor*.

62. Joe Soss, Richard C. Fording, and Sanford F. Schram, "Governing the Poor: The Rise of the Neoliberal Paternalist State," paper presented at the 2009 annual meeting of the American Political Science Association, Toronto.

63. Suzanne Mettler and Andrew Milstein, "American Political Development from Citizens' Perspective," *Studies in American Political Development* 21, no. 1 (2007): 130.

64. Lawrence R. Jacobs and Theda Skocpol, *Inequality and American Democracy* (New York: Russell Sage Foundation, 2005), 1.

65. Larry M. Bartels, *Unequal Democracy: The Political of the New Gilded Age* (Princeton, NJ: Princeton University Press, 2008), 6.

66. Martin Gilens, "Inequality and Democratic Responsiveness," *Public Opinion Quarterly* 69, no. 5 (2005): 778.

67. Bruce Western, *Punishment and Inequality in America* (New York: Russell Sage Foundation, 2006), 193.

68. Loïc Wacquant, "Deadly Symbiosis: When Ghetto and Prison Meet and Mesh," *Punishment and Society* 3, no. 1 (2001): 116–17.

69. Wacquant, *Punishing the Poor*.

70. Tonry, *Punishing Race*.

71. Michelle Alexander, *The New Jim Crow: Mass Incarceration in the Age of Colorblindness* (New York: New Press, 2012).

72. Morris J. Blachman and Kenneth E. Sharpe, "The War on Drugs: American Democracy under Assault," *World Policy Journal* 7, no. 1 (1989): 136.

73. James Forman Jr., "Racial Critiques of Mass Incarceration: Beyond the New Jim Crow," *New York University Law Review* 87 (2012): 58.

74. Jacob S. Hacker and Paul Pierson, "Winner-Take-All Politics: Public Policy, Political Organization, and the Precipitous Rise of Top Incomes in the United States," *Politics and Society* 38, no. 2 (2010): 152–204.

75. Harold Dwight Laswell, *Politics: Who Gets What, When, How* (New York: Whittlesey House, 1936).

76. Mettler, *Soldiers to Citizens*, 13.

77. David Mayhew, *Congress: The Electoral Connection* (New Haven, CT: Yale University Press, 1974). See, for instance, David Epstein and Sharyn O'Halloran, *Delegating Powers: A Transaction Cost Politics Approach to Policy Making under Separate Powers* (New York: Cambridge University Press, 1999); Kathleen Bawn, "Choosing Strategies to Control the Bureaucracy: Statutory Constraints, Oversight, and the Committee System," *Journal of Law, Economics and Organization* 13 (1997): 101–26; Mathew McCubbins, Roger Noll, and Barry Weingast, "Administrative Procedures as Instruments of Political Control," *Journal of Law, Economics, and Organization* 3 (1987): 243–77, and "Structure and Process, Policy and Politics: Administrative Arrangements and the Political Control of Agencies," *Virginia Law Review* 75 (1989): 431–82.

78. A. M. Gulas, "The American Administrative State: The New Leviathan," *Duquesne Law Review* 28, nos. 489–90 (1990); Joseph Postell, "From Administrative State to Constitutional Government," Special Report 116, The Heritage Foundation, 2012; Richard A Epstein, "Government by 'Expert,'" *Defining Ideas: A Hoover Institution Journal* (March 6, 2012), http://www.hoover.org/publications/defining-ideas/article/110276; Richard A Epstein, *Design for Liberty: Private Property, Public Administration, and the Rule of Law* (Cambridge: Harvard University Press, 2011).

79. James Q. Wilson, "The Rise of the Bureaucratic State," *Public Interest* 41, no. 3 (1975): 77–103.

80. Hwang-Sun Kang, "Administrative Discretion in the Transparent Bureaucracy," *Public Administration Quarterly* 29, no. 12 (2005): 162–85.

81. Frank J. Thompson and Norma M. Riccucci, "Reinventing Government," *Annual Review of Political Science* 1, no. 1 (1998): 231–57.

82. Robin D. G. Kelley reminds us that "Politics is not separate from lived experience or the imaginary world of what is possible; to the contrary, politics is about these things," in *Race Rebels: Culture, Politics, and the Black Working Class* (New York: Free Press, 1994), 9.

83. We thank Melvin Rogers for alerting us to these points. Sharon Krause, "Agency, Inequality, and the Meaning of Freedom," working paper, http://ptw.uchicago.edu/Krause09.pdf.

84. Keally McBride, *Punishment and Political Order* (Ann Arbor: University of Michigan Press, 2007), 4; Max Weber, "Politics as a Vocation," in *Essays in Sociology*, ed. Howard Garth and Cynthia Mills (New York: Macmillan, 1946), 26–45.

Chapter Two

1. Based on authors' analysis of FBI Uniform Crime Report data online, http://ucrdatatool.gov.

2. William Novak, "The Myth of the 'Weak' American State," *American Historical Review* 13, no. 3 (2008): 760.

3. James Austin and Barry Krisberg, "NCCD Research Review: Wider, Stronger, and Different Nets: The Dialectics of Criminal Justice Reform," *Journal of Research in Crime and Delinquency* 38, no. 1 (1981): 165–96.

4. Jim Webb, "Mass Incarceration in the United States: At What Cost?" opening statement to Senate Joint Economic Committee, 110th Congress, 1st sess., Washington, DC, October 4, 2007

5. William J. Stuntz, *The Collapse of American Criminal Justice* (Cambridge: Harvard University Press, 2011), 264, italics in original.

6. James Forman Jr., "Community Policing and Youth as Assets," *Journal of Criminal Law and Criminology* 95, no. 1 (2004): 5.

7. Laurie Levenson, "Police Corruption and New Models for Reform," *Suffolk University Law Review* 35, no. 1 (2001): 15.

8. *Mahari Bailey et al. v. City of Philadelphia et al.*, "Plaintiffs' Third Report to Court and Monitor on Stop and Frisk Practices" (3rd Cir. 2010), US District Court, Eastern District of Pennsylvania, http://www.aclupa.org/downloads/Baileycomp.pdf.

9. Sara LaPlante and Christopher Dunn, "Stop-and-Frisk 2012," NYCLU Briefing Paper (2012), http://www.nyclu.org/publications/report-nypd-stop-and-frisk-activity-2012-2013; Center for Constitutional Rights, "Racial Disparity in NYPD Stops-and-Frisks: The Center for Constitutional Rights Preliminary Report on UF-250 Data from 2005 through June 2008," January 15, 2009, available at http://ccrjustice.org/files/Report-CCR-NYPD-Stop-and-Frisk.pdf.

10. *Bailey et al. v. City of Philadelphia et al.*, "Plaintiffs' Third Report to Court and Monitor on Stop and Frisk Practices."

11. Other outcomes include a citation or warning, a field interview, or another unspecified outcome. Christopher Stone, Todd Foglesong, and Christine M. Cole, "Policing Los Angeles Under a Consent Decree: The Dynamics of Change at the LAPD," Program in Criminal Justice Policy and Management, Working Paper Series, Harvard Kennedy School (2009); US Census Bureau, State and County QuickFacts, Los Angeles (CA), http://quickfacts.census.gov/qfd/states/06/06037.html.

12. Peter Moskos, *Cop in the Hood: My Year Policing Baltimore's Eastern District* (Princeton, NJ: Princeton University Press, 2009), 55, cited in Natapoff, "Misdemeanors," 124.

13. Authors' calculations from data provided by Todd R. Clear, Michael D. Reisig, and George F. Cole, *American Corrections* (Belmont, CA: Wadsworth, 2011), 134.

14. As in adult cases, the minority of juveniles who come in contact with the courts are ultimately found guilty of a crime. About 81% of juvenile cases are referred by law enforcement, but some are referred by other sources, including social service agencies, parents, probation officers, and victims. Of all cases referred to the juvenile court system, about half (44%) are dealt with informally. In these cases, no formal adjudication occurs and cases are either dismissed (18%) or youth are given informal probation (8%) or other voluntary sanctions (17%). When a formal petition is filed, less than 1% are waived to criminal court. The rest are adjudicated in the juvenile justice system and, as in adult cases, a minority of juvenile suspects is ever found to be guilty of their alleged crime: of every 100 cases that enter the juvenile court system, only a minority (about 37) are determined delinquent. Authors' calculations from data provided by Clear, Reisig, and Cole, *American Corrections*, 134.

15. Louis Morgan and Edmund M. Joughin, *The Legacy of Sacco and Vanzetti* (New York: Harcourt, Brace, 1948), 220.

16. In addition, at least some of those who are convicted of crimes are later found innocent. Only 266 people have been formally exonerated with DNA evidence. However, the number of exonerees has increased over time, as forensic sciences improve and greater resources are invested in this pursuit. Others have been exonerated through other types of evidence, and a significantly larger number of convictions are overturned on appeal. Samuel R. Gross, Kristen Jacoby, Daniel J. Matheson, Nicholas Montgomery, and Sujata Patil, "Exonerations in the United States, 1989 through 2003," *Journal of Criminal Law and Criminology* 95, no. 2 (2005): 523–60. Estimates suggest that about 20% of the time, appeals result in a reversal of lower court decisions. In these cases, 35% are resentenced and 32% are granted a new trial, but almost 10% result in acquittal. Joy A. Chapper and Roger A. Hanson, *Understanding Reversible Error in Criminal Appeals* (Williamsburg, VA: National Center for State Courts, 1989). The systemic problems identified in cases of successful appeal and exoneration are numerous: mistaken identity, biased eyewitness testimony, false confessions, ineffective counsel, police and prosecutorial misconduct, and careless forensics. Moreover, these types of wrongful convictions have likely become increasingly common, as the aggressive pursuit of criminal wrongdoing in America has intensified. As one study argues: "by injecting public morals and fears [into criminal justice], the public's willingness to tolerate more 'false positives' increases" and the system becomes "a manufacturing line without quality control. Perhaps 90 to 95% of the cases are moved routinely from station to station, from police to prosecution to plea bargain, and so on in a continuing stream. Few are plucked from the assembly line for close scrutiny. Errors are unlikely to be detected anywhere along the line, but the errors of earlier steps in the process are ratified by later stages." Arye Rattner, "Convicted but Innocent: Wrongful Conviction and the Criminal Justice System," *Law and Human Behavior* 12, no. 3 (1988): 292–93.

17. Crutchfield et al., "Racial Disparities in Early Criminal Justice Involvement."

18. Rod K. Brunson and Jody Miller, "Young Black Men and Urban Policing in the United States," *British Journal of Criminology* 46, no. 4 (2006): 635.

19. E.g., Jeffrey Fagan and Garth Davies, "Street Stops and Broken Windows: Terry, Race and Disorder in New York City," *Fordham Urban Law Journal* 28 (2000): 457–504; Andrew Gelman, Jeffrey Fagan and Alex Kiss, "An Analysis of the New York City Police Department's 'Stop-and-Frisk' Policy in the Context of Claims of Racial Bias," *Journal of the American Statistical Association* 102, no. 479 (2007): 813–23.

20. Sean Gardiner, "'Stop and Frisk' on the Rise," *Wall Street Journal*, June 1, 2011.

21. Jeffrey A. Fagan, Amanda Geller, Garth Davies, and Valerie West, "Street

Stops and Broken Windows Revisited: The Demography and Logic of Proactive Policing in a Safe and Changing City," in *Race, Ethnicity, and Policing: New and Essential Readings*, ed. Stephen K. Rice and Michael D. White (New York: New York University Press, 2010), See also Gelman, Fagan, and Kiss, "An Analysis of the New York City Police Department's 'Stop-and-Frisk' Policy." In that report based on 1998–99 data, blacks made up 51% and Latinos 33% of all stops, while their share of the population was just 26% and 24% respectively. Racial disparities in stop rates remained even after taking into account precinct-level differences and crime rates; blacks were still 23% more likely and Latinos 39% more likely to be stopped by police than whites and *less likely* to be found engaged in wrongdoing (as measured by "hit rates").

22. Center for Constitutional Rights, "Racial Disparity in NYPD Stops-and-Frisks"; "2010 State and County QuickFacts: New York," US Census Bureau, last modified March 14, 2013, http://quickfacts.census.gov/qfd/states/36000.html.

23. Fagan et al., "Street Stops and Broken Windows Revisited."

24. *Bailey et al. v. City of Philadelphia et al.*, "Plaintiffs' Third Report to Court and Monitor on Stop and Frisk Practices."

25. Stone, Foglesong, and Cole, "Policing Los Angeles Under a Consent Decree."

26. Ian Ayres and Jonathan Borowsky, "A Study of Racially Disparate Outcomes in the Los Angeles Police Department," report prepared for the ACLU of Southern California, 2008, 5, accessed online at http://www.aclu-sc.org/documents/view/47.

27. Wesley G. Skogan and Lynn Steiner, "Crime, Disorder and Decay in Chicago's Latino Community," *Journal of Ethnicity in Criminal Justice* 2, nos. 1–2 (2004): 7–26.

28. Ronald Weitzer, Steven Tuch, and Wesley Skogan, "Police-Community Relations in a Majority-Black City," *Journal of Research in Crime and Delinquency* 45 (2008): 398–428.

29. Reenah Kim, "Legitimizing Community Consent to Local Policing: The Need for Democratically Negotiated Community Representation on Civilian Advisory Council," *Harvard Civil Rights–Civil Liberties Review* 36 (2001): 461.

30. Based on author calculations using publically available police stops data from the NYPD. www.nyc.gov/html/nypd/html/analysis_and_planning/stop_question_and_frisk_report.shtml.

31. *Bailey et al. v. City of Philadelphia et al.*, "Plaintiffs' Third Report to Court and Monitor on Stop and Frisk Practices."

32. Fagan et al., "Street Stops and Broken Windows Revisited," 323.

33. David Harris, "Factors for Reasonable Suspicion: When Black and Poor Means Stopped and Frisked," *Indiana Law Journal* 69 (1994): 681.

34. Natapoff, "Misdemeanors," 118–19.

35. Fagan and Davies, "Street Stops and Broken Windows," 457.

36. Fagan et al., "Street Stops and Broken Windows Revisited," 330. Specifically, their analysis controlled for homicide arrests in the police precinct and neighborhood the preceding year, concentrated neighborhood disadvantage (percentage of households receiving public assistance), residential turnover, ethnic heterogeneity of neighborhood (these are all measures of perceived disorder and crime risk), physical disorder, vacancy, and neighborhood fixed effects.

37. Ayres and Borowsky, "A Study of Racially Disparate Outcomes in the Los Angeles Police Department."

38. Fagan and Davies, "Street Stops and Broken Windows," 496.

39. "New York City Sued over Discriminatory Policing Policy in Public Housing," *Defenders Online*, February 2, 2010, http://www.naacpldf.org/news/nyc -sued-over-unlawful-and-discriminatory-policing-public-housing.

40. Jason Alcorn, "Legal Fight Brews over Public Housing Arrests," *The Uptowner*, January 5, 2011, http://theuptowner.org/2011/01/05/legal-fight-brews -over-public-housing-arrests/.

41. *Davis et al. v. The City of New York and New York City Housing Authority*, www.clearinghouse.net/chDocs/public/PN-NY-0013-0002.pdfF.

42. Entire paragraph is from this source: "Class Action Lawsuit Challenges NYPD Patrols of Private Apartment Buildings," New York Civil Liberties Union, last modified March 28, 2012, http://www.nyclu.org/news/class-action -lawsuit-challenges-nypd-patrols-of-private-apartment-buildings.

43. Center for Constitutional Rights, "Racial Disparity in NYPD Stops-and-Frisks," 151, 152.

44. Christine Eith and Matthew R. Durose, "Contacts between Police and the Public, 2008," Special Report of the USDOJ, Bureau of Justice Statistics, October 2001, http://www.bjs.gov/content/pub/pdf/cpp08.pdf.

45. "Lingering Questions about Stop and Frisk," *New York Times*, February 18, 2010, http://www.nytimes.com/2010/02/19/opinion/19fri3.html.

46. Based on authors' calculations. Howard N. Snyder and Joseph Mulako-Wangota, Bureau of Justice Statistics, "Arrests by Age in the U.S., 2001," generated using the Arrest Data Analysis Tool at www.bjs.gov.

47. Marc Mauer and Ryan S. King, *The War on Marijuana: The Transformation of the War on Drugs in the 1990s* (Washington, DC: The Sentencing Project, 2006).

48. Andrew Golub, Bruce Johnson, and Eloise Dunlap, "The Race/Ethnicity Disparity in Misdemeanor Marijuana Arrests in New York City," *Criminology and Public Policy* 6 (2007): 1.

49. Natapoff, "Misdemeanors," 107, 116.

50. Ibid., 138.

51. Ibid., citing studies by the Vera Institute for Justice and legal scholar Josh Bowers.

52. Ibid.

53. Ibid., 105, 107, 125.

54. Golub, Johnson, and Dunlap, "Race/Ethnicity Disparity in Misdemeanor Marijuana Arrests."

55. Natapoff, "Misdemeanors," 153.

56. Ryan S. King and Marc Mauer, *Distorted Priorities: Drug Offenders in State Prisons* (Washington, DC: The Sentencing Project, 2002); Federal Bureau of Investigation, Uniform Crime Reports, www.fbi.gov/anpit-us/cjis/ucr/ucr.

57. Tonry, *Punishing Race.*

58. King and Mauer, *Distorted Priorities*, 1.

59. Ibid.

60. Alison Lawrence, "Probation and Parole Violations: State Responses," National Conference of State Legislators, 2008, www.ncsl.org/print/cj/violations report.pdf.

61. John Schmitt, Kris Warner, and Sarika Gupta, "The High Budgetary Cost of Incarceration," Center for Economic and Policy Research, June 2010, http://www.cepr.net/documents/publications/incarceration-2010-06.pdf.

62. John Schmitt, Kris Warner, and Sarika Gupta, "The High Budgetary Cost of Incarceration," Center for Economic and Policy Research, 2010, 8, http://www.cepr.net/documents/publications/incarceration-2010-06.pdf .

63. King and Mauer, *Distorted Priorities*. See Human Rights Watch, "Decades of Disparity: Drug Arrests and Race in the United States," 2009, http://www.hrw.org/sites/default/files/reports/us0309web_1.pdf for info on possession vs. sales arrests.

64. Ryan S. King, *Disparity by Geography: The War on Drugs in America's Cities* (Washington, DC: The Sentencing Project, 2008).

65. Human Rights Watch, "Decades of Disparity."

66. Natapoff, "Misdemeanors," 112–13.

67. Human Rights Watch, "Decades of Disparity." In truth, this racial gap is actually even more divergent. These statistics do not separate out Latinos, who (like blacks) have higher rates of criminal justice contact than whites. It is thus likely the case that were Latinos removed from the white rate, the black/white disparities would be even greater.

68. Tonry, *Punishing Race*, 54.

69. Ibid.

70. Ibid., 59–67 specifically. See also Jamie Fellner and P. Vinck, "Targeting Blacks: Drug Law Enforcement and Race in the United States," Human Rights Watch, 2008, http://www.hrw.org/sites/default/files/reports/us0508_1.pdf .

71. Beckett et al., "Race, Drugs and Policing"; Beckett et al., "Drug Use, Drug Possession Arrests, and the Question of Race."

72. Stuntz, *Collapse of American Criminal Justice*, 273.

73. Michael H. Tonry, *Thinking about Crime: Sense and Sensibility in American Penal Culture* (New York: Oxford University Press, 2004); Gottschalk,

Prison and the Gallows. Tonry finds that the United States is more in the middle on property crime and on some other crimes lags behind Europe.

74. Alexia Cooper and Erica L. Smith, "Homicide Trends in the United States, 1980–2008," Bureau of Justice Statistics, US Department of Justice, November 2011, http://bjs.gov/content/pub/pdf/htus8008.pdf.

75. This is the figure for 2011. The homicide rate is 4.8 per 100,000 in 2010. Ibid.

76. Special Report, Bureau of Justice Statistics, US Department of Justice, "Violent Victimization and Race, 1993–1998," March 2001.

77. Cooper and Smith, "Homicide Trends in the United States, 1980–2008"; Lisa Miller, "Power to the People: Violent Victimization, Inequality, and Democratic Politics," *Theoretical Criminology* 17, no. 3 (2013): 283–313; Ruth D. Peterson and Lauren J. Krivo, *Divergent Social Worlds: Neighborhood Crime and the Racial-Spatial Divide* (New York: Russell Sage Foundation, 2010), 13.

78. Rucker Johnson, presentation at the Detaining Democracy? Conference at Yale University, November 8–9, 2012; Forman, "Racial Critiques of Mass Incarceration."

79. Cooper and Smith, "Homicide Trends in the United States, 1980–2008."

80. Anne C. Spaulding, Ryan M. Seals, Victoria A. McCallum, Sebastian D. Perez, Amanda K. Brzozowski, and N. Kyle Steenland, "Prisoner Survival Inside and Outside of the Institution: Implications for Health-care Planning," *American Journal of Epidemiology* 173, no. 5 (2011): 479–87; Christopher Wildeman, "Imprisonment and (Inequality in) Population Health," *Social Science Research* 41, no. 1 (2012): 74–91.

81. Peterson and Krivo, *Divergent Social Worlds*, 19.

82. Stuntz, *Collapse of American Criminal Justice.*

83. Cooper and Smith, "Homicide Trends in the United States, 1980–2008."

84. Mary Pattillo-McCoy, *Black Picket Fences: Privilege and Peril in the Black Middle Class Neighborhood* (Chicago: University of Chicago Press, 1999).

85. Authors' analysis of the first round of the 1997 NLSY.

86. "That Woman Is Not Adam Lanza's Mother, and She's Distracting Us from the Real Issue," *Jezebel,* http://jezebel.com/5968971/that-woman-is-not -adam-lanzas-mother-and-shes-distracting-us-from-the-real-issue.

87. Authors' analysis of Cathy J. Cohen, "Black Youth Culture Survey," Black Youth Project, Chicago, IL, 2005. Dataset accessed at http://www.blackyouth project.com.

88. "African-American Men Survey," Washington Post/Kaiser Family Foundation/Harvard University, June 2006, http://www.kff.org/kaiserpolls/upload/ 7526.pdf.

89. Johnson, presentation at the Detaining Democracy? Conference.

90. Forman, "Racial Critiques of Mass Incarceration," 128.

91. Randall Kennedy, *Race, Crime, and the Law* (New York: Vintage Books, 1997).

92. Stuntz, *Collapse of American Criminal Justice*, 22.

93. Miller, "Power to the People."

94. Elijah Anderson, "The Code of the Streets," *Atlantic Monthly*, May 1994, 80–94.

95. Forman, "Racial Critiques of Mass Incarceration," 129–30.

96. Based on authors' analysis of the National Longitudinal Survey of Youth, 1997.

97. Authors' analysis of Cohen, "Black Youth Culture Survey."

98. Miller, "Power to the People," 8.

Chapter Three

1. Robert Dahl, *Democracy and Its Critics* (New Haven, CT: Yale University Press, 1991), 311.

2. Ibid., 1.

3. Verba, "Fairness, Equality, and Democracy," 505.

4. Sidney Verba, *Thoughts about Political Equality: What Is It? Why Do We Want It?* (New York: Russell Sage Foundation, 2001), 2.

5. Verba, "Fairness, Equality, and Democracy."

6. King and Lieberman, "American Political Development," 3.

7. Eric Luna, "Transparent Policing," *Iowa Law Review* 85, no. 4 (2000): 1121.

8. Robert Dahl, *How Democratic Is the American Constitution?* (New Haven, CT: Yale University Press, 2003).

9. Nicola Lacey, *The Prisoner's Dilemma: Political Economy and Punishment in Contemporary Democracies* (Cambridge: Cambridge University Press, 2008), 7.

10. *Ruffin v. Commonwealth*, 62 Va. 790, 796 (1871).

11. Quoted in David M. Alderstein, "In Need of Correction: The Iron Triangle of the Prison Litigation Reform Act," *Columbia Law Review* 101 (2001): 1689 n. 39.

12. *Wolff v. McDonnell*, 418 U.S. 539, 555–56 (1974).

13. Mettler, "The Development of Democratic Citizenship," 239.

14. Luna, "Transparent Policing," 1108.

15. Kim, "Legitimizing Community Consent to Local Policing," 461.

16. Myriam Gilles, "Reinventing Structural Reform Litigation: Deputizing Private Citizens in the Enforcement of Civil Rights," *Columbia Law Review* 6 (2000): 1385, 1397 n. 45.

17. Ibid., 1385 n. 2.

18. Alison L. Patton, "The Endless Cycle of Abuse: Why 42 U.S.C. S 1983 Is Ineffective in Deterring Police Brutality," *Hastings Law Journal* 44 (1992): 787.

19. Justice Marshall, dissenting opinion, *City of Los Angeles v. Lyons*, 461 US 95 (1983).

20. Gilles, "Reinventing Structural Reform Litigation."

21. Decision quoted in ibid., 1398.

22. Ibid., 1399 n. 57.

23. Patton, "Endless Cycle of Abuse."

24. Levenson, "Police Corruption and New Models for Reform."

25. Allyson Collins, *Shielded from Justice: Police Brutality and Accountability in the United States* (New York: Human Rights Watch, 1998).

26. Ibid.

27. Patton, "Endless Cycle of Abuse," 787–89.

28. Quoted in ibid., 792.

29. Quoted in Stephen Clarke, "Arrested Oversight: A Comparative Analysis and Case Study of How Civilian Oversight of the Police Should Function and How It Fails," *Columbia Journal of Law and Social Problems* 43 (2009): 10.

30. The Louima case ultimately went to criminal trial and one of the officers involved was convicted and sentenced to prison. Several others were indicted and convicted for perjury and for conspiracy to cover up the assault. Louima also subsequently filed a successful civil suit, in which he was awarded the largest policy brutality settlement in the history of the city.

31. Harvey Gee, "The First Amendment and Police Misconduct: Criminal Penalty for Filing Complaints against Police Officers," *Hamline Law Review* 27 (2004): 227.

32. Clarke, "Arrested Oversight."

33. "Some courts have found that qualified immunity protects even malicious or intentional misconduct." David Rudovsky, "Running in Place: The Paradox of Expanded Rights and Restricted Remedies," *University of Illinois Law Review* 5 (2005): 1217 n. 116.

34. Ibid., 1224.

35. Thorne Clark, "Protection from Protection: Sec. 1983 and the ADAs Implications for Devising a Race-Conscious Police Misconduct Statute," *University of Pennsylvania Law Review* 150, no. 5 (2002): 1600.

36. Collins, *Shielded from Justice.*

37. Patton, "Endless Cycle of Abuse," 760.

38. Collins, *Shielded from Justice.*

39. Levenson, "Police Corruption and New Models for Reform," 22.

40. Clarke, "Arrested Oversight." As Human Rights Watch observes, "district attorneys are elected and are aware that the powerful police unions and their supporters may withdraw their support if a police officer is prosecuted." Collins, *Shielded from Justice*, 86.

41. Clark, "Protection from Protection," 1596–1597.

42. Gilles, "Reinventing Structural Reform Litigation," 1387.

43. An attorney general quoted in Margaret Johns, "Reconsidering Absolute Prosecutorial Immunity," *Brigham Young University Law Review* (2005): 123.

44. Ibid. Though Johns notes that the circuit courts have been split on whether some of these situations trigger absolute immunity or not.

45. Ibid., 145.

46. Ibid., 133.

47. Rudovsky, "Running in Place."

48. Johns, "Reconsidering Absolute Prosecutorial Immunity."

49. Rudovsky, "Running in Place."

50. Johns, "Reconsidering Absolute Prosecutorial Immunity," 82.

51. Quoted in ibid., 61.

52. Ibid., 60.

53. Rudovsky, "Running in Place," 1216.

54. Johns, "Reconsidering Absolute Prosecutorial Immunity."

55. Rudovsky, "Running in Place."

56. Erving Goffman, "Some Characteristics of Total Institutions," in Goffman, *Asylums* (New York: Anchor Books, 1962). Defined as "1) a single authority with a single organization designed to fulfill official aims; 2) all aspects of life continuing in the same place with large groups of individuals treated alike; 3) extensive amounts of scheduling and regulation; 4) large numbers of people supervised by a relatively small staff; 5) supervision of conduct which is so pervasive that conduct at one place and time can be used by the staff to control conduct elsewhere; and 6) only minimum opportunity for privacy, property, or family." Sidney Zonn, "Inmate Unions: An Appraisal of Prisoner Rights and Labor Implications," *University of Miami Law Review* 32, no. 3 (1978): 613–35.

57. Margo Schlanger and Giovanna Shay, "Preserving the Rule of Law in America's Jails and Prisons: The Case for Amending the Prison Litigation Reform Act," *University of Pennsylvania Journal of Constitutional Law* 11, no. 1 (2008): 139.

58. *Stroud v. Swope*, 187 F. 2d. 850 (9th Circuit, 1951).

59. The first of these cases occurred in 1941 in Ex parte Hull, ruling that prisoners had a right to access to the federal courts. Katherine J. Bennett and Craig Hemmens, "Prisoner Rights," in *Handbook of Criminal Justice Administration*, ed. M. A. DuPont-Morales, Michael K. Hooper, and Judy H. Schmidt (New York: Marcel Dekker, 2000), 303–18.

60. *McCarthy v. Madigan*, 503 U.S. 140, 153 (1992).

61. Michael Mushlin notes that "a series of Supreme Court decisions has radically enlarged the scope of deference accorded to prison administrators and proscribed the conditions under which poor treatment of prisoners—even objectively brutal treatment—can be considered justiciable." Michael B. Mushlin,

"Getting Real about Race and Prisoner Rights," *Pace Law Faculty Publications*, Paper 549 (2009), http://digitalcommons.pace.edu/lawfaculty/549.

62. Schlanger and Shay, "Preserving the Rule of Law," 139.

63. Giovanna E. Shay and Johanna Kalb, "More Stories of Jurisdiction-Stripping and Executive Power: Interpreting the Prison Litigation Reform Act (PLRA)," *Cardozo Law Review* 29, no. 20 (2007): 295, available at SSRN: http://ssrn.com/abstract=968486.

64. The PLRA applies to Section 1983 claims, which are civil claims, not criminal. Section 1983 provides: "Every person who, under color of any statute, ordinance, regulation, custom, or usage, of any State or Territory or the District of Columbia, subjects, or causes to be subjected, any citizen of the United States or other person within the jurisdiction thereof to the deprivation of any rights, privileges, or immunities secured by the Constitution and laws, shall be liable to the party injured in an action at law, suit in equity, or other proper proceeding for redress."

65. One article suggests that the PLRA applies to drug treatment facilities. Shay and Kalb, "More Stories of Jurisdiction-Stripping," 317.

66. Bureau of Justice Statistics, "Jail Inmates at Midyear 2012—Statistical Tables," http://www.bjs.gov/index.cfm?ty=pbdetail&iid=4655.

67. Alderstein, "In Need of Correction," 1686–87.

68. Michael Mushlin, *Rights of Prisoners*, 4th ed., vol. 2 (St. Paul, MN: West, 2009), 290.

69. This is called the "procedural default rule" and was established through the Court's decision in *Woodford v. Ngo*. Shay and Kalb, "More Stories of Jurisdiction-Stripping."

70. John Boston, "The Prison Litigation Reform Act: The New Face of Court Stripping," *Brooklyn Law Review* 67 (2001): 431.

71. Shay and Kalb, "More Stories of Jurisdiction-Stripping," See 321 n. 228.

72. There are numerous cases of failure to exhaust in which prisoners were placed in isolation and not given grievance application materials. In *Latham v. Pate*, for example, a lower court dismissed the case of a prisoner who filed suit against a group of correctional guards, claiming that he had suffered serious injuries during a beating at their hands. The prison rejected his grievance because it had been filed over a year late. The prisoner appealed, citing as the reason for his failure to exhaust that he had been confined in segregation since the incident and had not been provided grievance forms there. His case was still dismissed, as the court deferred to the prison on whether the claimant had followed their protocols. In another case, *Mendoza v. Goord*, an inmate filed a grievance for excessive force; upon not hearing anything, the inmate filed another grievance form. The court ruled that the inmate's case had been denied and his failure to exhaust resulted from his not appealing the decision about which he was never notified.

73. Human Rights Watch, "No Equal Justice: The Prison Litigation Reform

Act in the United States," Washington, DC, 12, http://www.hrw.org/sites/default/ files/reports/us0609webwcover.pdf; Kermit Roosevelt, "Exhaustion under the Prison Litigation Reform Act: The Consequence of Procedural Error," *Emory Law Journal* 52 (2003): 1771.

74. Shay and Kalb, "More Stories of Jurisdiction-Stripping," 326.

75. Only three states (Hawaii, Iowa, and Nebraska) handle inmate claims through an independent ombudsman. Van Swearingen, "Imprisoning Rights: The Failure of Negotiated Governance in the Prison Inmate Grievance Process," *California Law Review* 96 (2008): 1353.

76. Ibid., 1372.

77. One author notes the possibility that "correctional departments engage in practices that nominally signal compliance with the rule of law but fail to provide substantive protection." Ibid., 1355.

78. Ibid., 1378.

79. Alderstein, "In Need of Correction," 1696 n. 84; Bennett and Hemmens, "Prisoner Rights."

80. *Garcia v. Glover*, 197 F. App'x 866, 867 (11th Cir. 2006)

81. Boston, "Prison Litigation Reform Act," 431.

82. Quoted in Alderstein, "In Need of Correction," 1696 n. 84: "The potential for abuse in this [grievance] process is clear. Not only does having to ask their jailers for grievance forms very likely deter inmates from filing grievances, but after having filled out the form, the inmate cannot be assured that the grievance will be delivered and received."

83. There is one exception: if the prisoner is in "imminent danger of serious physical injury."

84. Boston, "Prison Litigation Reform Act," 433; Michael B. Mushlin and Naomi Roslyn Galtz, "Getting Real about Race and Prisoner Rights," *Fordham Urban Law Journal* 36 (2009): 35.

85. Boston, "Prison Litigation Reform Act."

86. Lynn S. Braham, "Toothless in Truth? The Ethereal Rational Basis Test and the Prison Litigation Reform Act's Disparate Restrictions on Attorney's Fees," *California Law Review* 89 (2001): 999–1053.

87. Ibid.

88. But see Shay and Kalb, "More Stories of Jurisdiction-Stripping," 295 n. 16, who find that courts have assumed the PLRA applies to state court, too, where federal constitutional claims are made.

89. Human Rights Watch, "No Equal Justice," 3.

90. Schlanger and Shay, "Preserving the Rule of Law," 2.

91. Toqueville, quoted in Robert Putnam, *Bowling Alone: The Collapse and Revival of American Community* (New York: Simon and Schuster 2000), 338–41.

92. Ibid.; Robert Putnam, *Making Democracy Work* (Princeton, NJ: Princeton University Press, 1994), 182–83

93. *NAACP v. Alabama ex rel. Patterson*, 357 U.S. 449, 460 (1958)

94. Edward Bond, "Freedom of Association—for Gangs?" *Los Angeles Times*, February 11, 1997.

95. Julie Gannon Shoop, "Gang Warfare: Legal Battle Pits Personal Liberty against Public Safety," *Trial* 34, no. 3 (March 1, 1998): 12–16.

96. "Gang Injunctions," Los Angeles City Attorney's Office, http://atty.lacity .org/our_office/criminaldivision/ganginjunctions/index.htm (last modified 2013).

97. Cheryl L. Maxson, Karen Hennigan, David Sloane, and Kathy A. Kolnick, "Can Civil Gang Injunctions Change Communities? A Community Assessment of the Impact of Civil Gang Injunctions," Final Report Submitted to the National Institute of Justice, US Department of Justice, Grant #98-IJ-CX-0038 (2005).

98. In San Diego, the city attorney who pressed the case asserted that the injunction brought "an overnight result" and that "after the injunction was served, immediately people began to come out of their homes again, and gang members disappeared from the area. The problem essentially went away." Shoop, "Gang Warfare."

99. Gary Stewart, "Black Codes and Broken Windows: The Legacy of Racial Hegemony in Anti-Gang Civil Injunctions," *Yale Law Review* 107, no. 7 (1998): 2249–79.

100. *People ex rel. Joan R. Gallo v. Acuna*, 14 Cal.4th 1090, 60 Cal.Rptr.2d 277, 929 P.2d 596 (1997).

In contesting the finding that the freedoms of the individual should be subjugated for the safety of the many, he argued that "the majority would permit our cities to close off entire neighborhoods to Latino youths who have done nothing more than dress in blue or black clothing or associate with others who do so; they would authorize criminal penalties for ordinary, nondisruptive acts of walking or driving through a residential neighborhood with a relative or friend. In my view, such a blunderbuss approach amounts to both bad law and bad policy."

101. Jeffrey Grogger, "The Effects of Civil Gang Injunctions on Reported Violent Crime: Evidence from Los Angeles County," *Journal of Law and Economics* 45, no. 1 (2002): 73.

102. Matthew Mickle Werdegar, "Enjoining the Constitution: The Use of Public Nuisance Abatement Injunctions against Urban Street Gangs," *Stanford Law Review* 51, no. 2 (1999): 409–45. In a study of civil gang injunctions in Los Angeles, Jeffrey Grogger notes that "although civil procedures result in less stringent penalties, they have the advantage (as viewed by the prosecutor) that their penalties can be imposed without criminal due process." Grogger, "Effects of Civil Gang Injunctions," 72.

103. Katherine Beckett and Steve Herbert, *Banished: The New Social Control in Urban America* (Oxford: Oxford University Press, 2009), 17, 57.

104. Ibid., 88.

105. Ibid., 146.

106. Ibid., 11, 105.

107. Article 20 of the UN Universal Declaration of Human Rights (1948), available at http://www.un.org/en/documents/udhr/index.shtml.

108. In cases such as *Kentucky Department of Corrections v. Thompson* (1989) and *Overton v. Bazzetta* (2003), prisons retained broad leeway to limit free association so long as regulations bore a rational relation to legitimate penological objectives—promoting internal security, protecting child visitors from harm, preventing future crimes, and deterring prisoners' use of alcohol and drugs. Courts have also ruled that prisoners have no liberty rights pertaining to remaining with inmates at a particular prison institution. Prison officials may therefore transfer an inmate within or across prison systems, so long as it is not in retaliation for exercising a right protected by the constitution.

109. Burt Useem and Peter Kimball, *State of Siege U.S. Prison Riots: 1971–1986* (Oxford: Oxford University Press, 1991).

110. Susan Blankenship, "Revisiting the Democratic Promise of Prisoners' Labor Unions," *Studies in Law, Politics, and Society* 37 (2005): 242.

111. James L. Regens and William Hobson, "Inmate Self-Government and Attitude Change: An Assessment of Participation Effects," *Evaluation Quarterly* 2, no. 3 (1978):, 455–79.

112. Mushlin, *Rights of Prisoners*. See also Zonn, "Inmate Unions."

113. Zonn, "Inmate Unions," 621 n. 63.

114. S. M. Singleton, "Unionizing America's Prisons—Arbitration and State-Use," *Indiana Law Journal* 48 (1973): 3; R. Montoya and P. Coggins, "The Future of Prisoners' Unions: Jones v. North Carolina Prisoners' Labor Union," *Harvard Civil Rights—Civil Liberties Law Review*, 13, no. 3 (1978): 799–826, citing Virginia McArthur, "Inmate Grievance Mechanisms: A Survey of 209 American Prisons," *Federal Probation* 38 (1974): 41; see also Zonn, "Inmate Unions." For a detailed account of the formation of an inmate union, see Clarence Ronald Huff, "Unionization behind the Walls: An Analytic Study of the Ohio Prisoners' Labor Union Movement," PhD diss., Ohio State University, 1974. https://etd.ohiolink.edu/.

115. Fay Knopp, "Instead of Prisons: A Handbook for Abolitionists," Prison Research Education Action Project, 1976, http://www.prisonpolicy.org/scans/instead_of_prisons.

116. Mushlin, *Rights of Prisoners*.

117. Ibid., 285.

118. Blankenship, "Revisiting the Democratic Promise of Prisoners' Labor Unions," 245.

119. Quoted in Montoya and Coggins, "The Future of Prisoners' Unions," 801.

120. Zonn, "Inmate Unions," 627.

121. They argued that "prisoners eventually would be stripped of all constitutional rights, and would retain only those privileges that prison officials, in their 'informed discretion,' designed to recognize. The sole constitutional constraint on prison officials would be a requirement that they act rationally." Quoted in ibid., 629.

122. Bradley B. Falkoff, "Prisoner Representative Organizations, Prison Reform, and Jones v. North Carolina Prisoners' Labor Union," *Journal of Criminal Law and Criminology* 70, no. 1 (1979): 47.

123. One case held that prisons had to allow legal communication from lawyers on union-related matters. Another upheld an inmate's right to wear a union pin. See Mushlin, *Rights of Prisoners*.

124. Susan B. Anthony, "The Status of Women, Past, Present and Future," *The Arena* 902 (1897).

125. Verba, "Fairness, Equality, and Democracy," 532.

126. *McLaughlin v. City of Canton*, 947 F. Supp. 954, 971 (S.D. Miss. 1995), cited in Ewald, "Civil Death," 1045–1132.

127. Manza and Uggen, *Locked Out*.

128. Christopher Uggen, Jeff Manza, and Angela Behrens, "Felon Voting Rights and the Disenfranchisement of African Americans," *Souls: A Critical Journal of Black Politics, Culture, and Society* 5 (2003): 47–55.

129. Manning Marable, Ian Steinberg, and Keesha M. Middlemass, *Racializing Justice, Disenfranchising Lives: The Racism, Criminal Justice and Law Reader* (New York: Palgrave Macmillan, 2007).

130. Vikram Amar, "Jury Service as Political Participation Akin to Voting," *Cornell Law Review* 80 (1995): 218.

131. Lord Windlesham, *Politics, Punishment, and Populism* (Oxford: Oxford University Press, 1998).

132. Alexis de Tocqueville, *Democracy in America*, ed. J. P. Mayer and Max Lerner, trans. George Lawrence (1835; New York: Harper and Row, 1966), 249–53.

133. Opinion in *Powers v. Ohio*, quoted in Amar, "Jury Service as Political Participation," 203.

134. James M. Binnall, "Sixteen Million Angry Men: Reviving a Dead Doctrine to Challenge the Constitutionality of Excluding Felons from Jury Service," *Virginia Journal of Social Policy and the Law* 17, no. 1 (2009): 2.

135. Brian C. Kalt, "The Exclusion of Felons from Jury Service," *American University Law Review* 53, no. 1 (2003): 65–189. "A leading estimate suggests that felon exclusion affects from 2% to 6.5% of adult citizens nationally, but 7% to 21% of black citizens, and 12% to 37% of black men." The lower numbers reflect those felons currently serving while the higher numbers include all felons.

136. Darren Lee Wheelock, "A Jury of 'Peers': Felon Jury Exclusion, Racial

Threat, and Racial Inequality in United States Criminal Courts," PhD diss., University of Minnesota, 2006, http://search.proquest.com/docview/305304950 ?accountid=15172.

137. *Jones v. North Carolina Prisoners' Union*, 433 US 119 (1977).

138. Morris, *Jailhouse Journalism*, 163, 164.

139. Ibid.

140. *Pell v. Procunier*, 417 US 817 (1974).

141. *Sandin v. Conner*, 515 US 472, 115 S.Ct. 2293, 132 L.Ed.2d 418 (1995).

142. Morris, *Jailhouse Journalism*, 196.

143. Ibid., 195.

144. *Shakur v. Selsky*, 391 F.3d 106, 2nd Circuit (2004).

145. *Murphy v. Missouri*, 814 F.2d 1252, 1256–57 (8th Cir. 1987) (holding a total ban on Aryan Nation materials too restrictive, but stating a policy restricting materials that advocate violence or that are racially inflammatory would be valid); *Winburn v. Bologna*, 979 F. Supp. 531, 534 (W.D. Mich. 1997) (prison mail policy withholding material that promotes violence and racial supremacy reasonable and valid); *Thomas v. United States Secretary of Defense*, 730 F. Supp. 362 (D. Kan. 1990) (regulation rejecting mail that communicates information designed to encourage prisoners to disrupt institutions by strikes, riots, racial or religious hatred does not violate First Amendment).

146. Mushlin, *Rights of Prisoners*, 290.

147. In one case, inmates were instructed to swallow unfiltered stool suspension in order to allow researchers to study the transmission of a deadly stomach bug. In another study, conducted at Philadelphia's Holmesburg Prison, an inmate "agreed to have a layer of skin peeled off his back, which was coated with searing chemicals to test a drug. He did that for money to buy cigarettes in prison. . . . [I]n an interview with The Associated Press . . . he recalled the beginning of weeks of intense itching and agonizing pain." Mike Stobbe, "Horrific US Medical Experiments Come to Light," Associated Press, February 27, 2011.

148. *Pell v. Procunier*, 417 US 817 (1974).

149. Ibid.

150. In her comparative account of criminal justice in the United States and Britain, Nicola Lacey notes that "the state of criminal justice—the scope and content of criminal law, the performance of criminal justice officials, public attitudes to crime, and the extent and intensity of the penal system—is often used as a broad index of how 'civilized,' 'progressive,' or indeed 'truly democratic' a country is." Lacey, *Prisoner's Dilemma*, xv, 3.

151. Alexis de Tocqueville and Gustave de Beaumont, *On the Penitentiary System in the United States and Its Application in France* (Carbondale: Southern Illinois University Press, 1979).

152. Gary T. Marx, "Police and Democracy," in *Policing, Security and De-*

mocracy: Theory and Practice, vol. 2, ed. Menachem Amir and Stanley Einstein (Hunstville, TX: Office of International Criminal Justice, 2001).

153. Gottschalk, *Prison and the Gallows*.

154. Jamie Fellner and Marc Mauer, *Losing the Vote: The Impact of Felony Disenfranchisement Laws in the United States* (Washington, DC: The Sentencing Project; New York: Human Rights Watch, 1998).

155. Andre Blais, Louis Massicotte, and Antoine Yoshinaka, "Deciding Who Has the Right to Vote: A Comparative Analysis of Election Laws," *Electoral Studies* 20 (2001): 41–62.

156. Reuven Ziegler, "Legal Outlier, Again? U.S Felon Suffrage," *Boston University International Law Journal* 29 (2011): 210.

157. Decision of Canadian Supreme Court Justice quoted in Courtney Artzner, "Check Marks the Spot: Evaluating the Fundamental Right to Vote and Felon Disenfranchisement in the United States and Canada," *Southwestern Journal of Law and Trade in the Americas* 13 (2006): 423, 437.

158. Beckett, *Making Crime Pay*; Natasha A. Frost, *The Punitive State: Crime, Punishment and Imprisonment across the United States* (New York: LFB Scholarly Publications, 2006); Julian V. Roberts, Loretta J. Stalans, David Indermaur, and Mike Hough, *Penal Populism and Public Opinion: Lessons from Five Countries* (New York: Oxford University Press, 2003).

Chapter Four

1. Kumlin, "Institutions–Experiences–Preferences," 20–50.

2. Mettler, *Submerged State*.

3. Kumlin, "Institutions–Experiences–Preferences," 26.

4. *Preiser v. Rodriguez*, 441 US 475, 492 (1973).

5. Cohen, *Semi-Citizenship in Democratic Politics*.

6. Ewald, "Civil Death," 1045–1132.

7. Michael Owens, "The Problem Is Not Punishment Per Se: Punitive Policies and Attitudes towards Felons as Polity Members," unpublished paper presented at the University of Virginia, April 2009, as part of the symposium on "The Problem of Punishment: Race, Inequality, and Justice."

8. Paul Samuels and Debbie Mukamal, *After Prison: Roadblocks to Reentry—A Report on State Legal Barriers Facing People with Criminal Records* (New York: Legal Action Center, 2004).

9. Devah Pager, "The Mark of a Criminal Record," *American Journal of Sociology* 108, no. 5 (2003): 937–75.

10. Numerous other policy designs also reinforce the stigma of custodial status, including the termination of parental rights under the Adoption and Safe Families Act, the seizure of assets of drug suspects through forfeiture laws, au-

tomatic deportation of convicts, and the loss of property and marriage rights through individual state laws.

11. Simon, *Governing through Crime.*

12. Ericka S. Fairchild, "Politicization of the Criminal Offender: Prisoner Perceptions of Crime and Politics," *Criminology* 15, no. 3 (1977): 287–318.

13. Rod Brunson and Ronald Weitzer, "Police Relations with Black and White Youths," *Urban Affairs Review* 44, no. 6 (2009): 858–85.

14. Soss, "Making Clients and Citizens," 314. Stigmatization is even more pronounced for those convicted of particularly heinous or repetitive crimes. For example, in the public imagination, the sexual offender maintains a unique position of disdain, considered at best to be a clinically incurable deviant and at worst a manifestation of evil. In response to these public perceptions, many localities have adopted laws designed to track and monitor sexual offenders for life, including publicly accessible electronic databases that provide the names, addresses, and, in some cases, the photos of sex offenders. Laws regarding community notification of sex offenders, or Megan's Laws, have in some cases led to Frankenstein-esque scenes of vigilantism: the beheading of a dog belonging to one offender, the burning down of another offender's house, and the beating of a New Jersey man who was mistakenly identified as a sex offender. Eric Lotke, "Politics and Irrelevance: Community Notification Statutes," *Federal Sentencing Reporter* 10, no. 2 (1997): 64–68.

15. Owens, "Problem Is Not Punishment Per Se."

16. Soss, "Making Clients and Citizens."

17. See, for example, Julianna Sandell Pacheco, "Political Socialization in Context: The Effect of Political Competition on Youth Voter Turnout," *Political Behavior* 30 (2008): 415–36; Paul Allen Beck and M. Kent Jennings "Pathways to Participation," *American Political Science Review* (1982): 76, 94–108; M. Kent Jennings and Gregory B. Markus, "Partisan Orientations over the Long Haul: Results from a Three Wave Political Socialization Panel Study," *American Political Science Review* (1984): 78, 1000–1008; Duane F. Alwin and Jon A. Krosnick, "Aging, Cohorts, and the Stability of Sociopolitical Orientations over the Life Span," *American Journal of Sociology* (1991): 97, 169–96.

18. Data from the 2004 Survey of Inmates in State and Federal Corrections Facilities, presented in Steven Raphael, "Improving Employment Prospects for Former Prison Inmates: Challenges and Policy," Working Paper 15874 National Bureau of Economic Research, http://www.nber.org/papers/w15874.pdf.

19. Becky Pettit and Bruce Western, "Mass Imprisonment and the Life Course," *American Sociological Review* 69, no. 2 (2004): 151–69.

20. Bureau of Justice Statistics, US Department of Justice, "Correctional Populations in the United States, 2010," appendix table 3, December 2010.

21. Alice Goffman, "On the Run: Wanted Men in a Philadelphia Ghetto," *American Sociological Review* 74, no. 3 (2009): 343.

22. Data from the Fragile Families Survey, a large panel study of 5,000 mostly poor families, reveal similar results. If we remove the EITC, men in that study were more likely to have contact with the punitive than the redistributive side of the state. While men are much less likely to receive public assistance than women, even still, by the third wave, 25% of mothers in the Fragile Families study had received welfare compared to 11% that had ever had any contact with criminal justice.

23. Lawless and Fox, "Political Participation of the Urban Poor," 376.

24. Shawn Bushway, Hui-Shien Tsao, and Herbert L. Smith, "Has the US Prison Boom Changed the Age Distribution of the Prison Population?," Working paper, University at Albany, Albany, NY, 2011.

25. Bureau of Justice Statistics, US Department of Justice, "Profile of Jail Inmates 1996," April 1998; US Department of Justice, Survey of State Prison Inmates, 1991 (1993), http://bjs.ojp.usdoj.gov/ content/pub/pdf/SOSPI91.PDF.

26. "African-American Men Survey."

27. Becky Pettit, *Invisible Men: Mass Incarceration and the Myth of Black Progress* (New York: Russell Sage Foundation, 2012).

28. Manza and Uggen, *Locked Out*, chap. 6. For ethnographic research on criminal justice, see Goffman, "On the Run," 339; Brunson and Weitzer, "Police Relations with Black and White Youths in Different Urban Neighborhoods," 858–85; Victor Rios Jr., *Punished: Policing the Lives of Black and Latino Boys* (New York: NYU Press, 2011); Megan Comfort, *Doing Time Together: Love and Family in the Shadow of the Prison* (Chicago: University of Chicago Press, 2009); Elijah Anderson, *Code of the Street: Decency, Violence, and the Moral Life of the Inner City* (New York: W. W. Norton, 2000); Donald Braman, *Doing Time on the Outside: Incarceration and Family Life in Urban America* (Ann Arbor: University of Michigan Press, 2004).

29. CQ Press, "City Crime Rankings by Population," 2011–2012, http://os.cqpress.com/citycrime/2011/CityCrimePopRank2011.pdf.

30. State of New Jersey Department of Corrections, http://www.state.nj.us/corrections/pages/contactus.html.

Chapter Five

1. Fairchild, "Politicization of the Criminal Offender," 296.

2. Anderson, "Code of the Streets," 80–94.

3. Caroline Wolf Harlow, "Defense Counsel in Criminal Cases," Bureau of Justice Statistics, Special Report, 2000, http://www.bjs.gov/content/pub/pdf/dccc.pdf.

4. Brian Pinaire, Milton Heumann, and Laura Bilotta, "Barred from the Vote: Public Attitudes Toward the Disenfranchisement of Felons," *Fordham Urban Law Journal* 30 (2003): 1519–50.

5. Harry J. Holzer, *What Employers Want: Job Prospects for Less-Educated Workers* (New York: Russell Sage Foundation, 1996).

6. Soss, "Making Clients and Citizens."

7. Devah Pager, *Marked: Race, Crime, and Finding Work in an Era of Mass Incarceration* (Chicago: University of Chicago Press, 2007).

8. Other studies have noted a similar trend. A team of sociologists found in their interviews with inmates and ex-felons that many felt having a criminal record was an all-encompassing aspect of their identity and viewed their conviction status as so totalizing that it outweighed even a college degree or wealth. One respondent remarked that the felon label had "branded" him with an "F" for life. Christopher Uggen, Jeff Manza, and Angela Behrens, "'Less than the Average Citizen': Stigma, Role Transition and the Civic Reintegration of Convicted Felons," in *After Crime and Punishment: Pathways to Offender Reintegration*, ed. Shadd Maruna and Russ Immarigeon (Portland, OR: Willan Publishing, 2004), 258–90.

9. We included controls for race, gender, age, education, military, homeowner, religiosity, born outside United States, region, welfare receipt, marital status, employed, and enrolled in college. In the models, we also include controls for parental socioeconomic background (education, household income, and parental homeownership), given the youthful nature of the sample. Due to high rates of missing data on parental income, our analysis is based on multiple imputation using Amelia II (Honaker, King, and Blackwell). Paul R. Rosenbaum, "The Consequence of Adjustment for a Concomitant Variable That Has Been Affected by the Treatment," *Journal of the Royal Statistical Society*, series A (General) 147, no. 5 (1984): 656–66.

10. Amy Guttman, *Democratic Education* (Princeton, NJ: Princeton University Press, 1987), 287.

Chapter Six

1. Regression analysis available from authors.

2. Beckett et al., "Drug Use, Drug Possession Arrests, and the Question of Race." Fellner and Vinck, "Targeting Blacks."

3. Eric Baumer, "Poverty, Crack, and Crime: A Cross-city Analysis" *Journal of Research in Crime and Delinquency* 31, no. 3 (1994): 311–27; Elliott Currie, *Reckoning: Drugs, the Cities, and the American Future* (New York: Hill and Wang, 1994); Troy Duster, "Pattern, Purpose and Race in the Drug War," in *Crack in America: Demon Drugs and Social Justice*, ed. Craig Reinarman and Harry G. Levine (Berkeley: University of California Press, 1997), 260–87; John Hagan, *Crime and Disrepute* (Thousand Oaks, CA: Pine Forge Press, 1994).

4. Alfred Blumstein, "Racial Disproportionality of US Prison Populations

Revisited," *University of Colorado Law Review* 64 (1993): 751–73; Duster, "Pattern, Purpose and Race in the Drug War"; Erich Goode, "Drug Arrests at the Millennium," *Society* 39, no. 5 (2002): 41–45; Weldon T. Johnson, Robert E. Peterson, and Edward Wells, "Arrest Probabilities for Marijuana Users as Indicators of Selective Law Enforcement," *American Journal of Sociology* 83 (1977): 681–99; Eric E. Sterling, "Drug Policy: A Smorgasbord of Conundrums Spiced by Emotions around Children and Violence," *Valparaiso Law Review* 32 (1997): 597–645; Michael Tonry, *Malign Neglect: Race, Crime, and Punishment in America* (New York: Oxford University Press, 1995).

5. Margaret Levi and Laura Stoker, "Political Trust and Trustworthiness," *Annual Review of Political Science* 3, no. 1 (2000): 475–507.

Chapter Seven

1. "Shapes racial experience and conditions meaning": Michael Omi and Howard Winant, *Racial Formation in the United States: From the 1960s to the 1990s*, 2nd ed. (New York: Routledge, 1994), 59; "defines racial identities and membership": Aliya Saperstein and Andrew M. Penner, "The Race of a Criminal Record: How Incarceration Colors Racial Perceptions," *Social Problems* 57, no. 1 (2010): 92–113; "positions racial groups": Loïc Wacquant, "Race as Civic Felony," *International Social Science Journal* 57, no. 183 (2005): 127–42.

2. I. Bennett Capers, "Policing, Race, and Place," *Harvard Civil Rights–Civil Liberties Law Review* 44 (2009): 46.

3. Ibid., 68. Capers quotes Peggy C. Davis, "Law as Microaggression," *Yale Law Journal* 98 (1988): 1559.

4. Lani Guinier, "From Racial Liberalism to Racial Literacy: Brown v. Board of Education and the Interest-divergence Dilemma," *Journal of American History* 91, no. 1 (2004): 94.

5. Ibid., 96.

6. Cedric Merlin Powell, "Rhetorical Neutrality: Colorbindness, Frederick Douglass, and Inverted Critical Race Theory," *Cleveland State Law Review* (2008): 831–32.

7. Guinier, "From Racial Liberalism to Racial Literacy," 102.

8. Ibid.

9. Naomi Murakawa and Katherine Beckett, "The Penology of Racial Innocence: The Erasure of Racism in the Study and Practice of Punishment," *Law and Society Review* 44, nos. 3–4 (2010): 695–730.

10. Ashby E. Plant and B. Michelle Peruche, "The Consequences of Race for Police Officers' Responses to Criminal Suspects," *Psychological Science* 16, no. 3 (2005): 180–83.

11. Richard R. Banks, Jennifer L. Eberhardt, and Lee Ross, "Discrimina-

tion and Implicit Bias in a Racially Unequal Society," *California Law Review* 94 (2006): 1169–90. See also Jennifer Eberhardt et al., "Seeing Black: Race, Crime, and Visual Processing," *Journal of Personality and Social Psychology* 87 (2004): 876–93.

12. Jeffrey J. Rachlinski et al., "Does Unconscious Racial Bias Affect Trial Judges?" *Notre Dame Law Review* 84, no. 3 (2009): 1195–1246.

13. The defendants in the two exercises were juvenile shoplifters or juvenile armed robbers. The only exception to the finding was when the race of the offender was made explicit, prompting judges to engage in corrective behavior. Black judges did not show greater bias against blacks.

14. Dorothy Roberts, "The Social and Moral Cost of Mass Incarceration in African American Communities," *Stanford Law Review* (2004): 1279.

15. Ryan P. Haygood, "Disregarding the Results: Examining the Ninth Circuit's Heightened Section 2 'Intentional Discrimination' Standard in Farrakhan v. Gregoire," *Columbia Law Review Sidebar* 111 (2011): 56.

16. Quoted in ibid., 57.

17. Mary Fainsod Katzenstein, Leila Mohsen Ibrahim, and Katherine D. Rubin, "The Dark Side of American Liberalism and Felony Disenfranchisement," *Perspectives on Politics* 9, no. 4 (2010): 1038.

18. *McLaughlin v. City of Canton*, 947 F. Supp. 954, 971 (S.D. Miss. 1995).

19. *McCleskey v. Kemp* (No. 84–6811), 753 F.2d 877, affirmed.

20. Ian F. Haney-Lopez, "Post-Racial Racism: Racial Stratification and Mass Incarceration in the Age of Obama," *California Law Review* 98 (2010): 1023–73.

21. Ibid., 1062.

22. Marc Mauer, "Racial Impact Statements as a Means of Reducing Unwarranted Sentencing Disparities," *Ohio State Journal of Criminal Law* 5, no. 19 (2007): 28.

23. Guinier, "From Racial Liberalism to Racial Literacy," 100.

24. Haney-Lopez, "Post-Racial Racism," 1048.

25. Bill Cosby, "Address at the NAACP on the 50th Anniversary of Brown v. Board of Education," May 17, 2004, Washington, DC.

26. "Optimism about Black Progress Declines: Blacks See Growing Values Gap between Poor and Middle Class," Pew Research Center, November 2007, http://pewsocialtrends.org/files/2010/10/Race-2007.pdf.

27. Haney-Lopez, "Post-Racial Racism," 1058.

28. John P. McKendy, "'I'm very careful about that': Narrative and Agency of Men in Prison," *Discourse and Society* 17, no. 4 (2006): 474.

29. This dual education is similar to what Benjamin Justice and Tracey Meares insightfully refer to as the "overt" and "hidden" curriculum of the criminal justice system. In their elegant framework, while the overt education portrays criminal justice as egalitarian and democratic, the hidden curriculum to which

inmates and suspects are exposed offers an adverse education—who is a citizen and who is not and their proper roles. Benjamin Justice and Tracey Meares, "How the Criminal Justice System Educates Citizens," *Annals of the American Academy of Political and Social Science* 651, no. 1 (2014): 159–77.

30. John Hagan, Carla Shedd, and Monique R. Payne, "Race, Ethnicity, and Youth Perceptions of Criminal Injustice," *American Sociological Review* 70, no. 3 (2005): 381–407.

31. Jon Hurwitz and Mark Peffley, "Explaining the Great Racial Divide: Perceptions of Fairness in the US Criminal Justice System," *Journal of Politics* 67, no. 3 (2005): 780.

32. Racial differences on other items also emerge strongly. For example, 54% of black youth agreed that blacks receive a poorer education on average than whites, as compared to 31% of whites. There are similar racial gaps on the question of whether "the government treats most immigrants better than it treats most Black people in this country." On this question, 48% of blacks and 29% of whites agreed.

33. Michael Dawson, *Behind the Mule: Race and Class in African-American Politics* (Princeton, NJ: Princeton University Press, 1994), 57.

34. We use the standard demographic controls described earlier (gender, age, education, military, homeowner, religiosity, parental background (mother's education, father's education, parents owned home), born outside the United States, region, welfare receipt, marital status, employment status, and currently enrolled in college). In the BYP models, controls for parental socioeconomic background (education, household income, and parental homeownership) are included, given the youthful nature of the sample. In addition, we control for welfare receipt, not available in AAMS. Due to high rates of missing data on parental income, our analysis is based on multiple imputation using Amelia II (Honaker, King, and Blackwell). Rosenbaum, "Consequence of Adjustment," 656–66.

35. Hagan, Shedd, and Payne, "Race, Ethnicity and Youth Perceptions of Criminal Justice," 384. See also Dennis P. Rosenbaum, Amie M. Schuck, Sandra K. Costello, Darnell F. Hawkins, and Marianne K. Ring, "Attitudes toward the Police: The Effects of Direct and Vicarious Experience," *Police Quarterly* 8, no. 3 (2005), on the "desensitivity hypothesis."

36. Rosenbaum et al., "Attitudes toward the Police," 362.

37. Luna, "Transparent Policing," 1117–18.

Chapter Eight

1. Lyndon B. Johnson, "Remarks in the Capitol Rotunda at the Signing of the Voting Rights Act," August 6, 1965, accessed at John T. Woolley and Gerhard

Peters, The American Presidency Project [online]. Santa Barbara, CA; available from http://www.presidency.ucsb.edu/ws/?pid=27140.

2. Christopher Uggen and Sarah Shannon. "State-Level Estimates of Felon Disenfranchisement in the United States, 2010," The Sentencing Project, July 2012, http://www.sentencingproject.org/doc/publications/fd_State_Level_Estimates_of_Felon_Disen_2010.pdf

3. On disenfranchised black men: The US Census reported 2,303,263 black men in America in 1870 ("Ninth Census," vol. 1, Government Printing Office, Washington, DC). Estimates from *Harper's Weekly* suggest that one-sixth of blacks in 1869 lived in areas where blacks remained enfranchised. "The Fifteenth Amendment: Creation," Black Voting Rights: The Creation of the Fifteenth Amendment, *Harper's Weekly*, http://15thamendment.harpweek.com/HubPages/CommentaryPage.asp?Commentary=03Creation.

On Native Americans and suffrage: Many Native Americans had already become citizens by this time under the Dawes Act. Others were still unable to vote for decades after the Citizenship Act, as they lived in states that retained restrictions denying suffrage to Indians. Theodore H. Haas, "The Legal Aspects of Indian Affairs from 1887 to 1957," *Annals of the American Academy of Political and Social Science* 311, no. 1 (1957): 12–22.

On the Twenty-sixth Amendment: "Census of Population Supplementary Reports," US Bureau of the Census, 1970.

4. Warren et al., *One in 100: Felony Disenfranchisement Laws in the United States*; The Sentencing Project, "Criminal Justice Primer: Policy Priorities for the 111th Congress" (2009).

5. Uggen and Manza, "Democratic Contraction?," 777–803.

6. See, for instance, Manza and Uggen, *Locked Out*.

7. Fellner and Mauer, *Losing the Vote*.

8. Pinaire, Heumann, and Bilotta, "Barred from the Vote," 1526–27.

9. Cohen, *Democracy Remixed*, 195.

10. Ibid., 196.

11. Ibid., 195–96.

12. Goffman, "On the Run," 339.

13. Julilly Kohler-Hausmann, "'The Crime of Survival': Fraud Prosecutions, Community Surveillance and the Original 'Welfare Queen,'" *Journal of Social History* 41, no. 2 (2007): 329–54.

14. Barbara Ehrenreich, "A Homespun Safety Net," *New York Times*, July 12, 2009.

15. Kohler-Hausmann, "Crime of Survival."

16. Kaaryn Gustafson, "The Criminalization of Poverty," *Journal of Criminal Law and Criminology* 99, no. 3 (2009): 670.

17. Ibid.

18. Phelps and Tenney, "Operation Talon."

19. Gustafson, "Criminalization of Poverty."

20. Goffman, "On the Run," 344.

21. American Civil Liberties Union, "Camden Agrees to Pay $3.5M to Victims of Police Corruption," January 10, 2013, https://www.aclu.org/criminal-law-reform/camden-agrees-pay-35m-victims-police-corruption.

22. Verba, "Fairness, Equality, and Democracy," 525.

23. James C. Scott, *Domination and the Arts of Resistance: Hidden Transcripts* (New Haven, CT: Yale University Press, 1990).

24. Cathy J. Cohen, "Deviance as Resistance: A New Research Agenda for the Study of Black Politics," *Du Bois Review* 1, no. 1 (2004): 27.

25. Ibid., 39. See also Scott, *Domination*, and Kelley, *Race Rebels*.

26. Cohen, "Deviance as Resistance," 29.

27. Ibid., 31.

28. Paul Butler, "Racially Based Jury Nullification: Black Power in the Criminal Justice System," *Yale Law Journal* 105, no. 3 (1995): 713.

29. Cohen, "Deviance as Resistance," 32.

30. Ibid., 40.

31. Ibid., 38.

32. Our analysis follows a long line of criminal justice scholars who use self-reported data. We discuss this issue in detail in the data and methods appendix.

33. Because we have no way of validating the self-reported measures we use here with actual voting and registration records of respondents (name and address of respondents is confidential and not available), we cannot be certain that some of our dependent variables do not contain measurement error. We discuss this issue in detail in the data and methods appendix.

34. In Add Health, we account for personality traits that predict criminal activity by including a scale of self-control items; research has established impulsivity to be one of the key determinants of violent offending; see, e.g., David P. Farrington, "Predictors, Causes, and Correlates of Male Youth Violence," *Crime and Justice* 24 (1998): 421–75; Michael R. Gottfredson and Travis Hirschi, *A General Theory of Crime* (Stanford, CA: Stanford University Press, 1990). We also include measures of self-reported violent and nonviolent criminal activity over the past twelve months. In Fragile Families, we use a similar index of self-control items, as well as history of domestic violence (as reported by the mother) and drug use.

35. We use CLARIFY to interpret the coefficients of the logistic regressions. Gary King, Michael Tomz, and Jason Wittenberg, "Making the Most of Statistical Analyses: Improving Interpretation and Presentation," *American Journal of Political Science* 44, no. 2 (2000): 347–61; Michael Tomz, Jason Wittenberg, and Gary King, "CLARIFY: Software for Interpreting and Presenting Statistical Results, Version 2.1," Harvard University, Cambridge, MA, 2003.

36. In the Wave III sample, approximately 54% of respondents reported having recently taken illegal drugs, including 16% who reported using "hard" drugs (excluding marijuana, steroids and prescription medication without a doctor's order). However, many of those who reported illegal drug use had never been caught or punished for any type of crime; for instance, 71% of drug users and 58% of serious drug users, respectively, reported having no contact with the police or criminal justice authorities. Thus we can divide the sample into a four-fold typology: non–drug users who have had no custodial contact, non–drug users who have had contact, drug users who have not had contact, and drug users who have had contact.

37. Similar results for voter turnout are obtained when the sample is further restricted to include only serious illegal drug users, excluding those who report using only marijuana, steroids, or prescription drugs. We have also conducted nonparametric analyses that use weights from genetic matching to create a matched set of convicted and never-convicted drug users, ensuring that the two groups are well balanced on the full set of covariates that we describe in the preceding parametric models, as well as on a propensity score that predicts having been convicted of a crime. After matching, there are no significant differences on baseline covariates in the matched sample between illegal drug users who have been convicted of a crime and those who have not. However, there are differences between the two groups in the outcomes of interest. Among self-reported drug users, having a criminal conviction lowers trust in government by about 3% and reduces voter registration and turnout by roughly 13% each. We find similar effects of other types of contact, and the effects are larger as contact becomes more severe. Details of this analysis can be found in Vesla Weaver and Amy Lerman, "Political Consequences of the Carceral State," *American Political Science Review* 104, no. 4 (2010): 817–33.

38. Kay Lehman Schlozman, Benjamin I. Page, Sidney Verba, and Morris Fiorina, "Inequalities of Political Voice," in *Inequality and American Democracy*, ed. Lawrence R. Jacobs and Theda Skocpol (New York: Russell Sage Foundation, 2005), 19.

39. Judith N. Shklar, *American Citizenship: The Quest for Inclusion* (Cambridge: Harvard University Press, 1991), 56.

40. Manza and Uggen, *Locked Out*.

41. Soss, "Making Clients and Citizens," 292.

42. Schlozman et al., "Inequalities of Political Voice," 29.

Chapter Nine

1. Butler, "Racially Based Jury Nullification," 713.

2. Rebecca Zietlow, "Giving Substance to Process: Countering the Due Process Counterrevolution," *Denver University Law Review* 75, no. 9 (1997): 14.

3. Gabriel Almond and Sidney Verba, *The Civil Culture: Political Attitudes and Democracy in Five Nations* (Boston: Little, Brown, 1963), 498.

4. Schlozman et al., "Inequalities of Political Voice," 19.

5. For instance, the AAMS shows those who have been incarcerated to be somewhat less tolerant of homosexual intercourse than those who have not spent time in prison, and shows custodial citizens generally to be less critical of having children out of wedlock. (There is no significant difference in the AAMS between custodial citizens and others on available questions related to interracial marriage or abortion.) Custodial citizens are also distinct in other politically salient ways. They are more likely to have had a friend of a different race, or to have had a gay friend. They are no more likely to consider themselves born-again Christians, but are less likely to attend church and more likely to pray. And somewhat surprisingly, they are no more likely to call themselves Democrats.

6. Based on author's analysis of the BYP, AAMS, NLSY, and Add Health.

7. Howard Rosenthal, "Politics, Public Policy, and Inequality: A Look Back at the Twentieth Century," in *Social Inequality*, ed. Kathryn Neckerman (New York: Russell Sage Foundation, 2004), 861–93.

8. Lisa L. Miller, "Power to the people: Violent victimization, inequality and democratic politics," *Theoretical Criminology* 17, no. 3 (2013): 291.

9. Lisa L. Miller, "The Invisible Black Victim: How American Federalism Perpetuates Racial Inequality in Criminal Justice," *Law and Society Review* 44, nos. 3–4 (2010): 805–42

10. The Political Participation Group of the NAACP Legal Defense and Education Fund, Inc., "Captive Constituents: Prison-Based Gerrymandering and the Distortion of Our Democracy," May 2010, http://www.naacpldf.org/files/publications/Captive%20Constituents%20Report.pdf.

11. Verba, "Fairness, Equality, and Democracy," 503–4, paraphrasing Judith Shklar, *The Faces of Injustice* (Ann Arbor, MI: Edward Brothers, 1990).

12. Forman, "Community Policing and Youth as Assets," 7.

13. Shklar, *American Citizenship*, 56.

14. Alan S. Gerber, Donald P. Green, and Ron Shachar, "Voting May Be Habit-Forming: Evidence from a Randomized Field Experiment," *American Journal of Political Science* 47, no. 3 (2003): 540–50.

15. Christopher Uggen and Jeff Manza, "Voting and Subsequent Crime and Arrest: Evidence from a Community Sample," *Columbia Human Rights Law Review* 36 (2004): 193–215.

16. Pinaire, Heumann, and Bilotta, "Barred from the Vote," 1526–27.

17. Owens, "Problem Is Not Punishment Per Se."

18. Washington Post/Kaiser/Harvard Racial Attitudes Survey, March 2001. iPOLL Databank, The Roper Center for Public Opinion Research, University of Connecticut, http://www.ropercenter.uconn.edu/data_access/ipoll/ipoll.html.

19. Nicole D. Porter, "Expanding the Vote: State Felony Disenfranchisement

Reform, 1997–2010," The Sentencing Project, Washington, DC, 2010; available at http://www.sentencingproject.org/doc/publications/publications/vr_expanding theVoteFinalAddendum.pdf.

20. http://www.brennancenter.org/legislation/democracy-restoration-act.

21. Porter, "Expanding the Vote."

22. In fact, at least one study suggests that barring inmates from voting may increase recidivism. Uggen and Manza, "Voting and Subsequent Crime and Arrest."

23. Verba, "Fairness, Equality, and Democracy," 517–18.

24. Luna, "Transparent Policing," 1117, 1108.

25. Ibid., 1132.

26. "Combating Prisoner Abuse," New York Times, December 20, 2009, http://www.nytimes.com/2009/12/21/opinion/21mon3.html.

27. Swearingen, "Imprisoning Rights," 1353.

28. Allan E. Lind and Tom R. Tyler, The Social Psychology of Procedural Justice (New York: Plenum Press, 1988); Tom R. Tyler, "Social Justice: Outcome and Procedure," International Journal of Psychology 35, no. 2 (2000): 117–25.

29. Patton, "Endless Cycle of Abuse," 787.

30. Clarke, "Arrested Oversight," 1.

31. Collins, Shielded from Justice. This is from the section of the report "External Review: Citizen Review Mechanisms"; available at http://www.columbia .edu/itc/journalism/cases/katrina/Human%20Rights%20Watch/uspohtml/uspo 22.htm.

32. Clarke, "Arrested Oversight."

33. Kim, "Legitimizing Community Consent to Local Policing."

34. Collins, Shielded from Justice.

35. Luna, "Transparent Policing," 1178.

36. Roberts, "The Social and Moral Cost of Mass Incarceration in African American Communities," 1273; See also Aman McLeod, Ismail K. White, and Amelia R. Gavin, "The Locked Ballot Box: The Impact of State Criminal Disenfranchisement Laws on African American Voting Behavior and Implications for Reform," Virginia Journal of Social Policy and the Law 11, no. 1 (2003): 66–88.

37. Martin Luther King Jr., "I Have a Dream," August 28, 1963, transcription accessed online at http://abcnews.go.com/Politics/martin-luther-kings-speech -dream-full-text/story?id=14358231.

38. Tonry, Punishing Race.

39. Mauer, "Racial Impact Statements," 33.

40. Judith Green, Kevin Pranis and Jason Ziedenberg, "Disparity by Design: How Drug-Free Zone Laws Impact Racial Disparity—and Fail to Protect Youth," Justice Policy Institute. Available at: http://www.justicepolicy.org/ research/1991.

41. Marc Mauer and Ryan Scott King, "Schools and Prisons: Fifty Years after

Brown V. Board of Education," *The Sentencing Project Briefing Sheet*, 2004, http://
www.sentencingproject.org/doc/publications/rd_brownvboard.pdf; Julie C. Kun-
selman, Kathrine A. Johnson, and Michael C. Rayboun, "Profiling Sentence Enhancement Offenders: A Case Study of Florida's 10–20-Lifers," *Criminal Justice
Policy Review* 14, no. 2 (2003): 229–48.

42. Richard S. Frase, "What Explains Persistent Racial Disproportionality
in Minnesota's Prison and Jail Populations?," *Crime and Justice* 38, no. 1 (2009):
201–80.

43. Mauer, "Racial Impact Statements," 19.

44. Citing a 1997 survey of inmates by Eric Sevigny. Ibid., 42.

45. Jerry Kang and Mahzarin R. Banaji, "Fair Measures: A Behavioral Real-
ist Revision of 'Affirmative Action,'" *California Law Review* 94, no. 4 (2006): *su-
pra* note 80, at 1090–91.

46. Mauer, "Racial Impact Statements."

47. See especially Jerry Kang, "Trojan Horses of Race," *Harvard Law Review* 118, no. 5 (2005): 1489–1593; also Alex C. Geisinger, "Rethinking Profiling:
A Cognitive Model of Bias and Its Legal Implications," *Oregon Law Review* 86,
no. 3 (2007): 657–78.

48. Sheri Lynn Johnson, "Race and Recalcitrance: The *Miller-El* Remands,"
Ohio State Journal of Criminal Law 5 (2007): 158.

49. Pamela M. Casey, Roger K. Warren, Fred L. Cheesman II, and Jennifer K. Elek, "Helping Courts Address Implicit Bias: Resources for Education,"
National Center for State Courts, Williamsburg, Virginia, 2012.

50. Email correspondence with Phil Goff. See also Nilanjana Dasgupta and
Anthony G. Greenwald, "On the Malleability of Automatic Attitudes: Combat-
ing Automatic Prejudice with Images of Admired and Disliked Individuals,"
Journal of Personality and Social Psychology 81, no. 5 (2001): 800–814.

51. Antony Page, "Batson's Blind-Spot: Unconscious Stereotyping and the
Peremptory Challenge," *Boston University Law Review* 85 (2005): 155–262.

52. John Irwin and Daniel L. Real, "Unconscious Influences in Judicial
Decision-Making: The Illusion of Objectivity," *McGeorge Law Review* 42 (2010): 7.

53. Kang, "Trojan Horses of Race," 1563.

54. Ibid., 1585.

55. Alexander, *New Jim Crow*, 211.

56. Western, *Punishment and Inequality*, 197.

57. Clear envisions that this justice reinvestment strategy will lead to the development of community justice organizations, and that communities will pros-
per as fewer of their members cycle back and forth between communities and
prison. Moreover, all of the savings from diverted incarceration will be spent
in the community itself, helping to further economic development of depleted
and blighted areas. Justice Reinvestment therefore has the potential to create
jobs, income, infrastructure, and stability in communities that desperately need

it, while simultaneously reducing the community-level harms that flow from high rates of imprisonment.

58. Todd Clear, "A Private-sector, Incentives-based Model for Justice Reinvestment," *Criminology and Public Policy* 10, no. 3 (2011): 585–608.

59. "North Carolina: Implementing the Strategy," Justice Reinvestment, http://justicereinvestment.org/states/north_carolina/how-nc/.

60. "Texas: Identify Options to Generate Savings and Increase Public Safety," Justice Reinvestment, http://justicereinvestment.org/states/texas/how -tx/provide-tx .

61. The Sentencing Project, "Downscaling Prisons: Lessons from Four States," http://sentencingproject.org/doc/publications/publications/inc_Downscaling Prisons2010.pdf

62. Marc Mauer, "Sentencing Reform: Amid Mass Incarcerations—Guarded Optimism," *Criminal Justice* 26, no. 1 (2011): 27–36.

63. "Realignment Report: A One-year Examination of Offenders Released from State Prison in the First Six Months of Public Safety Realignment," California Department of Corrections and Rehabilitation, http://www.cdcr.ca.gov/ realignment/docs/Realignment%206%20Month%20Report%20Final_5%20 16%2013%20v1.pdf.

64. Joseph Goldstein, "Police Stop-and-Frisk Encounters Plunged in Second Quarter of 2013, Data Show," *New York Times*, August 27, 2013, http://www .nytimes.com/2013/08/28/nyregion/data-show-steep-decline-in-police-stops-in -new-york-city-this-year.html?_r=0.

65. Phillip Reese, "Misdemeanor Drug Arrests Plummet Following Marijuana Law Change," *Sacramento Bee*, October 24, 2013, http://www.sacbee .com/2013/07/30/5610049/misdemeanor-drug-arrests-plummet.html.

66. Ian Urbina, "Blacks Are Singled Out for Marijuana Arrests, Federal Data Suggest," *New York Times*, June 3, 2013, http://www.nytimes.com/2013/06/04/us/ marijuana-arrests-four-times-as-likely-for-blacks.html?emc=eta1.

67. Jesse Walker, "David Simon Says," Reason.com, October 2004, http:// reason.com/archives/2004/10/01/david-simon-says/1.

Appendix A

1. The Fragile Families and Child Wellbeing Study was supported by grant R01HD36916 from the Eunice Kennedy Shriver National Institute of Child Health and Human Development (NICHD). The contents of this book are solely the responsibility of the authors and do not necessarily represent the official views of the NICHD. The National Longitudinal Study of Adolescent Health was a program project designed by J. Richard Udry, Peter S. Bearman, and Kathleen Mullan Harris, and funded by grant P01-HD31921 from the Eunice

Kennedy Shriver NICHD, with cooperative funding from seventeen other agencies. Special acknowledgment is due Ronald R. Rindfuss and Barbara Entwisle for assistance in the original design. Persons interested in obtaining data files from Add Health should contact Add Health, Carolina Population Center, 123 W. Franklin Street, Chapel Hill, NC 27516-2524 (addhealth@unc.edu). No direct support was received from grant P01-HD31921 for this analysis.

2. Parents were interviewed in seventy-five hospitals in twenty-two cities using a stratified random sample in the United States. Cities were sampled based on welfare generosity, child support enforcement, and strength of local economy. Hospitals were sampled based on the proportion of nonmarital births to achieve the desired oversample. The sample is representative of children born in large cities with more than 200,000 population.

3. Cities were sampled based on welfare generosity, child support enforcement, and strength of local economy. Hospitals were sampled based on the proportion of nonmarital births to achieve the desired oversample.

4. "African-American Men Survey"; Cohen, "Black Youth Culture Survey," http://www.blackyouthproject.com.

5. Kim Chantala, William D. Kalsbeek and Eugenio Andraca, "Non-Response in Wave III of the Add Health Study," 5, http://www.cpc.unc.edu/projects/addhealth/data/guides/W3nonres.pdf.

6. Robert F. Belli, Michael Traugott, and Matthew N. Beckman, "What Leads to Voting Overreports? Contrasts of Overreporters to Validated Voters and Admitted Nonvoters in the American National Election Studies," *Journal of Official Statistics* 17, no. 4 (2001): 479–98; Michael P. McDonald, "The True Electorate: A Cross-Validation of Voter Registration Files and Election Survey Demographics," *Public Opinion Quarterly* 71, no. 4 (2007): 588–602.

7. Traci Burch, "A Study of Felon and Misdemeanant Voter Participation in North Carolina," The Sentencing Project. February 2007, www.sentencingproject.org/doc/publications/fd_northcarolina.pdf; Michael V. Haselswerdt, "Con Job: An Estimate of Ex-felon Voter Turnout Using Document-based Data," *Social Science Quarterly* 90, no. 2 (2009): 262–73; Thomas J. Miles, "Felon Disenfranchisement and Voter Turnout," *Journal of Legal Studies* 33 (2004): 85–129.

8. Roger Tourangeau and Tom W. Smith, "Asking Sensitive Questions: The Impact of Data Collection, Mode, Question Format, and Question Context," *Public Opinion Quarterly* 60 (1996): 275–304; D. P. Farrington, "The Effects of Public Labelling," *British Journal of Criminology* 17 (1977): 112–25; M. J. Hindelang, T. Hirschi, and J. G. Weis, *Measuring Delinquency* (Beverly Hills, CA: Sage, 1981); D. G. Rojek, "Social Status and Delinquency; Do Self-reports and Official Reports Match?" in *Measurement Issues in Criminal Justice*, ed. Gordon P. Waldo (Beverly Hills, CA: Sage, 1983), 71–88. For a comprehensive treatment of the reliability and validity of self-reported data see Terence P. Thornberry and Marvin D. Krohn, "The Self-report Method for Measuring De-

linquency and Crime," *Criminal Justice* 4, no. 1 (2000): 33–83; and Josine Junger-Tas and Ineke Haen Marshall, "The Self-report Methodology in Crime Research," *Crime and Justice* 25 (1999): 291–367.

9. Thornberry, and Krohn, "Self-report Method for Measuring Delinquency and Crime," 33–83.

10. Ibid.; Roger Tourangeau and Ting Yan, "Sensitive Questions in Surveys," *Psychological Bulletin* 133, no. 5 (2007): 859–83.

Appendix B

1. 2013 statistics available at http://www.state.nj.us/corrections/pdf/offender_statistics/2013/By%20Ethnicity_Race%202013.pdf.

2. http://www.36odegrees.org/ddata/voting/index.html.

3. Ashley Nellis, "Throwing Away the Key: The Expansion of Life without Parole Sentences in the United States," *Federal Sentencing Reporter* 23, no. 1 (October 2010), http://www.sentencingproject.org/doc/publications/inc_federal sentencingreporter.pdf.

Appendix C

1. Farrington, "Predictors, Causes, and Correlates of Male Youth Violence," 421–75; Gottfredson and Hirschi, *General Theory of Crime*.

2. Walter R. Mebane and Jasjeet S. Sekhon, "Genetic Optimization Using Derivatives," *Political Analysis* 7, no. 1 (1998): 187–210; Alexis Diamond and Jasjeet S. Sekhon, "Genetic Matching for Estimating Causal Effects: A General Multivariate Matching Method for Achieving Balance in Observational Studies," *Institute of Governmental Studies, UC Berkeley* 1, no. 2 (2006): 23–50; Jasjeet S. Sekhon, "Alternative Balance Metrics for Bias Reduction in Matching Methods for Causal Inference," technical report, University of California, Berkeley, 2006, http://sekhon.berkeley.edu/papers/SekhonBalanceMetrics.pdf.

3. For all bootstrapping, nboots = 1000.

4. Sekhon, "Alternative Balance Metrics"; Diamond and Sekhon, "Genetic Matching for Estimating Causal Effects."

5. Jasjeet S. Sekhon, "Multivariate and Propensity Score Matching Software with Automated Balance Optimization: The Matching Package for R," *Journal of Statistical Software* (2011). http://sekhon.berkeley.edu/papers/Matching JSS.pdf.

6. Paul R. Rosenbaum and Donald B. Rubin, "The Central Role of the Propensity Score in Observational Studies for Causal Effects," *Biometrika* 70, no. 1 (1983): 41–55.

7. Sekhon, "Multivariate and Propensity Score Matching Software with Automated Balance Optimization."

8. See Rosenbaum, "Consequence of Adjustment," 656–66, for a discussion of bias that results from adjustment for a concomitant variable affected by treatment. While empirical studies of wealth transmission from parents to children offer varying estimates of the extent of economic mobility (Gary Solon, "Intergenerational Income Mobility in the United States," *American Economic Review* 82, no. 3 [1992]: 393–408) and are limited by existing data (Lisa A. Keister and Stephanie Moller, "Wealth Inequality in the United States," *Annual Review of Sociology* [2000]: 63–81), there is empirical evidence that poverty is transmitted across generations (Solon, "Intergenerational Income Mobility"; David J. Zimmerman, "Regression toward Mediocrity in Economic Stature," *American Economic Review* 82, no. 3 [June 1992]: 409–29), with education serving as an important mediator. See also Lisa A. Keister and Stephanie Moller, "Wealth Inequality in the United States," *Annual Review of Sociology* 26 (2000): 63–81; David J. Zimmerman, "Regression toward Mediocrity in Economic Stature," *American Economic Review* 82, no. 3 (1992): 409–29.

Index

Add Health survey, 51, 153–55, 217, 219–20, 222, 224–25. *See also* National Longitudinal Study of Adolescent Health

African-American Men Survey (AAMS), 54, 102, 173, 175, 194, 263–64, 309n34, 313n5

Alexander, Michelle, 24–25, 252American exceptionalism, 5

American institutions: racial membership, cultivating and structuring of, 16

American National Election Studies, 100

American national state, expansion of, 19

American political behavior, large-*n* surveys, 100, 102

AmeriCorps, 240

Anderson, Elijah, 112–13

Angola prison, 181

Angolite (newspaper), 87

antidemocratic features, 5–6, 28, 32, 58, 62, 91–92, 252, 259; avoidance, as mark of, 214; and crime control, 9; of criminal justice institutions, 7, 10, 61, 107, 138, 232, 237; in police agencies and prisons, 62

Antiterrorism and Effective Death Penalty Act (AEDPA), 71

Aristotle, 12

arrestees/misdemeanants, 45–48, 57; plea bargaining, 35; quality-of-life issues, 35

Attica prison, 82

avoidance tactics, 107, 207–8, 210–12, 215, 233; antidemocratic system, as mark of, 214; as survival mechanism, 216

Bartels, Larry, 21

Beckett, Katherine, 50, 80–81, 155, 245

black culture narrative, 167

black custodial citizens. *See* custodial citizens, as defined

black incarceration, 3; and criminal justice contact, 102, 195–97; explanations for, 194–95; rates of, 99; reasons for, 183–84; and structural inequities, 194–96. *See also* blacks; black youth; custodial citizens, as defined

blacks, 259, 260; bias against, as subconscious, 250; black America, portrait of, as bleak, 23; crime, as normalized by, 192, 193; crime, news reporting on, overrepresentation of, 251; in criminal justice, overrepresentation of in, 23; and criminal justice contact, 55–56; disempowerment of, 193; drug arrest rate of, increase in, 49–50; and drug charges, 9; drug-related offenses, and disproportionate arrests for, 49, 155; felon disenfranchisement of, 84–85, 199; government, attitudes toward, 170–71; government neglect of, perception of, 171–73; homicide rate of, 52; incarceration of, higher chances of, reasons for, 183–84; incarceration rates of, 99, 192–93; involuntary police encounters of, 9, 40–45; and lack of choices, 194; law enforcement, contact with, and diminished faith in racial equality, 16; literacy tests, 85; marginalization of,

blacks (*continued*)
246; negative imagery of, as criminals, 251–52; poll taxes, 85; quality of life policing, 47; and race, 180; race, as guiding factor in, 159; race, as scapegoat, 160; race, role of, as difficult to pinpoint, 178; racial differences, 309n32; racially pessimistic view of, 174; racial progress of, as fiction, 184; right to vote, loss of, 84–85; as second-class citizens, 23; "shadowy form of citizenship," as occupying, 165; stop-and-frisk rates of, 40–41; trespass admonitions and, 81; unequal status of, 177–78; violent victimization of, as catastrophic, 52. *See also* black incarceration; black youth

black youth, 169; and criminal justice contact, 102; downward shift in, expectations of, 53; high rates of violence among, 53; police, earlier encounters with, 157; political disengagement of, 208. *See also* black incarceration; blacks

Black Youth Project (BYP) surveys, 54, 102, 129, 135–37, 150–51

Bloomberg, Michael, 209

Boston, John, 77

Brennan, William, 83, 165

Britain, 11, 302n150. *See also* United Kingdom

broken windows policing, 45, 48; broken windows theory, 43

Brown v. Board of Education, 66, 162–63

Bureau of Justice Statistics, 100

Butler, Paul, 215

California, 49, 66–67, 201, 209, 247, 256; misdemeanor drug arrests in, 257; prisoner unions in, 82–83; prison newspapers in, 87–88; state prison inmates, reduction of in, 256

Camden (New Jersey), 213

Campbell, Andrea, 13

Canada, 90–91

Capers, I. Bennett, 157–58

capital punishment, as racially biased, 165–66

carceral lifeworld, definition of, 15–16

carceral state, 4, 59, 96, 141, 156, 252, 256;

and American political development, 19; civic and political marginality, 23; expansion of, as anti-democratic, 8–9; expansion of, political consequences of, 10; political marginalization of, 22; polity, splintering of, 230; reach of, 30–31, 230; reform of, 236; rise of, 246–47; size of, 30; as term, 20

causality, 107–9, 155, 223; strategies of, 275–79

Center for Constitutional Rights, 44

Charlottesville (Virginia), 14, 105, 108, 149; demographics of, 103; jail inmates of, as minorities, 103; population of, 103

Chicago (Illinois): murder rates in, 53; stop-and-frisk in, 41

Chicago Tribune (newspaper), 71

Christopher Commission, 66

citizenship, 5; and citizen participation, 78; citizen-state relationship, and social welfare programs, 14; and citizen voice, 78, 84; civil and political rights, as tenets of, 6; current notions of, 26; and democracy, 12, 21, 27–29; ethnographic citizenship, 29; government, character of, as tied to, 137; as lived experience, change in, 7; prisons, and citizenry, controlling of, 23; purging of, 6; right to vote, as pivotal, 84; socialization of, 111, 232; tenets of, 6; voting and participation, 229–30

Citizenship Act (1924), 199–200, 310n3

civic education, 137

Civic Engagement Project, 255

civil injunctions, 79–80

Civil Rights Act, 246

civil rights movement, 260; civil and voting rights acts, 6; criminal justice policies, as stymied, 23

class, 19, 118, 175, 258; and race, 9, 22, 24, 119, 147, 159

Clear, Todd, 253–54

code of prohibitions, 15, 112–13, 115, 117–18, 159, 189

"code of the street," 54

Cohen, Cathy, 202, 208, 215–16

collateral consequences, 7, 45, 200

colorblindness, 166, 168; and criminal justice, 158, 163; felon disenfranchisement laws, effects of on, 164; and political culture, 25; racial effects of, as disastrous, 247; and systemic racial inequality, 164

community action programs, as empowering citizens, 12

community-based organizations (CBOs), 254–55

Connecticut, 249, 257

Convention for the Protection of Human Rights and Fundamental Freedoms, 91

convicted offenders. *See* incarcerated offenders

Cornerstone Builders, 240, 255

Cosby, Bill, 167

Council of State Governments, 254

Covington (Louisiana), 1–2, 121

crime: and crime rates, 31; and criminal suspects, 35–40; politicizing of, responses to, 234–35; punishment, as focus of, 235; and state power, 19

crime control, 20, 59; as anti-democratic, 9; "colorblind" approach to, 25; and coercive state expansion, 18; crime policy, disadvantaged population, 23; crime policy, legislative agenda of, 33–34; and custodial citizens, 32; custodial citizens, as non-serious offenders, 35; draconian sentences, 34; federal government, and states, financial support to, 34; ghetto neighborhoods, viable economy in, promoting of, 253; and justice reinvestment, 253–55; mass imprisonment, reversal of, 253; and policing, 45; as "postracial," racial bias of, 25; "professional model" of, 36; and punishment, 29; punitive approach to, 34; "warrior" approach to, 36

criminal behavior: criminal justice, contact with, as tenuous, 3, 35

criminal justice: and American democracy, 4–6, 58, 89–90; American democracy, harming of, 233; American democracy, threat to, 253; Americans and state, contact between, 13; black community, cumulative effects of and, 246; black population, and poverty, as mired in, 23; blacks, overrepresentation of in, 23; as central state activity, 18–20; character of, 9; citizenship, delimiting of,

28; and civil rights movement, 23; as "colorblind," 158, 163; contact with, at young age, 96–97; contact with, growth of, 31; implicit bias, and judicial decision making, effect on, 164; implicit bias in, 163; intentional discrimination, and personal responsibility, gray area between, 25; and linked fate, 197–98; and negative rights, 63; and personal responsibility, 158–59; and political order, 19; polity, citizens' relationships to, 16; poor, managing of, 20; and race, 24, 166–67; race, role of in, 158; race, role of in, and personal responsibility narrative, 25; and racial disparities, 163; racial fairness, different perceptions of, 170; racialized civic stratification, as maintaining, 23; and racial knowledge, 26, 157; racial learning, 159; and racial liberalism, 165; racial organization, earlier forms of, as distinct from, 25; racial socialization of, 158; reforms of, and second-class citizenship, forming of, 231; repressive character of, 141; and social welfare, 209–10; state, as strong arm of, by definition, 259. *See also* criminal justice contact; criminal justice institutions; criminal justice policies; criminal justice practices; criminal justice reforms

criminal justice contact, 103, 225; and black incarceration, 195–97; and black youth, 102; and civic participation, 220–22; collective action, as less likely to engage in, 198; collective efficacy, negative relationship between, 137; criminal violence, as coupled with, 54–55; and custodial citizens, 55–56, 98–99, 108, 136, 156; custodial citizens, and "equal protection of interests," undermining of, 233; demobilizing effects of, 228; democratic elections, participation, effect on, 219, 227–28; disadvantaged racial groups, heightened identification with and, 173; effects of, as direct and secondary, 97; equality, generalized beliefs about, associated with, 175; likelihood of, 40; and linked fate perceptions, 173; as lived experience, 45; and political behavior, 226–27; political

criminal justice contact (*continued*)
    engagement, as diluted, 216–17; as
    politically socializing, 200. *See also*
    criminal justice; criminal justice insti-
    tutions; criminal justice policies; crim-
    inal justice practices; criminal justice
    reforms
criminal justice institutions, 2, 10, 21, 33,
    192; antidemocratic character of, 7, 91,
    107, 138, 259; citizenship, (un)learning
    of, 138; civic education, 137; custodial
    citizens, near total control over, as hav-
    ing, 141; democratic nature of, as topic
    of debate, 245; institutional features,
    changes in, 7; and political socializa-
    tion, 97; and popular will, 91; punitive-
    ness, of system, 107; and race, 169; and
    racial inequality, 25, 169; reforming
    of, 237; secrecy of, 242; and state gov-
    ernment, 19. *See also* criminal justice;
    criminal justice contact; criminal jus-
    tice policies; criminal justice practices;
    criminal justice reforms
criminal justice policies: criminal behavior,
    and criminal justice contact, discon-
    nect between, 25, 32, 36; minor offend-
    ers, increased share of, 32; nonoffend-
    ers and minor offenders, and American
    government, as anti-democratic, 32;
    number of citizens represented, in-
    crease of, as never been found guilty
    of crime, 32; as punitive, 194. *See also*
    criminal justice; criminal justice in-
    stitutions; criminal justice practices;
    criminal justice reforms
criminal justice practices: accountability
    and responsibility, 7, 60, 63–64, 236–45,
    253; citizen voices, restricting of, 7;
    democratic norms, 6–7; equality, un-
    dermining of, 7; shifts in, 3. *See also*
    criminal justice; criminal justice insti-
    tutions; criminal justice policies; crimi-
    nal justice reforms
criminal justice reforms, 256–57; alterna-
    tive policy options, 248; blind jury se-
    lection, 251; complexity of, 258; crack-
    to-cocaine sentencing disparity, 249;
    crime control, 253–55; custodial citi-
    zens, and racial disparities, 247; cus-
    todial citizens, and right to vote, re-
    storing of, 238–39; custodial citizens,
    political banishment, ending of, 238;
    democratic accountability and trans-
    parency, increasing of, 236–41; dem-
    ocratic responsiveness, and voice, in-
    creasing of, 236; diversity or sensitivity
    training, possible backlash of, 251; fel-
    ony disenfranchisement, opposition to,
    238–39; implicit bias, 250; implicit bias,
    and judges, 251; implicit biases, and
    public policy innovations, 252; incarcer-
    ation, scaling back of, 237; justice rein-
    vestment, 253–55; law enforcement and
    sentencing policies, and racial dispari-
    ties, 247; racial disproportionality, 246;
    racial equality, discourse of, and color-
    blind jurisprudence, 246; racial equal-
    ity, increasing of, 236, 246–53; racial
    equality, and racial order, government
    role in, as maintaining, 246; racial jus-
    tice movement, and prevailing system
    of control, challenging of, 252; sentenc-
    ing, and racial impact, considering of,
    249–50; sentencing policies and polic-
    ing practices, as prime areas of, 247–48;
    650 Lifer law, 248, 250; transparency
    and accountability, 241–45, 253; war on
    drugs legislation, 249. *See also* crimi-
    nal justice; criminal justice institutions;
    criminal justice policies; criminal jus-
    tice practices
Criminal Justice Reinvestment Act, 254
criminal justice system. *See also* crimi-
    nal justice; criminal justice institution;
    criminal justice practices; criminal jus-
    tice reforms
Current Population Survey and Panel
    Study of Income Dynamics, 100
custodial citizens, as defined, 8, 32

Dahl, Robert, 6, 58–59, 78
Dawes Act, 310n3
death penalty. *See* capital punishment, as
    racially biased
democracy: accountability and responsive-
    ness, 60, 63–64; active avoidance in, as
    antidemocratic, mark of, 214; in Ameri-
    can criminal justice, 6, 231; antidemo-

cratic institutions, effect on, 232; citizen
participation in, as healthy sign of, 199;
and citizenship, 10, 12, 27–29; custodial
citizens, as pariahs, 22; democratic participation, individual faculties, and development of "democratic" personality, 12; disempowered and alienated,
growing class of, 230; equality before
the law, 6; essential features of, 60; and
fair elections, 60; freedom of the press,
60; freedom to organize politically, 6,
60; free speech, 6; ideal character of,
58–59; as incomplete, 6; and political
equality, 59–60; political expression, 6,
60; and political institutions, 60–61; as
restricted, 6; and transparency, 60; and
tyranny of majority, 234; universal suffrage, 6, 60
Democracy and Its Critics (Dahl), 58
Democracy Restoration Act, 239
democratization: backsliding of, 5–6; as
gradual progress, 5–6; as unsteady
march, 6
Denmark, 90
Department of Labor, 240
Dewey, John, 91
DNA evidence, and wrongful convictions,
289n16
drugs: and blacks, 9, 24; crack cocaine, 191;
drug offenders, sentencing of, and violence, as reaction to, 50–51; nonviolent
offenders, 48–49; sentencing laws, as
harsh, 51; use of, 224–25
drug zone laws, 166
DuBois, W. E. B., 230

Eighth Amendment, 73, 165
equality, 5, 25, 162–63, 173
Escobedo v. Illinois, 62
European Court of Human Rights, 91
Ewald, Alec, 28

Fagan, Jeffrey, 40, 42–43
Fair Sentencing Act, 256
Farrakhan v. Gregiore, 164
felon disenfranchisement, 86, 90, 165,
184, 199, 216, 228, 238–39; as antidemocratic, 28; colorblindness, effect on, 164; mass black imprisonment

and, 199–200; and political participa-
tion, 222–23; politics, withdrawal from,
205–7; racial effect of, 84–85; stigma-
tized status of, 201–5
felon jury exclusion, 85–86, 301n135. *See
also* jury service
felons: and "civil death," 7
Fifteenth Amendment, 199, 257
First Amendment, 81, 86
Florida, 239, 247, 256
Floyd v. City of New York, 257
Folsom Prison, 82
food stamps. *See* National Food Stamp
Program
Fording, Richard, 20
Forman, James Jr., 25, 54
Foucault, Michel, 23
Fourteenth Amendment, 165; Equal Protection Clause of, 84, 201
Fourth Amendment, 42, 257
Fox, Richard, 11, 97
Fragile Families and Child Wellbeing
Study, 101, 217, 219–22, 305n22
freedom of association, 78–79; and gang
activity, 79–80; geographic banish-
ment, disturbing aspects of, 81; during
incarceration, 81–84; social marginality, increase of, 81; spatial segregation,
reinforcement of, 81; trespass admonishments, 81
Freedom Press (newspaper), 88
free speech and information, restrictions
on, 86
FYSK (Facts You Should Know) (newspaper), 87

gangs: and freedom of association, 79–80;
injunctions against, 79–80, 166,
299n102; loitering ordinances against,
248; as "public nuisance," 80
Garcia v. Glover, 76
General Social Survey, 100
Georgia, 85, 165–66
GI Bill: civic obligation, promoting of, 11;
political participation, of soldiers, in-
crease of, 12
Gideon v. Wainwright, 62
Gilens, Martin, 21
Gilles, Myriam, 66, 69

Goffman, Alice, 96, 208, 210
Goffman, Erving, 73
Gore, Al, 209
Gottschalk, Marie, 19, 90
grievance applications, 66–67, 69, 78, 141,
    211–12, 243; of prisoners, 8, 74–76, 107,
    135, 244, 297n72, 298n82
Grogger, Jeffrey, 299n102
Guinier, Lani, 162, 166
Gutmann, Amy, 137

Hacker, Jacob, 26
Hagan, John, 169
Haney-López, Ian, 166–67
Harlan, Justice, 79
Hawaii, 243, 298n75
Herbert, Steve, 80–81
Hirst v. United Kingdom, 91
Hispanics. *See* Latinos
Holder, Eric, 256
Holmesburg Prison, 302n147
HOPE, 256
Human Rights Watch, 66, 75, 155

Illinois, 49, 209
Imbler v. Pachtman, 71
implicit bias, 250–52; and criminal justice,
    163–64
incarcerated offenders, 35–36, 48–51
incarceration: as racial caste system, 24;
    scaling back of, 237. *See also* criminal
    justice; criminal justice contact; crim-
    inal justice institutions; criminal jus-
    tice policies; criminal justice practices;
    criminal justice reforms
inmate councils, 82
Iowa, 243, 249, 298n75
Israel, 90

Jacobs, Lawrence, 21
Jim Crow, 163, 197, 252–53; and ghetto, 24;
    and slavery, 24–26
Johnson, Lyndon B., 199
Johnson, Rucker, 53
Jones v. Bock, 75–76
Jones v. North Carolina Prisoner Union,
    83–84
jury nullification, 215
jury participation, blacks, exclusion from,
    85–86

jury service, 85. *See also* felon jury
    exclusion
Justice, Benjamin, 308–9n29
Justice Integrity Act, 249
Justice Mapping Institute, 253
Justice Reinvestment Act, 253–54
justice reinvestment strategies, 256, 315–
    16n57; communities, reinvestment in,
    253–55; community-based organiza-
    tions (CBOs), and voucher system,
    254; democracy, as enhancing, 255; in-
    frastructure, building of, 255; inno-
    vation of, 253–54; prison admittance
    rates, and recidivism, plans for reduc-
    ing and, 253

Kang, Jerry, 251; "disinfection" technique
    of, 252
Kansas, 256
Katzenstein, Mary, 28
Kelley, Robin, 215
Kennedy, Anthony, 85
Kennedy, Randall, 54
Kentucky, 239
Kentucky Department of Corrections v.
    Thompson, 300n108
King, Desmond, 5
King, Martin Luther, Jr., 247
King, Rodney, 67
Krause, Sharon, 29
Krivo, Lauren, 52
Kumlin, Staffan, 13, 93

Lacey, Nicola, 61, 302n150
Landy, Marc, 10
Latham v. Pate, 297n72
Latinos: and criminal justice contact,
    55–56, 292n67; individual, and free-
    doms of, 299n100; involuntary police
    encounters with, 40–45; neighborhoods
    of, violence in, 53, 167; stop-and-frisk
    rates of, 40–41
Lawless, Jennifer, 11, 97
Lieberman, Robert, 5
linked fate, 173–75, 180; and criminal jus-
    tice, 197–98
Lipsky, Michael, 10
Locke, John, 78
Los Angeles (California), 51; arrest rates
    in, 37; chokeholds, use of, by police in,

65; gang injunctions, 79, 299n102; homicide rate of in, 52; police abuse in, 66, 244; police stops in, 41, 43; Rampart scandal in, 244
Los Angeles v. Lyons, 64–66
Louima, Abner, 67, 295n30
Lousiana, 179
Louisiana State Penitentiary, 87
Luna, Eric, 60, 64, 242

Maine, 257
Malik v. Coughlin, 88
mandatory minimum penalties, 34, 248–50, 256, 270
Mansbridge, Jane, 13
Manza, Jeffrey, 238
Mapp v. Ohio, 62
Marshall, T. H., 6, 10–11, 21
Marshall, Thurgood, 83
Mauer, Marc, 247, 249
McCarthy v. Madigan, 73
McCleskey v. Kemp, 165–66
McKendy, John, 168
McWhorter, John, 167
Meares, Tracey, 308–9n29
Megan's Laws, 304n14
Mendoza v. Goord, 297n72
Mettler, Suzanne, 11–13, 20, 27, 62
Michigan, 248, 256
Mill, John Stuart, 12
Miller, Lisa, 54–55, 234
Milstein, Andrew, 20
Minnesota, 49, 67, 247, 249
Miranda rights, 63
Miranda v. Arizona, 62
misdemeanor drug arrests, 38; racial disparity in, 257
misdemeanor justice, 47
Mississippi, 25
Mosk, Stanley, 80
Moskos, Peter, 38
MPV (smoking marijuana in public), 45–47
Murphy v. Missouri, 302n145
Mushlin, Michael, 88, 296n61
mutual aid leagues, 82

NAACP v. Alabama ex rel. Patterson, 79
Natapoff, Alexandra, 43, 46–47
National Association for the Advancement

of Colored People (NAACP), Legal Defense Fund, 43
National Center for State Courts, and National Campaign to Ensure the Racial and Ethnic Fairness of America's State Courts, 251
National Food Stamp Program, 95; and Operation Talon, 209
National Longitudinal Study of Adolescent Health, 101, 149. *See also* Add Health survey
National Longitudinal Survey of Youth (NLSY), 101, 149, 226
National Prisoners' Reform Association, 83
Native Americans, 199, 310n3
Nebraska, 49, 243, 257, 298n75
Nevada, 67
New Jersey, 248, 255
New Jersey State Parole Board, Community Programs Division of, 240
New Orleans (Louisiana), 14, 103, 149, 202, 229, 240, 255; crime rate in, 104; demographics of, 104; incarceration rate in, 104; population of, 104
New York City, 51, 67, 69, 97; blacks and Latinos, stop-and-frisk rate of in, 40–41, 289–90n21; broken windows policing in, 45; Operation Clean Halls program, 44; police stops, of young black men, 3; public housing, police stops in, 43–44; quality-of-life policing in, 47; stop-and-frisk practices in, 36–37, 40–43, 257
New York Civil Liberties Union, 44
New York State, and Rockefeller laws, 248, 256
North Carolina, 254

Obama, Barack, 180–81, 187, 200, 203, 256; and speech on race, 5
Ohio, 67
Oregon, 49, 249
Osborne, Thomas Mott, 82
Overton v. Bazzetta, 300n108
Owens, Michael, 28

Pateman, Carole, 12
Pell v. Procunier, 87–89
People ex rel. Gallo v. Acuna, 79–80

personal responsibility narrative, 165; and criminal justice, 158–61, 167–69, 179, 185–92, 252–53; failure of, 25

Peterson, Ruth, 52

Philadelphia (Pennsylvania), 51, 208; stop-and-frisk practices in, 37, 40–41

Pierson, Paul, 26

Pinaire, Brian, 201

plea bargains, 72, 119

police: accountability of, 243–44; accountability of, court-erected hurdles of, 64–65; chokeholds, use of, 65; citizen complaints toward, barriers of, 67–69; citizen oversight committees, 244–45; detailed data, making public of, importance of, 245; gang injunctions, use of by, 79–80; qualified immunity defense, use of by, 67–68, 70; racial minorities, as disproportionately stopped by, 2–3, 9, 41; wide-ranging authority of, 64; wrongdoing of, as financial accountability, as rarely held, 66. *See also* police abuse; police discretion; policing; stop-and-frisk practices; Terry stops

police abuse: citizen complaints of, discouraging of, 67; and courts, 65–66; in Los Angeles, 66, 244; and strict standing test, 65–66. *See also* police; police discretion; policing; stop-and-frisk practices; Terry stops

police discretion, 8, 46. *See also* police; police abuse; policing; stop-and-frisk practices; Terry stops

policing, 32; and crime control, 45; and criminal suspects, 36; drug possession, and sentencing policies, shift in, 48; forceful tactics of, 36; "location plus evasion" and, 42; off-limits orders, 80; parks exclusion orders, 80–81; and police stops, 159; quality of life, and low-level offenders, focus on, 45–47; as racially disparate, 41–43; and "racial tax," 54; and "reasonable suspicion," 42; trespass admonitions, 80–81; vertical patrols, 43–44. *See also* police; police abuse; stop-and-frisk practices; Terry stops

political culture: as "colorblind," 25; as "postracial," 25, 181

political learning, 92, 94, 99–101, 112, 137, 159

political participation, 15, 22, 198, 205, 216–17, 220, 223–27, 263, 267, 276, 278; civic education, 137; felon disenfranchisement, 203; GI Bill, 12; prisoners' unionization, 83; withdrawal from, 207, 222

political socialization, 13, 59, 92, 137; and avoidance, 212; and criminal justice, 97, 100, 111–12

politics: as "electoral spectacle," 26; as lived experience, 28

Powell, Cedric, 162

Prison Abuse Remedies Act (PARA), 242–43

prisoners, 98; constitutional protections, surrendering of, 62, 73; courts, access to, 73–74; criminal record, as all-encompassing, 306n8; and drug offenses, 48; experiments on, 302n147; free association, restrictions against, 81–82; grievance applications, 8, 74–76, 107, 135, 244, 297n72, 298n82; non-violent drug offenders, growth of in, 48–49; political organizations of, 82; poor treatment of, as justifiable, 296n61; prison activism, 73–74; prisoner rights movement, 62–63

prison labor unions, 82, 90; abolishing of, 83–84; purpose of, 83

Prison Litigation Reform Act (PLRA), 7, 74, 243, 297n64; exhaustion provision, 75; federal court fees, 77; government redress, curtailing of, 77; three-strikes provision, and *in forma pauperis* claims, 76–77

prison newspapers, 86–87; censorship in, 88; free speech restrictions of, 88–89; and protected speech, 88; and unpopular views, 88

prisons, 32; abuse in, 243; antidemocratic practices in, 62–63; due process reforms, 63; early release from, abolishing of, 34; expansion of, and government, restructuring of, 19; free speech, restrictions of in, 241; grievance process, and institutions, lack of independence between, 76; and independent agencies, 243; internal prison grievance systems, deference to, 75–76; lack of accountability and responsibility in, 73; population of, growth of, 30; population of, reduction in, 256–57; pretrial detention, 73; procedural barriers, 75–76; procedural rights, 46–47, 62–63, 69, 71; self-help psychology programs, 168; as "total institutions," 73; writing in, restriction of, 86–87

prosecutors: absolute immunity of, 70–71; harmless error doctrine, 70–71; prosecutorial misconduct, 70–72

punishment, 32, 59, 64, 200; and crime control, 29; and criminal justice reforms, 241; and early modern state, 19; punitive activities, phenomenal growth of, 17

quality-of-life offending, and MPV (smoking marijuana in public), 45–47

race-making institutions, 25, 157, 159, 198
racial domination narrative: agency, robbing of, 198; and poor, 179–89; and white power, 179
racial impact statements, 248–49
racial inequality, 23–24, 162, 169; and criminal justice institutions, 25; and personal choice, 25; racialized poverty, 163; as systemic, colorblindness of, 164
racial learning, 159, 176
racial liberalism, 162–63, 166; and criminal justice, 165
racial profiling, 157, 188, 245
racism, 175–76; as episodic or intentional, 162–63; as structural, 162–63
representational biases, 21
Rhode Island, 257
Richardson v. Ramirez, 84, 201
Richmond (Virginia), 87
Rizzo v. Goode, 65
Robles v. Prince George's County, 68
Rockefeller laws, 248–50, 256
Rosenthal, Howard, 234
Ruffin v. Commonwealth, 62

San Diego (California), 299n98
San Francisco (California), 79
Schmitt, John, 48
Schram, Sanford, 20

Scott, James, 215
Scott, Robert, 242
Seattle (Washington), 50, 81, 245
Second Chance Act, 256
semi-citizenship, 4, 94
sentencing policies: law enforcement, and racial disparities, 247; racial impact of, 249–50; reforms of, and diversion programs, move toward, 256
Sentencing Project, 247
sexual offenders, stigmatization of, 304n14
Shklar, Judith, 229–30, 235
Simon, David, 231, 258
Simon, Jonathan, 19
Skocpol, Theda, 13, 21
slavery: and ghetto, 24; and Jim Crow, 24–26
"smart on crime" movement, 257
SNAP, 95
Social Capital Community Benchmark Survey, 100
Social Security Disability Insurance (SSDI), 11
social welfare programs, and citizen-state relationship, 14
Soledad Prison, 82
Soss, Joe, 11, 13, 20, 94, 230
South Africa, 90, 230
stop-and-frisk practices, 64, 166; and Latinos, 40–41; in New York City, 36–37, 40–43, 257, 289–90n21; in Philadelphia, 37, 40–41; surging of, 36–37; in Washington, DC, 41. *See also* police; police abuse; police discretion; policing
Stuntz, William, 35, 50–51
submerged state, 19, 93, 99, 162, 173
Supreme Court, 42, 71, 79, 83–84, 165, 201, 296n61. *See also individual cases*
Sweden, 11, 90

Talley v. Stephens, 62
TANF, 95
Terry, John, 42
Terry stops, 42, 64, 248. *See also* police; police abuse; police discretion; policing
Terry v. Ohio, 42
Texas, 255–56
Thomas v. United States Secretary of Defense, 302n147
Tocqueville, Alexis de, 12, 78, 85, 89

Tonry, Michael, 249
Trenton (New Jersey), 14, 110, 149, 191; demographics of, 103; high crime rate in, 104; population of, 103
truth-in-sentencing grants, 34
Tulia (Texas), 72
Twenty-sixth Amendment, 200

Uggen, Chris, 238
United Kingdom, 91. *See also* Britain
United Nations, 81
United Prisoner's Union, 82–83
United States, 5–6, 32, 90, 159, 302n150; authoritarian enclaves in, 6; democratization in, backsliding of, 5–6; disenfranchisement in, 199; felon disenfranchisement in, as exceptional, 90; murder rate in, 52; prisons in, 242; state's role, transformation of, 20–21; violent crime in, 52

Verba, Sidney, 6, 60, 84, 214, 235, 241
vertical patrols, 248
victimization, 9, 168, 267; and criminal justice contact, 53–54; rates of, for blacks, as catastrophic, 52
Virginia, 87, 206, 239, 258

Voting Rights Act (1965), 164–65, 246; gains of, as dismantled, 199–200

Wacquant, Loïc, 18–20, 23–25
war on drugs, 48–49
Warren, Earl, 62
Washington, DC, 244; stop-and-frisk in, 41
welfare: recipients of, as "undeserving," 12; and welfare fraud, 209
welfare institutions: political orientations, affecting of, 11; welfare reform, 209
welfare state, 11, 95; penal state, as replacement of by, 19–20; as term, 20
Wells, Reverend E. M., 82
Western, Bruce, 23, 253
Wheelock, Darren, 85
Wichita Falls (Texas), 79
Williams, Juan, 167
Wilson, James Q., 27
Winburn v. Bologna, 302n145
Wire, The (television program), 258
Wisconsin, 67
Wolff v. MacDonnell, 62
Woodford v. Ngo, 75–76

Younger v. Harris, 71